BRIEF WRITING
&
ORAL ARGUMENT
Ninth Edition

By

EDWARD D. RE
Chief Judge Emeritus
United States Court of International Trade
Distinguished Professor of Law Emeritus
St. John's University

and

JOSEPH R. RE
Of the New York and California Bars
Partner
Knobbe, Martens, Olson & Bear, LLP
Irvine, Newport Beach, California

2005
OCEANA PUBLICATIONS, INC.®

You may order this or any other Oceana publication by visiting Oceana's website at http://www.oceanalaw.com

Library of Congress Control Number: 2004110666

ISBN 0-379-21533-0

© 2005 by Oceana Publications, Inc.

Manufactured in the United States of America on acid free paper.

TABLE OF CONTENTS

PART ONE: LEGAL WRITING

PART TWO: OPINION LETTERS AND CLAIM OR DEMAND LETTERS, TRIAL AND POST-TRIAL BRIEFS, AND MEMORANDA OF LAW

PART FIVE: LEGAL CITATOR

APPENDICES

INDEX

FOREWORD[1]

by

THE HONORABLE WARREN E. BURGER

Chief Justice of the United States, 1969-1986

Chairman of the Commission on the Bicentennial of the United States Constitution, 1985-1992

More than thirty-five years ago, the first edition of this book was published, declaring its "modest" purpose of setting forth "fundamental principles underlying an effective brief and a convincing oral argument." With each new edition and revision, it has become more useful and valuable to law students and lawyers. In the words of Dean Robert B. McKay of New York University School of Law, reviewing the fifth edition, "the short of it is that this book, already a classic in the field, is simply the best guide to the work of every litigating lawyer." With the publication of this new edition of *Brief Writing and Oral Argument,* Chief Judge Edward D. Re has made available to law students and the bar a work that effectively fulfills an urgent need in legal education and in the practice of law.

The success of this book, in the teaching of legal writing skills, the writing of effective briefs, and the presentation of persuasive oral arguments, is attributable in large measure to the unique background of its author. A distinguished law teacher, Chief Judge Re writes with the rich experience of a trial judge of almost twenty years who, sitting by designation on the various United States Courts of Appeals, has also heard countless appeals and oral arguments. He thus has an appreciation for the role of advocacy in ensuring the proper functioning of the adversary system.

Drawing upon his diversified experience as a lawyer, teacher, and judge, Chief Judge Re offers the law student and lawyer a wealth of valuable information on advocacy in general and legal writing and reasoning in particular. Particularly useful to law students are Chief Judge Re's discussions of *stare decisis,* the evaluation of authority, the analysis of cases, legal reasoning, and legal research. If lawyers understood and complied with the lessons contained in this valuable manual, they would undoubtedly contribute to the more effective functioning of our judicial process.

Teaching the fundamental principles, techniques, and skills of written and oral advocacy is but one goal of the work. What especially appeals to me about the book is that in teaching these skills it also highlights professional responsibility and the public service function of the lawyer. One of the book's principal themes is that, although the litigation process may be adversarial, ethical norms and pro-

---

1   This foreword was written by Chief Justice Burger for the sixth edition of *Brief Writing & Oral Argument* (1987).

fessional responsibility must be foremost in the performance of the lawyer's duties. Judge Re makes it clear that advocacy must remain within the bounds of ethical standards and of the law, and that training a lawyer in the skills of the profession without equal emphasis on the moral and ethical standards is a bit like handing a small boy a loaded pistol to play with on the schoolground. I am pleased that law schools and, to some extent, the profession itself are also moving in this direction.

Dean McKay has aptly summarized my own view of this work:

> We can all be grateful for this excellent book—legal educators, litigators, judges and the client public. If it did not exist, someone would have to invent it. Fortunately, Judge Re got there first.

FOREWORD[1]

by

WHITNEY NORTH SEYMOUR, SR.

Former President, American Bar Association

The development of this excellent book has now proceeded for more than 21 years and it can properly be viewed as having reached full maturity. Each edition has added valuable new qualities and the present edition also contains new contributions. Among others, it makes readily available the portions of the Code of Professional Responsibility which particularly affect the advocate. Starting as a book primarily intended to help law students in their moot court work, when there were few practical guides, it has become as well a valuable guide to the practitioner who acts as advocate in a trial or appellate court.

The development of the book parallels the unfolding of the author's interesting career. Originally written when he was devoting much of his time to teaching at St. John's University Law School, where he observed the need for such a guide for law students, later editions have increasingly served the needs of the practicing bar as his own observations of those needs have developed. The Third Edition was brought out when he was the distinguished Chairman of the Foreign Claims Settlement Commission of the United States and responded to the practitioner's needs as they could be seen from high posts in government. Now he has been drafted for the bench and as the Chief Judge of the United States Court of International Trade, designated from time to time to sit in United States District Courts and the Courts of Appeals, he has observed from a new angle the need for a comprehensive guide to written and oral advocacy in important trial and appellate courts. Even if fate beckons him to other tasks, already this varied background has taught him what needs of the advocate must be met and he has met them very well.

This new edition comes when advocacy is buffeted in many ways, from many directions. The need for good advocacy is clear and the shortage of good advocates is the subject of frequent comment. The adversary system is obviously the genius which makes the judicial system work and, indeed, the entire governmental system works best when all points of view are fairly and properly presented. Experienced judges know and, indeed, many proclaim that the quality of their performance depends heavily on the skill and breadth of the advocacy which they can consider in reaching their judgments. And the need for skilled advocates is not just static. With the increased emphasis on criminal law and the right to counsel there, great new fields for advocacy have developed and everyone recognizes that there is a tragic shortage of trained advocates to take up the slack. Where for-

---

1   This foreword updates the foreword written by Mr. Seymour for the fourth edition of *Brief Writing & Oral Argument* (1977).

merly law schools rather assumed that advocacy was an easily acquired skill, many now recognize the need for teaching it and for exposing students to clinical materials and experiences where advocacy plays an important role. Paradoxically, the need for better advocacy and for more advocates is paralleled by what sometimes seems to amount almost to an allergy to oral argument in some appellate courts. This takes the form of vigorous encouragement of submissions in some courts, along with sharp reduction in the time allowed for oral argument except by special leave, which is grudgingly granted. Of course, some of this attitude is attributable to the crushing burdens of increased business on some courts, but I fear that more is due to the decline in the character of advocacy and increase in the illusion that judges can do as well or better without what they regard as wasting time on oral argument. In my view, this is a deplorable result; it sacrifices some of the values of the adversary system, and the bar should do all it can to reverse the tide. Those who use this book and profit by its use can help for only better advocacy will convert some judges to its importance.

Business in the English courts is increasing too, though not nearly so fast. Largely because the quality of advocacy by the English barrister remains of a high order and the judges' experience of good advocacy enables them to take full advantage of it, the English show no signs of giving up the benefits of oral argument or turning to briefs alone for counsel's views. We should benefit by this experience. We should, of course, help to encourage well-written briefs, for they supplement and support good oral argument, and this book contains much excellent advice on that subject. We should also actively recruit talented young lawyers to specialize in advocacy (or at least do it well when they must act as advocates) and this book will be extremely valuable to them. And we should help keep the experienced, older advocates in the courtroom to remind the young lawyers what good advocacy is, for observation and experience, as the writer recognizes, must go hand in hand with the guidance which this manual provides.

Perhaps one who has spent almost fifty years of his professional life as an advocate may be forgiven a few parting words. There is no thrill like that which comes from the sense of a case well tried or an appeal well argued. There is hardly any congenial atmosphere to equal the feeling in a courtroom when the judge knows and shows that he knows that the lawyers are doing their best and that he can trust absolutely what they say. One of the great virtues of this book is to emphasize the standards which insure that such trust can be justified. The spirit of brotherhood between such lawyers and with judges who appreciate the traditions of the Bar is one of the great joys and rewards of the profession. Finally, in these days when retirement systems often drain off talents in education, industry and the judiciary much too early, it is pleasant to recall the story about John W. Davis, surely the greatest advocate and one of the most delightful companions of my time. Chief Judge Re obviously shares the same high opinion of him for he frequently cites his fine lecture, "The Argument of an Appeal." When, at 83, Mr. Davis had just argued a case in the Supreme Court, a reporter asked him how it felt to argue a case at his age, and he replied: "I was glad to find that there's still a tune in the old violin."

This book will help to provide the right pitch for the tune, whatever the age of the instrument.

PREFACE

BRIEF WRITING & ORAL ARGUMENT
Ninth Edition

This ninth edition of *Brief Writing & Oral Argument* has its origins in a brief text on brief writing and oral argument first published in 1951. It was written because of the firm conviction that legal writing and oral advocacy can be taught, and learned by conscientious law students and lawyers. It was intended, as is the present book, as a standing introduction to legal writing and advocacy for law students and lawyers about to write a legal document, memorandum or brief, or argue an appeal.

The first edition has been expanded and has developed through succeeding editions and revisions into a comprehensive text on brief writing and oral argument. The text of all editions was designed to assist both the law student and the practicing lawyer in the writing of a variety of legal documents, such as opinion and claim letters, diverse memoranda of law, and trial and appellate briefs.

The ninth edition is intended to serve as a text and assist the law student in courses on legal writing. It will also be invaluable in the preparation of the appellate brief for law school Moot Court participation. It is a book that offers guidance both for the preparation and writing of effective appellate briefs as well as the presentation of an effective oral argument.

This ninth edition of *Brief Writing & Oral Argument* is a thorough text on brief writing and oral argument with countless suggestions and examples. Many of the modifications and additions in the text were dictated by the authors' personal experiences; others reflect the contributions of some of the ablest law professors, judges, and lawyers who are experts in the trial and appeal of cases. In addition to comprehensiveness, all materials have been updated and all references are to the most recent rules of court.

Beyond retaining all areas deemed essential for law students, it also includes new areas that will be helpful in the writing of briefs, legal writing in general, and the study of law. These areas include an explanation of the trial and appellate function, the structure of appellate courts, standards of appellate judicial review, frivolous appeals and the imposition of sanctions, *stare decisis,* legal reasoning, the distinguishing and analysis of cases, and a section on the interpretation and application of statutes. A mastery of these materials will be most helpful for success both in law school and in the practice of law.

This edition also reflects the amendments to the Federal Rules of Appellate Procedure, effective December 1, 1998, and to the Supreme Court of the United States Rules, effective May 1, 1997. In addition, this edition emphasizes the federal courts' widespread use of local rules at both the trial and appellate levels. As a result, this edition highlights many of the practical considerations necessary for briefs and oral arguments to comply with court local rules. For example, new material has been added concerning local rules governing motion practice, appellate briefs, and the proper use of visual aids at oral argument. This ninth edition updates all of the materials in the book by adding new sources that constitute the current literature on the particular subject covered. It also reflects changes and recent developments in all statutes, rules, and case law. Moreover, this edition fully conforms to the seventeenth edition of *The Bluebook: A Uniform System of Citation.*

The Appendix contains illustrative examples of the various legal documents that an attorney may be required to prepare. They are included in this edition of *Brief Writing & Oral Argument* because they are also excellent legal writing exercises for legal writing classes.

In recognition of the importance of correct, concise, and complete citations in all legal writing documents, the authors have included a revised chapter on "Citation of Authorities." The instructions and sample citations contained in this Legal Citator constitute an abridged citator that covers most of the citation problems likely to be encountered when writing a brief or memorandum of law.

All of the materials included in this book are designed to teach skills that are necessary for the professional competence of the advocate. Appellate judges readily detect inadequate research, faulty legal reasoning, bad grammar or citation form, and are particularly sensitive to violations of applicable court rules. Judges can sense, almost immediately, whether counsel has prepared a brief and oral argument designed to be helpful to the court in deciding the question presented. Indeed, as stated in the text, a brief will only be as effective as it is helpful to the court.

The Preface is an appropriate place for the authors to record their gratitude to those who have played a part in the publication of this book. At the outset, reference must be made to the late Mr. Philip F. Cohen, Chairman of the Board and Publisher, Oceana Publications, whose friendly suggestion led not only to the publication of the first edition, but also the earlier subsequent editions. Beyond the jurists and scholars whose contributions are acknowledged in the footnotes to the text, the authors are greatly indebted to all of the lawyers and law professors who have urged that the book be revised as an effective manual or handbook for law students and lawyers. Judge Re assumes full responsibility for all changes, omissions and innovations in the book. For this ninth edition a special debt of gratitude is owed to Prof. William H. Manz of St. John's University School of Law Library, and a member of the New York Bar, for having undertaken the major burden of checking and updating the many references to statutes and rules of court as well as the countless citations found in the book.

The Preface to this edition may well conclude with the following paragraph from the Preface to the sixth edition. It will be repeated here because it highlights professional responsibility and the functions of the lawyer in the administration of justice.

"As in all prior editions, this most recent edition highlights professional responsibility and the prominent role of the lawyer in the adversary system. By applying their professional skills, lawyers will succeed in accomplishing several important goals. First, they will discharge their professional duties to their clients. Second, by the submission of well-written pleadings and effective briefs, they will help the judge or court render well reasoned and well written decisions. Third, by their written submissions and competent presentation of cases, they will contribute to the substantive aspects of judicial opinions and decisions. Fourth, by the competent and effective presentation of cases, lawyers can play a vital role in giving impetus and guidance to the law itself. Indeed, by the competent practice of the profession, a lawyer is also truly a lawmaker."

The authors believe that this book will help the reader achieve these goals, and in the process also help bridge the gap between law school and the practice of law.

Edward D. Re
Joseph R. Re

New York City
May 1, 2005

ABOUT THE AUTHORS

Edward D. Re, Distinguished Professor of Law Emeritus at St. John's University, Chief Judge Emeritus of the United States Court of International Trade, served in the administrations of both President John F. Kennedy and President Lyndon B. Johnson as Assistant Secretary of State for Educational and Cultural Affairs, and as Chairman of the Foreign Claims Settlement Commission of the United States. He was appointed a federal judge by President Johnson in 1968, and, by appointment of President Carter, served as Chief Judge from 1977 to his retirement from the federal bench in 1991. Among other books, he is the author of *Remedies* (Foundation Press), and *Freedom's Prophet* (Oceana), a *liber amicorum* in honor of Professor Zechariah Chafee, Jr.

Joseph R. Re is a graduate of Rutgers University College of Engineering, and St. John's University School of Law, where he was an editor of the Law Review. He served as law clerk to the Honorable Howard T. Markey, Chief Judge of the United States Court of Appeals for the Federal Circuit, and is a partner in the law firm of Knobbe, Martens, Olson & Bear of Newport Beach, California, where he manages an intellectual property litigation practice. He is a member of the New York and California bars.

ABOUT THE BOOK

"If lawyers understood and complied with the lessons contained in this valuable manual, they would undoubtedly contribute to the more effective functioning of our judicial process."—*The Honorable Warren E. Burger, Chief Justice of the United States Supreme Court, 1969–1986*

"By actively combining academic and judicial experience, Judge Re provides a truly unique work to assist in this worthwhile area of education."—*Judge J. Clifford Wallace, U.S. Court of Appeals*

"Succinct writing, clear instructive quality, brilliant organization and practical wisdom pervade this volume . . . the benchmark of the written and spoken word of an eminent jurist."—*Benjamin Busch, New York Law Journal*

"Holds the reader's interest and can be reread and studied time and again by law students, neophyte lawyers or experienced advocates. Judge Re not only teaches and enlightens, but challenges and inspires."—*Judge Gerald Scarboro, Circuit Court of Cook County, Illinois, ABA Journal*

"We can all be grateful for this excellent book—legal educators, litigators, judges and the client public. If it did not exist, someone would have to invent it."—*Robert B. McKay, IJA Report*

BRIEF WRITING
&
ORAL ARGUMENT

Ninth Edition

Part One

LEGAL WRITING

I

PRELIMINARY CONSIDERATIONS

A. The Nature and Importance of Legal Writing

In order to attain competence in the law, the lawyer must be able to communicate. Hence, no skill can be of greater value to the law student than the ability to communicate by writing and speaking.

For law students, the ability to write well is an essential skill.[1] All law schools today require students to take courses to improve their writing skills.[2] A law student who wants to write well must be willing to work at being a good writer.[3] A law student cannot become a good legal writer without first becoming skilled in the use of language.

Professor Zechariah Chafee, Jr., a scholar of exceptional talent, once wrote: "Words are the principal tools of lawyers and judges, whether we like it or not."[4] This observation on the relationship of law and language is confirmed by other scholars who have noted that "[t]he law is a profession of words,"[5] and that "words in their proper order are the raw materials of the law."[6]

Once the function of language is appreciated, the lawyer's need for linguistic skill becomes apparent.[7] Too often an effort is made to build a superstructure of legal draftsmanship upon the shaky foundation of a poor vocabulary and a deficient knowledge of English grammar.[8] All writing requires knowledge of grammar and a command of words. Students who wrote effective essays, short stories,

---

1 *See* Robert L. Clare, *Teaching Clear Legal Writing—The Practitioner's Viewpoint*, 52 N.Y. St. B.J. 192 (1980).

2 *See* Hans J. Gottlieb, *Teaching English in a Law School*, 49 A.B.A. J. 667 (1963); *see also* Robert B. McKay, *Critics Say Lawyers Should Speak and Write in Clearer English*, 48 LAW & FACT 9 (1976).

3 WILLIAM ZINSSER, ON WRITING WELL 13 (2d ed. 1980). "To emphasize the importance of thought, effort and rewriting, we are told that for most mortals there is no good writing, but only good rewriting." Edward D. Re, Appellate Opinion Writing (Seminar for Federal Appellate Judges, Federal Judicial Center, FJC-ETS-77-4) (Mar. 1975).

4 Zechariah Chafee, *The Disorderly Conduct of Words*, 41 COLUM. L. REV. 381, 382 (1941). On Chafee, see EDWARD D. RE, FREEDOM'S PROPHET (1981).

5 DAVID MELLINKOFF, THE LANGUAGE OF THE LAW vii (1963).

6 Norman Birkett, *Law and Literature*, in EUGENE C. GERHART, THE LAWYER'S TREASURY 127, 135 (1956).

7 One must be "intent on improving" one's language. I. BERNARD COHEN, BENJAMIN FRANKLIN, HIS CONTRIBUTION TO THE AMERICAN TRADITION 77 (1953).

8 NORMAN BRAND & JOHN O. WHITE, LEGAL WRITING viii (1976).

and compositions as undergraduates should have little difficulty adapting their talent to the art of good legal writing.

B. Words, Language, the Legal Profession, and the "Vanishing Trial"

For members of the legal profession words and language are the very heart of their work. To give a specific example, lawyers should not state that their clients were found guilty of <u>misstating</u> their earnings or expenses on a tax return. Their clients did not merely <u>misstate</u>. Their clients <u>falsified</u> income and expenses on their tax return.

In all areas of the law a mastery of words is an indispensable requirement. It is absolutely essential for lawyers to speak and write with accuracy, especially when the particular words used may have a special meaning or importance in determining the rights and duties of the parties. There are occasions when the choice of a word may seriously affect the legal consequences, and the professional responsibility for choosing the right word is that of the lawyer. Therefore, a knowledge of words and language is indispensable for members of the legal profession.

In this manual the authors write of the ABCs of Legal Writing, ABC referring to Accuracy, Brevity and Clarity. The attainment of the goal of Accuracy, Brevity and Clarity of necessity requires the use and choice of the right word. Many examples may be given. "Has your client 'avoided' paying a toll or has your client 'evaded' paying a toll?" Countless examples can be given of the importance of words and language in the profession of the law.

A rather recent development in the practice of law, that has been called the "vanishing of trials," emphasises in a dramatic way the <u>importance of writing</u> for the legal profession. As stated in a front page article in the New York Times of December 14, 2003, *US suits multiply, but few ever go to trial.*[9] The article states that, notwithstanding the tremendous increase in cases that are brought to court, the trial in court is becoming "uncommon." The article reports of a study that revealed that most cases are disposed of in court "on papers submitted." The study indicates that "in 1920, . . . 11.5% of all civil cases in federal court went to trial but last year that number had dropped to 1.8%," and "even though there are five times as many law suits today, the raw number of such trials has dropped too."

Some refer to the recent trend as the "passing of the common law adversarial system." In the words of Professor Arthur Miller of Harvard, "this is a cultural shift of enormous significance." Many lawyers and judges state that the "vanishing trial" reflects a "growing antagonism to trials by lawyers and judges, who consider them costly and risky." The article can best be summarized by a state-

---

9   N.Y. TIMES, Dec. 24, 2003, at 1, 50. *See also* Patricia Lee Refo, *Opening Statement: Trial Rescue*, LITIGATION, Spring 2004, at 1.

ment that most cases are now "decided on papers" submitted to the court. Although law schools in recent years have devoted more attention to the teaching of legal writing, the implications of this professional cultural shift has not yet been fully understood by the academic community or by all members of the legal profession.

C. Demands of the Legal Writing Process

Before beginning to write, all authors must answer two questions:

1. *Why* do we write, and

2. For *whom* do we write?

Differently stated, the author must think of the *purpose* of the composition, and the *audience* for whom it is written.

Too often law students, as well as lawyers, begin writing a document without knowing exactly what it is they wish to say or write. Hence, one cannot overemphasize the importance of giving careful thought to a writing project *before* the writing begins.

Is the document intended to be an objective presentation of the facts or law; or is it designed to persuade the reader to adopt a particular view of the facts or law? These are two very different forms of communication. The proper presentation of the material will depend on the objective that the writer seeks to achieve.

The *legal* writing process has additional demands.[10] The lawyer author cannot take liberties with the text, which consists of the facts and the law. Hence, the legal writing process implies an exactness or precision that distinguishes legal writing from other literary compositions. The additional essential element is that of responsibility. Counsel can neither say nor imply that "the sky was well-lit and clear," when it was cloudy and dark, or that "plaintiffs walked calmly and normally," when they were running and pushed and shoved.

Hence, due to the demands of the legal writing process, legal composition may be more difficult than other forms of literary composition. In legal writing, the author is constrained to record what the facts accurately reveal and must conform to the restraints of style, length and form mandated by rules of court.[11]

D. Essentials of Legal Writing

The lawyer confronted with the task of writing a legal document would do well to remember what may be called the ABC's of legal writing. These letters repre-

---

10   Edward D. Re, *Demands of the Legal Writing Process*, N.Y. St. B.J. Dec. 1984, at 20, 21–24.

11   *See id.*

sent three indispensable requirements of brief writing in particular and legal writing in general—Accuracy, Brevity, and Clarity.

1. Accuracy

In all legal writing the importance of accuracy cannot be overemphasized. The lawyer must set forth the facts and law with honesty, candor, and specificity.

If unfavorable facts or precedents are omitted from a brief, opposing counsel will surely point out the omission; if a fact or precedent is misstated, the court will question the value of the brief and counsel's integrity.[12] In either instance, the reviewing court will view all other statements, whether accurate or not, with a degree of skepticism.[13] Frankness and honesty, on the other hand, inspire confidence. For example, all assertions of fact in a brief must be supported by the record.

The "Statements of Facts" in a brief should relate everything in the record that is necessary to understand the case.[14] Damaging evidence or testimony cannot be ignored.[15] This does not mean that the brief writer should repeat every fact in the record regardless of its relevance. In the words of Justice Cardozo: "There is an accuracy that defeats itself by the over-emphasis of detail. . . . The sentence may be so over-crowded with all its possible qualifications that it will tumble down of its own weight."[16] The brief writer must examine the record, discern the material facts, and, using only those facts that are essential, construct a precise narrative of the facts of the case.

Although the statement of facts must be fair, the brief writer should never fail to stress the equities of the client's cause. The facts should be stated in such a way that the court will feel that, by deciding in favor of the advocate's client, justice will be done.

---

12 "There is no sense in withholding unfavorable facts or law from the attention of the court. Opposing counsel, or the diligent law clerk, will ferret out such material. If there is unfavorable precedent it is best to admit and distinguish your case." George K. Rahdert & Marc Roth, *The Appellate Practitioner and the Fifth Circuit Brief*, 51 FLA. B.J. 264, 270 (1970); *see also* McKeon v. Sherman, 166 N.Y.S. 133 (App. Div. 1st Dep't 1917).

13 "If it is revealed that what he says or writes cannot be believed, he forfeits the confidence which he seeks to create. The court's distrust of him may taint his next appeal as well." John C. Godbold, *Twenty Pages and Twenty Minutes—Effective Advocacy on Appeal*, 30 Sw. L.J. 801, 816–17 (1976).

14 George Rose Smith, *Arkansas Appellate Practice: Abstracting the Record*, 31 ARK. L. REV. 359, 361 (1977).

15 J. Paxton Blair, *Appellate Briefs and Advocacy*, 18 FORDHAM L. REV. 30, 37 (1949).

16 BENJAMIN N. CARDOZO, LAW AND LITERATURE 7 (1930). "The picture cannot be painted if the significant and the insignificant are given equal prominence." *Id.* at 8.

2. Brevity

Many persons consider lawyers to be "slaves of verbosity." This is unfortunate, for lawyers ought to be the masters of words rather than their slaves.[17] Briefs should be brief.[18]

Lengthy, poorly organized briefs are ineffective and unpersuasive.[19] Overwhelming caseloads simply do not allow appellate judges the time to wander through page after page of meandering prose.[20] Occasionally, appellate courts have reacted to poorly written briefs with more than mere annoyance. In one case, the Supreme Court of the United States ordered that new briefs be filed and that the old briefs not be used. The Court issued the severe warning that "the new briefs shall conform to the rules of this Court, be compact, logically arranged with proper headings, concise, and free from burden-some, irrelevant, and immaterial matter."[21] The lawyers in that case were fortunate. More often, brief writers do not have the opportunity to rectify their mistakes. The long, burdensome brief is never read with sympathy—if it is read at all.

Achieving brevity is a difficult, time-consuming task. The writer must first master the facts and law, and then summarize them without distorting the true picture.[22] In brief writing, the advocate cannot choose the escape of Lady Mary Wortley Montagu's daughter, who wrote a long letter because she did not have time to write a short one.[23]

---

17 "The influences most responsible for wordiness in the law . . . lost their original force. The redundancies of primitive word magic and metaphysical ritual; the solemn repetitions coaxing barbarians to accept an unestablished law; the need and fashion of bilingual duplications; the involvements brought on by the translation of Latin; by Elizabethan literary styles, and by the pay-by-the-word legal economy; the overcautious repeating of the repeated to circumvent the harshness of the law to mask an ignorance of its content . . . —all of these have burdened the law with language unnecessary, confusing, and wasteful." MELLINKOFF, *supra* note 5, at 399.

18 "A brief should be clean and clear, as taut as a violin string and as terse as a rifle shot. It should not contain an ounce of fat or an excess word." Godbold, *supra* note 12, at 816.

19 *See* SUP. CT. R. 24.6.

20 Because of expanding caseloads at the appellate level, judges are considering "oral decisions from the bench, the use of short unpublished opinions, . . . and the imposition of time limits on oral argument and prehearing conference." Eugene A. Wright, *Introduction: Essays from the Bench*, 52 IND. L.J. 97 n.4 (1976).

21 The case was *Gilchrist v. Interborough Rapid Transit Co.*, 279 U.S. 159 (1929). *See* SUP. CT. R. 24.6; *see also* Felic Frankfurter & James M. Landis, *The Business of the Supreme Court at October Term, 1928*, 43 HARV. L. REV. 33, 57 (1929). "The state of the docket demands that arguments be closely focused upon essential issues and that briefs serve as compact and artistic expositions of the contentions of the parties." *Id.* at 56.

22 "Wordiness in all its forms is a widespread modern disease: its characteristics are length, repetition, vague abstractions which cannot be pinned down, muddled and confused verbiage. It needs real determination to be short, concrete and to the point." John Munkman, *Some Thoughts on Drafting*, 114 L.J. 420 (1964).

23 "All of us have known lawyers of great ability and surpassing acuteness of mind . . . who, when they attempted to put their thoughts on paper, immediately became the slaves of verbos-

Brevity is not simply equated with the number of pages in the brief. Brevity is a flexible standard of conciseness in relation to the complexity of the case. A brief statement of facts, for example, is not necessarily a statement containing a few short paragraphs. Everything germane must be included. It will not suffice, however, to state that Jones testified to this effect, and that Smith testified that these events occurred. Events must be described succinctly; testimony compressed. There must be an economy of words. A lazy presentation of the facts does not help the court or the advocate's case.[24]

Brevity and clarity of expression can be attained by the elimination of "clutter." Clutter is the conglomeration of "unnecessary words, circular constructions, pompous frills and meaningless jargon" that permeates American language.[25]

Although most courts by rule limit the length of briefs, the legal writer should strive for brevity even in the absence of a specific rule. The goal is to achieve maximum brevity consistent with accuracy and clarity.[26]

3. Clarity

In legal writing, clarity is of paramount importance.[27] Briefs, contracts, wills, and all other legal documents must be clearly written if they are to serve their intended purpose. The reader of a legal document should have no doubt about the facts and ideas the writer wishes to convey.

Clarity begins with "straightforward thinking."[28] Clarity of understanding must precede clarity of expression. "No knowledge, however thorough, of the art [of legal composition] will compensate for the want of knowledge of the facts and the law with which the practitioner has to deal."[29]

Once the lawyer has the facts clearly in mind, the task begins of conveying that knowledge to the reader. The advocate must now select the *mot juste*—the right

---

ity. Pages of their briefs may be turned without a restful stop or even a fatigue relieving comma." Walter P. Armstrong, *A Practicing Lawyer Looks at Legal Education*, 9 AM. L.SCH. REV. 775 (1940).

24 "A short brief is the result of careful planning, condensation and attention to essentials. . . . Such a brief is more effective because it is actually a better brief, but also because it conserves the time and energies of the court." FREDERICK C. HICKS, MATERIALS AND METHODS OF LEGAL RESEARCH 373 (3d ed. 1942).

25 ZINSSER, *supra* note 3, at 7.

26 For example, in the United States Court of International Trade there is no limit, by rule, as to the length of briefs.

27 "A brief should be well written, but . . . it must be clearly written." FREDERICK B. WIENER, BRIEFING AND ARGUING FEDERAL APPEALS 64 (1967).

28 REED DICKERSON, LEGISLATIVE DRAFTING 13 (1954).

29 E. J. G. Mackay, *Introduction to an Essay on the Art of Legal Composition Commonly Called Drafting*, 3 L.Q. REV. 326, 337 (1887).

word.[30] What is the precise word that conveys the exact meaning intended? How will the context in which the word is used affect its meaning? Justice Holmes eloquently expressed in a judicial opinion the thought that:

> A word is not a crystal, transparent and unchanged, it is the skin of a living thought and may vary greatly in color and content according to the circumstances and the time in which it is used.[31]

This vivid description highlights the need to exercise care in word selection. Professor S.I. Hayakawa[32] points out that:

> Nothing is so important to clear and accurate expression as the ability to distinguish between words of similar, but not identical, meaning. There are occasions in which we have to make choices between *transient and transitory, mutual* and *reciprocal, gaudy* and *garish, inherent* and *intrinsic, speculate* and *ruminate, pinnacle* and *summit,* because in a given context one is certain to be more appropriate than the other. To choose wrongly is to leave the hearer or reader with a fuzzy or mistaken impression. To choose well is to give both illumination and delight. The study of synonyms will help the [author] come closer to saying what [the author] really wants to say.[33]

If the writer has reason to believe that a particular word may convey an unintended or undesired meaning or implication, the author should ascertain the etymology of the word to avoid using a word that may cast doubt upon the intended meaning. The search is for the word that expresses the precise thought that the author wished to express and convey.

Frequently, the word selection process is not only choosing one word instead of another, but rather selecting the right word from an array of nearly or almost right words. "English has the largest vocabulary and the most synonyms of any language in the world."[34] An example of the writer's predicament is found in the synonyms listed in *Webster's Third New International Dictionary* (1981) for the word "assert": declare, profess, affirm, aver, protest, avouch, avow, predicate, warrant. Yet, "assert" is not listed as a synonym of "declare" as are announce, publish, advertise, proclaim, promulgate, and broadcast. The *shade* or *difference* of meaning between these "synonyms" is substantial.

The use of the right word may have a special significance in the law. For example, in a brief, a statement that "the court said" is not the same as "the court held." The word "said" may give the impression that the statement was dictum. The

---

30   "The search is for the just word, the happy phrase, that will give expression to the thought . . . ." BENJAMIN N. CARDOZO, GROWTH OF THE LAW 89 (1924).

31   Towne v. Eisner, 245 U.S. 418, 425 (1918).

32   Professor Hayakawa also served as a United States Senator from California.

33   S.I. HAYAKAWA, USE THE RIGHT WORD: A MODERN GUIDE TO SYNONYMS vii (1968).

34   *Id.* at v. "This richness is due to the fact that the English language has grown over the centuries by constantly incorporating words from other languages." *Id.*

word "held" tells the reader about the *holding* of the case. The *holding* embodies an authoritative legal precept, rule, or principle.

In referring to cases, brief writers often write: "In *Jones v. Brown* the court stated. . . ." The word "stated" is a general or neutral term. Unless the general word was chosen deliberately, the brief writer ought to select a more precise word. For example, did the court "declare" or "enunciate" a principle of law? Did it make a "finding" of either law or fact? Often, it is more accurate and more meaningful to say that the court "intimated," "reasoned," "suggested," "noted," "concluded," or "decided."

Many examples can be given to show the importance of using the precise word. A good example is the difference between a *misstatement* and a *falsehood*. Did a person *misstate* or *falsify* a fact? Under a criminal statute, when is a statement made to a government agency "false?" When is a tax return "fraudulent?" Has a taxpayer "avoided" or "evaded" taxes? Whereas "avoidance" connotes lawfulness, "evasion" implies unlawfulness.

An extensive vocabulary is of value to any professional person. When possessed by the advocate, however, it is an asset that pays the most generous dividends. It may be encouraging to bear in mind that the willingness to devote time to the search for the precise word is perhaps a more important trait than glibness of tongue and facility with words. One cannot underestimate the value of the unabridged dictionary and thesaurus. These two writing tools are excellent supplements to a basic knowledge of English grammar and composition. Together with a standard law dictionary and a manual of standard legal citations,[35] these books comprise the indispensable minimum kit of writing tools for the brief writer.

E. Gender Neutral Language

Whether required by law, or as matter of policy or good judgment, legal writers ought to write in language that is gender neutral. The goal is to avoid the generic "he," and other usages that may be regarded by the reader as sexist. Some states have begun the task of drafting or re-writing statutes in gender neutral language.

The goal of gender neutral language is not accomplished simply by removing the word "he" and substituting a noun for the pronoun. While retaining or preserving the precise meaning, the writer must use language that is neither stilted nor

---

35 THE BLUEBOOK: A UNIFORM SYSTEM OF CITATION (17th ed. 2000), is by far the most widely used legal citator. As a result, many courts have enacted rules requiring that all briefs comply with the citation format of that 391-page book. *See, e.g.,* 11TH CIR. R. 28-1(k); U.S. CT. MILITARY APP. R. 37(c)(2); *see also* Swedish Am. Hosp. v. Midwest Operating Eng'rs Fringe Benefit Funds, 842 F. Supp. 1039, 1043 n.7 (N.D. Ill. 1993) (admonishing counsel to conform briefs to *Bluebook* rules); Priess v. Fisherfold, 535 F. Supp. 1271, 1272 n.1 (S.D. Ohio 1982) (same). For convenience, an abbreviated legal citator has been included in this text showing the most commonly used forms of citation, all of which conform to *The Bluebook. See infra* Part Five, Chapter XII.

awkward. In addition to the use of a plural expression for the singular "he," the writer will soon learn several methods or techniques that will result in elegant gender neutral language. A few examples may be helpful:

1. If the attorney requests a stay, the court should grant ~~his~~ *the* request unless it prejudices the opposing party.

2. Any person who ~~has in his possession~~ *possesses* an unlicensed firearm is guilty of a felony.

3. ~~If the~~ *An* attorney *who* wishes to file a reply brief ~~he~~ may do so within ten days.

4. ~~When the board approves of the applicant he~~, *After having been approved by the board, the applicant* may participate in committee meetings.

5. When a public officer sues or is sued in ~~his~~ *an* official capacity, ~~he~~ *the officer* may be described as a party by ~~his~~ *the* official title rather than by ~~his~~ name.

6. Only an attorney admitted to the bar of the court may practice before the court, except that an individual may *be self*-represented ~~himself~~ in an action.

F. Literary Style

It has been stated that style "has to do with choice of words, choice of sentence length and structure, and with the pattern of ideas in writing."[36] The literary style of the brief is quite as much an individual matter with each brief writer as the writer's attire or views concerning surrealistic art. However, just as there is a noticeable distinction between a well-dressed person and one who is not, in matters of literary style, the distinction is often equally pronounced.

It is the goal of all writers to attain a cultured literary style. Its attainment, however, is difficult and elusive.[37] The observation or study of the style and manner of expression of those judges and authors endowed with a gift of literary expression may be helpful.[38] It is encouraging to know that many of these authors will readily admit that their "felicitous phrases" represent many hours of hard work

---

36 BRAND & WHITE, *supra* note 8, at 109. This textbook, subtitled "The Strategy of Persuasion," in the words of its authors, is "an application of the principles of expository prose and the rhetoric of persuasion to the kind of writing required in law school." *Id.* at viii.

37 For "some suggestions and cautionary hints that may help the beginner find his satisfactory style," see WILLIAM STRUNK & E. B. WHITE, THE ELEMENTS OF STYLE 66–85 (3d ed. 1979). *See also* ZINSSER, *supra* note 3, at 19–25.

38 The success of La Rochefoucauld's "maximes" has been attributed to his "taste for the right word [and] the fear of archaic, pedantic or provincial terms." FRANÇOIS, DUC DE LA ROCHEFOUCAULD, MAXIMES xvii (1927).

and, perhaps, the second or third draft rather than phrases glibly dictated to a stenographer.[39]

A comparison of judicial opinions indicates the importance of a pleasing, yet forceful style. Some opinions can be read from beginning to end with the same degree of interest with which one would read a delightful short story.[40] The reader will do well to analyze these opinions in order to ascertain the elements that have made them outstanding examples of legal writing.[41] Additional examples of effective legal writing can be found in *The Lawyer's Treasury*,[42] which contains "some of the best literary work and legal thought printed by the *American Bar Association Journal*."[43]

A lack of a literary gift should not deter the diligent advocate. It is entirely possible to *learn* to write effectively. Many distinguished legal authors commenced their literary career without any particular desire to write. Professor Williston, in his autobiography, *Life and Law*, writes that in his youth he had no thought of writing "either as a vocation or an avocation."[44] He adds:

> While in college I not only never offered a contribution to the *Harvard Advocate* or to the *Crimson*, but never thought of doing so. I wrote the themes and "forensics" that were part of the required course, but neither enjoyed the practice nor obtained good marks. A contributing cause may have been that I had nothing of interest that I desired to express.[45]

A rich vocabulary, clarity of expression, and a literary style can be acquired. They will flow from the experience acquired in the actual writing of legal documents.[46]

---

39   "[T]he stature of the great writers was the end result of hard labor, unstinted self-criticism, unremitting self-discipline and endless revision." Harold G. Pickering, *On Learning to Write: Suggestions for Study and Practice*, 41 A.B.A. J. 1121, 1122 (1955). "Never dictate a brief. The pen is a great analyzer." Alfred C. Cox, *Is Brief-Making a Lost Art?*, 17 YALE L.J. 413 (1908).

40   For the citations to the opinions of Justice Cardozo in the United States Supreme Court, see SELECTED WRITINGS OF BENJAMIN NATHAN CARDOZO 435 (Margaret E. Hall ed., 1947).

41   See excerpts of the writing of Maine, Pollock, Salmond, Dicey, Holmes, Maitland, and Cardozo in George John Miller, *On Legal Style*, 43 KY L.J. 235, 262 (1955) ("Appendix A—Some Fine Passages of Legal Writing"). Compare the majority opinion in *Haddock v. Haddock*, 201 U.S. 562 (1906), with the dissenting opinion by Justice Holmes, which commences: "I do not suppose that civilization will come to an end whichever way this case is decided." *Id.* at 628.

42   EUGENE C. GERHART, THE LAWYER'S TREASURY (1956).

43   *Id.* at 7; *see also* Edward D. Re, *Legal Writing as Good Literature*, 59 ST. JOHN'S L. REV. 211 (1985).

44   SAMUEL WILLISTON, LIFE AND LAW 254 (1941).

45   *Id.*

46   A brief writer can avoid some of the more common violations of the rules of usage and principles of composition by becoming familiar one or more of the following reference manuals: WILLIAM STRUNK & E. B. WHITE, THE ELEMENTS OF STYLE (4th ed. 2000), THE CHICAGO

A student beginning to learn how to write legal documents should try to write succinct sentences, primarily in the active voice. This fundamental writing style will assist the student to prepare briefs that are easy for the reader to understand. This style forms the foundation of every well-written brief. In an age when briefs must be read and understood at record pace, it is in every lawyer's interest to write a brief that can be quickly understood by judges and their staffs.

G. Ornamental Language

The belief that language is not lawyer-like unless it is interspersed with a generous quantity of "whereas," "wherefores," "and/ors," "passims," "supras," "infras," "contras," "ergos," and "hereinafters" is a grave mistake, which ought to be dispelled very early in the advocate's professional career.[47] No document should be written in such a manner as to have it sound "legalistic." Because the historical reasons or causes that made the language of the law and legal writing stilted and redundant have expired, there is no reason why all legal writing today cannot attain a high level of literary quality.[48]

There are in the legal vocabulary certain words that convey a definite meaning to the lawyer and to the court. These are *words of art*, which make for understanding and clarity. They are professional shortcuts to express certain concepts. Consequently, in a legal document addressed to lawyers and judges, it is entirely proper and usually necessary to use words that serve as "conceptual labels."[49] The law has many such words as "corpus," "certiorari," "dictum," and "recognizance." The same may also be said of certain Latin maxims that are in common usage. In a legal document, the word "vested" or "contingent" before the word "remainder" conveys a definite meaning to the lawyer. The use of terms of art, however, is not to be confused with the use of stilted words that needlessly disrupt otherwise smooth language. Some words not only impair smooth reading but also are pretentious. "An ornate, pretentious, grandiose style, replete with superfluous frills and rhetorical extravagances, can act only as an undesirable distraction."[50]

In brief writing, the excessive use of the words *supra* and *infra* should be avoided. If it is desirable to refer the reader to specific language previously used

---

MANUAL OF STYLE (15th ed. 2003), and TERRI LECLERCQ, GUIDE TO LEGAL WRITING STYLE (3d ed. 2004).

47   "A discussion of some words that don't belong in briefs could probably be condensed into this concise statement: about fifty percent of them. This comment could not accurately be made in regard to judicial opinions; it would be necessary to omit 'fifty percent' and substitute 'sixty-five percent.'" Mortimer Levitan, *Some Words That Don't Belong in Briefs*, 1960 WIS. L. REV. 421 (1960).

48   *See generally* Re, *supra* note 42.

49   Miller, *supra* note 40, at 255. This article makes specific basic suggestions that are very helpful.

50   Horace Stern, *The Writing of Judicial Opinions*, 18 PA. B.A. Q. 40 (1947).

or quoted, it is proper to summarize, and to refer the reader to the previous discussion by setting forth the specific page number in the brief.

Counsel should also refrain from the excessive use of footnotes in a brief. Footnotes in a brief often are distracting. If a particular matter is important to the discussion, its substance should be skillfully woven into the text. Matter that is merely peripheral to the discussion does not warrant inclusion in the brief.

Occasionally, some distracting information must be included in a brief. In those rare circumstances, a footnote may be appropriate. For example, if a long, cumbersome citation to the record is necessary, a footnote may be useful. A footnote may also be appropriate to explain or define the use of certain abbreviations or citations. For example, a footnote explaining that "JA at ___" refers to a page in the joint appendix would be proper.

H. The Brief as Preparation for Oral Argument

The brief submitted to the court reflects counsel's professional competence. It demonstrates the amount of research, preparation, and thought given to the problem that must be solved by the appellate tribunal. The careful writing of the brief also prepares the advocate to deliver a persuasive and convincing oral argument. Having done exhaustive research, having mastered the facts of the case and the record on appeal, and having prepared an effective brief, the attorney is uniquely qualified to argue the case orally.[51] The problem of oral argument is then essentially one of selection and presentation. The presentation, to be effective, must be concise, clear, and convincing. It affords the last opportunity to win a case that up to that time may have been lost.

Rarely should oral argument be a time to say anything that has not already been included in the brief. Therefore, the brief should include any and all information and arguments that the lawyer wishes to convey to the court. The brief writer should not refrain from including information in the brief on the assumption that oral argument will present a second opportunity to convey that information or argument to the court. Moreover, because litigants are not guaranteed the opportunity to have an oral argument, it is simply too risky to save anything solely for oral argument. The only time new information should be provided at oral argument is if, for some acceptable reason, that information was not known at the time the briefs were submitted, or it is necessary to answer a question by the court.

I. Counsel's Professional Responsibility

When trying a case or arguing an appeal, a lawyer has a professional duty vigorously to assert the client's cause in an effort to win the case. A second, and equally important, responsibility, however, is the lawyer's duty to assist the court in de-

---

51   *See* Edward D. Re, *The Lawyer as Lawmaker*, 52 A.B.A. J. 159 (1956).

ciding the case justly and according to law.[52] What, then, is a lawyer to do when to assist the court may produce an unfavorable result for the client, or when vigorously to assert the client's cause may produce an unjust result? The occasional conflicts between the professional responsibilities associated with the dual roles of "advocate" and "officer of the court" give rise to some of the most important and troublesome ethical questions confronting the legal profession.[53]

A compilation of the ethical premises and problems of the legal profession are found in the "Model Rules of Professional Conduct." In the Preamble of the "Model Rules," it is stated that:

> [i]n the nature of law practice . . . conflicting responsibilities are encountered. Virtually all difficult ethical problems arise from conflict between a lawyer's responsibility to clients, to the legal system and to the lawyer's own interest in remaining an upright person while earning a satisfactory living. The Rules of Professional Conduct prescribe terms for resolving such conflicts. Within the framework of these Rules, many difficult issues of professional discretion can arise. Such issues must be resolved through the exercise of sensitive professional and moral judgment guided by basic principles underlying the Rules.[54]

Hence, the "Model Rules" address such areas as the attorney-client relationship, the lawyer as counselor, the lawyer as advocate, law firms and associations, public service, and maintaining the integrity of the profession. By offering guidelines in these areas, the "Model Rules" seek to promote the highest standards of professional competence and ethical conduct by the attorney.[55]

J. Attorney as Agent of the Client

In drafting a brief or any other litigation paper, or in oral argument, an attorney must always be aware that counsel's words may be used against the client. Although an attorney's statements in court are not considered evidence, nevertheless, they may be introduced as vicarious party admissions under Federal Rules of Evidence 801(d)(2).[56] As long ago as 1880, the Supreme Court recognized

---

52　*See* Edward D. Re, *The Partnership of Bench and Bar,* 16 CATH. LAW, 194, 207–08 (1970).

53　The art of advocacy is "beset with perils of a very special kind, and for that reason the first quality beyond all others in the advocate . . . is that he must be a man of character. The Court must be able to rely on the advocate's word." The Right Honorable Lord Justice Birkett, *quoted in* Julius J. Marke, *The Art of Advocacy—A Bibliographical Commentary,* N.Y.L.J., July 19, 1977, at 4.

54　The "Model Rules" may be found in Martindale-Hubbell Law Digest, pt. IV.

55　*See* Bruce A. Green, *The Ten Most Common Ethical Violations,* 24 LITIGATION 48 (1998).

56　*See, e.g.,* United States v. McKeon, 738 F.2d 26, 31–33 (2d Cir. 1984). *See* discussion of opening statements and closing arguments *infra* pp. 27–29.

that an attorney's statement of fact in court could constitute an admission on behalf of the client.[57]

For example, a brief submitted in an administrative proceeding relating to the market for a company's products could be introduced by an adversary in an unrelated proceeding as evidence of the plaintiff's marketing practices. Superseded pleadings may also be introduced to impeach a party's version of events.[58] Indeed, it is not uncommon for counsel in a major litigation to obtain and analyze the opposing party's submissions to the court in other proceedings that involve similar questions of law or fact in the hope of finding material that may be used to counsel's advantage. Thus, when preparing any written document for submission to a court, it is well to remember that, as the agent of a client, the attorney may bind the client. A careless phrase or statement can have serious consequences.

---

57 Oscanyan v. Arms Co., 103 U.S. 261, 263 (1880); *see also* Link v. Wabash R.R., 370 U.S. 626, 633–34 (1962).

58 Contractor Util. Sales Co., v. Certain-Teed Prods. Corp., 638 F.2d 1061, 1084 (7th Cir. 1981); Raulie v. United States, 400 F.2d 487, 526 (10th Cir. 1968).

Part Two

OPINION LETTERS AND CLAIM OR DEMAND LETTERS, TRIAL AND POST-TRIAL BRIEFS, AND MEMORANDA OF LAW

This part of the book will introduce a variety of important documents that are essential in the practice of law and in the trial of cases. As in other parts of this book, the purpose is to illustrate the importance of effective writing in the drafting of all legal documents. In this part, the documents relate to pretrial and trial practice.

II

OPINION LETTERS AND CLAIM OR DEMAND LETTERS

A. Opinion Letter

The opinion letter is an informal memorandum of law in letter form. It sets forth with professional objectivity and candor the answer to the specific question that must be answered. In the practice of law, it is addressed to a client and, in clear and understandable language, states the specific answer to the legal question asked by the client.

There is no limit to the types of questions that counsel may be asked to answer in the opinion letter. The client may ask a very specific legal question, or may seek advice and counsel. For example, may the client follow a certain course of action or conduct? What is the legal meaning of certain words, phrases, or clauses in a legal document? On the particular facts stated, does the client have a cause of action? On the particular facts stated, is the client violating a particular clause or paragraph of a lease? On the particular facts stated, is the client's tenant violating a particular clause or paragraph of the lease?

The opinion letter, notwithstanding its informality as a legal document, is very important and of great value to both client and attorney. It is of value to the client because it is responsive and offers the client reasonable certainty and confidence. It is of value to the lawyer because it states the precise factual basis for counsel's legal opinion. Hence, there can be no misunderstanding as to the basis for counsel's answer or advice.

Clients are generally not interested in the citation of authority or other documentation for counsel's opinion. Accordingly, legal citations should not be included in the letter. Clients wish to know the answer to the specific question that has been asked. The letter, in clear and understandable language, must set forth counsel's answer.

In the sample opinion letter, reproduced in Appendix H of the text, counsel answers the question whether the words "Executive Brand" may be registered with the U.S. Patent and Trademark Office as a trademark for men's suits. The opinion letter answers the question directly and succinctly: "As a result of our research, we have concluded that an application for the registration of the mark 'Executive Brand' is likely to be refused."

Although the letter reproduced in the appendix contains a reference to the case upon which counsel relies, and explains its pertinence to the inquiry, neither the name of the case nor its citation is included. The client is primarily interested in counsel's opinion that the client "would probably not be able to register the mark 'Executive Brand.'"

B. Claim or Demand Letter

An important letter that is often ignored or overlooked as a valuable legal document, both in the settlement and litigation processes, is the claim or demand letter. Unlike the opinion letter, which is a communication between a client and its counsel, a claim or demand letter is a communication between potentially adverse parties. These letters serve to notify an adverse party of the sender's legal rights, and demand that the recipient of the letter modify its course of conduct in some way. While these letters are typically written and sent by lawyers on behalf of clients, often it is appropriate and more helpful if the letter is written or reviewed by counsel, but signed and sent by the client.

In the absence of special circumstances, such as a contractual provision, there is no requirement for a plaintiff to advise a defendant that the plaintiff intends to institute suit. Hence, the claim letter ought not to be sent unless it is sent for a particular purpose. What does counsel wish to accomplish?

The initial letter by the client may show that the client does not really wish to bring suit, but was "constrained" by circumstances or the unreasonable attitude of the other party. An attitude of conciliation and reasonableness may be helpful and, indeed, decisive in a close case in which the adversary has been abusive, and defiant.

The appropriate and effective claim letter is always, expressly or impliedly, an invitation to a settlement of the dispute. If written by the client, the response, even if not entirely favorable, will usually foretell a defense, and will also reveal the attitude of the potential adversary. This initial response places counsel in a better position to evaluate the client's grievance or case and the difficulties that may be expected or encountered. Surely, it is helpful to know of the adversary's defense through a letter written by the adversary.

Counsel should not draft the claim or demand letter in tone and terms that are intimidating and threaten litigation unless the client is prepared to litigate. The more cautious and preferred approach is to draft a letter that will give notice to the recipient but will not make the recipient reasonably fearful of suit. The letter ought to be courteous, moderate in tone, and exploratory.

Beyond an appropriate tone, the claim letter should set forth the specific claim or demand that is being made and the legal basis for that claim or demand. Without necessarily referring to any legal action that the client may contemplate taking, the letter should indicate what the recipient must do to comply with the claim or demand. As in all legal documents, and letters in particular, the ABC's of legal writing are applicable.

An example of a claim or demand letter may be found in Appendix E. At this juncture, however, two brief illustrative examples may be helpful to the law student. The first is written by the client, and the second by counsel.

———————

John Landers
2100 5th Ave
New York, NY 10036
May 16, 2004

Mr. William Tenant
14 Madison Ave.
New York, NY 10017

Dear Mr. Tenant:

It has been brought to my attention by several tenants that, in apartment 4H, which you occupy at 14 Madison Avenue, you are violating clause 16 of your lease, which prohibits the keeping of pets. Specifically, I am told that you have acquired a dog, which has been described as a bull terrier.

This letter is notice that the harboring of a dog violates the terms of the lease, and that, unless the dog is immediately removed from the apartment, I will be constrained to commence eviction proceedings.

I do hope you will notify me as soon as you have removed the dog so that your eviction will not be necessary. Thank you for your cooperation.

Sincerely,

John Landers

———————

Law Office of
James Warren
21 K Street, NW
Washington, DC 20571

July 27, 2004

Mr. Donald Debtor
1900 Eades Street
Arlington, VA 20079

Dear Mr. Debtor:

My client, Ms. Linda Loaner, has informed me that the promissory note you executed on April 1, 1998, when she made the $5000.00 loan that you requested, was due and payable on June 30, 1998, and that payment has not been made.

Please send me a bank check or money order, payable to Ms. Linda Loaner, for the full amount due plus interest. If you have any question as to the exact amount due, please telephone me.

Your cooperation will be greatly appreciated.

Sincerely,

James Warren

III

THE TRIAL BRIEF

The nature and content of the trial brief and of the legal memorandum are not as well defined as those of the appellate brief. Their form and content are determined by the purpose to be served. For example, one trial brief may be for the exclusive benefit of counsel while another may be primarily for the purpose of assisting the court in following the proceedings of the trial. The trial "brief" submitted to the court is often referred to as a "trial memorandum" for the court.[1] Regardless of nomenclature, it is evident that the trial brief drafted for counsel's own benefit and guidance will be different in content and scope from the trial memorandum that will be submitted to the court.

Likewise, the memorandum that the research assistant submits to trial counsel or to a partner of a law firm in answer to the question: "On the above facts, does Pryor have a cause of action for deceit against Donaldson?" will be different in form, length, and content from the memorandum that is submitted to a court upon a point of law. In the former, only the accuracy of the answer may be important, while in the latter, the form, the citation of authorities, and the discussion of the propositions of law are also important.

A. Generally

1. Definition; Nature and Purpose

When used generally, "trial brief" refers to any brief that will be used in the trial of a case, as distinguished from a brief on appeal. The trial brief may be used in a trial before a judge and jury, a judge without a jury, in a hearing or trial before a referee or an administrative law judge, in the argument of a motion or an interlocutory question, or in any type of special proceeding. It is trial counsel's blueprint of the trial. In the process of preparing the trial brief, counsel is actually preparing to conduct the trial competently. The trial brief may also serve to assist special trial counsel to try the case. It serves as an effective checklist for lawyers by indicating all that they must know and prove in order to succeed at trial.[2]

The trial memorandum submitted to a court at the beginning or during a trial differs from counsel's trial brief in that the trial memorandum is designed to help the court understand and conduct the trial. It should not be exhaustive or exhausting.

---

1   The trial brief for counsel's own use during trial is also referred to as the trial notebook, trial outline, trial manual, and trial file. Joseph P. Zammit, *The Trial Brief and the Trial Memorandum,* PRAC. LAW., Mar. 1978 at 75; *see also* RALPH C. MCCULLOUGH & JAMES L. UNDERWOOD, CIVIL TRIAL MANUAL 573 (2d ed. 1980).

2   "A proper trial brief consists of a compilation of practically everything that may be usable and valuable in the conduct of the case." Leo R. Friedman, *The Trial Brief in a Criminal Case,* PRAC. LAW., Mar. 1963, at 61.

The trial memorandum should merely indicate the type of case to be heard and recite the general nature of the evidence that counsel intends to introduce. It should be obvious to the advocate that the trial memorandum need not set forth the names, statements, and expected testimony of all of the witnesses that will be called, although this information would be appropriate and necessary in counsel's trial brief.

Although counsel's trial brief is solely for the benefit of counsel or special trial counsel, it may sometimes be helpful to submit certain portions of that trial brief to the court and opposing counsel. For example, if a question concerning the admissibility of certain documents or testimony into evidence arises during the trial, a lawyer prepared to submit that portion of the trial brief that deals with the question will have a distinct advantage. For this reason, it is of the utmost importance that counsel anticipate the questions that will arise during trial. These matters should be discussed or treated on sheets separate from the rest of the trial brief and, if the opportunity arises, may be submitted to the court and opposing counsel.

2. Necessary Preparation

a. Investigation of Facts

If the trial brief is to serve a useful purpose, it must be drafted only after counsel has made a thorough investigation of the case. Counsel must know the facts as maintained by the plaintiff and the points that may be contradicted or disputed by the defendant. The lawyer's investigation and analysis of the facts must commence the moment the attorney is retained. After having listened to the client's story, counsel must check those "facts," and must interview witnesses, verify the charges, assertions and statements of the client, examine relevant documents, and attend to many other similar matters. This has been referred to as "marshalling the evidence."[3]

b. Search for the Applicable Law

Having ascertained and learned the facts, counsel may begin the search for the applicable law. From the facts of the case, counsel should answer certain questions that will facilitate the legal research. What word or words describe:

i) the party or parties to the case?

ii) the subject matter of the case?

iii) the cause of action and relief sought by the plaintiff, or the defendant's defense?

iv) the legal issue or question of law?

---

3   *See* HARRY S. BODIN ET AL., MARSHALLING THE EVIDENCE (1962). This monograph contains helpful suggestions as to the content and organization of the lawyer's "file" of a case. It is indicated that the file should include the "trial memorandum for the court" and "counsel's trial brief." It is no small or easy task, but it is an indispensable phase of the preparation for trial.

The answers to the questions asked will give descriptive words that will lead to authorities and cases in point.

The word that describes the party or parties should refer to the particular group or class of the person or persons involved in the action. Examples are words such as heirs, distributees, and infants.

In considering subject matter, counsel should find the word or words that describes places, things, or objects that relate to or caused the dispute or injury that led to the cause of action. Examples of words that describe subject matter are automobiles, derricks, and sidewalks. The cause of action is usually easily described by words such as assault, battery, breach of contract, ejectment, negligence, and trespass. The relief sought may include declaratory judgment, injunction, damages mandamus, replevin, restitution, specific performance, or abatement of nuisance. Some examples of words that describe defenses are lack of or failure of consideration, infancy, laches, unclean hands, and statute of limitations.

Apart from the nature of the cause of action itself, the word that describes the disputed legal question or point of law will be very helpful in leading to other cases in point. Some examples are suppression of evidence, probable cause for search, and search warrant.

Having analyzed the facts and determined how they can be proven in court, the attorney can begin to "research" the legal problem and to formulate a legal theory for the prosecution or trial of the case.

c. Legal Research Materials—Where to Find the Law

As a result of the ever-increasing scope of legislative activity, the statutory law of the appropriate jurisdiction is an excellent place to begin the search for an answer to the legal problem presented. It is a great time-saving device to know initially if the controversy will ultimately be resolved by the interpretation and application of a statute. If a relevant statute exists, the annotations to it will serve as an introduction to the important cases in that field of law. Furthermore, although the search for statutory authority may prove futile, the researcher's time will not have been wasted. A search for statutory authority is always necessary because it is no longer realistic to assume that there is no pertinent statute.

Alternative starting points for the legal researcher include legal encyclopedias, treatises, and law reviews. These publications act as refreshers, furnish a legal framework applicable to the facts, and also supply valuable leads to case law. Legal digests are an additional source of relevant case law. In specialized fields such as taxation, administration of estates, antitrust, labor law, and the like, special sources[4] are available that will save many hours of tedious research in seeking cases and materials "in point."

---

4   Looseleaf reporter services of the Bureau of National Affairs, Commerce Clearing House, and Prentice-Hall are examples.

Computer assisted legal research has now become the preferred method of research for many attorneys. Westlaw and LexisNexis, and a variety of lower-cost commercial services[5] provide the researcher with expedient and efficient research methods for retrieving cases and other materials. In essence, the researcher combines words and phrases that the researcher believes will appear in relevant cases. In the search for cases, the search can be further narrowed by limiting the jurisdiction, year, or particular judge's opinion to be researched. A large amount of case law is now also available on free Internet sites. However, since even the best of these sites do not offer search features that are as sophisticated as those provided by LexisNexis and Westlaw, they are usually most valuable as document retrieval services for opinions already known to the researcher.

In addition to case law, both of these systems offer methods for researching statutory, administrative, and secondary authorities. Authority can also be updated using the KeyCite feature for Westlaw and the Shepard's feature for LexisNexis. Most law students also have access to these systems, and training manuals and courses are offered so that students can become proficient in their usage.

A word of caution, however, is required. What has been said, pertaining to the use and advantages of computer-assisted legal research, is not intended to minimize the importance of the traditional methods of legal research. It is still vital for the law student and lawyer to be thoroughly familiar with the use of traditional sources in the discovery of the applicable law, and in bringing cases and other authorities up to date. Proficiency and skill in the traditional methods of legal research are essential, quite apart from the cost or expense that may be associated with the use of computer-assisted legal research. Hence, it may be suggested that, prior to taking advantage of computer-assisted legal research, the student use traditional methods in the search for the applicable law.

The analytical approach taken or the search technique used by the advocate is an individual matter. Some researchers prefer to see the general picture first and then see where the particular problem fits into that picture. Others prefer to examine the most recent materials first because "a recent case may make further research unnecessary, whereas an ancient one would not."[6] Usually a combination of techniques must be employed.[7]

---

5   Examples of such subscription services are LawProbe, Loislaw, National Law Library, and VersusLaw.

6   GEORGE TROSK, BRIEF WRITING AND APPEALS 4 (1962).

7   See discussion under "Legal Research," *infra* pp. 79–90 and recommended books dealing with legal research and legal method.

d. Nature of Cause of Action or Claim

Just as important as a thorough investigation of the facts and law is counsel's choice of the nature of the cause of action or claim upon which the case will be tried.[8] Does the action sound in tort or contract? Is the action properly a suit in equity or at law? Based on the facts, precedents, and statutes that have been reviewed, the lawyer must discern the legal basis upon which the client is most likely to prevail. The course that the litigation will take may be determined by the lawyer's choice or decision.

A clear exposition of the nature of the cause of action will focus the court's attention on the significant features of the case. It will prevent the court from becoming bogged down in peripheral issues and allow the court to move forward expeditiously toward a just result. A wrong choice, though not always fatal to an action,[9] will certainly make less obvious the merits of a client's cause, and the lawyer who chooses poorly risks losing a case that might have been won. Furthermore, the cause of action selected will, in all likelihood, be adhered to on any subsequent appeal.[10]

An important factor to consider in selecting the cause of action upon which to proceed is the kind of relief sought by the plaintiff. For example, a plaintiff who is suing for breach of contract to sell land may insist upon specific performance of the contract, rather than damages or rescission. Counsel must prepare the case with special reference to the relief requested. Even if specific performance lies, it is counsel's duty to inform the client of the various legal consequences flowing from the demand for "equitable" or "extraordinary relief."[11] Furthermore, the choice may also determine whether the right to a jury trial will be lost, the applicability of a different statute of limitations, the applicability of the statute of frauds, and several other matters such as measure of damages and burden of proof.

---

8   "Not only must all the facts be marshalled and the law reviewed, but it is also necessary to evolve a definite theory for the action." A. HAROLD FROST, PREPARATION OF A NEGLIGENCE CASE 43 (1962). "The first aim in the search for authorities is the ascertainment of a proper theory of the case." ROGER W. COOLEY, BRIEF MAKING AND THE USE OF LAW BOOKS 418 (5th ed. 1926).

9   Trial courts will not dismiss a case merely because a plaintiff has misconceived the proper legal theory, if, based on the facts alleged, the plaintiff might obtain relief on a different legal theory. Jenkins v. Fidelity Bank, 365 F. Supp. 1391, 1398 (E.D. Pa. 1973). "[T]he court is under a duty to . . . determine if the allegations provide for relief on any possible theory." Bramlet v. Wilson, 495 F.2d 714, 716 (8th Cir. 1974); see also Lane v. Mercury Record Corp., 252 N.Y.S.2d 101 (App. Div. 1st Dep't 1964).

10 E.g., Universe Tankships, Inc. v. United States, 528 F.2d 73, 76 (3d Cir. 1975).

11 This consultation with the client may save counsel embarrassment, if not despair, at a later date when the client may ask: "Why didn't you tell me?" "Failure to keep clients fully advised is one of the principal causes of dissatisfaction with lawyers. Malpractice claims against lawyers are often the result of this client dissatisfaction." Charles R. Richey, A Federal Trial Judge's Reflections on the Preparation for a Trial of Civil Cases, 52 IND. L.J. 111 (1976).

B. Trial Brief for Counsel

Having carefully investigated the facts and thoroughly examined the law, counsel is prepared to draft the *trial brief*. It must be remembered that this trial brief is solely for the benefit of trial counsel. It, therefore, contains material that would not be included if it were a trial memorandum to be submitted to the court and opposing counsel.

The trial brief for counsel, in addition to an identifying caption or title, should contain:

(1) Table of Contents and Authorities Cited;

(2) Statement of Facts;

(3) Digest of Pleadings;

(4) Grounds for Challenging Jury or Jurors;

(5) Evidence Required to Establish the Case;

(6) List of Witnesses and Exhibits;

(7) Digest or Statements of Witnesses;

(8) Proof Required by Opposing Counsel; Cross-Examination;

(9) Brief on the Legal Questions Presented;

(10) Requested Charges to the Jury;

(11) Opening Statement of Counsel;

(12) Closing Argument of Counsel; and

(13) Other Possible Contents.

These headings represent what may be termed the essential parts of a useful trial brief. No dogmatic rule, however, prevents counsel from modifying the form of the brief to meet the needs of the particular case. For example, if the case involves the application or interpretation of a constitutional provision, statute, or administrative regulation, it is advisable to have a heading, perhaps after the facts, to include those materials. It has been suggested that these materials be placed in a single volume, either bound or looseleaf, with the various headings indicated by tabular indices.[12] A looseleaf binder seems preferable because it provides flexibility and permits the addition of new materials.

1. Table of Contents and Authorities Cited

The "Table of Contents and Authorities" should be sufficiently detailed to serve the purpose of an index to the various headings and subdivisions of the trial brief. This ready reference to the contents of the brief, which includes all that is essen-

---

12   Friedman, *supra* note 2, at 62.

tial for the competent handling of the trial, instills confidence in the advocate. It makes readily available to counsel all the materials gathered as a result of investigation and legal research. It enables counsel to proceed with the trial knowing that the major problems that will be encountered have been considered, and that any unforeseen problems will not create a crisis.

2. Statement of Facts

The "Statement of Facts" should be a brief summary of all of the material facts of the case. It is recommended that the facts be stated in the order in which they occurred. This chronological narration of the facts should also indicate the facts that are disputed by the defendant. Because the statement of facts will refresh counsel's recollection of the case, this statement should be read anew before the trial begins.

3. Digest of Pleadings

The "Digest of Pleadings" must be terse and, if possible, should be contained on one page so that counsel can visualize the pleadings at a glance and know which factual assertions have been admitted and which have been denied.[13] It is advisable to set forth the digest of pleadings as follows:

Complaint	Answer
1. Residence of Plaintiff	Admitted
2. Defendant is New York corporation doing business in this county	Admitted
3. On 6/1/99 plaintiff delivered parcel to defendant and received stub or coupon	Admitted
4. On 6/25/99 plaintiff presented coupon and defendant refused to return parcel	Denied
5. Reasonable value of parcel $1000	Denied

In the same manner, the digest should indicate any new matter that may be set forth in the answer such as an affirmative defense or counterclaim. If the pleadings have been amended, the digest should indicate the amendments. Appropriate page references to the actual pleadings should also be included.

4. Grounds for Challenging Jury or Jurors

Under this heading, counsel should include the various grounds allowed by the law of the particular jurisdiction to challenge the jury or individual jurors. This section should include all grounds whether permitted by statute or by decisional law with the appropriate citation of authority. Since this heading can be used in all future jury cases, it is advantageous to make a thorough outline as a separate document that can be included in future trial briefs.

---

13   Zammit, *supra* note 1, at 73.

It is also advisable to include under this heading questions that are helpful in examining the jury.[14] "Wherever prospective jurors may be examined by counsel on the voir dire, counsel's trial brief may profitably contain notes as to the subjects to be covered in the questioning."[15]

5. Evidence Required to Establish the Case

Under this heading counsel should state the evidence that must be introduced to establish the cause of action alleged in the pleadings. In the first instance it implies that counsel is familiar with the elements of the prima facie case that must be established.[16] It also implies that counsel knows how to phrase appropriate questions to be asked of the witnesses in order to establish the necessary elements.[17] If documents or exhibits are to be introduced into evidence, counsel should be familiar with the rules of evidence permitting the introduction of the various exhibits. If counsel experiences difficulty in phrasing appropriate questions to lay the necessary foundations for such evidence, the phraseology of questions should be included under this heading. Until counsel knows what questions to ask of the witness, it is preferable to sacrifice brevity and to write out the questions that must be asked. These questions must be learned. The phraseology of key questions cannot be left to the inspiration of the moment. Even experienced counsel is advised to write out all crucial questions.

It is generally inadvisable to read the questions verbatim since the examination of the witness may thereby lose much of its effectiveness. It may, however, be necessary to read technical questions to be asked of an expert witness. No matter how well an attorney may have prepared certain technical, nonlegal aspects of a case, it is not advisable to rely exclusively upon memory or ingenuity to phrase

---

14   "The principal purpose of the examination of the jury on the *voir dire* is to obtain information about the jurors which will enable counsel to eliminate jurors who cannot or are not likely to be fair in the consideration of the case. This is the essence of the selection of a jury." HARRY S. BODIN, SELECTING A JURY 1 (1954). For suggestions in the selection of a jury in a criminal action, see IRVING MENDELSON, CRIMINAL CASES 26 (1953). *See also* Reynolds v. Benefield, 931 F.2d 506 (8th Cir. 1991).

15   HARRY S. BODIN, FINAL PREPARATION FOR TRIAL 7 (1954). For suggestions on "the art of jury persuasion," see FRANCIS X. BUSCH, LAW AND TACTICS IN JURY TRIALS (1949).

16   "The proof of facts is one of the most important fields of practice. The ultimate facts upon which the right of the parties rest are usually in dispute. In such cases it becomes necessary to introduce evidentiary matter to prove them. Upon their proper proof depend success or failure in the litigation." PERCIVAL W. VIESSELMAN, ABBOTT ON FACTS iii (5th ed. 1937).

17   For helpful suggested questions in the various types of actions, see HOWARD H. SPELLMAN, HOW TO PROVE A *PRIMA FACIE* CASE (3d ed. 1954). "The proof of a prima facie case is the keystone in the arch of successful litigation. After the issues have been framed by the pleadings, it is incumbent upon the plaintiff to demonstrate his right to remain in court by the establishment of certain minima of proof, without which there is neither necessity for the defendant to state his side of the case nor power for the court to give a plaintiff's judgment, should the defendant remain silent." *Id.* at 3. For suggestions on the trial of a civil action, see McCULLOUGH & UNDERWOOD, *supra* note 1.

accurate questions to be asked of an expert. This would apply, for example, in proving medical phases of cases.[18]

The evidence required to prove plaintiff's case can be set forth in narrative form or in the form of a diagram. The following diagram, illustrating a simple bailment case, indicates the facts that counsel for the plaintiff must establish, the witnesses who will testify to establish the facts, the page in the trial brief where the statement of the witness appears, the status of the pleadings in relation to the facts, and the documents to be introduced.

Prima Facie Case

Facts to be Established	Witness	Page	Pleadings	Documents
1. Delivered parcel	Plaintiff	8	Admitted	
2. Received coupon	"	8	"	Coupon
3. Presented coupon on demand; refusal	"	8	Denied	
4. Value of parcel	Jones	9	"	

If counsel represents a defendant, the same form of diagram should be used in order to visualize the defense and to make sure that all the facts necessary to establish the defense will be proven through the witnesses at the trial.

6. List of Witnesses and Exhibits

The "List of Witnesses and Exhibits" in a case of considerable complexity is very important. In a simple case, with one or two witnesses in addition to the plaintiff, the problem of remembering the names and the testimony of the witnesses may not be difficult. In more complex cases, this list is an invaluable aid to counsel.

The witnesses should be listed in the order in which they are to be called. This depends upon the natural order for the presentation of evidence. If necessary, the names of the witnesses should also be listed alphabetically with the page reference to their statements or digest of their testimony.

If the exhibits or documents are numerous, it is also wise to list each exhibit with the name of the witness through whom the particular exhibit will be introduced into evidence.

---

18   For assistance in cases having medical aspects, see WILLIAM J. CURRAN & E. DONALD SHAPIRO, LAW, MEDICINE, AND FORENSIC SCIENCE (3d ed. 1982).

7. Digest or Statements of Witnesses[19]

If the statements of the witnesses are not unduly long, they should be reproduced in full. If a statement contains much that is irrelevant, counsel should include only the pertinent portions. These statements should be placed under this heading in the order in which the witnesses will be called, i.e., in the order in which the testimony will be presented. If statements of hostile witnesses are available, they should also be included. These latter statements will be valuable for purposes of cross-examination.[20]

8. Proof Required by Opposing Counsel; Cross-Examination

Under this heading, counsel should indicate the matters that must be proved by the defendant in order to establish a defense. It is a great advantage for counsel to be able to anticipate the evidence that the defendant will endeavor to introduce. The trial brief of the plaintiff should indicate not only what matters would have to be proven by the defendant, but also what objections could be raised. If a particular question is doubtful, counsel should follow the notation of the objection with appropriate citation of authorities. If the point is sufficiently important, counsel would do well to prepare a discussion of that point, adequately documented, in such a manner that it can be separated from the rest of the brief, if necessary, for submission to the court.

Counsel should also include in this section all that can be anticipated about the case of opposing counsel. It is often said that a lawyer who is going to try a case must prepare not only the plaintiff's case, but also the defendant's. In this way, weaknesses and omissions in the adversary's case can be more readily detected, and counsel is better prepared to cross-examine hostile witnesses.

On the important subject of cross-examination of witnesses, preparation, rather than intuition or "telepathic insight," is the "golden key." In the words of Professor McCormick: "Improvisation is often necessary but its results are small compared to those from planned questions based on facts dug out before trial."[21]

---

19   Judge Joiner considers the digest or statements of witnesses as "perhaps the most important part of the trial brief." Charles W. Joiner, *The Trial Brief—The Lawyer's Battle Plan and Ammunition*, PRAC. LAW., at 53. 58 Oct. 1955. He adds that this "resume of testimony" has a five-fold-purpose: "1. It will be the organization of your case. 2. It will organize the testimony of each witness. 3. It will help the lawyer to remember important details during the trial. 4. It serves as the basis for the conduct of the examination of a witness. 5. It will relieve the trial lawyer or his assistant of some of the burden of note-taking during the trial." *Id.*

20   For a delightful and instructive book containing the fundamental principles of cross-examination together with famous examples from selected cases, see FRANCIS WELLMAN, THE ART OF CROSS-EXAMINATION (4th ed. 1936).

21   Charles T. McCormick, *The Scope and Art of Cross-Examination*, 47 NW. L. REV. 177, 193 (1952).

9. Brief on the Legal Questions Presented

This portion of the trial brief for counsel represents the result of counsel's legal research. If the trial brief is for the exclusive use of counsel, this heading should objectively set forth the state of the law. The discussion should be expository rather than argumentative. If, on the other hand, counsel wishes to submit this segment of the brief to the court, as part of a trial memorandum, cases and authorities clearly opposed to counsel's position should be analyzed and carefully distinguished. If a statute is involved, it, too, should be set forth under this heading together with a digest of pertinent cases.

Organizing the discussion of authorities under appropriate point headings will add immeasurably to the usefulness of this part of the trial brief. In the event of an appeal, this section of the trial brief will be particularly helpful and time-saving.

10. Requested Charges to the Jury

The trial brief should include a draft of those instructions that counsel desires the court to give to the jury. "An instruction is an explanation by the trial judge to the jury of the rules applicable to the case in general, or to some branch or phase of the case."[22] This draft should be accompanied by the authorities upon which the request for the instructions is based. The requests should be numbered for purposes of identification. They should be short and clear. The language should be sufficiently simple so that the jury will have no difficulty understanding exactly what is meant by the charge. Although the judge will not charge the jury as requested if the request is legally incorrect, the refusal to charge the jury as requested, when the charge is correct, may be reversible error.

Three copies of the requested charges ought to be readily available. One copy is to be submitted to the court, one to opposing counsel, and the remaining copy forms a part of counsel's trial brief or file.

11. Opening Statement of Counsel

The opening statement of a case "is a matter of great importance to the outcome of the litigation."[23] Its purpose is to inform the court and jury, in a general way, of the nature of the action and the basic facts intended to be proved. It is the preview presented by counsel to the court or jury before any evidence is

---

22   1 EDWARD R. BRANSON, THE LAW OF INSTRUCTIONS TO JURIES IN CIVIL AND CRIMINAL CASES 1 (Alexander Hamilton Reid ed., 3d ed. 1960).

23   Arthur T. Vanderbilt, *The Six Factors in the Work of the Advocate*, 7 WASH. & LEE L. REV. 123–30 (1950), *reprinted in* 1 FANNIE J. KLEIN & JOEL LEE, SELECTED WRITINGS OF ARTHUR T. VANDERBILT 7, 14 (1967); *see also* Edward D. Re, *The Role of the Lawyer in Modern Society*, 30 S.D. L. REV. 501 (1985).

introduced.[24] An effective opening will help the judge and jury understand the significance of the testimony that they are about to hear.

In trials before a jury, scholars and lawyers may differ as to the importance of the opening statement, and the influence it may have on jurors in reaching the verdict that they will ultimately render. It is to be noted, however, that the "issue" or difference of opinion is not whether the opening statement is *important*, but rather, the "power of the opening statement."[25] For example, it has been stated, that "80 to 90 percent of all jurors do reach their ultimate verdict during or immediately after opening statements." It has been stated that studies "consistently provide support for the significance of the opening statement. Again and again, jurors—actual, surrogate, or simulated—rely on key portions of the opening statement in their deliberations. Trial verdicts are almost always connected in a juror's mind to points made in the opening."[26]

Regardless of the specific degree of "power" or "influence" of the opening statement in cases tried before a jury, no lawyer can ignore the great benefits that flow from a well-prepared, effectively delivered opening statement. The opening statement is important in all cases.

In cases tried without a jury, the trial judge welcomes an opening statement that introduces the case and states the issue that must be decided. It is helpful to counsel and facilitates the work of the court in understanding the case. Even when a trial brief or trial memorandum has been submitted, the opening statement refreshes the recollection of the court and sets the stage for the trial that will follow.

After stating that "the first impression you make on the jury is crucial," an exceptionally gifted and experienced lawyer added: "And whatever you say in your opening statement, you had better be prepared to prove. Make sure you're absolutely right on the law and the facts."[27] Careless statements made by counsel during the trial may very well adversely affect the outcome of the case.

---

24 *See* Re, *supra* note 22, at 501–08 (Lawyer as Advocate).

25 Vinson & Hanley, *Do Not Ignore This Opening Statement—Or any Others: A Reply to Professor Zeisel*, LITIGATION, Winter 1989 at 1, 2.

26 *Id.* at 2, 54.

27 Priscilla Anne Schwab, *Interview with Edward Bennett Williams*, LITIGATION, Winter 1986, at 28, 62; *see* discussion of vicarious admissions by lawyers *supra* p. 13.

12. Closing Argument of Counsel

The closing argument is counsel's opportunity to summarize what has occurred at trial and to indicate the facts that counsel believes have been proven. Counsel "re-states the evidence, and . . . reasons from the evidence."[28] It is the only time that counsel may address the members of the jury directly in an effort to persuade them of the validity of the client's claim.

The obvious importance of the closing argument necessitates their inclusion in the trial brief. Although the closing argument will almost certainly require revision based on what has occurred during the trial, the basic outline or text of the closing argument should be written before the trial. It is unlikely that counsel will have adequate time to compose a cogent closing argument after the trial has started.

An additional reason for the careful preparation of the closing argument is that, although counsel is allowed wide latitude, there are restrictions upon the statements and assertions that counsel can make during trial. Professor Wigmore, in his classic work on evidence, states:

> A counsel's argument is in its purpose a connected *presentation of the conclusions of fact* supposed to have been *proved by the evidence* tending in favor of his client. . . . He is not a witness. He may have testified as a witness; but in his argument he has solely the functions and rights of counsel. Any representation of fact, therefore, which is made by him *in the argument, must not be an assertion made upon his own credit*; it must be based solely upon those matters of fact of which evidence has already been introduced or of which no evidence need ever be introduced because of their notoriety as judicially noticed facts. To bring forward in argument an assertion of fact not of those two sorts is to become a witness; and to be a witness without being subjected to cross-examination is to violate the fundamental principle of the Hearsay rule.[29]

13. Other Possible Contents

The preceding headings are not necessarily exhaustive. The necessities of the case or the needs of counsel may require the inclusion of additional materials. For example, counsel who is not entirely familiar with the conduct of a trial may decide to include notations of the various motions that can be made during the trial. For the defendant, these may include a motion to dismiss after the plaintiff's opening address, a motion to dismiss at the close of plaintiff's case, a motion to dismiss at the close of the whole case, or a motion for a directed verdict. By including these matters in the trial brief, counsel is unlikely to overlook any necessary technical step during the trial.

---

28   6 JOHN HENRY WIGMORE, EVIDENCE § 1806 (3d ed. 1940).

29   *Id.* (emphasis in original).

Although initially an arduous task, the drafting of the trial brief will add immeasurably to the preparation for trial. Its presence on counsel's table during the trial offers rewards far in excess of the time and effort necessarily expended in its preparation.

C. Trial Memorandum for the Court

Rules of court may not require that counsel submit a trial brief or trial memorandum for the court. It is a good practice, however, to submit a trial memorandum to the court in all but the simplest cases.[30]

As indicated previously, certain materials in the trial brief for counsel should not be included in the trial brief or trial memorandum for the court. To the extent applicable, however, the order of the headings in both documents may be similar. Generally, the trial memorandum for the court, in addition to an identifying caption or title, should contain:

(1) Table of Contents and Authorities Cited;

(2) Statement of Facts;

(3) Digest of Pleadings;

(4) Synopsis of Evidence;

(5) Brief on Legal Questions Presented; and

(6) Requested Charges to the Jury.

The trial memorandum is designed to assist the court by providing the trial judge with the essential facts and law applicable to the particular case. It must not be so lengthy or detailed as to burden the court.

It must be remembered that the trial memorandum to be submitted to the court is a partisan document. It is designed to present the case about to be tried in a light most favorable to the party on whose behalf it is being submitted. Since it will present the facts and the law in a way that will be as favorable as possible, it is comparable to an appellate brief. Clearly, therefore, such a document will not contain certain matters that may be essential for the trial brief that has been prepared for counsel's own guidance during the trial.

For example, the document submitted to the court will not contain the specific questions that counsel proposes to ask witnesses on direct or cross-examination. Neither will it contain the statements of the various witnesses. It may, however, give a "Synopsis of Evidence" in addition to the "Statement of Facts." Whereas

---

30 "The Trial Memorandum is usually the judge's first exposure to what the case is all about and it facilitates his understanding of the issues and the proof. Moreover, if the opponent files a Trial Memorandum and counsel does not, his will be the only view of the case that the court will have until counsel presents his evidence." Zammit, *supra* note 1, at 79.

the "Statement of Facts" may set forth what occurred, i.e., narrate the facts, the "Synopsis of Evidence" will summarize the testimony of the various witnesses who will be called at trial.

If the trial memorandum is submitted to the court at the conclusion of the trial, counsel ought to state precisely what has been proved at trial. From the testimony and other evidence introduced at trial, counsel may draw reasonable inferences that will benefit the case.

The following headings are merely suggestions and should be modified to meet the needs of the particular case. If the facts are agreed upon or essentially not in dispute, the trial memorandum for the court may summarize the facts and deal solely with the legal questions presented. In such a case, under an appropriate heading, it ought to state the specific legal questions presented, followed by the legal argument in support of the position urged by counsel. A copy must also be served upon opposing counsel.

1. Table of Contents and Authorities Cited

The purpose of this table is to enable the trial judge to refer to the contents of the trial memorandum and the legal authorities upon which counsel will rely. Counsel must be sure that all references are accurate.

2. Statement of Facts

The "Statement of Facts" in the trial memorandum may be similar to, or a modified version of, the statement of facts in counsel's trial brief. It should contain all material facts, including those that are disputed. Counsel must not omit or misstate any material fact. By directing the court's attention to disputed facts, counsel can gain a psychological advantage since a candid presentation always inspires confidence.

3. Digest of Pleadings

The "Digest of Pleadings" should succinctly set forth the contentions of the plaintiff and defendant. This digest tells the judge "why" the case is before the court for adjudication. It is recommended that the digest of pleadings be written in simple narrative form and follow the chronological order of the pleadings filed by the parties.

4. Synopsis of Evidence

The "Synopsis of Evidence" tells the court what counsel intends to prove. It contains elements of the "Evidence Required to Establish the Case," "List of Witnesses and Exhibits," and "Digest or Statements of Witnesses" in counsel's trial brief. Counsel thereby informs the court of the evidence that will be produced while maintaining trial flexibility. The "Synopsis of Evidence" permits the trial judge to follow the relationship of the various strands of proof to the whole fabric of counsel's case.

5. Brief on Legal Questions Presented

Under this heading all relevant legal authority should be brought to the attention of the trial court. Cases that detract from counsel's position should be analyzed and distinguished. A complete and candid discussion of disputed cases gains for counsel the same psychological advantage as a candid presentation of the facts.

6. Requested Charges to Jury

Frequently, attorneys will not submit requested charges to the jury until the end of the trial so that they may phrase the requested charges in light of the evidence educed at trial. Nevertheless, it may be advantageous to include requested charges to the jury in the trial memorandum. For a brief discussion of requested charges to the jury, the reader is referred to the section dealing with the trial brief for counsel.[31]

D. Post-Trial Briefs; Findings of Fact and Conclusions of Law

A post-trial brief or memorandum may be submitted even in cases in which counsel has already submitted a trial memorandum. This post-trial brief or memorandum, submitted after the case has been tried, may be of the utmost importance to counsel who wishes to urge upon the court a particular view of the facts and the law.

The post-trial brief affords counsel the excellent opportunity to comment upon the evidence presented at the trial and suggests the inferences that should be drawn by the court. In effect, this post-trial document states counsel's view of the case. In this document, counsel may indicate factual findings deemed warranted by the evidence presented at the trial, as well as the suggested or proposed conclusions of law in an effort to persuade the court to reach a favorable decision.

In the post-trial brief, counsel will have several opportunities to set forth what Professor Llewellyn would call "the proffered, phrased opinion-kernel." These are passages that must be so clear that they "can be quoted verbatim by the court . . ., practically demanding to be lifted into the opinion."[32] The goal is to submit a post-trial brief that is so well written that it "does the needed work" of deciding the case. An effective post-trial brief may greatly influence the judicial opinion and decision of the court.

Sometimes, at the conclusion of a trial, a court may request counsel to submit proposed "Findings of Fact and Conclusions of Law." Even when a specific re-

---

31 *See supra* pp. 29.
32 KARL N. LLEWELLYN, THE COMMON LAW TRADITION 24 (1960).

quest is not made, it is nevertheless useful and helpful to submit a post-trial brief, which, in effect, contains proposed findings of fact and conclusions of law.

In submitting proposed findings of facts and conclusions of law, the advocate should not exaggerate or overreach. The proposed findings of fact and conclusions of law must be justified by the evidence presented at trial and by the applicable law. Even if the trial court is persuaded to accept or adopt unfair, unjustified, or highly partisan findings, the court's judgment, although subject to the "clearly erroneous" or other appropriate standard of review, on appeal may be susceptible to a more searching scrutiny.[33]

---

33 *See* CPG Prods. Corp. v. Pegasus Luggage, Inc., 776 F.2d 1007, 1022 (Fed. Cir. 1985) (Rich, J., dissenting in part); Pentec, Inc. v. Graphic Controls Corp., 776 F.2d 309, 318–19 (Fed. Cir. 1985) (Harvey, J., concurring); discussion of Anderson v. City of Bessemer City, 470 U.S. 564 (1985), and appellate review of factual findings *infra* pp. 67–68.

IV

MEMORANDUM OF LAW

A. Generally

Just as there is no fixed rule that determines the exact form and content of a trial brief or a trial memorandum, there is no established rule that governs the form and content of a memorandum of law or a "legal memorandum." The nature of the memorandum of law, and the formality of appearance of the final draft, depend upon the purpose for which the memorandum is drawn.

Law students may be more familiar with the memorandum of law than they may at first realize. Many law school essay examinations either expressly ask for a memorandum of law, or the question is phrased in language that requires the submission of a terse memorandum of law. The question might be: "What advice would you give Adams?"; "Does Brown have a good defense?"; or "Should the motion to dismiss the complaint upon the ground that it does not state facts sufficient to constitute a cause of action be granted?" The answer sought is the legal conclusion to an inquiry regarding the application of the law to a specific factual statement.

This *opinion* of the law, or the *legal* conclusion to a similar inquiry, is embodied in a memorandum of law. In practice, the problem will be real. "Adams" or "Brown" will become an actual client—or the examiner may become a senior partner in a law office who wishes to know: "On the above facts does Mr. Farnsworth have a cause of action against the Acme Corporation?"; but the legal problem is essentially the same. Counsel is not asked to write an abstract expository monograph, but is asked to give an opinion of the correct legal solution to the specific legal problem presented.

Knowing the facts, the advocate must examine all the legal factors upon which the answer depends. Once these factors have been considered, and the answer is clear in the mind of the lawyer, the problem is one of transcribing the essential mental steps into the written answer. This written "answer," consisting of an analysis of the legal questions presented together with a "conclusion," expressed in a scholarly and professional manner, is called a *memorandum of law.*

Memoranda of law generally fall into two classes. The first is to be used by the lawyer for the purpose of advising a client on a legal question. The second is to be submitted to a court to assist it in deciding a legal question that may have arisen before or during trial, or as a supplement to a trial memorandum or appellate brief. The specific purpose for which the memorandum will be drawn will determine its form and content.

B. Office Memorandum of Law

1. Nature and Purpose

The memorandum of law that lawyers draw for their own use in advising clients, or at the request of another attorney, is commonly called an *office memorandum of law.* Since this memorandum is for office use only, although it may be the basis for an important decision such as whether to prosecute an action, it may be an informal document. It contains an answer to a particular question, together with the legal basis for the answer submitted. The question asked may be broad, such as: "Does Wood B. Client have a valid cause of action against Dawson?", or it may be a specific question of law, such as: "Has Wood B. Client's cause of action been barred by the statute of limitations?" The memorandum is the vehicle whereby a legal researcher conveys the answer to an employer. It is also the means by which the advocate advises the client—either by submitting the memorandum or, ordinarily, by informing the client orally or by letter of its content. The substance of this memorandum may also be conveyed to the client in the form of an *opinion letter*.[1] Generally, only the conclusion is of interest to the client.

2. Form of Office Memorandum of Law

Although no particular format is mandated for an office memorandum of law, the attorney should make certain that the form chosen includes all necessary information. The following outline or form, suggested in prior editions of this book, is widely used:[2]

Memorandum of Law

TITLE:
REQUESTED BY:
DATE SUBMITTED:

QUESTION PRESENTED
* * *

BRIEF ANSWER
* * *

STATEMENT OF FACTS
* * *

DISCUSSION
* * *

CONCLUSION
* * *

Respectfully submitted,
Robert Reeves,
Attorney for Plaintiff

---

1   *See* discussion of opinion letter *supra* pp. 15–16. An example of an opinion letter may be found in Appendix H of this book.

2   For an example of a completed Office Memorandum of Law, see *infra* Appendix G.

a. Title

The "Title" identifies the particular matter in relation to which the memorandum is drawn. If it is drawn for a pending action, or in contemplation of the commencement of suit, the title may be a caption such as is used in an appellate brief, or in the pleadings.

b. Question Presented

The "Question Presented" should indicate exactly what question of law the memorandum proposes to answer. This not only informs the reader of the scope and content of the memorandum but also facilitates the filing and indexing of a copy of the memorandum for future use.

c. Brief Answer

The "Brief Answer" is included as a timesaver for the busy advocate who wishes to know the conclusion or specific answer immediately without the necessity of reading the discussion and conclusion. This "Brief Answer" serves as a ready reference to the law on the question discussed. It is a summary of the conclusion.

d. Statement of Facts

The "Statement of Facts" in the memorandum should include only the facts necessary for the resolution of the question presented. The memorandum is not an abstract monograph; it gives an answer to a specific question based upon a specific set of facts. Superfluous details should be omitted. If the memorandum is drawn pursuant to the request of a senior partner in a law firm, and the author of the memorandum has not interviewed the client, the facts must be stated as given but, again, only to the extent that they are relevant to the resolution of the question.

e. Discussion

The "Discussion" evidences the fruits of counsel's labor and research. Under this heading, counsel should include the relevant portions of any statute that may be pertinent to the answer, followed by an analysis of the cases that have interpreted the statute. If no statute is involved, counsel should proceed to discuss all factors that are pertinent to the answer.

The length of the discussion is determined by its adequacy and completeness. Has counsel overlooked any aspect of the question? If the question is: "Does Pryor state a cause of action?", has counsel examined the requirements for a prima facie case? Are all of the necessary elements present in the facts stated? If not, counsel should indicate what element is lacking. What legal theory has counsel evolved? Does Pryor have several causes of action that may be brought? If so, which will afford the most effective remedy? Are there any differences regarding matters of proof or measure of damages? Considering matters of jurisdiction, venue, and availability of witnesses, can any action be prosecuted?

This discussion should include an analysis of the state of the law. What are the leading cases in point? What do they hold? These cases should be analyzed skillfully so that the reader will have no doubt as to the holding of the cases.

If the question has several facets or points, the discussion may properly be broken down into a discussion of its various points. Counsel must remember, however, that this is not an argumentative document. The form used in an appellate brief in relation to points and point headings may be borrowed, but not the argumentative nature of the brief. The goal of the memorandum is to present, in an orderly, logical fashion, an objective picture of the applicable law. The perspective should not be jaundiced by the partiality of the author.

If the memorandum were to be submitted to a court in support of a motion or counsel's position on a legal question that arose during a trial or an appeal, then, obviously, different considerations would govern. This latter type of memorandum of law is similar to an appeal brief on the limited question presented. While this "court" memorandum is designed primarily to *persuade*, the "office" memorandum must simply *inform*.

The goal of a lawyer drafting an office memorandum of law is not necessarily to emerge with an answer that Pryor or Wood B. Client has an unassailable cause of action. Rather, the lawyer must objectively answer the question: "Based on the facts, does the client have a cause of action?"

The same attitude should prevail if, for example, Mary Donaldson states a "defense" to a claim that someone has made against her. She has received a claim letter advising her that a claim against her has been entrusted to an attorney for appropriate legal action. Ms. Donaldson has stated her reasons to counsel why she has not paid the claim. If a memorandum is drawn, the conclusion may very well be that "under the law of this jurisdiction Donaldson is liable for the full amount."

f. Conclusion

The "Conclusion" should contain a specific and clear answer to the question presented, and a summary of the grounds upon which the answer is based. This conclusion must, in all cases, be supported by the authorities and materials found in the discussion. To submit a memorandum of law based upon inadequate research and faulty analysis is an unprofessional practice unworthy of the advocate.

If the law on a given question is not certain, the uncertainty should be indicated in the conclusion. The conclusion may be prefaced: "Although no cases have been found in this jurisdiction that are controlling, cases in other jurisdictions lead to the conclusion that such and such would be the answer to the question presented." If there is a conflict of authority, or the jurisdictions have reached conflicting conclusions, this, too, should be noted. If no cases can be found in any jurisdiction that are directly in point, counsel should nevertheless state a conclusion as to the likely outcome if the issue were litigated.[3] A treatise or periodical may have indicated the path. In all cases, based upon the available authorities, counsel should state an opinion. Legal training and skill can be demonstrated by the ability to analyze the factors that will influence a court if the issue will ultimately be judicially determined. The conclusion will set forth a prediction of that judicial determination.

C. Memorandum of Law for the Court

1. Nature and Purpose

The memorandum of law that counsel will submit to a court is a more formal document than the office memorandum and is generally a document of equal dignity to an appellate brief. It differs from the appellate brief in that the discussion in the memorandum of law usually is limited to a specific question of law.

The occasion for the submission of a memorandum of law may arise during a trial, on the argument of a motion, or during an appeal.[4] In each instance, a difficult or unanticipated question of law will have arisen, and, in support of, or as a basis for, the oral argument, counsel will have volunteered the submission of a memorandum of law on the particular question. The matter may be considered of sufficient importance by the court that it may ask for the memorandum of law on its own initiative.

The memorandum of law contains the suggested solution to the problem that confronts the attorney who, during oral argument, is asked a question by the court that raises an "undigested difficulty." Under the discussion of the oral argument on appeal, in the section that deals with questions asked by the court, this memorandum is referred to as a *supplemental memorandum.*[5]

As the title indicates, this document supplements the appellate brief submitted. The supplemental memorandum discusses a question that arises during oral argument and is submitted to present counsel's position on a matter that, in all probability, was not discussed in the brief. The memorandum may complete an inadequate discussion in the brief of a point of law that the court deems important. Because this type of memorandum of law is akin to the appellate brief, or is the

---

3   *See* Detlev Vagts, *Legal Opinions in Quantitative Terms: The Lawyer as Haruspex or Bookie,* 34 Bus. Law. 421 (1979).

4   "A memorandum of law should be prepared upon issues that will be the subject of dispute at the trial, and present questions of law for the court to decide." 1 Sydney C. Schweitzer, Cyclopedia of Trial Practice 7 (1954). For examples of a trial brief or trial memorandum for the court, see *infra* Appendix F.

5   *See* discussion under "Questions by the Court," *infra* p. 160, and under "Briefs After Oral Argument," *infra* p. 175.

basis for oral argument of a motion or reargument of a case, a copy must be submitted to opposing counsel.

2. Form and Content

The guide that counsel may follow in drafting a memorandum of law to be submitted to a court is the appellate brief. The task is one of modifying the form and content of the appellate brief to meet the needs of the memorandum. What is the specific question or matter that the court wishes to be discussed? Unlike the office memorandum of law, counsel cannot simply state the results of legal research. Counsel must analyze the authorities and distinguish unfavorable precedents. It must be remembered that the brief, as well as this memorandum, represents a partisan effort. The memorandum of law may be the decisive factor in the ultimate decision of the case. It cannot be taken lightly.

The memorandum of law should contain the following main parts:

(a) Title;

(b) Question Presented;

(c) Argument; and

(d) Conclusion.

The "Title" should be identical with the title of the pending case. If the memorandum is to be submitted to an appellate court, the title is identical to the title of the brief as found on the cover or front page, except that, instead of stating "Brief for Appellant-Respondent," it will state "Memorandum of Law for Appellant-Respondent." The name of counsel, or the firm name above the recital "Attorneys for Appellant-Respondent," together with the signature of counsel following the conclusion, will also indicate on whose behalf the memorandum of law is being submitted.

The "Question Presented" should be an accurate statement of the question that counsel either volunteered to answer or was requested to discuss. The question will not be an abstract legal inquiry, but a specific question in relation to the case under consideration.

It is advisable that the supporting reasons for the answer to the question be discussed under an appropriate point heading such as "Argument." If a thorough answer requires a discussion of several subordinate matters, these may be discussed in outline form or, if they are sufficiently important, under several point headings. In writing the argument or discussion of the question in the memorandum of law, counsel should constantly keep in mind the principles of effective advocacy. These principles apply to clarity of expression, persuasiveness of the discussion, soundness of conclusion, and manner and quantity of citations of authority. The psychology of persuasion is as effective in a memorandum of law as it is in an appellate brief.

The "Conclusion" represents counsel's reply to the "Question Presented." It is not simply a reply that is favorable to counsel's legal position. It should be supported by the discussion of the authorities contained in the memorandum. Counsel cannot be satisfied with a memorandum of law that avoids answering the question directly or evades a discussion of apparently unfavorable or hostile authority. Thorough research will usually indicate a path that will lead to a favorable solution. Counsel can never be satisfied with a "Conclusion" that "did the case no harm." Unless the "Conclusion" affirmatively supports the case, it probably *did* do harm. It is ineffective unless it strengthens the case, and lends additional support to the contentions of counsel.

As in the appellate brief, the memorandum of law to be submitted to the court will be signed by counsel under the appropriate recital that it has been "Respectfully submitted."

D. Motion Papers

In general terms, a motion may be defined as an application to the court for an order. The supporting documents of a motion consist of the following:

(1) notice of motion in which counsel advises the opposing party that a motion for an order of the court is being made;

(2) the motion itself, which consists of counsel's request for an order granting specific relief;[6]

(3) a memorandum of law which sets forth precedential cases and statutory authority in support of the relief sought; and

(4) proof of service which is usually an affidavit attached to the moving papers that asserts that the papers were served on the opposing party.

The papers may also include:

(5) a proposed form of an order; and

(6) evidentiary materials and other documents appropriate to the motion such as affidavits, depositions, discovery responses, transcripts of related proceedings and stipulations.

Essentially, the memorandum of law in support of a motion should contain:

(1) a statement of the relief requested, e.g., if the motion is one to dismiss for lack of personal jurisdiction, the memoranda should set that forth precisely at the outset;

(2) summary of the argument;

(3) statement of facts; and

---

6   *See* FED. R. CIV. P. 7(b)(1).

(4) argument, i.e., a statement of the applicable law and its application to the particular case.

The ABC's of legal writing, of course, also apply to a memorandum of law in support of a motion. Brevity is especially important in drafting this document. "Rarely if ever should it be necessary to exceed . . . 25 pages. . . . Avoid voluminous supporting documentation; the larger the motion, the less its chance for success."[7]

1. Satisfying Meet-and-Confer Requirements

Virtually every court requires that counsel meet and confer before filing any motion. These courts enacted various local rules requiring these conferences in an effort to eliminate motions that the parties should be able to resolve without court intervention. These rules basically encourage pre-motion conferences to occur in person and be used as an opportunity to narrow or eliminate the issues for the court's consideration. Assuming that the motion is still necessary, courts require that the movant specifically state when the conference occurred, and in many courts, no motion may be filed until a certain period of time has elapsed since the conference.[8] Failure to satisfy a court's meet-and-confer requirements will doom even the most meritorious motion for failure to comply with the rules.

2. Requesting Oral Argument on a Motion

Counsel may wish to request oral argument on a motion that has been presented. Usually, in most jurisdictions, "there is no oral argument unless requested and granted by the court in its discretion."[9] The local rules must be examined to determine the proper time and manner for the making of a request for oral argument. Because most motions are decided without oral argument, every brief should be written as if no oral argument will be allowed.

3. Opposing a Motion

When faced with a motion, the first question counsel must answer is whether the motion should be opposed. The fact that a motion has been made does not necessarily mean that the motion must be opposed. Opposing a motion may serve no useful purpose and may, in certain cases, be "frivolous." Counsel for the moving party may be entitled to the relief requested in the motion papers, and no purpose will be served by opposition.

Certain motions must be opposed. If opposition is warranted, it is then necessary for counsel to prepare appropriate opposition papers. Essentially, these papers

---

7   William W. Schwarzer, *Guidelines for Discovery Motion Practice and Trial*, 117 F.R.D. 273, 278 (1987).

8   *See, e.g.*, C.D. CAL. R. 7–3 (twenty-day period after conference).

9   1 McCUTCHEN, DOYLE, BROWN & ENERSEN, FEDERAL LITIGATION GUIDE ¶ 2.08 (1989).

may consist of a memorandum in opposition and any supporting documentation, an affidavit of service, and a proposed order for the court. Specifically, these papers should set forth the reason for the moving party not being entitled to the relief requested. The reasons for the opposition are to be stated together with the supporting authority.

Obviously, principles of good legal writing apply to the memorandum in opposition. In general, in drafting a memorandum in opposition, counsel should call the court's attention to the facts and legal authorities that support the position urged. This can be accomplished by distinguishing or refuting the opposition's arguments, without necessarily repeating them, and by stating affirmatively what counsel considers the "'true' state of the law, i.e., those cases which are clearly relevant and which govern the outcome of the pending motion."[10]

Counsel need not refute every statement or proposition contained in the opposition's motion papers. Certain propositions made may be true, and it enhances counsel's credibility to acknowledge them. Other statements may simply be irrelevant. Depending upon the particular case, counsel may either ignore the irrelevant statements or explain why they are irrelevant.[11]

---

10   *Id.* § 2.13.
11   *See id.*; *see also* "Refutation of Appellant's Argument," *infra* p. 138.

Part Three
APPELLATE BRIEF WRITING

V
APPELLATE REVIEW

A. Nature and Importance of Appellate Review

1. The Appeal

The term "appeal," in general, signifies the removal of a cause, for purposes of re-hearing or review, from an inferior to a superior court. It is not limited solely to questions of law. The appeal may include questions of fact, questions of law, or questions of both fact and law.

Counsel who is contemplating the taking of an appeal must have a clear concept of the nature of the appeal and the judicial appellate process. For the appellant, the decision to take an appeal is itself a very important one.[1]

Although the appeal is regarded as an important element of procedural fairness, it has not been held to be an essential requirement within the due process guarantee of the United States Constitution.[2] Nevertheless, it has been the general policy of legislatures to grant to aggrieved parties the right to at least one appeal in actions involving the merits of a case. Since the courts favor the right of appeal, an aggrieved party will not be deprived of the right of appeal without just cause.

What is the function of the appellate court? It may be said generally that an appellate court serves a dual function. First, the appellate court serves a *review for correctness* function, i.e., a review of the case on appeal to assure that substantial justice has been done.[3] Second, the appellate court is said to serve an *institutional* function, i.e., the progressive development of the law for general application in the

---

1   *See* Fred I. Parker, *Appellate Advocacy and Practice in the Second Circuit*, 64 BROOK. L. REV. 457 (1998).

2   "The due process clause does not guarantee to the citizen of a state any particular form or method of state procedure. Under it he may neither claim a right to trial by jury nor a right of appeal." Dohany v. Rogers, 281 U.S. 362, 369 (1930).

3   In Charles Alan Wright, *The Doubtful Omniscience of Appellate Courts*, 41 MINN. L. REV. 751, 779 (1957), Professor Wright cautioned that "we should refrain from agreeing that appellate courts are to do justice until we have seen the price we must pay for this concept." He adds: "There is no way to know for sure whether trial courts or appellate courts are more often right. But in the absence of a clear showing that broadened appellate review leads to better justice, a showing which I think has not been made and probably cannot be made, the cost of increased appellate review, in terms of time and expense to the parties, in terms of lessened confidence in the trial judge, and in terms of positive injustice to those who cannot appeal, seems to me clearly exorbitant." *Id.* at 782. He concludes by quoting Justice Jackson of the United States Supreme Court who observed that "we are not final because we are infallible, but we are infallible only because we are final." Brown v. Allen, 344 U.S. 443, 540 (1953) (Jackson, J., concurring); *see infra* p. 177.

judicial system. Differently stated, the *review for correctness* function is concerned with the justice of the particular case, and the *institutional* function is concerned with the articulation and application of constitutional principles, the authoritative interpretation of statutes, and the formulation of policy within the proper sphere of the judicial function.

Professors Carrington, Meador, and Rosenberg, in their splendid volume entitled *Justice on Appeal*, state the following of the dual functions of appellate adjudication:

> On the one hand, appellate justice is preoccupied with the impact of decisions on particular litigants, but on the other it is concerned with the general principles which govern the affairs of persons other than those who are party to the cases decided.[4]

The dual function of appellate adjudication also relates to the dual function of all adjudication in the common law system. The first pertains to the doctrine of *res judicata*, which decides the case and settles the controversy. The second is the doctrine of *stare decisis*, which pertains to the precedential value of the case, which assists in deciding future similar cases by the application of the rule or principle derived from the earlier case.[5]

It has been stated that with each level or rise of the appellate structure, the *review for correctness* function diminishes, and the *institutional* function, which concerns itself with uniformity of judicial administration and the progressive development of the law, increases.

Since the appeal is predicated upon the aggrieved party's belief that errors have been committed by the lower court, the success of the appeal depends upon the ability of the advocate to indicate these errors to the reviewing court. The appellate court may reverse, affirm, or modify the judgment or order on appeal. It may also remand or remit the case to another court for further proceedings.[6]

The advocate contemplating the taking of an appeal must first ascertain whether an appeal will lie. Whether the particular adverse ruling or determination is

---

4   PAUL D. CARRINGTON, DANIEL J. MEADOR & MAURICE ROSENBERG, JUSTICE ON APPEAL 3 (1976).

5   Edward D. Re, *Stare Decisis*, 79 F.R.D. 509 (1979); *see* discussion of *Stare Decisis*, *infra* pp. 83–86.

6   *See, e.g.*, New York CPLR 5522 (McKinney 1995) ("A court to which an appeal is taken may reverse, affirm, or modify, wholly or in part, any judgment, or order before it, as to any party. The court shall render a final determination or, where necessary or proper, remit to another court for further proceedings. A court reversing or modifying a judgment or order without opinion shall briefly state the grounds of its decision."). *See generally* 28 U.S.C. § 1291 (2000) ("The courts of appeals . . . shall have jurisdiction of appeals from all final decisions of the district courts . . . .").

appealable is often a very difficult question.[7] It is no exaggeration to observe that "the questions of what orders, judgments and decrees are appealable and who can appeal therefrom are not always easy of solution."[8] These questions, however important, are beyond the scope of this book.[9]

Conceding that the particular judicial determination is appealable, the importance of the appeal cannot be minimized. First of all, it should be pointed out that, although "the party aggrieved" in the court below is generally the *party who lost*, occasionally, even the "successful" litigant (in whose favor a judgment was awarded) may feel "aggrieved," if, for example, the damages awarded by the trial court are deemed inadequate.

The appeal is of equal importance to all parties. For the appellant, who seeks a reversal of the judgment, the appeal represents the last opportunity to procure a favorable determination by convincing the court to reverse or modify the judgment. For the respondent, success on the appeal is necessary to retain the benefits gained. As stated by one author: "The argument of an appeal is, in most cases, the last, and frequently the most important step in the trial of a lawsuit. In the appellate court, a case which up to that point has been lost, may still be won."[10]

Remarks to the effect that the appeal is to be won in the trial court should not be misunderstood. They refer to the competent handling of cases at all stages of the litigation.[11] No one will deny the importance of trial practice and the necessity for the preparation of a "good record" in the event that an appeal is necessary. There is no doubt that the thorough preparation of a case precedes even the drawing of the complaint. However, the skills necessary for the successful prosecution of an appeal cannot be minimized, nor can the advocate afford to neglect them. As has been aptly stated, the appeal is a "breathless moment for the lawyer and the client alike."[12]

---

7   For errors pertaining to the admissibility or exclusion of evidence at the trial, see 1 JOHN HENRY WIGMORE, EVIDENCE § 21 (3d ed. 1940). "An erroneous ruling having been made . . . the great question on appeal then becomes: *Shall a new trial be granted because of the erroneous admission or exclusion of the particular piece of evidence?" Id.* § 21, at 364–65.

8   Fred H. Kelly, *Right to Appellate Review*, 1952 U. ILL. L. REV. 24, 27.

9   For a reference to certain manuals dealing with such matters, see *infra* p. 58.

10 Raymond S. Wilkins, *The Argument of an Appeal*, 33 CORNELL L.Q. 40 (1947). For a book that is helpful in understanding the nature of the appellate process, see DELMAR KARLEN, APPELLATE COURTS IN THE UNITED STATES AND ENGLAND (1963).

11 *See* Robert H. Jackson, *The Advocate: Guardian of Our Traditional Liberties*, 36 A.B.A. J. 607 (1950). "The success or failure of young lawyers will be determined by the way they investigate and prepare and present cases to the triers of the facts. A surprising number of cases every term are thrown out of our Court because counsel in the trial courts have not made adequate records, have not preserved crucial questions or have not asked appropriate instructions or findings. The place to win an appeal, as well as a verdict, is in the trial court." *Id.* at 610.

12 John W. Davis, *Foreword* to FREDERICK BERNAYS WIENER, EFFECTIVE APPELLATE ADVOCACY v (1950).

2. Necessity of Indicating Error

The word "review" conveys the correct concept in that it implies that it is a second look at the case. The appellate court is not a court of original jurisdiction, and the appeal is not a retrial of the case in an appellate forum. It is not a repeat performance of the trial on the record made in the trial court.

The function of the appellate court is to determine whether the trial court correctly decided the issues presented at the trial, or in deciding and issuing any other appealable order, such as one granting a motion to dismiss or a motion for summary judgment.

Furthermore, the appeal is not a general scrutiny, examination, or reexamination of all of the proceedings that have taken place up to the moment of the appeal. Appellate counsel must remember that, in all but the most unusual situations, the basic function of the appellate court is to determine whether *error* has been committed by the trial court. Indeed, it is a rule of appellate practice that appellate courts will consider only questions and contentions that were initially presented for consideration and determination by the trial court. By requiring the parties to submit their case fully to the trial court, this rule strengthens the authority of the trial court and reduces the number of appeals.

If error has been committed, the court must then determine whether the error was of sufficient gravity or magnitude to necessitate the *reversal* or the setting aside of the judgment of the trial court. Veteran appellate lawyers will say that the place to win a lawsuit is at the trial, and that the appellate court is the place for the correction of errors committed by the trial court.

Although the appellate court may, under certain circumstances, on its own initiative, examine or search the record for error, counsel cannot rely upon this possibility.

Some appellate courts, by rule of court, may consider issues not raised by the parties. For example, the rules of court may provide that the court may, at its option, consider a plain error not specified in appellant's brief. Rule 52 of the Federal Rules of Criminal Procedure is entitled "Harmless Error and Plain Error," and reads as follows:

> (a) Harmless Error. Any error, defect, irregularity or variance which does not affect substantial rights shall be disregarded.

> (b) Plain Error. Plain errors or defects affecting substantial rights may be noticed although they were not brought to the attention of the court.

Rule 14.1(a) of the Rules of the Supreme Court of the United States provides, in part, that a petition for a writ of certiorari shall contain the questions presented by the appeal. It states that the petition should contain:

> [t]he questions presented for review, expressed concisely in relation to the circumstances of the case, without unnecessary detail. The questions should be short and should not be argumentative or repetitive. If the petitioner or respondent is under a

death sentence that may be effected by the disposition of the petition, the notation "capital case" shall precede the questions presented. The questions shall be set out on the first page following the cover, and no other information may appear on that page. The statement of any question presented is deemed to comprise every subsidiary question fairly included therein. Only the questions set out in the petition, or fairly included therein, will be considered by the Court.

In Rule 24.1(a) of the Rules of the Supreme Court it is provided that:

[t]he phrasing of the questions presented need not be identical with that in the petition for a writ of certiorari or the jurisdictional statement, but the brief may not raise additional questions or change the substance of the questions already presented in those documents. At its option, however, the Court may consider a plain error not among the questions presented but evident from the record and otherwise within its jurisdiction to decide.

The American Bar Association Commission on Standards of Judicial Administration, in its *Standards Relating to Appellate Courts*, has declared that an appellate court:

should consider an issue that was not raised in the court below only where necessary to prevent manifest injustice or where it concerns the court's jurisdiction or that of the court below.[13]

Generally, an appellate court will not peruse a record for the purpose of uncovering some error that may justify a reversal. It is the function of counsel to allege the specific error or errors that warrant a reversal of the judgment on appeal. In all but the most exceptional cases it is the function of counsel for the appellant to indicate to the appellate court the error committed and to demonstrate that it was a *reversible* error, i.e., sufficiently serious or grave that a reversal is warranted or required.

Counsel, therefore, must persuade the appellate court that the trial court committed error, and that the error was prejudicial to the substantial rights of the appellant.

3. Is the Error Harmless or Reversible?

Error must be sufficiently serious to be deemed "reversible." In 1877, a reviewing court stated:

The court erred in some of the legal propositions announced to the jury; but all the errors were harmless. Wrong directions which do not put the traveler out of his way, furnish no reasons for repeating the journey.[14]

---

13   A.B.A. COMM'N ON STANDARDS OF JUDICIAL ADMINISTRATION: STANDARDS RELATING TO APPELLATE COURTS § 3.11 (1977) [hereinafter A.B.A. COMM'N].

14   Cherry v. Davis, 59 Ga. 454, 456 (1877), *quoted in* ROBERT A. LEFLAR, APPELLATE JUDICIAL OPINIONS 117 (1974).

Since error may be harmless, counsel must demonstrate that the error which is alleged is not merely *error*, but is *reversible* error because it affected the substantial rights of the appellant. In the words of the Supreme Court of the United States, did the appellant suffer "substantial prejudice?"[15]

Whether error is sufficiently serious to be deemed "reversible" is in itself a difficult question. The difficulty in determining whether error is "harmless" or "reversible" may be gathered from the most useful discussion by former Chief Justice Roger J. Traynor of the California Supreme Court, in his book, *The Riddle of Harmless Error*. Justice Traynor wrote:

> Concededly, it is not for an appellate court to retry cases on appeal or to substitute its judgment of the probabilities for that of the trier of fact, whatever it might find in the record. . . . Strictly speaking, the so-called trier of fact is really a trier of probabilities. In turn, an appellate court ponders probabilities in determining whether or not an error affected the judgment below.[16]

On the scope of judicial review, the American Bar Association Commission on Standards of Judicial Administration, in its *Standards Relating to Appellate Courts*, states that the appellate court:

> should reverse only when there has been a denial of substantial justice or a serious departure from established procedure. Recognition should be given to the trial court's opportunity to assess conflicting testimony, to resolve conflicting inferences that might be drawn from the evidence, and to apply general legal standards to the particular circumstances at issue. Appropriate respect should be given the trial court's exercise of discretionary authority.[17]

These standards, in their commentary defining the proper role of an appellate court, also state that:

> an appellate court should disturb a trial court judgment only when the proceeding, taken as a whole, can be said to have resulted in a denial of substantial justice or involved a serious departure from established procedure.[18]

The Supreme Court has stressed on several occasions that "the Constitution entitles a criminal defendant to a fair trial, not a perfect one."[19] Thus, even when a "constitutional" error has occurred at trial, an otherwise valid conviction will not be set aside if the reviewing court is convinced beyond a reasonable doubt that the constitutional error was harmless.[20] It is important to note, however, that some errors, such as denying the defendant the assistance of counsel at trial, "are

---

15 Kotteakos v. United States, 328 U.S. 750, 752 (1946).

16 ROGER J. TRAYNOR, THE RIDDLE OF HARMLESS ERROR 27, 29–30 (1970).

17 A.B.A. COMM'N, *supra* note 13.

18 *Id.*

19 Delaware v. Van Arsdall, 475 U.S. 673 (1986); *see also* United States v. Hastings, 461 U.S. 499, 508–09 (1983); Bruton v. United States, 391 U.S. 123, 135 (1968).

20 *See, e.g., Hastings,* 461 U.S. at 508–09; Moore v. Illinois, 434 U.S. 220, 232 (1977); Harrington v. California, 395 U.S. 250, 254 (1969).

so fundamental and pervasive that they require reversal without regard to the facts or circumstances of the particular case."[21]

In attempting to demonstrate reversible error, the advocate will not find it fruitful to seize upon minor errors or imprecisions in the phrasing of the court's opinion when these perceived errors are not central or necessary to the court's ultimate judgment or decision. As the Supreme Court has made clear, an appellate court "reviews judgments, not opinions."[22]

4. Is There a Right to Appeal?

Although it may seem obvious, one of the most fundamental questions that must be answered is whether an appeal may be taken at all. In other words, does the aggrieved party have a right to appeal? The answer is not always simple.

An important distinction must be made between appeals as of right and what may be termed discretionary appeals. An appeal as of right is one in which the party has a right to have an appeal heard and decided on the merits by a higher tribunal. A discretionary appeal is an appeal that the appellate tribunal may choose to hear or not. As a rule, most jurisdictions allow at least one appeal as of right from a final order or judgment. An appeal to the highest tribunal in the jurisdiction, however, is usually by leave of the court.[23]

5. Filing a Notice of Appeal

If counsel contemplates taking an appeal, it is of the utmost importance that a Notice of Appeal be filed timely, i.e., within the period of time prescribed by the applicable statute or rule. For example, Rule 4(a)(1) of the Federal Rules of Appellate Procedure provides:

Appeal as of Right—When Taken

(a) Appeal in a Civil Case (1) Time for Filing a Notice of Appeal (A) In a civil case, except as provided in the Rules 4(a)(1)(B), 4(a)(4), and 4(c), the notice of appeal required by Rule 3 must be filed with the district clerk within 30 days after the judgment or order appealed from is entered.

Although the view has been criticized, federal and state courts have characterized timing defects in notices of appeal as jurisdictional defects. Hence, appeals have been dismissed as untimely even though the parties themselves have over-

---

21 *Van Arsdall*, 475 U.S. at 681; Chapman v. California, 386 U.S. 18, 23 (1967); Gideon v. Wainright, 372 U.S. 335 (1963).

22 Chevron U.S.A., Inc. v. Natural Resources Defense Council, Inc., 467 U.S. 837, 842 (1984); *see also* King Instrument Corp. v. Otari Corp., 767 F.2d 853, 862 (Fed. Cir. 1985) ("This court passes on judgments, not opinions."); Jones v. Hardy, 727 F.2d 1524, 1531 (Fed. Cir. 1984).

23 *See* Sup. Ct. R. 10.

looked the defect or error. These courts have raised the timing defects on their own motion and have dismissed these appeals as untimely.

It has been submitted that "appeal periods are like original jurisdiction limitation periods: they involve primarily the interests of the immediate parties, not fundamental societal interests. They should, therefore, be subject to waiver by the parties."[24] Hence, the suggestion that: "[t]he Supreme Court, either by case decision or rule amendment, should clarify that the mandatory nature of Rule 4(a) is a question entirely distinct from its jurisdictional nature."[25]

Regardless of the merit of the views expressed and the suggestion, counsel desiring to take an appeal should file the required notice of appeal as soon as possible and, surely, within the prescribed time.

6. Penalties for "Frivolous Appeals"

Occasionally, counsel may be faced with the professional responsibility of informing a client that the taking of an appeal in a particular case is unwarranted because an appeal would be "frivolous." Furthermore, that there may be a right to appeal does not immunize counsel and the client from sanctions for filing the appeal, if the appeal is frivolous. If there is no error to be brought to the attention of the appellate court, and the appeal is clearly devoid of merit, the appeal is *frivolous*.

Although a successful appeal cannot be said to be frivolous, merely *losing* on the appeal is no proof that the appeal was frivolous. A useful work, devoted entirely to litigation abuse, states that an appeal is frivolous "only if the result is obvious and the arguments of error are wholly without merit."[26] Among the many definitions or phrases intended to describe when an appeal is frivolous, perhaps the best are those that state that an appeal is frivolous if it lacks "any support in law or the record,"[27] is "brought without the slightest chance of success,"[28] advances a "claim [that] is unreasonable, or . . . is not brought with a reasonably good faith belief that [the claim] is justified,"[29] or is "contrary to established law and unsupported by a reasoned, colorable argument for change in the law."[30]

---

24 Mark A. Hall, *The Jurisdictional Nature of the Time to Appeal*, 21 GA. L. REV. 399, 399–400 (1986).

25 *Id.* at 427.

26 GREGORY P. JOSEPH, SANCTIONS: THE FEDERAL LAW OF LITIGATION ABUSE 415 (1989).

27 Chalfy v. Turoff, 804 F.2d 20, 23 (2d Cir. 1986).

28 Banker's Trust Co. v. Publicker Indus., 641 F.2d 1361, 1367 (2d Cir. 1981).

29 Clark v. Green, 814 F.2d 221, 223 (5th Cir. 1987) (quoting Stelly v. Commissioner, 761 F.2d 1113, 1116 (5th Cir. 1985)).

30 Coleman v. Commissioner, 791 F.2d 68, 71 (7th Cir. 1986). *See* JOSEPH, *supra* note 26, at 417–18, for "factual indicia of frivolousness identified by courts in particular cases."

The taking of a frivolous appeal is a serious matter that may result in the imposition of sanctions or costs. For example, Rule 38 of the Federal Rules of Appellate Procedure provides that:

> If a court of appeals determines that an appeal is frivolous, it may, after a separately filed motion or notice from the court and reasonable opportunity to respond, award just damages and single or double costs to the appellee.

Rule 38 should be read together with 28 U.S.C. § 1912. Section 1912, entitled "Damages and Costs on Affirmance," provides:

> Where a judgment is affirmed by the Supreme Court or a court of appeals, the court in its discretion may adjudge to the prevailing party just damages for his delay, and single or double costs.

Appellate Rule 38 and § 1912 authorize the imposition of a monetary sanction for the filing and prosecution of a frivolous appeal. Although Rule 38 is entitled "Damages for Delay," under the rule, even without showing that the appeal resulted in delay, the courts of appeals may allow damages, attorney's fees and other expenses incurred by an appellee if the appeal is frivolous.

Rule 38 in effect codifies the interpretations that courts had given § 1912 that, notwithstanding the language of "delay," sanctions may be imposed for frivolous appeals without a showing of delay.

If a court is unable to deter a lawyer from repeatedly filing frivolous appeals, the court may suspend the lawyer from practicing before the court.[31]

7. The Imposition of Sanctions

When lack of candor is sufficiently serious, the court may properly impose sanctions upon the attorney who signed the brief, since the "duty of candor is a necessary corollary of the certification request by Rule 11."[32]

When originally adopted in 1938, Rule 11 of the Federal Rules of Civil Procedure was intended and designed to discourage the filing of frivolous or dilatory pleadings. Since the rule was rarely invoked, it did not deter abuses.

In 1983, the rule was amended to include motions and other papers, and also provided for the imposition of "appropriate" sanctions for its violation. Under the

---

31   *In re* Solerwitz, 848 F.2d 1573 (Fed. Cir. 1988). In an effort to reduce litigation and "taking aim at the nation's trial lawyers and . . . a glut of unnecessary legal actions," on September 14, 2004 the House of Representatives approved a measure requiring "sanctions against lawyers who file law suits deemed frivolous." Carl Hulse, *Bill to Require Sanctions on Lawyers Passes House*, N.Y. TIMES, Sept. 15, 2004 at A 20.

32   Golden Eagle Distrib. Corp. v. Burroughs Corp., 103 F.R.D. 124, 127 (N.D. Cal. 1984), *rev'd*, 801 F.2d 1531 (9th Cir. 1986); *see* William W. Schwartzer, *Sanction Under New Federal Rule 11—A Closer Look*, 104 F.R.D. 181, 193 (1985); *see also* Edward D. Cavanagh, *Developing Standards Under Amended Rule 11 of the Federal Rules of Civil Procedure*, 14 HOFSTRA L. REV. 499 (1986).

rule, sanctions may be imposed upon the client, the attorney, or both. The Advisory Committee states that the rule expands the equitable doctrine that permits the court to award expenses, including attorney's fees, to a litigant whose opponent acts in bad faith in instituting or conducting litigation.[33]

In addition to their deterrent value, sanctions have made lawyers aware of the seriousness of departing from acceptable standards of professional responsibility.[34]

a. Lawyer Sanctions by State Courts

The judicial attitude of imposing sanctions upon attorneys is not limited to the federal courts pursuant to Rule 11 of the Federal Rules of Civil Procedure. Judicial intolerance for "frivolous conduct" is also manifested by the state courts. For example, since January 1, 1989, New York judges have been able to impose sanctions upon attorneys for "frivolous conduct" in civil cases.[35] The sanctions may include awarding attorney's fees and expenses to the other party or by imposing a fine of up to $10,000 a case.[36]

"Frivolous conduct" in civil litigation is defined in the Rules of the Chief Administrator of the Courts as conduct that "is completely without merit in law or fact and cannot be supported by a reasonable argument for an extension, modification or reversal of existing law; or . . . undertaken primarily to delay or prolong the resolution of the litigation or to harass or maliciously injure another."[37]

In addition to New York, California has also established a statutory framework for dealing with attorney misconduct:

> Every trial court may order a party, the party's attorney, or both to pay any reasonable expenses, including attorney's fees, incurred by another party as a result of bad-faith actions or tactics that are frivolous or solely intended to cause unnecessary delay.[38]

In a 3 to 2 decision, the Indiana Supreme Court disciplined a lawyer, "ruling that a footnote in a brief, that criticized a lower court undermined the public's confidence in the administration of justice."[39] In its opinion, the court stated that the statements of counsel, "violated Indiana's Professional Conduct Rule 8.2(a) and warrant the respondent's suspension from the practice of law in this state [for thirty days].[40]

---

33   1983 Amendments of the Federal Rules of Civil Procedure, Advisory Committee, 97 F.R.D. 165, 198 (1983).

34   *See* FED. R. CIV. P. 11(c).

35   *See Top State Court Adopts Sanction Rules*, N.Y.L.J., Oct. 26, 1988, at 1; *see also* Aaron J. Broder, *Imposition of Sanctions on Lawyers*, N.Y.L.J., Jan. 12, 1989, at 3.

36   *See* 22 NYCRR § 130-1.2.

37   *Id.* § 130.1(c)(i)–(ii).

38   CALIF. CODE CIV. PROC. § 128.5(a).

39   *Indiana Court Bars Lawyer for Criticizing an Opinion*, N.Y. TIMES, Nov. 3, 2002, at 31.

40   *In re* Wilkins, 77 N.E.2d 714, 714 (Ind. 2002).

b. Proper Professional Conduct and Contempt

The judicial attitude of insisting upon proper professional conduct is also manifested by the readiness with which courts will resort to the power of contempt. For example, a United States judge in New York City left no doubt that extensive lack of consideration and disrespect would not be tolerated, and held a lawyer in contempt for refusing to attend trial. After repeated tardiness, the judge ordered the lawyer to spend nights in jail in a nearby federal detention facility to ensure the lawyer's attendance during the final days of a multi-defendant narcotics trial.[41]

On the responsibility of counsel to the court, another instructive case is *United States v. Agajanian*,[42] in which the Court of Appeals for the Second Circuit upheld the conviction of a lawyer on two counts of criminal contempt. The defendant was found guilty of criminal contempt, 18 U.S.C. § 401, for unexcused lateness, and for making misleading and incomplete statements to the court.

Reference may also be made to lawyers who believe that they have been treated unfairly or improperly by a judge and with to express their displeasure and complain. An article with the subtitle "Lawyers Who Badmouth Judges Could Face Sanctions" cautions lawyers that there is a risk that what [counsel may say or write about the judge] may violate a rule of ethics that may lead to discipline [against counsel]. The author cites four rules of the ABA Model Rules of Professional Conduct that may possibly have been violated by counsel's expression of criticism.[43]

B. Appellate Procedure

1. Introduction

Counsel must prosecute the appeal in conformity with the procedural rules that prevail in the particular jurisdiction and court where the appeal is taken. Consequently, it is important to ascertain the applicable procedural provisions that govern appeals and the applicable rules of court. Procedural rules, although similar in broad outline, differ from one jurisdiction to another. Not only will the rules of court differ in the various states, but they may also differ within the various appellate courts within the same state.

2. Mechanics for the Prosecution of Appeals

The mechanics of the appeal ought to present no particular challenge. Rules of practice and procedure deal with the methods devised for the orderly protection

---

41   *See* Deborah Squiers, *Lawyer Jailed to Get Her to Court on Time*, N.Y.L.J., Aug. 19, 1988, at 1.

42   852 F.2d 56, 59 (2d Cir. 1988).

43   Kathleen Maher, *Gag the Gripes*, A.B.A. J., Feb. 2002, at 54.

and vindication of legally protected interests. Judicial procedure has been described as "the mode of proceeding by which a legal right is enforced, as distinguished from the law which gives or defines the right, and which by means of the proceeding the Court is to administer . . . the machinery as distinguished from its product."[44]

a. Practice Manuals and Handbooks

Each jurisdiction has rules governing not only the orderly *trial* of cases but also the prosecution of *appeals*. Practice manuals set forth the manner in which the attorney must proceed. These volumes also contain helpful forms.[45] They explain the steps that must be taken, the documents that must be filed with the court, and the time limitations that will govern. Practice manuals also discuss what determinations are appealable, who may appeal, proceedings necessary to perfect an appeal, and other matters pertaining to the mechanics of appellate practice. The law of the particular jurisdiction will likewise provide the time within which to take an appeal.[46]

Appeals to the United States courts of appeals are governed by the Federal Rules of Appellate Procedure. These rules, applied in conjunction with local rules adopted by the various courts of appeals, provide uniform and simplified procedures for appeals taken to the United States courts of appeals.

Pursuant to these rules the timely filing of a simple notice of appeal is the only procedural step required to take an appeal.[47] The rules also provide for a cost bond in civil cases,[48] the filing of the record on appeal,[49] the docketing of the appeal,[50] and the filing of the brief and appendix.[51]

The various appellate courts may have prepared pamphlets or booklets that contain the Rules of Court and other pertinent information. In addition to the Rules of Court, there may also be available a manual or handbook that describes the practice and procedure before the court. These manuals may contain helpful text and suggestions on the processing and prosecution of an appeal. An inquiry as to the

---

44 Poyser v. Minors, [1881] 7 Q.B. 329, 333 (Lush, L.J.); *cf.* Jerome Michael & Mortimer J. Adler, *The Trial of an Issue of Fact,* 34 COLUM. L. REV. 1224 (1934). "The rules of procedural law regulate the trial of an issue of fact. A trial resolves disputes about matters of fact." *Id.* at 1228.

45 *See* WEST'S FEDERAL FORMS, COURTS OF APPEALS (1995); 4B BENDER'S FEDERAL PRACTICE FORMS (1999) (containing forms based on Federal Rules of Appellate Procedure and Local Rules).

46 *See, e.g.,* N.Y. CPLR 5513. (McKinney Supp. 2004).

47 FED. R. APP. P. 3(a).

48 *Id.* 7.

49 *Id.* 12(c).

50 *Id.* 12(a).

51 *Id.* 25(a)(2)(B).

availability of these manuals should be made to the office of the appropriate Clerk of Court or "Circuit Executive."

b. Record and Papers on Appeal

The applicable procedural code or rules of the jurisdiction where the appeal is taken will indicate what papers are necessary on the appeal. For example, in the state of New York, as soon as an attorney has decided to prosecute an appeal on behalf of an aggrieved party, the road to be followed is clear. New York Civil Practice Law and Rules 5525 through 5532 govern the preparation of the papers necessary to prosecute the appeal. The physical nature and format of the appellate brief are also covered by rule.[52]

For the United States courts of appeals, Rule 10(a) of the Federal Rules of Appellate Procedure defines the record on appeal. Rule 10(a) provides:

> The following items constitute the record on appeal: (1) the original papers and exhibits filed in the district court; (2) the transcript of proceedings, if any; and (3) a certified copy of the docket entries prepared by the district clerk.

c. Appendix Method

The New York CPLR, as well as the law of other states, also provides for an appendix method of prosecuting an appeal. Instead of reproducing all of the papers that constitute the record on appeal,[53] the appellant may now reproduce only such portions "as are necessary to consider the questions involved, including those parts the appellant reasonably assumes will be relied upon by the respondent."[54] Under this abbreviated "appendix" method, counsel may be selective in determining the portions of the record and the transcript of the trial that need to be reproduced as necessary on the appeal. The greatest saving of time and money can be effected if the parties can agree upon a statement in lieu of a record on appeal.[55]

In all cases, counsel must examine the specific rules of the particular court to which the appeal is taken.

In summary, an appeal in New York, as well as in many other jurisdictions, may be prosecuted on the complete record, on an abbreviated appendix, or on an agreed statement.

3. Rules Regarding Oral Argument

The length, manner, and availability of oral argument are determined by local court rules. In response to the pressure of burgeoning caseloads, many of these rules have been amended to allow appellate courts to restrict or eliminate oral ar-

---

52   *See, e.g.*, N.Y. CPLR 5528–5529 (McKinney 1995 & Supp. 2005).
53   N.Y. CPLR 5526 (McKinney 1995) (setting forth precisely what shall be the content of the record on appeal).
54   *Id.* 5528(a)(5).
55   *Id.* 5527.

gument on a discretionary basis.[56] The impact of these changes, and other aspects of oral argument, are discussed in Chapter 9 of this book.

4. Procedural Rules and Content of Brief

Enough has been said to highlight the importance of procedural rules and rules of court. The applicable rule may set forth explicitly the content of the appellate brief. In New York, the applicable rules are set forth in Rule 5528 of the New York Civil Practice Law and Rules.

Rule 28 of the Federal Rules of Appellate Procedure governs the submission of appellate briefs in the United States courts of appeals.[57]

5. Compliance with Rules of Court

Many cases can be cited that illustrate the importance of compliance with the rules of the particular court to which the appeal is taken.[58] On occasion a court may do more than merely express its displeasure and may order the submission of a new brief or even the imposition of costs.

The following statement from a case in which counsel failed to prosecute an appeal with due diligence highlights counsel's responsibility:

> Henceforth, on facts showing such inexcusable neglect as we find here, an appeal will be dismissed. If the party whose appeal is thus dismissed is thereby aggrieved, his remedy will be against his attorney. . . .

> If any appellee is required to move for the dismissal of an appeal in a civil case, the cost of his doing so will be assessed against the appellant or, in the proper case, against appellant's attorney.[59]

C. Scope of Appellate Brief and Appellate Review

Appellate counsel must appreciate the special function of the record in limiting the matters that may properly be treated in the appellate brief and considered by the appellate court. The record, as settled by the lower court, is controlling on the appellate court, and if it is maintained that there is some error in the record, the application to correct the error is usually addressed to the court below. As in other matters, however, the appropriate rule of court must be consulted. An example is Rule 10(e) of the Federal Rules of Appellate Procedure.

The general principle may be stated that the appellate court may consider only matters contained in the record. Hence, the court will not consider matters set forth in the brief that have no basis in the certified record. Likewise, a brief can-

---

56 *See, e.g.,* FED. R. APP. P. 34.

57 Rule 28 is set forth in Appendix A.

58 *See* United States v. Raimondi, 760 F.2d 460 (2d Cir. 1985).

59 Gilroy v. Lackawanna R.R., 421 F.2d 1321 (2d Cir. 1970).

not go beyond the record by the inclusion of quotations from the minutes of a former trial, or by the inclusion of reflections and comments concerning opposing counsel. Furthermore, in the brief, counsel can neither state nor intimate that something is a fact unless the statement is based upon evidence that appears in the record.[60]

If the counsel does include in the brief matter extraneous to the record with knowledge of its impropriety, the extraneous matter will be deleted, and the court may censure counsel for unprofessional and reprehensible conduct. If counsel misstates the facts or otherwise attempts to mislead the appellate court, in addition to rebuking counsel, the court may strike the entire brief from the records of the court.

1. General Structure of Appellate Courts

A party to a case or proceeding may seek appellate review of an adverse decision of a trial court, an intermediate or lower appellate court, or an administrative agency. Counsel for the litigants must give thought to how and where the appeal may be taken. Hence, counsel must be familiar with the procedural steps that must be followed, the controlling standard of review, and the hierarchy of courts that may hear the appeal. The following overview may be helpful.

a. Federal Appellate Review

i. The United States Courts of Appeals

Title 28 of the U.S. Code provides for 13 courts of appeals, representing 13 judicial circuits, which include 11 courts of appeals for the various states, one for the District of Columbia, and one for the Federal Circuit. The courts of appeals review decisions of the district courts and of administrative agencies and commissions, and may issue prerogative writs in certain cases.[61]

In a foreword to *Distinctive Practices of the Second Circuit*, designed to introduce the reader to the practice of the Second Circuit Court of Appeals, former Chief Judge Wilfred Feinberg wrote:

> There are 12 regional federal courts of appeals in the nation, including one covering only the area of the District of Columbia. And there is another Article III court of appeals—for the Federal Circuit—whose jurisdiction is defined by type of case

---

60   *See, e.g.*, Genentech, Inc. v. Chiron Corp., 112 F.3d 495, 497 n.1 (Fed. Cir. 1997) (striking affidavit from joint appendix because it was never before the district court); Laitram Corp. v. Cambridge Wire Cloth Co., 919 F.2d 1579, 1582–84 (Fed. Cir. 1990) (sanctioning counsel in part for improperly citing to an exhibit not before the district court, for improperly arguing about that exhibit, and for relying upon deposition excerpts never identified to the district court).

61   For a discussion and overview of the federal courts and their jurisdiction, see HENRY M. HART & HERBERT WECHSLER, THE FEDERAL COURTS AND THE FEDERAL SYSTEM (4th ed. 1996), and CHARLES A. WRIGHT & MARY KAY, LAW OF FEDERAL COURTS (6th ed. 2002).

rather than by geography. These 13 federal Article III appellate courts have only 168 authorized active judges.

With so few courts and so small a group of judges handling almost all of the nation's federal appellate jurisdiction (with the exception of the Supreme Court), one would think that the workings of these courts and their personnel would be well known to practicing lawyers, if not to the citizenry at large. Yet this is not so.[62]

Appeals from the district courts of the United States and the other federal trial courts and federal administrative agencies are taken to the regional United States Courts of Appeals or the United States Court of Appeals for the Federal Circuit.

Although appeals from the various district courts of the United States are taken to the court of appeals for the circuit in which the district court is located, appeals from district court decisions in cases that "arise under" the patent laws are taken to the Court of Appeals for the Federal Circuit.[63]

ii. The United States Supreme Court

The Supreme Court, which is established expressly by Article III of the Constitution, has limited original jurisdiction. Generally, the Court has appellate jurisdiction, by virtue of the discretionary writ of certiorari, over the district courts, the courts of appeals, and the highest courts of the states.[64] The Court may issue the writ "upon the petition of any party to any civil or criminal case, before or after rendition of judgment or decree."[65]

Until June 1988, a party could bring an appeal to the United States Supreme Court "if any court of the United States . . . [held] an Act of Congress unconstitutional,"[66] or if "a State statute [was] held by a court of appeals to be invalid as repugnant to the Constitution, treaties or laws of the United States,"[67] or if the highest court of a State put into "question the validity of a treaty or statute of the United States and the decision is against its validity."[68] In recognition of the ever-increasing case load of the Supreme Court, Congress virtually eliminated all of the Court's "mandatory" appellate jurisdiction.[69] Instead, these cases are now left to the Court's discretionary or certiorari jurisdiction.[70] Hence, the Court can now decide for itself whether a case in any of the repealed provisions is important enough to warrant being considered by the Supreme Court.

---

62   RICHARD L. REVESZ, DISTINCTIVE PRACTICES OF THE SECOND CIRCUIT (1989).

63   28 U.S.C. § 1295(a)(1) (2000).

64   *See* ROBERT L. STERN ET AL., SUPREME COURT PRACTICE 26–27 (7th ed. 1993).

65   28 U.S.C. § 1254(1) (2000).

66   Ch. 646, 62 Stat. 928 (1948) (repealed 1988) (formerly codified at 28 U.S.C. § 1252).

67   *Id.* (formerly codified at § 1254(2)).

68   *Id.* (formerly codified at § 1257(1)).

69   Pub. L. No. 100-352, §§ 1–3, 102 Stat. 662, 662 (1988).

70   *See* SUP. CT. R. 10.

Rule 10 of the Rules of the Supreme Court, entitled "Considerations Governing Review on Certiorari" expressly states:

> Review on a writ of certiorari is not a matter of right, but of judicial discretion. A petition for a writ of certiorari will be granted only for compelling reasons. The following, although neither controlling nor fully measuring the Court's discretion, indicate the character of the reasons the Court considers:

These "considerations," set forth in the rule, refer to conflicts among the U.S. Courts of Appeals, important conflicts on questions of federal law by state courts of last resort, and a decision by a state or U.S. Court of Appeals that conflicts with governing Supreme Court precedent. The rule emphasizes not only the existence of a "conflict" but also that the "conflict" must be over an important question of federal law.

Rule 10 concludes with the statement that a petition for a writ of certiorari "is rarely granted when the asserted error consists of erroneous factual findings or the misapplication of a properly stated rule of law." The petition will not be granted unless at least four justices approve.

In view of the extremely small number of petitions that are granted,[71] it is accurate to say that a "petitioner for certiorari bears a heavy burden to persuade the Court to select its case for review out of the many thousands of petitions filed."[72]

b. State Appellate Review

On the state level, general original jurisdiction over civil and criminal cases is lodged in the various trial courts or, in certain cases, with an administrative agency. In general, states also have intermediate courts of appeal. The highest court of the state is the Supreme Court in all states except New York[73] and Maryland where it is named the Court of Appeals.

2. The Applicable Standard of Appellate Review

The applicable standard of appellate review will determine the nature of the consideration and deference that the court will give to the question on appeal. Hence, at the risk of oversimplification, it may be said that "standard of review" refers to the degree of deference that a reviewing court will give or accord to the decision, action, or ruling being reviewed. The word "review" implies a second look at the case. The case has been decided by the trial court. On the appeal, it is incumbent

---

71 *See* Stephen M. Shapiro, *Certiorari Practice: The Supreme Court's Shrinking Docket*, LITIGATION, Spring 1998, at 25.

72 Timothy S. Bishop, *Opposing Certiorari in the U.S. Supreme Court*, LITIGATION, Winter 1994, at 31.

73 For a discussion of the New York courts, see ROBERT MACCRATE ET AL., APPELLATE JUSTICE IN NEW YORK (1982).

upon the appellant to indicate, i.e., state reasons, why that decision, action, or ruling should be disturbed.

The applicable standard of review will determine the degree of deference that the appellate court, on review, will accord the decision of the trial court. In broad terms, it also refers to the sharing of judicial or decision-making responsibility or power between the trial court and the appellate court. The standard of review will also determine both the nature and the degree of error that the appellant must prove or demonstrate in order to have the judgment or order reversed or modified on appeal.

Although a thorough examination of the various standards of review is beyond the scope of this book, it is of vital importance that the advocate develop a clear awareness of the applicable standard of review for the particular question or issue being reviewed by the appellate court.[74]

What is the specific allegation of error? Does the appellant challenge the constitutionality of a statutory enactment? Does the action attack the statute as written or merely its application in the particular case? Is the question on appeal the meaning of statutory language? Does the question on appeal pertain to the validity of the interpretation that an administrative agency has given to a statutory term?[75] Is the question on appeal one of law or fact, or a mixed question of law and fact?

The standard of review, as has been stated, will differ according to the particular nature of the question or issue presented. It is not sufficient to contend and argue that the decision on appeal was "wrong" or "incorrect." Rather, appellant must show that, under the appropriate and applicable standard of review, the judgment, action, or order on appeal should be reversed. Conversely, the appellee must emphasize that, because of the degree of deference that the reviewing court must give to the determination or decision of the lower court, that determination or decision should be affirmed.

a. Review of Questions of Law

Generally, it may be said that an appellate court has plenary jurisdiction to review a question of law. That is, in reviewing what may be termed a purely legal issue, an appellate court has the authority to decide the question presented as if it were the first to decide the issue. This rule, however, is not absolute. Counsel should not present the oral argument as if the lower court proceeding never took place. Thus, the appeal of a legal issue may not provide counsel with an opportunity to raise arguments never raised in the trial court. Counsel should keep in mind the admonition made by one appellate court that "no matter how independent an appellate court's review of an issue may be, it is still no more than that—a review."[76]

---

74   *See* Richard H. W. Maloy, *Standards of Review—Just a Tip of the Icicle*, 77 U. DET. MERCY L. REV. 603 (2000).

75   *See, e.g.*, NLRB v. Hearst Publ'ns, Inc., 322 U.S. 11 (1944).

76   Sage Prods., Inc. v. Devon Indus., Inc. 126 F.3d 1420, 1426 (Fed. Cir. 1997).

Moreover, a reviewing court must accord due weight to an administrative agency's interpretation of a statute that the legislature has directed the agency to administer.[77] Thus, although it might have reached a different result on its own, a court must defer to the agency's interpretation of the statute, provided the interpretation is "sufficiently reasonable."[78] The degree of deference will depend upon a variety of factors. The following language from a leading Supreme Court case may be helpful:

> We consider that the rulings, interpretations and opinions of the [administrative official], while not controlling upon the courts by reason of their authority, do constitute a body of experience and informed judgment to which courts and litigants may properly resort for guidance. The weight of such a judgment in a particular case will depend upon the thoroughness evident in its consideration, the validity of its reasoning, its consistency with earlier and later pronouncements, and all those factors which give it power to persuade, if lacking power to control.[79]

Notwithstanding the deference that a reviewing court must accord the interpretation of the administrative agency, counsel may nonetheless stress that:

> The judiciary is the final authority on issues of statutory construction and must reject administrative constructions which are contrary to clear congressional intent. . . . If a court, employing traditional rules of statutory construction, ascertains that Congress had an intention on the precise question at issue, that intention is the law and must be given effect.[80]

If a legislative enactment has been challenged as unconstitutional, it is well established that the wisdom of the statute is not before the court, only its legality or lawfulness. As long as the statutory enactment falls within the legislature's constitutional authority and is a proper subject matter for the exercise of legislative power, the statute need only bear a real and substantial relationship to a lawful purpose to survive judicial scrutiny.[81] Thus, as long as the statute may be considered a rational means of achieving the stated legislative purpose, the court will not disturb the legislative judgment. Of course, where fundamental rights are affected or if the statute discriminates against a suspect class, a more searching judicial scrutiny will take place.[82]

---

77   *See, e.g.,* Zenith Radio Corp. v. United States, 437 U.S. 443, 450–51 (1978); Udall v. Tallman, 380 U.S. 1, 16 (1964).

78   *See, e.g.,* Federal Election Comm'n v. Democratic Senatorial Campaign Comm., 454 U.S. 27, 39 (1981); American Lamb Co. v. United States, 785 F.2d 994 (Fed. Cir. 1986).

79   Skidmore v. Swift & Co., 323 U.S. 134, 140 (1944).

80   Chevron U.S.A., Inc. v. Natural Resources Defense Council, Inc., 467 U.S. 837, 843–44 n.9 (1984); *see also* Board of Governors of the Fed. Reserve Sys. v. Dimension Fin. Corp., 474 U.S. 361 (1986).

81   *See, e.g.,* Usery v. Turner Elkhorn Mining Co., 428 U.S. 1, 15 (1976); Nebbia v. New York, 291 U.S. 502, 525 (1934).

82   *See, e.g.,* Moore v. City of East Cleveland, 431 U.S. 494, 499 (1977); Wisconsin v. Yoder, 406 U.S. 205, 231–33 (1972).

b. Abuse of Discretion

Courts will not set aside ordinary factual findings of administrative agencies if they are supported by *substantial evidence*.[83] If the question on appeal relates to an exercise of discretionary authority by an administrative official, the courts will not set aside the discretionary finding or action unless the court concludes that there has been an *abuse of discretion*.[84] Thus, the appellant must show that the official abused the delegated discretionary authority by having acted arbitrarily, capriciously, or not in accordance with law.[85] It is also important to note that although the appellate court may set aside the discretionary findings or action of the administrative agency if there has been an abuse of discretion, the court will not substitute its discretion for that of the agency.

Under the Administrative Procedure Act ("APA"), a reviewing court may set aside discretionary agency action only if it is found to be "arbitrary, capricious, an abuse of discretion or otherwise not in accordance with law."[86] This is said to be a deferential standard that presumes the validity of agency action.[87] Clearly, the standard does not authorize the reviewing court to "substitute its judgment for that of the agency."[88] Under the abuse of discretion standard, the reviewing court's proper function is to determine whether the agency has "considered relevant factors and articulated a rational connection between the facts found and the choice made."[89]

In cases in which a court is faced with questions of statutory interpretation, the Supreme Court has stated that "[it] is by now commonplace that . . . 'this Court shows great deference to the interpretation given the statute by the officers or agency charged with its administration.'"[90] This is especially true in cases in which the decision on the interpretation, meaning, or reach of the statute involves reconciling conflicting policies clearly committed under the statute to the agency because of its unique expertise.[91] The cases also show that, if the statute is suscep-

---

83   *See, e.g.*, Universal Camera Corp. v. NLRB, 340 U.S. 474 (1951); ICC v. Union Pac. Ry., 222 U.S. 541, 547–48 (1912) ("[C]ourts will not examine facts further than to determine whether there was substantial evidence to sustain [them].").

84   Administrative Procedure Act § 10(e), 5 U.S.C. § 706(2)(A) (2000); *see, e.g.*, Heckler v. Chaney, 470 U.S. 821, 829 (1985).

85   5 U.S.C. § 706(2)(A) (2000).

86   *Id.*

87   Ethyl Corp. v. EPA, 541 F.2d 1, 34 (D.C. Cir.) (en banc), *cert. denied*, 426 U.S. 941 (1976).

88   Citizens to Preserve Overton Park v. Volpe, 401 U.S. 402, 416 (1971).

89   Baltimore Gas & Elec. Co. v. Natural Resources Defense Council, Inc., 462 U.S. 87, 105 (1983).

90   EPA v. National Crushed Stone Ass'n, 449 U.S. 64, 83 (1980) (quoting Udall v. Tallman, 380 U.S. 1, 16 (1965)); *accord* United States v. Riverside Bayview Homes, Inc., 474 U.S. 121 (1985).

91   Chevron U.S.A., Inc. v. Natural Resources Defense Council, Inc., 467 U.S. 837, 844 (1984).

tible to more than one interpretation, the court will accept the interpretation chosen by the agency if it is reasonable.[92]

Certain decisions, such as a motion to consolidate actions or a motion for rehearing, are committed by law to the sound discretion of the trial court. Thus, the appellate court will reverse those discretionary decisions only upon a showing of abuse of discretion.[93]

c. Judicial Review of Factual Findings

It is important to understand the role or review function of appellate courts in reviewing *factual findings* of a trial court. Although this discussion deals specifically with the interpretation and application of Rule 52(a) of the Federal Rules of Civil Procedure, its underlying reasoning applies to the review function of all appellate courts.

Rule 52(a) of the Federal Rules of Civil Procedure, *inter alia*, provides:

> Findings of fact, whether based on oral or documentary evidence, shall not be set aside unless clearly erroneous, and due regard shall be given to the opportunity of the trial court to judge of the credibility of the witnesses.

The phrase "whether based on oral or documentary evidence" was added to the rule, effective August 1, 1985, following the Supreme Court's decision in *Anderson v. City of Bessemer City*.[94] In that case, the Court of Appeals for the Fourth Circuit had reversed a district court's findings of sex discrimination. In reversing the Court of Appeals, the Supreme Court emphasized the limitations of the appellate court's role in reviewing factual findings, whether predicated upon documentary or oral evidence. It is significant that the Court stated:

> [The "clearly erroneous" standard of Fed. R. Civ. P. 52(a)] plainly does not entitle a reviewing court to reverse the finding of the trier of fact simply because it is convinced that it would have decided the case differently. The reviewing court oversteps the bounds of its duty under Rule 52 if it undertakes to duplicate the role of the lower court. "In applying the clearly erroneous standard to the findings of a district court sitting without a jury, appellate courts must constantly have in mind that their function is not to decide factual issues de novo." *Zenith Radio Corp. v. Hazeltine Research, Inc.*, 395 U.S. 100, 123 (1969). If the district court's account of the evidence is *plausible* in light of the record viewed in its entirely, the court of appeals may not reverse it even though convinced that had it been sitting as the trier of fact, it would have weighed the evidence differently. Where there are two permissible views of the evidence, the factfinder's choice between them cannot be clearly erroneous.[95]

---

92   *Id.*
93   *See, e.g.*, Evans v. Syracuse City Sch. Dist., 704 F.2d 44, 46–48 (2d Cir. 1983).
94   470 U.S. 564 (1985).
95   *Id.* at 573–74.

Indeed, the Court emphasized: "This is so even when the district court's findings do not rest on credibility determinations, but are based instead on physical or documentary evidence or inferences from other facts."[96]

Although the amendment to Rule 52(a) had been prepared prior to the *Anderson* decision, Judge Joseph F. Weis, Jr., of the United States Court of Appeals for the Third Circuit, in his testimony before a subcommittee of the House Committee on the Judiciary, as a member of the Advisory Committee on the Federal Rules of Civil Procedure, maintained that the amendment was still appropriate so that the Rule would reflect clearly the Supreme Court's interpretation of the Rule.

Appellate review of a jury's factual findings is also tightly constrained. Generally, in order to set aside a jury verdict, a reviewing court must find that the verdict "is against the clear weight of the evidence, or is based upon evidence which is false, or will result in a clear miscarriage of justice."[97]

d. Mixed Questions of Law and Fact

It is important to remember that not all determinations or findings that involve questions of historical fact, that is, that require a determination as to the existence of a particular fact or occurrence, are considered pure questions of fact subject to these restricted standards of review. Mixed questions of law and fact, and what have been termed "constitutional facts," require a more searching standard of review. No simple categorical rule can be set forth. As the Supreme Court recently explained: "At least in those instances in which Congress has not spoken and in which the issue falls somewhere between a pristine legal standard and a simple historical fact, the fact/law distinction at times has turned on a determination that, as a matter of the sound administration of justice, one judicial actor is better positioned than another to decide the issue in question."[98] Thus, depending on the type of interest implicated by a judicial determination, different standards of review will apply.

Certain determinations as to historical facts are treated as questions of law or are subject to more searching scrutiny on appellate review, because fundamental rights are affected. For example, in a federal habeas corpus proceeding, the statutory presumption of correctness that attaches to state court findings of fact does not apply to a review of the voluntariness of a confession.[99] Similarly, the Supreme Court has held that the clearly erroneous standard of Rule 52(a) does not prescribe the standard for reviewing a determination of "actual malice" in a libel

---

96   *Id.* at 574.

97   CVD, Inc. v. Raytheon Co., 769 F.2d 842, 848 (1st Cir. 1985).

98   Miller v. Fenton, 474 U.S. 104, 114 (1985); *see also* Harry P. Monoghan, *Constitutional Fact Review*, 85 COLUM. L. REV. 229, 237 (1985).

99   *Miller*, 474 U.S. at 111–12; *see also* 28 U.S.C. § 2254(d) (2000).

case.[100] Because of the important first amendment concerns at stake, the appellate tribunal must independently examine the evidence to determine whether actual malice has been proven with "convincing clarity."[101]

The rules of the court may require that the appellate brief contain a statement of the "standard or scope of review." For example, Rule 28.1 of the Rules of Court of the United States Court of Appeals for the Third Circuit provides that:

> The brief of appellant/petitioner shall include . . . the statement of the standard or scope of review for each issue on appeal, *i.e.*, whether the trial court abused its discretion; whether its fact findings are clearly erroneous; whether it erred in formulating or applying a legal precept, in which case review is plenary; whether, on appeal or petition for review of any agency action, there is substantial evidence in the record as a whole to support the order or decision, or whether the agency's action, findings and conclusions should be held unlawful and set aside for the reasons set forth in 5 U.S.C. § 706(2). . . .[102]

While it is important to state the relevant standard of review near the beginning of the brief, it is also vital that the appropriate standard of review be woven skillfully through the argument. By demonstrating specifically how the standard of appellate review applies to the alleged error in the case, the advocate provides the court with the legal framework for its decision and thus encourages a favorable result.

3. Interpretation and Application of Statutes

In order to assist the court, appellate counsel must appreciate and understand the role of the courts in the interpretation and application of statutes.

The outcome or decision of a case often may depend upon the meaning and application of a particular statute. Obviously, the first thing that the court must do is to read the statute carefully to ascertain its meaning.

If the specific language of the statute resolves the question presented, the function of the court is simply to give effect to the "plain meaning" of the language used. Most cases, however, are on appeal because the parties contend that the meaning of the statute or its application to the case is unclear. As has been stated elsewhere, the question is not always so clear "that the answer is to be found by a simple reading of the plain language of the statute. After all, if the specific question presented had been expressly answered by the explicit language of the statute, the problem would not be before the court. . . ."[103] Usually, counsel do not agree on the meaning of the words used in the statute and its application to the

---

100 Bose Corp. v. Consumers Union of United States, Inc., 466 U.S. 485, 511 (1984); *see also* Jacobellis v. Ohio, 378 U.S. 184, 190 (1964); Roth v. United States, 354 U.S. 476, 497–98 (1957).

101 *Bose Corp.*, 466 U.S. at 511.

102 3D CIR. R. 28.1(a)(i)(2).

103 Edward D. Re, *International Trade Law and the Role of the Lawyer*, CAL. W. INT'L L.J. 363, 374 (1983). On the interpretation and application of statutes, see ABNER MIKVA & ERIC LANE,

problem presented. The problem is often encountered in the interpretation and application of a new statutory provision. Hence, the importance of *statutory interpretation* or *construction*, i.e., *ascertaining* the meaning of the statute, and its *application* to resolve the question presented cannot be minimized.

Although the courts have expressed the thought or process in various ways, all courts will agree that, if the meaning is plain, the "plain meaning" of the statute must control and must be given effect by the court. To this seemingly precise and simple principle, the courts usually add a caveat by stating that the "plain meaning" ought not to be applied if it will lead to an "absurd result." This basic precept of statutory interpretation is set forth in *United States v. American Trucking Associations*.[104] In that case, the Supreme Court stated:

> There is, of course, no more persuasive evidence of the purpose of the statute than the words by which the legislature undertook to give expression to its wishes. Often these words are sufficient in and of themselves to determine the purpose of the legislation. In such cases we have followed their plain meaning. When that meaning has led to absurd or futile results, however, this Court has looked beyond the words to the purpose of the act.[105]

The explanation for the exception to the "plain meaning" principle is that, of course, Congress could not have intended the "absurd result." Nevertheless, it may be well to add that unless the result is truly "absurd," the words used are to be given their plain meaning, and it is not for the court to ignore or to frustrate the plain language of the statute.

If the language used is ambiguous, or leaves doubt as to what was intended by the legislature, it is the function of the court to interpret the statute so as to resolve the issue that is presented in the particular case. It is at this point that, to ascertain meaning, the courts resort to sources outside of the words or language of the statute itself.

Since the language of the statute did not resolve the question presented, reference is made to "legislative history," which usually consists of reports of committees of the legislature that have considered the legislation. These reports may be helpful because they state the precise problem that was addressed or resolved by the legislation, and the purpose or intent underlying the enactment of the statute. Hence, when the legislation is not clear, the courts may consult legislative history to ascertain the purpose of the statute and the underlying intent for its enactment. The process is usually referred to simply as "ascertaining legislative intent."

AN INTRODUCTION TO STATUTORY INTERPRETATION AND THE LEGISLATIVE PROCESS (1997); REED DICKERSON, THE INTERPRETATION AND APPLICATION OF STATUTES (1975).

104 310 U.S. 534 (1940).

105 *Id.* at 543 (footnote omitted).

Many cases have dealt with factual situations, circumstances, or problems that were not specifically considered by the legislature. These were cases in which the court was called upon to fill a void or *lacuna* in the statute. "This category represents that large area of decided cases in which it has been said that the judiciary is permitted to legislate 'interstitially,' that is, it may fill the interstices of the statute."[106] Justice Holmes stated: "I recognize without hesitation that judges do and must legislate, but they can do so only interstitially. . . . "[107] In the face of congressional silence, the court must "discern dispositive legislative intent by 'projecting as well as it could how the legislature would have dealt with the concrete situation if it had but spoken.'"[108]

4. Doctrine of Judicial Notice

The principle of appellate practice that an appellate court will not consider matters outside the record is qualified by the doctrine of judicial notice. This doctrine allows the appellate court to take judicial notice of all facts that are notorious and commonly known without any evidence having been introduced to prove them.[109] Although the doctrine is most frequently applied in trial courts, it is also implemented by appellate courts.[110]

It has been held that an appellate court may, in its discretion, take judicial notice of a fact that was not brought to the attention of the trial court, even for the purpose of reversing the judgment. Also, since the submission of the famous Brandeis brief,[111] it seems clear that a court may consider matters of a general factual nature consisting of published statistical data from official sources.

The doctrine of judicial notice also applies to matters of law. Every court is bound to take judicial notice of the law that prevails in its jurisdiction. In the absence of a statute, however, courts of one state need not take judicial notice of the law of another state or of a foreign country. By statute, the courts of New York are required

---

106   Re, *supra* note 103, at 374.

107   Southern Pac. Co. v. Jensen, 244 U.S. 205, 221 (1917) (Holmes, J., dissenting).

108   District of Columbia v. Orleans, 406 F.2d 957, 958 (D.C. Cir. 1968) (quoting City of Chicago v. FPC, 385 F.2d 629, 635 (D.C. Cir. 1967)).

109   *See* FED. R. EVID. 201. *See, e.g.*, Seminole Tribe of Fla. v. Butterworth, 491 F. Supp. 1015, 1019 (S.D. Fla. 1980) (taking judicial notice that bingo was largely a senior citizen pastime), *aff'd*, 658 F.2d 310 (5th Cir. 1981).

110   *See* Neeld v. Nat'l Hockey League, 594 F.2d 1297, 1300 (9th Cir. 1979) (taking judicial notice that ice hockey is a very rough physical contact sport).

111   The "Brandeis Brief" was submitted in the case of *Muller v. Oregon*, 208 U.S. 412 (1908). It contained socioeconomic data drawn from more than ninety different committee reports concerning the effects of long hours of labor on women and was submitted in support of the validity of a state statute. See the discussion of the use in briefs of extra-judicial sources of information *infra* pp. 126–28.

to take judicial notice of the public laws of the United States and of sister states, and may take judicial notice of the laws of foreign countries.[112]

In the federal courts, Rule 44.2 of the Federal Rules of Civil Procedure provides for the determination of foreign law.

5. Matters of a Jurisdictional Nature

There are situations in which a person cannot be deemed bound, for all purposes, by the judgment or proceedings of a court. For example, in order to determine the applicability of the full faith and credit clause of the Constitution, it may be shown that the court that rendered the judgment did not have jurisdiction.[113] Likewise, it has been held that if a person, by habeas corpus, collaterally attacks a judgment of conviction, alleging the denial of the assistance of counsel, it may be shown by proof outside the record that such assistance had not been waived.[114] It has been pointed out that in these situations, "it would be clearly erroneous to confine the inquiry to the proceedings and judgment of the trial court."[115] The petitioned court has the power to inquire into the jurisdiction of the inferior court, either with respect to the subject matter or the person, even if the inquiry involves an examination of facts that are outside the record.[116]

6. New Questions Barred on Appeal

A question or issue not raised in the trial court will not ordinarily be considered on the appeal.[117] It is fundamental in appellate practice that the lower court should have the opportunity to consider and pass upon all dispositive issues and avoid or correct any alleged errors before those issues or errors become the basis for an appeal. This rule is "essential in order that parties may have the opportunity to offer all the evidence they believe relevant to the issues."[118]

In *Luria Brothers & Co. v. Allen*,[119] Chief Judge Aldisert explained the rationale for this rule:

> In *Newark Morning Ledger Co. v. United States*, Justice Clark, writing for this court, stated our position that, absent the prospect of a gross miscarriage of justice, we will not consider arguments raised for the first time on appeal. . . . Behind our

---

112 N.Y. CPLR 4511 (McKinney 1992) (judicial notice of law); *see* FED. R. CIV. P. 44.1; Cunard S.S. Co. v. Salen Reefer Servs. AB, 773 F.2d 452, 460 (2d Cir. 1985).

113 *See* Thompson v. Whitman, 85 U.S. (18 Wall.) 457 (1874).

114 Johnson v. Zerbst, 304 U.S. 458 (1938).

115 Frank v. Mangum, 237 U.S. 309, 327 (1915).

116 *Zerbst*, 304 U.S. 458.

117 Hormel v. Helvering, 312 U.S. 552 (1941); *see also* Redwood Empire Sav. & Loan Ass'n v. Comm'r of Internal Revenue, 628 F.2d 516 (9th Cir. 1980) (refusing to decide whether attorney fees were deductible as a theft loss because issue was not raised in tax court).

118 *Hormel*, 312 U.S. at 556.

119 672 F.2d 347 (3d Cir. 1982).

disinclination to hear a newly raised theory is our belief that the district court should be allowed to consider the arguments, preside over the factual development, and thus create a complete record on appeal. . . .

It was [appellant's] responsibility to present this issue on the trial court level. Failing that, it cannot belatedly be heard on it on an appellate level. Our recognition of the division of competencies between trial and appellate courts compels us to forego consideration of a theory on which the trial court was not given a meaningful opportunity to develop a factual record.[120]

The rule, however, is not without exceptions.

Appellate courts do sometimes decide issues raised for the first time on appeal, but the circumstances under which they will do so are not clearly defined. Speaking of the United States courts of appeals, Justice Blackmun, in the case of *Singleton v. Wulff*,[121] stated that:

The matter of what questions may be taken up and resolved for the first time on appeal, is one left primarily to the discretion of the courts of appeals, to be exercised on the facts of individual cases. . . . Certainly there are circumstances in which a federal appellate court is justified in resolving an issue not passed on below, as where the proper resolution is beyond any doubt, . . . or where "injustice might otherwise result."[122]

Federal appellate courts have exercised their discretion in favor of deciding issues raised for the first time on appeal "where questions of public importance are involved,"[123] and when "the error is 'plain' and a refusal to treat it would result in the denial of fundamental justice."[124] It has also been held that new evidence that developed after trial may be presented to an appellate court if that evidence renders the appeal moot.[125]

7. Respectful Presentation of Error

Under the heading of "Necessity of Indicating Error,"[126] it was noted that, whether by specific rule or merely as a policy of appellate practice, an appellate court will not peruse a record to discover some error that may warrant a reversal of the judgment or order on appeal. It is the responsibility of the complaining party, generally the appellant, to point out to the appellate court the error or errors upon which it relies for a reversal.

---

120 *Id.* at 355.
121 428 U.S. 106 (1976).
122 *Id.* at 121 (citations omitted).
123 Cohen v. West Haven Bd. of Police Comm'rs, 638 F.2d 496, 500 n.6 (2d Cir. 1980) (determining that back pay is available as remedy in sex discrimination suit).
124 *E.g.*, United States v. Barge Shamrock, 635 F.2d 1108, 1111 (4th Cir. 1980).
125 *See, e.g.*, Matthews v. Marsh, 755 F.2d 182 (1st Cir. 1985).
126 *See supra* pp. 50–53.

The special purpose of this section is to highlight the respectful attitude that must prevail in the presentation of the alleged errors that are being brought to the attention of the appellate court. The brief is a dignified document respectfully submitted to an appellate court. Counsel must set forth allegations of error in a manner which reflects both professional competence and respect for the courts and the administration of justice. The more serious the alleged error, the greater the need for candor, objectivity, and restraint.

In pointing out error in an appellate brief, counsel should scrupulously avoid any tone or impression of disrespect, disdain or sarcasm. Above all, counsel should avoid an *ad hominem* attack either upon opposing counsel or the court whose judgment or order is on appeal. This important aspect of brief writing, which relates to the tone of the brief, is discussed more fully in the section entitled "Contents and General Tenor" of the brief.[127]

To refer to the lower court in a seemingly disrespectful manner is both professionally improper and poor strategy. Counsel wishes the brief to be read sympathetically. In pointing out error, counsel must stress the legal issue, the position on appeal, the applicable authority, and the relief requested. Moreover, since appellate courts will not reverse a judgment solely upon minor or "harmless" errors, an affirmative showing must be made that the error complained of was a "reversible error," that is, prejudicial to the substantive rights of the appellant.[128]

It should also be borne in mind that what is on appeal is the *judgment* or *order* of the court below. There may indeed be statements in the judicial opinion of the court below that are inaccurate or otherwise incorrect. The accuracy of the judicial opinion, however, is not the question presented on the appeal. The question presented is whether the issues presented below were resolved correctly, that is, in accordance with the applicable law. If the lower court judgment or order on appeal is *correct*, misstatements of fact and law in the judicial opinion of the court below are not grounds for reversal.[129]

The rule of the particular court may also require that the appellant, in the brief, present the reasons for each error assigned, together with a statement of the law applicable thereto and supporting authorities. Consequently, the appellant must state the points relied upon for a reversal and must argue them either in the brief or at oral argument.

---

127 *See infra* pp. 94–95.

128 *See supra* pp. 50–53.

129 *See* Stratoflex, Inc. v. Aerocorp Corp., 713 F.2d 1530, 1540 (Fed. Cir. 1983) ("We sit to review judgments, not opinions.").

VI

PREPARATION FOR APPELLATE BRIEF WRITING

A. Preliminary

1. Counsel's Decision to Appeal

The advocate's decision to appeal a cause is necessarily based upon several important considerations. First, the advocate must decide that the adverse determination is appealable.

Second, counsel must be certain that the case raises at least one arguable question that warrants the taking of the appeal. To appeal a case without legal basis is an indication of incompetency or insincerity. Other practical considerations, such as the retainer, need not be stressed here. However, it is necessary to warn the neophyte that the task should not be treated lightly. A great deal of hard work is involved.[1]

If the advocate about to prosecute the appeal was also trial counsel, the familiarity with the facts and the law of the case will be a most helpful start. If the advocate is not familiar with the case, the task, although ultimately no more difficult, entails the additional time-consuming element of becoming familiar with the facts and the law. However, there is no excuse for not acquiring a complete mastery of the case. A statement upon oral argument that someone else tried the case below is a defensive remark that may be construed by the court as an admission of inadequate preparation. Since the preparation of the brief necessarily precedes preparation for oral argument, the drafting of the brief will be treated first.

2. The Appellate Specialist

At the outset, it must be decided whether an appellate specialist should be engaged to prosecute the appeal. No categorical answer can be given as to the desirability of having the appeal handled by an appellate specialist. In each case, the question to be answered is, "who can prepare the most effective brief and deliver the most persuasive oral argument?"

In the chapter on "Preparation for Oral Argument," the question is discussed whether an appellate specialist ought to be engaged to present the oral argument.[2] Those materials may help answer the basic question whether an appellate specialist should be engaged to prosecute the appeal.

In his book, *Appellate Courts and Lawyers*, Thomas B. Marvell states that the "prevalence of new counsel on appeal indicates that the cases are often turned

---

[1]   For such "practical problems" as "relations with other counsel, fees, and retainers," see HERBERT M. LEVY, HOW TO HANDLE AN APPEAL ch. 2 (1968).

[2]   *See infra* p. 149 (Argument by Appellate Specialist).

over to appellate specialists after the trial."[3] This study revealed that there is no agreement among lawyers and judges "whether appeals should be handled by the trial lawyer or by an appellate specialist."[4]

With special reference to criminal appeals, Professors Carrington, Meador, and Rosenberg suggest that trial lawyers "argue most importantly to juries, appellate lawyers to judges. These are very different audiences, which respond to quite different personality traits."[5] They state that the argument for appellate counsel is based on a concern for fairness to defendants and indicate that:

> [w]hen the defendant is represented by able trial counsel who is also adept at appellate practice, the defendant is likely to be better served by retaining that lawyer throughout the appellate stages. It is when the defense attorney either did a poor job at trial or is not capable of good appellate work that a change of counsel between trial and appeal becomes important to protect the defendant's interest.[6]

3. Admission to Practice Before the Appellate Courts

Is counsel a member of the bar duly admitted to practice before the appellate court that will hear the appeal? Admission to the bar of a state confers the privilege of appearing before the appellate courts of that state, including its highest court. In the federal courts, however, counsel must apply for admission to practice before the United States court of appeals for each of the thirteen circuits.[7] Counsel must also apply for admission before the Supreme Court of the United States.[8]

A lawyer who, due to lack of time or other reasons, cannot be admitted to practice before the appellate court, may be admitted *pro hac vice*,[9] that is, for the one particular occasion. It has been noted that counsel admitted *pro hac vice* "who argues before a single judge is under a tremendous handicap." The suggestion is made that under these circumstances, "the visiting lawyer acquaint himself with as much of the judge's written output as possible."[10]

---

3   THOMAS B. MARVELL, APPELLATE COURTS AND LAWYERS, INFORMATION GATHERING IN THE ADVERSARY SYSTEM 53 (1978).

4   *Id.*

5   PAUL D. CARRINGTON ET AL., JUSTICE ON APPEAL 84 (1976).

6   *Id.*

7   *See* Rule 46 of the Federal Rules of Appellate Procedure, which pertains to admission to the bar of a court of appeals. .

8   *See* SUP. CT. R. 5.

9   *See* SUP. CT. R. 6.2 ("An attorney qualified to practice in the courts of a foreign state may be permitted to argue *pro hac vice*."); N.Y. CT. APP. R. § 520.11 ("An attorney . . . from another state, territory, district or foreign country may, in the discretion of any court of record, be admitted pro hac vice. . . .").

10 Simon H. Rifkind, *Appellate Courts Compared, in* COUNSEL ON APPEAL 165, 171 (Arthur A. Charpentier ed., 1968).

4. The Cross-Appeal

Litigants and counsel should consider very carefully whether it is necessary to file a cross-appeal. How will it help their case by filing a cross-appeal? Frequently, litigants file cross-appeals with little thought to the purpose and possible consequences of filing the cross-appeal.

It is not uncommon for both parties to be dissatisfied with the judgment rendered by the trial court. Trial courts sometimes decide partially in favor of one party, and partially in favor of the other party. In these situations, both parties may wish to appeal from that portion of the judgment which is adverse to that party. Thus, two appeals may be filed. The appeal that is filed second is designated a cross-appeal. In cases in which both parties have filed appeals, rules of court will indicate or designate which party is the appellant. In the federal courts, pursuant to the Federal Rules of Appellate Procedure, "if notices are filed on the same day, the plaintiff in the proceeding below is the appellant. These designations may be modified by agreement of the parties or by court order."[11]

Before filing a cross-appeal, of course, counsel should be sure that the portion of the judgment that is to be appealed presents an appealable question. The rules which govern appealability apply to both appeals and cross-appeals. In a nutshell, there must be something about the *judgment* that is adverse to the cross-appellant's claim. Without filing a cross-appeal, the prevailing party may defend the judgment on any ground that would not expand the relief that the lower court has already granted it.[12] Thus, a cross-appeal is necessary if a party hopes to improve or expand the relief that it has already obtained. If the judgment is entirely in favor of the party, obviously no cross-appeal is possible.

B. Thorough Understanding of the Case

The drafting of the brief should commence only after counsel has a thorough understanding of the facts and the law. Unless the facts are particularly interesting, acquiring a mastery of the facts may be a tedious task. It is a task that cannot be avoided.

The record on appeal must be read carefully to give the advocate a thorough understanding of every phase of the case. The record will generally consist of the pleadings, the transcript of testimony, exhibits, and the judgment and opinion of the court below. One author has stated: "[C]ounsel must adhere to the fundamental rule which permeates the whole subject of appeals: Know the record!"[13] The record and all its contents must be known so well that one can recall the page where the particular information is to be found. This has been referred to as "geo-

---

11 FED. R. APP. P. 28(h); *see also id.* 34(d).
12 *See* United States v. New York Tel. Co., 434 U.S. 159, 166 n.8 (1977).
13 Raymond S. Wilkins, *The Argument of an Appeal*, 33 CORNELL L.Q. 40, 41 (1947).

graphical familiarity"[14] with the record. It is no exaggeration to state that in the record lies the key to success.

1. Who Will Author the Brief?

Appellate lawyers may have associates or members of a research staff to undertake the initial research and draft a preliminary brief. Counsel will then personally perform the task of assembling the materials and writing the final draft. The brief, like all papers "of a party represented by an attorney, shall be signed by at least one attorney in his individual name, whose address shall be stated." This signature constitutes a personal certification that the document is "warranted by existing law or by a nonfrivolous argument for the extension, modification, or reversal of existing law [and] . . . is not being presented for any improper purpose, such to harass or cause unnecessary delay or needless increase in the cost of litigation. . . ."[15] Moreover, it has been established that the signature need not be handwritten and that typewritten or printed signatures may suffice.[16]

Lawyers who have done their own research, and who have a thorough knowledge of the record and the authorities, have a great advantage over counsel who will argue an appeal based upon a brief authored by someone else. Even appellate specialists will admit that there is no substitute for a knowledge of the record on appeal. Lawyers cannot be thoroughly prepared to argue an appeal if their knowledge of the case is limited to the appellate brief and the opinion below. They must have a knowledge of the record and the authorities upon which the briefs are founded.

2. Digest of Facts and Record

The task of becoming completely familiar with every fact contained in the record may be facilitated by the preparation of a digest or an abstract of the facts and the record of the case. This will prove to be of great help when the statement of facts is prepared for inclusion in the brief. If there is doubt whether a certain fact is sufficiently material to be included in the digest, it is preferable to include it. The final decision whether to include or exclude the particular fact from the "Statement of Facts" should be postponed until after the completion of the necessary legal research.

Usually the answer to certain self-imposed inquiries will reveal whether the advocate understands the factual core of the case. Precisely what occurred between the parties that gave rise to the litigation? What took place in the court below that culminated in the judgment of that court? Has counsel read all of the authorities cited in the decision of the lower court? What is the basis for the decision of the

---

14 *Id.*

15 FED. R. CIV. P. 11(1), (2); *see* discussion of "frivolous appeals" and sanctions, *supra* pp. 55–56.

16 *See, e.g.*, Thiem v. Hertz, 732 F.2d 1559 (11th Cir. 1984).

court below? What are the errors that the appellant maintains warrant a reversal? It is not until these questions can be answered in one's own words, without doubt or hesitation, that it can be said that one *knows the record*.

C. Legal Research

1. Search for the Experience of the Past

From one standpoint, the preparation for the appeal may be said to have commenced with the preliminary research leading up to the trial of the case presently on appeal. It was upon this knowledge of the case, and the applicable law, that the advocate probably relied to justify the determination to prosecute the appeal. Thereafter, the record was studied and digested, and a preliminary statement of the facts was drafted. The advocate thus came to *know* the record. Now commences the second phase of preparation: the search for legal authority to support the position taken on appeal.

Although the field of "Legal Research" as such is beyond the scope of this book, a few basic matters of vital importance will, nevertheless, be mentioned.[17]

Attorneys often commence their search for authorities with the belief that the facts of the case are unique and uncommon. They are usually surprised to learn that a great number of prior cases have dealt with the subject. No two cases are ever *identical*, but many cases are said, in the legal vernacular, to be "on point."

In addition to the computerized legal research services like LexisNexis and Westlaw, numerous indexes, digests, encyclopedias, treatises, and periodicals are available to aid the attorney in the search for authority. For specific jurisdictions, local publications are particularly helpful and timesaving. For example, *West's New York Digest* may afford an excellent point of departure if the law of the state of New York is to be examined. If a New York statute is relevant, the annotations found in the *Consolidated Laws Service* or *McKinney's* will lead to decisions that deal with the subject matter being investigated. Similar publications are available for other jurisdictions.

An attorney wishing to study federal case law may begin with *West's Federal Practice Digest,* which contains abstracts of cases decided by the federal courts. These abstracts, or case summaries, are arranged according to topic and allow the researcher to survey many federal cases dealing with the same subject in a relatively short period of time. Decisions of federal courts are also summarized in the

---

17   For a comprehensive discussion of legal research, the reader is referred to MORRIS L. COHEN, ROBERT C. BERRING & KENT C. OLSON, HOW TO FIND THE LAW (9th ed. 1989); J. MYRON JACOBSTEIN & ROY M. MERSKY, FUNDAMENTALS OF LEGAL RESEARCH (7th ed. 1998); and JULIUS J. MARKE & SLOANE, LEGAL RESEARCH AND LAW LIBRARY MANAGEMENT (1993). For a discussion of the use of computers in legal research, see CHRISTINA L. KUNZ, THE PROCESS OF LEGAL RESEARCH (5th ed. 2000).

Decennial and General Digests of the *American Digest System*. Federal statutes are reproduced with commentary and summaries of relevant cases in the *United States Code Annotated* and the *United States Code Service*.

In certain specialized areas, such as administrative practice and taxation, the researcher may consult various loose-leaf and other "Services" that are available.

These digests usually contain a brief statement of the holding of a case. Based upon the statement in a digest or annotation, a case may often appear to be directly on point. The advocate, however, should never cite a case as authority without having read the actual judicial opinion. A brief summary of a case in a digest may be misleading, and, at best, is incomplete.

Similarly, it is unprofessional to rely upon the statement of the case in the headnotes or syllabus found in the reports of the cases.[18] The case itself must be read and the factual situation must be understood. Not infrequently the statements in headnotes deal with the *law* of the case and sacrifice the *facts* that are the very basis of the decision. When the facts are stated "neatly" in one of the headnotes, the researcher should not yield to the temptation of taking for granted that the statement is accurate. There is simply no shortcut for reading the case.

2. Card Index; Digest of Materials Read

Since the process of legal research requires the unavoidable and tedious task of reading many cases and other materials, it is suggested that a card index or other record be kept of the cases and materials that have been read. Important cases and materials should be digested. If a particular statement is sufficiently clear and on point so that it is desirable to quote the statement in the brief, the citation of the case should be checked and the exact page on which the particular statement is to be found should be included in the citation.

3. Search for the Desirable Result

As has been stated in an excellent book that suggests methods of legal research: "An essential characteristic of all research is the requirement that all pertinent facts, including those opposed to one's hypothesis, be examined before venturing to assert a conclusion."[19] Hence, it cannot be said that one has completed legal research until all aspects of the question have been adequately explored. The advocate who, in addition to knowing the principles of law, is able to discuss intelligently the sociological, economic, and other implications of a case will be met

---

18   Special caution must be exercised when reading opinions of the Supreme Court of the State of Ohio. With respect to decisions of that court, "[o]nly what is stated in a syllabus or in an opinion *per curiam* or by the court represents a pronouncement of law." State v. Phillips, 151 N.E.2d 722, 724 (Ohio 1958). The syllabus referred to is that prepared by the court and must be distinguished from headnotes prepared by the editor of the reporter. *See also* Wiss v. Cuyahoga County Bd. of Elections, 401 N.E.2d 445 (Ohio 1980).

19   FREDERICK C. HICKS, MATERIALS AND METHODS OF LEGAL RESEARCH 24 (3d ed. 1942).

with great favor by judges who strive to decide the case correctly, not only as to the parties to the litigation but also in relation to society as a whole. The advocate, therefore, must bear in mind that a position that is most persuasive on appeal is one that is not only equitable as between the parties but also socially desirable to the community at large.[20]

The interests of the community, to some degree, are also affected by every judicial decision, and these interests must be considered in addition to those of the litigants. If these interests are ignored, there will exist additional justification for the "persistent feeling" that the "legal profession has shown insufficient interest in making law more responsive to social needs."[21]

4. Updating Authority

The goal of legal research is always to find the governing law of a given jurisdiction. Hence, finding cases "on point" is only the intermediate step. The next very important step involves ascertaining the present status of prior judicial authority. The step, popularly referred to as "Shepardizing" a case, requires the use of computer-assisted citator services or citation books which show the subsequent history of a case. They reveal whether the opinion has been appealed, affirmed, modified, reversed, distinguished, or overruled. The *Shepard's* print citators indicate such history by letter codes. The meaning of these letters is explained in a table of abbreviations that appears at the beginning of the volume. Both computer-assisted services, *KeyCite* on Westlaw and *Shepard's* on LexisNexis, also use color-coded "flags" to alert the researcher to subsequent negative treatment of a case.

The citation books or computer databases will also indicate whether a particular case has been cited in other cases and will show whether it has been followed, overruled, criticized, or distinguished. This information is of extreme importance in determining the current authority of a case. If the case has been followed and cited with approval, it is unlikely that its authority will be questioned. If, on the other hand, it has been limited or criticized, opposing counsel will surely *bring attention* to its doubtful precedential status. An advocate, therefore, should never cite a case without first Shepardizing it, i.e., ascertaining the treatment accorded

---

20   As indicated by Professor Hicks, this is a particularly effective presentation with judges who conceive their office "to be one of judicial statesmanship." *Id.* at 29. Surely, this broad sociological method of approach would have to be followed in cases involving "discretionary" remedies. For excellent examples of the importance of this approach, see *International News Services v. Associated Press*, 248 U.S. 215 (1918); *Mechanic's Foundry v. Ryall*, 17 P. 703 (Cal. 1888); *Sturges v. Bridgman*, 11 Ch.D. 852 (1878).

21   ESTHER LUCILLE BROWN, LAWYERS AND THE PROMOTION OF JUSTICE 215 (1938). For the various considerations or "influences" on the decisionmaking process, see RUGGERO J. ALDISERT, THE JUDICIAL PROCESS 415–28 (1996) ("Making the Decision"). Chief Judge Aldisert distinguishes between making the decision (the process of discovery) and the public explanation of it (the process of justification). *Id.* at 604–24.

the cited case by subsequent decisions to determine whether the earlier case still represents the law.

A word of caution, however, must be interposed. The advocate should know that a citator will only show a subsequent history if the case has been referred to or cited elsewhere. Thus, it is entirely possible that the authority of an earlier case has been considerably weakened (or perhaps overruled by implication) without the citator indicating that fact. Notwithstanding this possibility, Shepardizing is so important that the advocate must learn to Shepardize cases as a matter of professional habit.

Veteran appellate practitioners recount many stories about "the lawyer who rested on the case of "Whoosit v. Whatzit" only to be completely discomfited by the opposing counsel (usually the story-teller) who calmly and authoritatively informed the court that the case had been either reversed on appeal or overruled. Although none of these tales of legal victories will be repeated here, it seems appropriate to reproduce part of an advertisement that appeared on behalf of *Shepard's Citations*.

> When Stryker [Mr. Lloyd Stryker] opened the argument in court, he pointed out that the prosecution had cited a case as law in its brief when, in fact, it had been reversed by a higher court. He hammered the point home:
>
>> 'Before citing a case in a brief, every competent lawyer checks it in *Shepard's Citations* to make sure it hasn't been reversed. Every lawyer has a copy of *Shepard's* on his desk, and any first year law student knows that this simple check is absolutely necessary. It was very negligent of the prosecutor to fail to do this. But I am not asking his removal from office, nor am I asking his disbarment. How cruel it would be to ask that, for an unintentional offense. And yet, Your Honor, that is exactly what he is asking you to do to my client, for an error far less negligent, far less unusual, than his own!'
>
> The court was impressed with this argument and Stryker won a reversal.[22]

It is important to note that an advocate's responsibility to research the law on an issue does not end when the brief is filed. The court should be alerted to any pertinent and significant authorities that come to the attention of counsel after the filing of the brief but before decision, by means of a letter to the clerk of the court with copies to all counsel.[23]

5. Evaluation of "Authority"

In seeking authority to submit to the court to sustain one's position on the appeal, it is important to keep in mind that not all sources will carry equal weight in the effort to convince or constrain the court to decide as is urged. For example, in

---

22   For an interesting anecdote about how one lawyer learned to Shepardize after losing a case early in his career, see the autobiography of Jerry Giesler, THE JERRY GIESLER STORY 281–82 (1960).

23   *See* FED. R. APP. P. 28(j); *see also infra* p. 168 ("Recent or 'Late' Cases").

the case of the infant who purchased goods, the submission of a statute as authority is entirely different from the citation of the views of a text writer who offers an opinion that in such a case the infant should or should not be liable. Whereas the statute is of imperative authority, the view of the author of a treatise, however scholarly, is merely of persuasive authority. The statute would prevail over the words of a learned judge who, in a judicial opinion decided before the statute was enacted, wrote that "it is the strong policy of the law to protect the infant in all cases involving a contract that he has made, however reasonable or provident." Obviously, such "case law" on the subject would be superseded by the passage of the statute. However, in the absence of the statute, the utterance of the judge would carry greater weight *as authority* than the view of an author as expressed in a treatise or in a law review article. As among authors, the brief writer must evaluate their professional prestige and prominence, and the cogency and persuasiveness of their writings.

6. Stare Decisis: Authority of Cases as Precedents

In stating that "[t]he law must be stable, and yet it cannot stand still," Dean Roscoe Pound highlighted two ideals that require reconciliation: stability and change.[24] Stability requires a continuity with the past and is necessary to permit members of a society to conduct their daily affairs with a reasonable degree of certainty as to the legal consequences of their acts. Change implies a variation or alteration of that which is fixed and stable. Without change, however, there can be no progress. Basic to the discussion is the understanding that, in the common law world, a judicial decision serves a dual function. First, it settles the controversy, that is, under the doctrine of *res judicata* the parties may not relitigate the issues that have been decided. Second, in the common law system, under the doctrine of *stare decisis,* the judicial decision also has precedential value. The doctrine, from *stare decisis et non quieta movere*, "stand by the decision and do not disturb what is settled," is rooted in the common law policy that a principle of law deduced from a judicial decision will be considered and applied in the determination of a future similar case. In essence, this policy refers to the likelihood that a similar case arising in the future will be decided in the same way.

The doctrine of *stare decisis* was received in the United States as part of the common law tradition. In addition to fostering stability and permitting the development of a consistent and coherent body of law, it also served other beneficial functions. It preserved continuity, manifested respect for the past, assured equality of treatment for litigants similarly situated, spared judges the task of reexamining rules of law with each succeeding case, and afforded the law a desirable measure of predictability. These concepts, developed in the course of hundreds of

---

24 For a discussion of the doctrine of stare decisis and the judicial process, see Edward D. Re, *Stare Decisis*, 79 F.R.D. 509 (1979).

years of judicial experience, require further consideration as a result of today's massive legislative activity.

Although it is not altogether uncommon for an American court to overrule itself or ignore well-established precedents,[25] the authority of prior decided cases cannot safely be overlooked or understated. The precise limits of the doctrine of precedents, however, must be understood by the advocate.[26] Although it is probably true that judges prefer to "follow" cases rather than overrule prior "binding" authority, the advocate must remember that the doctrine is not absolute.

If the doctrine of precedents is regarded as the champion of stability and uniformity in law, it must, nevertheless, give way to progress, the needs of society in a subsequent era, and the overwhelming considerations of equity and justice.

Chief Justice Black of Pennsylvania remarked that "a palpable mistake, violating justice, reason and law, must be corrected, no matter by whom it may have been made."[27]

In the language of Chancellor Kent: "A solemn decision upon a point of law, arising in any given case, becomes an authority in a like case, because it is the highest evidence which we can have of the law applicable to the subject, and the judges are bound to follow that decision so long as it stands unreversed, unless it can be shown that the law was misunderstood or misapplied in that particular case."[28] As may be noticed, there are several prerequisites before a prior decision may be said to be "binding authority." The solemnity of the decision refers to the requirement that the proposition of law contended must actually have arisen in the prior case and *must have been necessary for the determination of that case.* Unless the proposition was stated in order to decide the case, the utterance of the judge is said to be *judicial dictum* or *obiter dictum* depending upon its relevance to the decision.

Precedents, therefore, are not to be applied blindly. The precedent must be analyzed carefully to determine whether there exists a similarity of facts and issues,

---

25 For example, see *Williams v. North Carolina*, 317 U.S. 287 (1942), which overruled *Haddock v. Haddock*, 201 U.S. 562 (1906); *Erie R.R. v. Tompkins*, 304 U.S. 64 (1938), which overruled the approximately 100-year-old doctrine established in *Swift v. Tyson*, 41 U.S. (16 Pet.) 1 (1842); and *Garvin v. Garvin*, 96 N.E.2d 721 (N.Y. 1951), which overruled *Goldstein v. Goldstein*, 27 N.E. 2d 969 (N.Y. 1940). It is of value to remember the factors that led to the overruling of the prior decision. For some of the "factors . . . [that] serve to tip the scales in favor of change," see Chief Judge Loughran's lecture on the *Authoritative Force of Precedents* in 10 BAR BULL. 125–34, 180–89 (1953).

26 *See* HENRY CAMPBELL BLACK, HANDBOOK ON THE LAW OF JUDICIAL PRECEDENTS 37 (1912). On the doctrine of *stare decisis*, see the materials in WILLIAM T. FRYER & CARVILLE D. BENSEN, CASES AND MATERIALS ON LEGAL METHOD AND LEGAL SYSTEM 357–72 (1950); JESSE F. BRUMBAUGH, LEGAL REASONING AND BRIEFING 168 *et seq.* (1917). Compare the doctrine of *stare decisis* with that of *res judicata*. *See* Baldwin v. Iowa State Traveling Men's Ass'n, 283 U.S. 522, 525–26 (1931).

27 *Quoted in* SIMEON E. BALDWIN, THE AMERICAN JUDICIARY 61 (1905).

28 1 JAMES KENT, COMMENTARIES 475 (12th ed. 1896).

and to ascertain the actual holding of the court in the prior case. The precedent is studied to determine whether the principle deduced therefrom is the *holding* of the case or merely *dictum*. Only the *holding* of the case is entitled to recognition and respect as binding authority. A *dictum* is only a remark or observation and, at best, is merely persuasive authority. The factors that affect or determine the degree of persuasiveness that is accorded to dicta are many and varied. How pertinent or relevant is the dictum to the decision in which it was uttered? Does the court or judge who authored the dictum enjoy a special respect for scholarship and wisdom? Is the dictum reasonable?

The distinction between the *holding* of a case and its *dicta* is warranted by the nature of the adversary system that prevails in the common law. The reason for the distinction was expressed as follows by Chief Justice John Marshall:

> It is a maxim, not to be disregarded, that general expressions, in every opinion, are to be taken in connection with the case in which those expressions are used. If they go beyond the case, they may be respected, but ought not to control the judgment in a subsequent suit when the very point is presented for decision. The reason of this maxim is obvious. The question actually before the court is investigated with care and considered in its full extent. Other principles which may serve to illustrate it, are considered in their relation to the case decided, but their possible bearing on all other cases is seldom completely investigated.[29]

Hence, the *holding* of a prior case is limited to the principle or rule that was necessary for the resolution of those factual and legal issues actually presented and decided. All utterances not necessary to that decision are *dicta*.

In summary, the "solemn decision" becomes an authority only in a "like case." Hence, if the advocate can demonstrate to the court a distinguishing feature, a different factual pattern, the prior decision is not binding authority although the facts, generally, may come within the same *genre* of cases. Here, the advocate has the greatest opportunity skillfully to analyze the factual situations and propositions of law. A case may be distinguished either on its facts or on the issue presented.[30]

Clearly, counsel must be aware of all of the factors that a judge will intuitively, deliberately, or unconsciously consider in determining the weight to be given to prior judicial pronouncements. Is the court dealing with an isolated precedent or a series of well-reasoned opinions? Has the precedent that is being urged upon the court been eroded by decisions that have restricted its application? Have changed conditions rendered the precedent obsolete? With what degree of authority may the court speak? Surely, if the court can speak with finality on a particular ques-

---

29 Cohens v. Virginia, 19 U.S. (6 Wheat.) 264, 399 (1821).

30 "The prior decided case stands only for a point actually necessary to the judgment. Anything else in the opinion is dictum. Even if the rule carefully laid down would lead to the decision in the case and was unmistakably meant to, the case is still 'distinguishable' if you can distinguish it on either the facts or the issue." KARL N. LLEWELLYN, COMMERCIAL TRANSACTIONS 16–17 (1921).

tion, it will determine for itself the particular balance that will be struck between stability and change. The court will make a value judgment as to the desirability of following the past or effecting change.[31]

7. Overruling Existing Authority

There is also the possibility of showing that the "law was misunderstood or misapplied." Justice Field has stated that "it is more important that the court should be right upon later and more elaborate consideration of the cases than consistent with previous decisions."[32]

A notable example is furnished by the case of *Gideon v. Wainwright*,[33] which held, by unanimous vote, that Florida must provide counsel for an indigent defendant accused of a felony. It thereby specifically overruled *Betts v. Brady*.[34] Justice Black, writing for the Court, stressed that, in denying that the right to counsel was fundamental, the *Betts* case had been incorrectly decided and that the absence of counsel was "shocking to the universal sense of justice."

Another interesting example is furnished by the 1967 case of *Camara v. Municipal Court*,[35] which overruled *Frank v. Maryland*,[36] a 1959 case that had upheld a Baltimore ordinance that required householders to permit inspections without a search warrant during daytime hours, whenever the health commissioner has "cause to suspect that a nuisance exists in any house, cellar or enclosure." Justice White, who delivered the opinion of the court in the *Camara* case, stated: "Having concluded that *Frank v. State of Maryland*, to the extent that it sanctioned such warrantless inspections, must be overruled, we reverse."[37]

The principles enunciated in the *Camara* case were held applicable in *See v. City of Seattle*,[38] which dealt with similar inspections of commercial structures not used as private residences. Justice Clark, who dissented in *Camara* and in *See*, wrote as follows:

> I shall not treat in any detail the constitutional issue involved. For me it was settled in *Frank v. Maryland, supra.* I would adhere to that decision and the reasoning therein of my late Brother Frankfurter. Time has not shown any need for change. Indeed the opposite is true, as I shall show later.[39]

---

31 "The infusion of morals into the law through the development of equity was not an achievement of legislation, it was the work of courts." ROSCOE POUND, THE SPIRIT OF THE COMMON LAW 184 (1921).

32 Barden v. Northern Pac. R.R., 154 U.S. 288 (1894).

33 372 U.S. 335 (1963).

34 316 U.S. 455 (1942).

35 Camara v. Municipal Court of the City & County of San Francisco, 387 U.S. 523 (1967).

36 359 U.S. 360 (1959).

37 *Camara*, 387 U.S. at 528.

38 387 U.S. 541 (1967).

39 *Id.* at 547.

Notwithstanding the 1967 *Camara* and *See* holdings, the Supreme Court in 1971 held that the Fourth Amendment does not invalidate a New York statute and regulation, which conditioned the receipt of AFDC (Aid to Families with Dependent Children) payments on periodic, warrantless visits by caseworkers to homes of recipients.[40] The majority held that "the visit does not fall within the Fourth Amendment proscription" since "it does not descend to the level of unreasonableness."[41] Justice Marshall, joined by Justice Brennan, in his dissent stated that the home visit is precisely the type of inspection proscribed by the *Camara* and *See* cases.

It is therefore apparent that the advocate's effort calculated to demonstrate that a prior decision, or even an entire line of cases, is inapplicable to the case at bar, is never a futile effort. Indeed, a failure to urge that prior decisions are not controlling in the instant case may very well indicate a lack of adequate preparation for the appeal.

If the appeal is before the Supreme Court of the United States, the fact that the decision of that Court is not reviewable by any other tribunal is of great significance. It has been stated that, as a consequence, "the Court is not bound by authorities to any greater extent than it wishes to be, and that the Court is much freer to reach what it regards as the correct or wise decision than any subordinate tribunal."[42] It seems fair to infer that, in arguing a case before such a tribunal, argument based on reason and principle may very well, in an appropriate case, be more effective than authority based on prior decisions. It is also true that "very few cases which reach the Supreme Court are completely indistinguishable from prior decisions, and *the Court has great facility in distinguishing cases it does not wish to follow.*"[43] Hence, the extent to which counsel may wish to argue what the law "ought to be," rather than what it is, depends upon the status of the tribunal. Before an intermediate appellate court, a lawyer can hardly afford to ignore the existence of governing authority.

A related inquiry pertains to what may be termed a request for judicial legislation. Is the relief requested founded upon existing judicial or legislative authority, or is counsel asking the court to create a right not previously established? Is counsel's argument, in effect, a request that the court enact legislation, or repeal or amend a controlling statute? To such an argument, the court, either expressly or

---

40 Wyman v. James, 400 U.S. 309 (1971).

41 *Id.* at 318.

42 Robert L. Stern et al., Supreme Court Practice 550 (7th ed. 1993).

43 *Id.* (emphasis added). "Decisions of this Court do not have equal intrinsic authority." Adamson v. California, 332 U.S. 46, 59 (1947) (Frankfurter, J.). *See* discussion of *Girouard v. United States,* 328 U.S. 61 (1946), *in* Edward D. Re, *supra* note 24, at 516–18.

impliedly, may very well respond that it should properly be addressed to the legislature and not to the court.[44]

8. The Adversary System: Influence and Importance of the Lawyer and the Lawyer's Brief

The adversary system that prevails in the common law world has been described as that competitive system for the administration of justice under which "the judge is relatively passive, listening, moderating, and passing on what is offered to him."[45]

Although, partially in response to the criticisms of the adversary system, judges are becoming less "passive," the description of the prevailing system should also highlight the importance of the role and contribution of the lawyer in the judicial process.[46]

Judge Bergan, of the New York Court of Appeals, noted that the lawyer's brief and the court's judicial opinion have "a common professional lineage." He added that good briefs "have patently influenced the writing of good opinions."[47]

All judges and lawyers are familiar with Mr. Justice Cardozo's *The Nature of the Judicial Process*. His incisive and penetrating "introspective searchings of the spirit" have been most helpful. They have offered insight to countless law students, and valuable instruction to many lawyers and grateful judges. It would be difficult to find a finer exposition or discussion of *"the* formula,"[48] insofar as it may be expressed, according to which American judges decide cases. But here again the analysis and effort center around the role and contribution of the judge. What remains to be done is to understand the contribution of the lawyer in that process properly called by Mr. Justice Cardozo, the *"judicial process."*

---

44 Many examples may be cited. One case that manifests the differing judicial views is *Bivens v. Six Unknown Named Agents of Federal Bureau of Narcotics*, 403 U.S. 388 (1971). In *Bivens*, the Supreme Court upheld a right of action against federal agents who allegedly violated fourth amendment rights while acting under color of their authority, even though no federal statute expressly authorizes damages in such a case. Justice Brennan, citing *Bell v. Hood*, 327 U.S. 678 (1946), writing for the majority, stated that "where federally protected rights have been invaded, it has been the rule from the beginning that courts will be alert to adjust their remedies so as to grant the necessary relief." Chief Justice Burger wrote a dissenting opinion to the effect that the Court's holding created a judicial remedy in damages not provided by the Constitution nor by Congress.

45 Elliott E. Cheatham, *The Lawyer's Role and Surroundings*, 25 ROCKY MT. L. REV. 405, 409 (1953).

46 For a discussion of the crucial role of the lawyer in the judicial process, see Edward D. Re, *The Partnership of Bench and Bar*, 16 CATH. LAW. 194 (1970); Edward D. Re, *The Law Professor and the Administration of Justice*, 23 N.Y.L. SCH. L. REV. 1 (1977); Edward D. Re, *The Lawyer as Counselor and the Prevention of Litigation*, 31 CATH. U. L. REV. 685 (1982).

47 FRANCIS BERGAN, OPINIONS AND BRIEFS—LESSONS FROM LOUGHRAN 42 (1970).

48 Benjamin N. Cardozo, *The Nature of the Judicial Process*, in *Selected Readings of Benjamin Nathan Cardozo* 110 (M. Hall ed., 1947).

One aspect of the lawyer's work that demonstrates clearly the lawyer's contribution to the judicial process, is the writing of briefs that are submitted to the court. When the crucial part that a brief plays in the decision of a case and the judicial opinion are appreciated, briefs will be written with greater care and thoroughness.

Justice Rossman, a former Justice of the Supreme Court of Oregon, noted the relationship between the lawyer's brief and judicial decision by asserting that: "If better briefs are written, the court will produce better decisions."[49]

It is the lawyer who, in the first instance, must prepare the case and submit the authorities to the court for adjudication.

9. Legal Reasoning and the Judicial Process

For the lawyer faced with the task of convincing a court that a particular view of the facts and the law is correct, an understanding of the judicial process is indispensable. Counsel must know the appellate decisional process, that is, what happens "when the judges take over after the brief writers and oral advocates complete their presentation."[50]

Chief Judge Ruggero J. Aldisert, author of the extremely valuable book, *The Judicial Process*, summarizes the judicial process in four parts: "finding the facts, choosing a legal precept, interpreting the precept, and applying the precept to the facts."[51]

The basic pattern of legal reasoning in common law jurisdictions is really *reasoning by example*. It may be regarded as a "three step process described by the doctrine of precedent in which a proposition descriptive of the first case is made into a rule of law and then applied to the next similar situation."[52] The process is described simply as "deciding like cases alike." This application of precedent is the keystone of legal reasoning. Despite its importance in the decision-making process, precedent is not the only factor or ingredient that influences judicial decision making.

Hence, the lawyer who is to succeed in the performance of this professional responsibility must possess a variety of skills and a broad background. Counsel must possess more than the ability to grasp the salient facts and to understand and apply the principles of law to the facts of the case. Counsel must possess a keen sense of justice and a knowledge of the political, economic, and social factors that also comprise the "facts" of the case.

---

49 George Rossman, *Appellate Practice and Advocacy*, 34 OR. L. REV. 73 (1955).

50 Aldisert, *supra* note 21, at xvii. For an interesting and informative collection of essays on the judicial role and function written by a number of outstanding jurists, see VIEWS FROM THE BENCH: THE JUDICIARY AND CONSTITUTIONAL POLITICS (Mark W. Cannon & David M. O'Brien eds., 1985).

51 Ruggero J. Aldisert, *Appellate Justice*, 11 MICH. J.L. REF. 317, 318 (1978) (citing 4 ROSCOE POUND, JURISPRUDENCE 56 (1959)).

52 EDWARD H. LEVI, INTRODUCTION TO LEGAL REASONING 1 (1948).

Professor Llewellyn refers to the role of the lawyer in appellate argument in terms that are particularly applicable here. He states that:

> the real and vital central job is to satisfy the court that sense and decency and justice require (a) the rule which you contend for in this *type* of situation; and (b) the result that you contend for, as between these parties. *You* must make your whole case, on law and facts, *make sense*, appeal as being *obvious* sense, inescapable sense, sense in simple terms of life and justice. If that is done, the technically sound case on the law then gets rid of all further difficulty: it shows the court that its duty to the Law not only does not conflict with its duty to Justice but urges to decision along the exact same line.[53]

---

53   Karl N. Llewellyn, *The Modern Approach to Counseling and Advocacy*, 46 COLUM. L. REV. 167 (1946), *quoted in* KARL N. LLEWELLYN, THE COMMON LAW TRADITION 238 (1960).

VII

THE APPELLATE BRIEF

A. Generally

As has been previously indicated, matters pertaining to the form, content, filing, and service of an appellate brief are governed by the rules of the jurisdiction and of the particular court to which the appeal is taken.[1]

The various parts of the appellate brief will be treated separately under appropriate sections.

1. Purpose and Definition

Although the word "brief" has acquired several meanings, both legal and nonlegal, the appellate brief is a written legal document upon the questions that the record brings before the appellate court for decison.[2]

It is written either in support of or in opposition to a particular appealable determination of the lower court. It may be regarded as the vehicle employed by the advocate to convey to the appellate court:

(a) the essential facts of the client's case;

(b) the issues raised on the appeal;

(c) the questions of law involved;

(d) the principles of law, discussed under appropriate points, that the advocate maintains govern the determination of the issues;

(e) the desired application by the court of the governing legal principles in the manner urged by the advocate; and

(f) the specific relief requested.[3]

The purpose of the brief is to present to the court, in concise form, the matters in controversy and, by appropriate argument on the facts and the law of the case, to assist the court in arriving at a just and proper conclusion.[4] The brief therefore states to the appellate court the specific grounds, supported by authority, to warrant an affirmance or reversal of the determination from which the appeal has been taken. Since the primary purpose of the brief is to persuade, by conveying

---

1   *See supra* pp. 57–59.

2   See Duncan v. Kohler, 34 N.W. 594 (Minn. 1887), wherein the court referred to the "brief" as synonymous with "points" and "authorities" and explained it to be a *condensed* statement of the propositions of law that counsel desire to establish together with the reasons and authorities that sustain their positions.

3   *See* Bell v. Germain, 107 P. 630 (Cal. Ct. App. 1910)

4   *See* 2 R.C.L. *Briefs and Arguments* 176 (1914); Hoover v. State, 175 P. 117 (Okla. 1918); Brunson v. Emerson, 124 P. 979 (Okla. 1912).

knowledge and information to the court, this purpose cannot be achieved unless the advocate states clearly and distinctly the facts that gave rise to the legal dispute and the governing propositions of law supported by authority.

a. Appellant's Brief, Respondent's Brief, and the Reply Brief

The appellant's brief will advise the court of the errors committed by the lower court and will urge a reversal of the unfavorable determination. This *opening brief*, as the appellant's brief is sometimes called, must bear the burden of demonstrating the error that warrants a reversal of the determination of the lower court.[5] Counsel for the appellant should know that studies have indicated "a strong presumption that the result of a civil or criminal appeal would be the affirmance of the judgment below."[6]

Much can be written to demonstrate the advantage possessed by the respondent on the appeal and the low percentage of reversals of the judgments of the lower court. Suffice it to say that the burden is upon the appellant to present prejudicial error.

The respondent's brief, on the other hand, will argue that no reversible error was committed, will cite authorities to sustain the determination of the lower court, and hence, will urge that it be affirmed or that the appeal be dismissed.[7] A reply brief is one filed by an appellant who deems it necessary to reply to some matter or argument set forth in the respondent's brief.[8]

b. Brief Amicus Curiae

The principles of effective brief writing are equally applicable to a brief *amicus curiae*. This brief, as indicated by the title, is submitted by a "friend of the court" and theoretically implies a disinterested bystander who wishes to make certain suggestions to the court on matters apparent upon the record. The brief *amicus curiae*, therefore, is submitted by someone not a party to the litigation.[9] In an attempt to ensure that amicus curie briefs have some degree of impartiality, the Supreme Court has amended its rules so that every *amicus curiae* brief must state in the first footnote on the first page of text "whether counsel for a party authored the brief in whole or in part and shall identify every person or entity . . . who made a monetary contribution to the preparation or submission of the brief.[10] Like all other briefs, its function is to help the court to decide the legal questions presented. Hence, it ought to bring to the attention of the court relevant matter

---

5   *See* discussion of "Respondent's Strategic Advantage," *infra* p. 135.

6   JAMES WILLARD HURST, THE GROWTH OF AMERICAN LAW 178 (1950).

7   *See* DELMAR KARLEN, PRIMER ON PROCEDURE 109–20 (1950).

8   For further treatment of respondent and reply briefs, see *infra* pp. 135–41.

9   *See* Northern Sec. Co. v. United States, 191 U.S. 555 (1903).

10   SUP. CT. R. 37.6.

"not already brought to its attention by the parties. . . ."[11] As a practical matter, a brief *amicus curiae* is submitted by persons or organizations who, although not parties, have a particular interest in the principle involved or feel that they may be affected by the decision of the appellate court.

A brief *amicus curiae* may be filed upon consent of the parties or by leave of court.[12] Obtaining leave of court is not automatic. In one case, Chief Judge Posner, on behalf of the United States Court of Appeals for the Seventh Circuit, denied leave to file an *amicus curiae* brief because the brief did not say anything not already said by the party that the amicus supported.[13] Judge Posner wrote that leave should be allowed only if (1) the party on whose behalf the brief will be filed is not represented or is not represented competently; (2) the amicus has an interest in some other case that may be affected by the decision in the case being appealed (though not enough interest to entitle the amicus to intervene); or (3) the amicus has "unique information or perspective" that can assist the court beyond the help the lawyers or the parties are able to provide. In denying the motion for leave, Judge Posner reminded counsel that *amicus curiae* means "friend of the court," not "friend of a party."

2. Importance of the Appellate Brief

Surely, extensive discussion is not required to stress the importance of brief writing in general and the appellate brief in particular. The following remarks by Justice Thurgood Marshall nevertheless serve to emphasize the important part played by the brief in the decision of the appeal:

> Regardless of the panel you get, [*i.e.* whether the court has read the briefs before or after oral argument] the questions you get, or the answers you give, I maintain it is the brief that does the final job, if for no other reason than that opinions are often written several weeks and sometimes months after the [oral] argument. The arguments, great as they may have been, are forgotten. In the seclusion of his chambers the judge has only his briefs and the law books. At that time your brief is your only spokesman.[14]

With increasing frequency, appeals are being submitted for decision without benefit of oral argument.[15] In these cases, counsel's only means of communicating with the court is the appellate brief. Counsel, therefore, has a professional obligation to use the utmost skill in the preparation of the brief.

---

11   SUP. CT. R. 37.1.

12   *See* FED. R. APP. P. 29.

13   Ryan v. Commodity Futures Trading Comm'n, 125 F.3d 1062, 1063 (7th Cir. 1997).

14   Thurgood Marshall, *The Federal Appeal,* in COUNSEL ON APPEAL 141, 146 (Arthur A. Charpentier ed., 1968).

15   For example, the United States Court of Appeals for the Fifth Circuit uses a screening procedure under which more than half of all appeals are decided without oral argument. *See* George K. Rahdert & Marc Roth, *Practice Before the Fifth Circuit: Briefs and Oral Advocacy—A Way To Do It,* 8 TEX. TECH L. REV. 847, 848 (1977).

3. Contents and General Tenor

The brief submitted to a court should be a fair reflection of the dignity and professional competence of its author. The inspiring observation has been made that the brief and the judicial opinion that it has helped shape and influence represent the preservation of the practitioner's professional skill.[16] As stated by a distinguished jurist, "if better briefs are written the court will produce better decisions."[17] It should be moderate in tone, fair to the opposing counsel, and respectful to the court from which the appeal is taken.

Rule 24.6 of the Rules of the Supreme Court of the United States describes briefs in the following terms and states the possible consequences of noncompliance:

> A brief shall be concise, logically arranged with proper headings, and free of irrelevant, immaterial, or scandalous matter. The Court may disregard or strike a brief that does not comply with this paragraph.

Candor and fairness of presentation ought to be the principal characteristics of the brief.[18] One aspect of the requirement of candor is counsel's duty to disclose to the court legal authority directly adverse to the client's case when not presented by opposing counsel.[19] The policy underlying this requirement is explained in the comment following Rule 3.3, "Candor Toward the Tribunal," of the Model Rules of Professional Conduct:

> The advocate's task is to present the client's case with persuasive force. Performance of that duty while maintaining confidences of the client is qualified by the advocate's duty of candor to the tribunal . . . .

> Legal argument based on a knowingly false representation of law constitutes dishonesty toward the tribunal. A lawyer is not required to make a disinterested exposition of the law, but must recognize the existence of pertinent legal authorities. Furthermore, . . . an advocate has a duty to disclose directly adverse authority in the controlling jurisdiction which has not been disclosed by the opposing party.

If an attorney violates this duty of candor, the court may properly impose sanctions upon the attorney who signed the brief.[20]

---

16   FREDERICK BERNAYS WIENER, BRIEFING AND ARGUING FEDERAL APPEALS 37 (1961).

17   George Rossman, *Appellate Practice and Advocacy*, 34 OR. L. REV. 73 (1955).

18   "Counsel's mistakes and, especially, lack of candor color the rest of his arguments in the eyes of many judges." THOMAS B. MARVELL, APPELLATE COURTS AND LAWYERS 35–36 (1978).

19   Rule 3.3, *"Candor Toward the Tribunal,"* of the *Model Rules of Professional Conduct* provides that "(a) [a] lawyer shall not knowingly: . . . (3) Fail to disclose to the tribunal legal authority in the controlling jurisdiction known to the lawyer to be directly adverse to the position of the client and not disclosed by opposing counsel . . . ." This, however, is a minimum standard. It is the authors' firmly held belief that full disclosure of authorities promotes understanding, inspires the confidence of the court, and contributes to the just resolution of the litigation.

20   *See* discussion of "frivolous appeals" and sanctions *supra* pp. 54–57.

Similarly, in a brief, it is a serious breach of ethics for counsel to misstate the facts and the evidence. A fair statement of the facts is of the greatest importance.[21] The unfair statement will doubtless be discovered and, if not construed as casting a reflection upon the integrity of the brief, will surely be regarded as a sign of professional incompetence.

If the brief contains scandalous matter, the appellate court may, in its discretion, refuse to award costs even though the party filing the brief is successful on the appeal.[22] Scandalous matter is always improper, whether the unjustifiable comments are aimed at the adverse party,[23] counsel,[24] or the trial court.[25] Furthermore, a brief containing unjustifiable accusations and criticisms may be removed from the files of the court.[26]

Sarcasm, disparagement, and *ad hominem* attacks are unworthy of counsel. In short, the brief is to be a dignified legal document, reflecting a mastery of the facts and law of the case. Its every phrase must indicate that it has been authored by a professionally competent ethical practitioner.

4. Selectivity

One of the advocate's most fundamental tasks in preparing a brief is selecting the best arguments to be made. In most cases, counsel should be able to devise many arguments capable of being presented to the appellate court. From these many arguments, however, counsel must select only those that are serious and substantial. The inclusion of weak arguments will dilute the force of stronger ones and detract from an advocate's persuasive points. In *Jones v. Barnes*, Chief Justice Burger emphasized this point:

> Experienced advocates since time beyond memory have emphasized the importance of winnowing out weaker arguments on appeal and focusing on one central issue if possible, or at most on a few key issues.[27]

Thus, it is imperative that counsel focus on those issues that are most helpful and effective in presenting the client's case.

---

21 "If a brief gives the reader a feeling of confidence, a conviction that the material is being fairly presented, he will pay far more attention to it than if it appears to consist of exaggeration and dubious statements." F. Trowbridge vom Baur, *The Art of Brief Writing*, 3 SCRIVENER 1 (1975–76); *see* discussion of post-trial briefs and proposed findings of fact *supra* pp. 34–35.

22 Hess v. Kennedy, 171 N.Y.S. 51 (Sup. Ct. App. T. 1st Dep't 1917).

23 *See* Joyce v. Katzenberg, 209 N.Y.S. 854 (App. Div. 2d Dep't 1925).

24 *See* Jamaica Estates v. Smith, 163 N.Y.S. 389 (App. Div. 1st Dep't 1917).

25 *See* Pelzer v. Perry, 196 N.Y.S. 342 (App. Div. 1st Dep't 1922); Pittsburgh, C.C. & St. L., Ry. v. Muncie & Portland Traction Co., 77 N.E. 941 (Ind. 1906).

26 Scholing v. O'Connor, 204 N.Y.S. 777 (App. Div. 3d Dep't 1924).

27 Jones v. Barnes, 463 U.S. 745, 752 (1983) (Burger, C.J.) (quoting Robert Jackson, *Advocacy Before the United States Supreme Court*, 25 TEMPLE L.Q. 115, 119 (1951)).

B. Component Parts of the Brief

1. Contents of the Brief

The applicable rules of the court to which an appeal is taken will dictate the form and content of the brief. Generally, however, the following are the essential parts of a brief:

(a) Title;

(b) Preliminary Statement;

(c) Questions Presented;

(d) Statement of Facts;

(e) Argument (consisting of the points of law discussed under appropriate point headings); and

(f) Conclusion and Signature of the Author.

These are the *essential parts* of the brief, and they are required regardless of any additional requirements enumerated by the rules of court. The court rules may call for additional matter such as a Table of Contents, a Table of Cases, and a Table of Statutes and Authorities.[28] The rules may also require a statement disclosing the basis upon which it is contended that the court has jurisdiction to review the judgment or decree in question.[29] The author of the brief may comply with this requirement by including a separate heading entitled "Jurisdictional Statement" or, if sufficiently brief, the statement may be set forth as part of the "Preliminary Statement."

The rules are likely to require a statement of the judgment or ruling of the lower court and may require a statement of the standard or scope of review applicable to that decision.

The specificity of rules governing the form and content of appellate briefs is exemplified by the rules that apply to briefs filed in United States circuit courts of

---

28 The Table of Contents should list by page number all of the essential parts of the brief. A list of all issues to be raised on appeal should also be stated in the Table of Contents. The Table of Cases should contain all cases cited in the brief, organized alphabetically, listing each page in the brief where the case is cited. All statutes, regulations, and rules should be similarly listed in the Table of Authorities. Finally, a listing of miscellaneous sources such as law review publications, treatises, and the like should be included. *See* Rahdert & Roth, *supra* note 15, at 851. It should be noted that the U.S. Supreme Court now requires a Table of Contents and a Table of Cited Authorities in all documents exceeding five pages. *See* SUP. CT. R. 24.1(c).

29 *See, e.g.*, SUP. CT. R. 24.1(e).

appeals. A brief filed in any United States court of appeals must comply with Rule 28 of the Federal Rules of Appellate Procedure, which provides, in part:

(a) *Appellants's Brief.* The appellant's brief must contain, under appropriate headings and in the order indicated:

(1) a corporate disclosure statement if required by Rule 26.1;

(2) a table of contents, with page references;

(3) a table of authorities—cases (alphabetically arranged,) statutes, and other authorities—with references to the pages of the brief where they are cited;

(4) a jurisdictional statement . . . ;

(5) a statement of the issues presented for review;

(6) a statement of the case briefly indicating the nature of the case, the course of proceedings, and the disposition below;

(7) a statement of facts relevant to the issues submitted for review;

(8) a summary of the argument, which must contain a succinct, clear, and accurate statement of the arguments made in the body of the brief, and which must not merely repeat the argument headings;

(9) the argument, which must contain:

(A) appellant's contentions and the reasons for them, with citations to the authorities and parts of the record on which the appellant relies; and

(B) for each issue, a concise statement of the applicable standard or review (which may appear in the discussion of the issue or under a separate heading placed before the discussion of the issues);

(10) a short conclusion stating the precise relief sought; and

(11) the certificate of compliance, if required by Rule 32(a)(7).

(b) *Appellee's Brief.* The appellee's brief must conform to the requirements of Rule 28(a)(1)-(9) and (11), except that none of the following need appear unless the appellee is dissatisfied with the appellant's statement:

(1) the jurisdictional statement;

(2) the statement of the issues

(3) the statement of the case;

(4) the statement of the facts; and

(5) the statement of the standard of review.

In addition, a brief filed in a United States court of appeals must conform to the local rule of court of the particular circuit. For instance, a brief filed in the

United States Court of Appeals for the Federal Circuit must comply with local rule 28(a), which provides:

(a) Contents of Brief; Organization of Contents; Addendum; Binding—Briefs must be bound as prescribed in Rule 32 of the Federal Rules of Appellate Procedure and must contain the following, in the order listed:

(1) the certificate of interest (see Federal Circuit Rule 47.4);

(2) the table of contents;

(3) the table of authorities;

(4) the statement of related cases (see Federal Circuit Rule 47.5);

(5) the jurisdictional statement;

(6) the statement of the issues;

(7) the statement of the case, including the citation of any published decision of the trial tribunal in the proceedings;

(8) the statement of facts;

(9) the summary of the argument;

(10) the argument, including statement of the standard of review;

(11) the conclusion and statement of relief sought;

(12) the judgment, order or decision in question, and any opinion, memorandum, or findings and conclusions supporting it, as an addendum placed last within the initial brief of the appellant or petitioner. This requirement is met when the appendix is bound with the brief. (See Federal Circuit Rule 30(c)(1) and (d) for a duplicative requirement of the appendix.);

(13) the proof of service (see Federal Rule of Appellate Procedure 25(d));

(14) the certificate of compliance, if required by Federal Rule of Appellate Procedure 32(a)(7).

The entire contents of the brief shall be bound in the manner prescribed in rule 32(b) of these Federal Circuit Rules.

Noncompliance with any of these provisions may lead to serious consequences including, but not limited to, striking the brief from the record, dismissal of the appeal, imposition of costs, and imposition of disciplinary sanctions against counsel.[30]

2. Cover; Caption; Names of Parties and Attorneys; Reproduction

Although there is no uniformity concerning the order and designation of parties in the title, the brief is always entitled in the court to which the appeal is taken. In

---

30 *See* Kushner v. Winterthur Swiss Ins. Co., 620 F.2d 404 (3d Cir. 1980) (dismissing appeal and imposing costs against appellant's counsel because appendix to brief did not comply with rules of court).

PRINT
NAME _Deborah Kim_

DATE _1-8-07_

TITLE	EDITION	AUTHOR

Brief Writing + Oral Arg. 9th

Supplement: LR + W 2

_7th Ed_
Wills + Trusts - Dukeminier

SIGNATURE _Deborah Kim_

Book Return Policy

NOTICE:
ALL RETURNS MUST BE
ACCOMPANYED BY THIS RECEIPT.

All Textbooks and Study Materials must be returned within 2 weeks of purchase or by the 3rd week of the semester, whichever is later, in order to receive full credit (text must be in the same condition as sold). All materials returned after the deadline will be considered used materials and their purchase will be at the discretion of the Bookstore Clerk. All Non-textbook or Study Materials purchased must be returned within 2 weeks of purchase and in the same condition as sold. – Trinity Bookstore

most jurisdictions it is the current practice not to reverse the names of the parties to a lawsuit. Some jurisdictions still adhere to the practice of placing the name of the appellant first, even though the appellant may have been the defendant in the trial court. The better practice is not to change the order of plaintiff and defendant in the caption but to indicate under the name of the party the status on appeal. All parties to the appeal are to be listed unless the number is too large, in which case the abbreviation *"et al."* may be substituted.

Counsel must be certain to comply with any rule specifying the color of the brief's cover. Different colors are used to indicate the party filing the brief. Thus, for example, the Federal Rules of Appellate Procedure provide that the cover of the appellant's brief should be blue; that of the appellee, red; that of an intervenor or amicus curiae, green; and that of any reply brief, gray.[31]

Permissible methods of reproducing appellate briefs are also specified by court rule. Typographical printing may be the preferred method of reproduction, but, generally, courts will accept briefs that have been duplicated by any process that produces a clear black image on white paper.[32]

If a defendant were to appeal to the Court of Appeals of the State of New York, the cover of the brief for the defendant-appellant would appear as follows:

To be Argued by
William Whitestone

COURT OF APPEALS

OF THE
STATE OF NEW YORK

Peter Pryor,
Plaintiff-Respondent,

against

David Donaldson,
Defendant-Appellant.

BRIEF FOR DEFENDANT-APPELLANT

William Whitestone
Alberts, Brown and Carlson
Attorneys for Defendant-Appellant
Office and Post Office Address
100 Court Square
Albany, New York 12207

---

31   FED. R. APP. P. 32(a)(2); *see also* SUP. CT. R. 33.1(g).

32   *See* SUP. CT. R. 33.1(a); N.Y. CPLR 5529 (McKinney Supp. 2004).

If the appeal were to be taken to the Appellate Division of the Supreme Court of the State of New York, the title of appellant's brief would be the same except that the name of the court would be set forth as follows:

To be Argued by
William Whitestone

SUPREME COURT

OF THE STATE OF NEW YORK
APPELLATE DIVISION—SECOND DEPARTMENT

The outside cover of a petition for certiorari in the Supreme Court of the United States would appear thus:

NO. 04-1437

IN THE

SUPREME COURT OF THE UNITED STATES

October Term 2004

Peter Pryor
Petitioner,

v.

Donald Donaldson
Respondent.

PETITION FOR WRIT OF CERTIORARI
TO THE UNITED STATES COURT OF
APPEALS FOR THE SECOND CIRCUIT

[Name and address of counsel.]

The title of the above petition for a writ of *certiorari* is the same as appears on the outside cover except that the calendar number of the appeal (No. 1437) would be given immediately below the term of court instead of above the name of the court.

Generally, the rules of court require that the name of the attorney who will argue the appeal be set forth in the upper right-hand corner of the first page of the brief. If there is a cover, the name will also appear on the cover of the brief.

The cover of the brief for the Supreme Court of the United States contains the calendar number of the appeal. When this number is required by the rules of court, it is generally placed immediately above the name of the court.

As indicated by the preceding facsimiles, immediately beneath the title there appears a statement indicating on whose behalf the brief is being submitted. For example, the brief for the appellant would state "Brief for Plaintiff-Appellant" or "Brief for Defendant-Appellant," as the case may be. Although it is also proper to state simply "Brief for Appellant" or "Appellant's Brief," the form suggested in the Court of Appeals facsimile is to be preferred since the inclusion of the word "plaintiff" or "defendant" clearly shows the history of the case.

In the body of the brief, it is not advisable to refer to the parties as "appellant" and "appellee." It is better to refer to the parties as "plaintiff" and "defendant," or by their names, or by abbreviations of their names. This practice is required in federal appellate courts by Rule 28(d) of the Federal Rules of Appellate Procedure, which provides:

> **(d) References to Parties.** In briefs and at oral argument, counsel should minimize use of the terms "appellant" and "appellee." To make briefs clear, counsel should use the parties' actual names or the designations used in the lower court or agency proceeding, or such descriptive terms as "the employee," "the injured person," "the taxpayer," "the ship," "the stevedore."

3. The Preliminary Statement; Nature of Case

The "Preliminary Statement," or simply "statement" as some advocates choose to call it, clearly and succinctly sets forth the history of the case and the general nature of the action or proceeding. The following information should be contained in the "Preliminary Statement" in one or two sentences:

(a) Who is taking the appeal;

(b) The court whose determination is being appealed;

(c) Whether the determination followed a trial;

(d) Whether the trial was before a judge or judge and jury;

(e) The determination or disposition of the case by the court or courts below; and

(f) The general nature of the action or proceeding.

While the cover and title of the brief inform the court of the names of the parties and on whose behalf it is submitted, the "Preliminary Statement" informs the appellate court generally of the nature of the cause of action and what has occurred up to the taking of the appeal. It is the first statement that tells the court something about "the kind of case" that is being appealed. This is the purpose of the "Preliminary Statement." Pertinent rules may modify the title or contents of the "Preliminary Statement." For example, the applicable rule of the New York Civil Practice

Law and Rules, which deals with the content of briefs, does not require a "Preliminary Statement." Rather, it requires "a concise statement of the nature of the case and of the facts which should be known to determine the questions involved."[33] Under such a requirement, much of the information usually contained in the "Preliminary Statement" may be recast in the statement of the "nature of the case." The heading in the brief to comply with this requirement may very well be "Nature of Action" or "Nature of Case." This section of the brief may then be followed by the "Statement of Facts." The rule also requires "supporting references to pages in the appendix."[34]

Read the following "Preliminary Statements":

I

"This is an appeal by the defendant from a judgment entered in the office of the Clerk of the County of Kings on May 10, 1990, in favor of the plaintiff, an attorney, who sued to recover for professional services rendered, against the defendant, in the sum of $2,500.00 after a trial before Justice James J. Johnson, without a jury, on April 15, 1990, in the Supreme Court, Kings County."

II

"This is an action, based on negligence and nuisance, to recover damages for severe and crippling injuries sustained by the plaintiff. The defendant appeals from a judgment of $200,719.50 entered upon a $200,000 verdict in favor of plaintiff after trial in the Supreme Court, Kings County, before Justice James J. Johnson and a jury, and from an order which denied a motion to set aside the verdict."

III

"This is an action to recover damages for personal injuries allegedly sustained by the plaintiff when she tripped and fell on a stairway in a building owned and operated by the defendant. The defendant appeals from a judgment rendered in favor of the plaintiff in the amount of Ten Thousand ($10,000) Dollars, which was entered on May 10, 1990, in the office of the Clerk of the County of Kings, after trial before Justice James J. Johnson, with jury, on April 15 and 16, 1990."

If there has been a determination by an intermediate appellate court, the "Preliminary Statement" may read as follows:

IV

"In this action to recover damages for an alleged breach of contract, the defendant appeals from an order of the Appellate Division of the Supreme Court, Second Judicial Department, entered on May 10, 1990, which order, two Justices dissenting, affirmed the order of the Supreme Court, which denied the defendant's motion to dismiss the complaint."

What suggestions, if any, could you offer to the brief writer to make the above "Preliminary Statements" clearer and more understandable?

---

33   N.Y. CPLR 5528(a)(3) (McKinney 1995).
34   *Id.*

Throughout the writing process, counsel must remember that the brief must be sufficiently flexible to permit an effective presentation of the case. Hence, in a particular case, whether or not required by rule, it is important to set forth the holding of the lower court. This is particularly helpful in a case in which the issue may be clearly demonstrated by stating the decision of the trial court that was reversed by the intermediate appellate court.

4. Questions Presented

a. Position in the Brief

The brief writer should inform the court of the questions presented on appeal at the earliest practicable opportunity. Hence, it is suggested that the "Questions Presented" follow the "Preliminary Statement" and precede the "Statement of Facts." Placing the questions presented at this juncture allows the court to read the facts *in light of the questions that must be determined.* The court, therefore, is in a better position to evaluate the salient facts in relation to the issues presented on the appeal. The court should not be made to guess, even for a moment, what issues it is being called upon to decide.

As with most matters of form, the position of the questions presented in the brief may be dictated by court rules. In briefs for the Supreme Court of the United States, the statement of the questions presented for review must precede all other matters, including the table of contents.[35] The position of the questions presented, as mandated by the applicable rule of the Supreme Court, underscores the importance of conveying this vital information to the court at the very beginning of the brief.

Rule 28(a) of the Federal Rules of Appellate Procedure sets forth "the order" in which the parts or "headings" of the appellate brief are to be set forth:

(2) a table of contents . . .;

(5) a statement of the issues presented for review;

(6) a statement of the case . . .;

(9) the argument . . .;

(10) a short conclusion stating the precise relief sought . . . .

In New York, the problem of precedence is resolved by the specific provisions of the applicable rule. Rule 5528(a) of the Civil Practice Law and Rules states that the brief shall contain *"in the following order . . . 2. a concise statement,* not exceeding two pages, *of the questions involved* without names, dates, amounts or particulars, with each question numbered, set forth separately and followed immediately by the answer, if any, of the court from which the appeal is taken." (emphasis added).

---

35   *See* SUP. CT. R. 24.1(a).

Subdivision 3 of Rule 5528(a) requires "a concise statement of the nature of the case and of the facts which should be known to determine the questions involved." Subdivision 4 sets forth the requirement "for the argument for the appellant [or respondent], which shall be divided into points by appropriate headings distinctively printed."

It is therefore clear that compliance with the rule requires that the questions presented or "involved" precede the statement of the nature of the case and the facts. The only additional requirement is that each question be followed immediately by the answer given by the court below. Compliance with this latter requirement may be achieved as follows:

QUESTIONS PRESENTED

Question 1: Whether testimony tending to show that the defendants had notice that in the past some of the patrons of their Skating Rink skated in a manner as to render it unsafe for the other patrons was sufficient to hold the defendants liable on the occasion in question without additional proof.

Answer of the court below: Yes, defendants were held liable.

Question 2: Whether the infant plaintiff had assumed the risk of injury of bodily contact with other skaters, in stopping five or six feet from the opening or exit from the rink when she admittedly knew that patrons skated off the rink at a fast rate of speed.

Answer of the court below: No, the infant plaintiff had not assumed the risk of bodily injury.

b. Purpose and Length

The purpose of the "Questions Presented" in the brief is to identify the issue or issues on appeal. It has been noted that "[t]he way an issue gets to be stated can have fateful consequences."[36] The statement of the questions presented is counsel's opportunity to focus the attention of the court on the specific question that counsel considers vital. For this purpose, a simple statement of the issue as an abstract proposition of law is too general to be of value. "The attention of the judge—catalyzed by the striking written or oral phrase—must be held through to the critical issue."[37]

The brief writer should frame the question in such a manner as to include the key facts of the case on appeal.[38] Inclusion of the facts will give substance and concreteness to an otherwise abstract proposition. For example, in an action to recover damages for injuries suffered as a result of an automobile accident that occurred while plaintiff was a guest in an automobile owned and driven by the defendant, the defendant contends that it was negligence as a matter of law for the

---

36 FRANCIS BERGAN, OPINIONS AND BRIEFS—LESSONS FROM LOUGHRAN 6 (1970).

37 *Id.*

38 *See* SUP. CT. R. 14.1(g), 24.1(g).

plaintiff to fall asleep in the automobile, even though the defendant had consented. If the defendant appeals from a decision for the plaintiff, the question on the appeal could be stated as follows:

> The question presented on this appeal is whether the plaintiff was guilty of negligence as a matter of law.

However, it would be more effective to state:

> Whether plaintiff's falling asleep with the consent of the driver, while riding as a guest in an automobile, constitutes negligence as a matter of law.

It is ineffective to set forth the question presented in the brief in general terms, such as:

> The question on this appeal is whether the complaint states a cause of action.

It is more effective to phrase the question in a way that places it in its factual setting, for example:

QUESTION PRESENTED

> Whether in an action on a negotiable instrument between the payee and the maker, the complaint is insufficient if it fails to contain an allegation of consideration.

It is difficult to predetermine the length of the statements that are to be made and the key facts that should be set forth in order to make the question applicable to the specific case. It is suggested that several drafts be made of the question or questions presented. Usually no one draft will be used as written, but rather, a part of one draft will be included in another, thereby giving a blended or telescoped finished product. The problem thereafter is the same as encountered with all parts of the brief. Having included the ideas, the language must itself be polished and rendered smooth.

c. Examples of Questions Presented

Often one will find excellent examples of the "Questions Presented" in the decision of the court. A reading of the statements found in judicial opinions will serve to illustrate the length and language of the "Questions Presented."

The following examples represent the court's statement of the issue presented on the appeal, or a suggested statement of the question presented:

QUESTION PRESENTED

I

> "Whether the trial court, after denying an injunction against the disturbance of easements of the plaintiffs, was warranted in directing that, in exchange for their property rights, the plaintiffs have judgment for a sum of money only."

II

> "Whether, in a criminal prosecution charging that the defendant did, feloniously and purposely and with premeditated malice, kill and murder a human being, the drunkenness of the accused, if it existed to the extent of depriving the accused of

the power of deliberation, might be considered by the jury as disproving an essential ingredient of the crime of murder in the first degree, viz., the deliberate intention to take human life."

III

"Whether equity will enforce the specific performance of an agreement for the making of repairs necessitated by fire, according to the provision of a lease between the plaintiff-lessee and the defendant-lessor."

IV

"Whether, in a contract for the purchase of real property where the vendee is to give back a purchase-money bond and mortgage, the vendor may be compelled to accept in place of the vendee anyone to whom the latter may have assigned the contract."

V

"Two questions are presented on this appeal:

"1. Whether a contract to give a mortgage on realty is a contract for the sale of an interest in real property within the meaning of Section 259 of the Real Property Law of the State of New York; and

"2. Whether there have been sufficient acts of part performance to relieve plaintiff from the production of a writing if such writing was necessary within the meaning of the aforementioned statute."

VI

"Whether the defendant shall be enjoined against using the word 'Waltham' or 'Waltham, Mass.,' upon the plates of its watches without some accompanying statement that shall distinguish clearly the defendant's watches from those manufactured by the plaintiff."

VII

"Whether the plaintiff, as one of several payees to whose order a check was drawn, may bring an action for its conversion though, at the time of the alleged conversion, the plaintiff was not the holder of the instrument."

VIII

"Whether the imported merchandise is to be assessed with duty as 'wood screens,' as classified by the customs officials, or whether it is entitled to free entry as 'paintings,' as claimed by plaintiffs."

d. Certified Questions

Occasionally, appellate courts will decide a legal question in an interlocutory order that is not yet appealable. To give permission to appeal from such an order, a trial court and the appellate court may certify the question for immediate appellate review.[39] If questions are certified to the appellate court, the brief should state the certified questions under the heading of the "Questions Presented." However, it should be

---

39   *See, e.g.,* 28 U.S.C. § 1292(b) (2000).

stated that "the following questions have been certified." The certified questions are usually simple and terse and often do not contain the facts that gave rise to the issue. These certified questions may be as follows:

"Does the complaint herein state facts sufficient to constitute a cause of action?"[40]

In the famous case of *Humphrey's Executor (Rathbun) v. United States*,[41] the plaintiff sued in the United States Court of Claims to recover salary allegedly due the deceased, a member of the Federal Trade Commission, from the date that the President undertook to remove him to the time of his death. The case involved the power of the President to remove a member of the Federal Trade Commission for causes other than those stated in the Federal Trade Commission Act.

The following questions were certified to the Supreme Court of the United States:

"1. Do the provisions of section 1 of the Federal Trade Commission Act, stating that 'any commissioner may be removed by the President for inefficiency, neglect of duty, or malfeasance in office,' restrict or limit the power of the President to remove a commissioner except upon one or more of the causes named?

"If the foregoing question is answered in the affirmative, then—

"2. If the power of the President to remove a commissioner is restricted or limited as shown by the foregoing interrogatory and the answer made thereto, is such a restriction or limitation valid under the Constitution of the United States?"

In an action by a plaintiff-holder of a negotiable promissory note signed "J. & G. Lippman, L.J. Lippman, Pres.," the plaintiff asked for judgment in the alternative against the corporation, maker of the note, or against the president personally, if, in signing the note on behalf of the corporation, he acted without authority. The Appellate Division certified this question:

"Does the complaint herein state facts sufficient to constitute a cause of action against the individual defendant, L.J. Lippman?"[42]

It seems clear that the certified question, *i.e.*, the statement of the matter to be decided by the appellate court, assumes meaning only after the reader has read the prior terse statement of facts. Hence, it may be more helpful to the court (therefore, more effective) if the certified questions be preceded by a condensed version of the facts in order to have the certified questions read in perspective. This statement of the facts should not be a complete statement. If it is complete, there is no reason for its repetition after the certified questions. This condensed statement should be no more than the setting of the stage for the certified questions. The picture of the facts is one painted with broad strokes so as to give what may be called a bird's eye view of the facts. It is designed to introduce the court to the case and

---

40 *See* Somberg v. Somberg, 188 N.E. 137 (N.Y. 1933).

41 295 U.S. 602 (1935).

42 New Georgia Nat'l Bank of Albany, Ga. v. J. & G. Lippman, 164 N.E. 108 (N.Y. 1928).

should result in clarity of presentation.[43] The technique of condensation is difficult and time consuming. However, it can be acquired, and it is possible to reduce the case to a few sentences.

This introductory statement of the facts is sometimes simply called "Facts." When this technique is employed, the headings of the various parts of the brief will be:

TITLE

*

Brief for Defendant-Appellant

*

FACTS

*

QUESTIONS CERTIFIED BY COURT [BELOW]

*

STATEMENT OF FACTS

*

POINT I

(Point Heading)

*

CONCLUSION

> Respectfully submitted,
> William Whitestone
> *Attorney for*
> *Defendant-Appellant*

Instead of the heading "Facts," some attorneys refer to this general introductory factual statement as "Special Statement" or "Introductory Statement." Regardless of its heading, its purpose is clear. It must enlighten the judge as to the issue to be decided, and must help clarify the certified questions in relation to their meaning in the specific case on appeal.

---

43 "Often clarity is gained by a brief and almost sententious statement at the outset of the problem to be attacked. Then may come a fuller statement of the facts, rigidly pared down, however, in almost every case, to those that are truly essential as opposed to those that are decorative and adventitious." Benjamin N. Cardozo, *Law and Literature, reprinted in* SELECTED WRITINGS OF BENJAMIN NATHAN CARDOZO 352–53 (Margaret E. Hall ed., 1947).

e. Headings of Brief Under New York CPLR 5528[44]

As indicated throughout this book, counsel must in all cases comply with the applicable rules of court. The following outline or headings of the various parts of the appellate brief, in the order indicated, will comply with New York CPLR 5528:

As indicated throughout this book, counsel must in all cases comply with the applicable rules of court. The following outline or headings of the various parts of the appellate brief, in the order indicated, will comply with New York CPLR 5528:

TITLE

*

Brief for Defendant-Appellant

*

TABLE OF CONTENTS

*

QUESTIONS PRESENTED

Question 1:

Answer of the court below:

Question 2:

Answer of the court below:

*

NATURE OF CASE

*

STATEMENT OF FACTS

*

POINT 1
(Point Heading)

*

POINT 2
(Point Heading)

*

CONCLUSION

Respectfully submitted,
[Name of attorney]

The appendix may be bound separately.

---

44   See headings of appellate briefs in Appendices B and D.

5. The Statement of Facts

a. Overwhelming Importance

Mastering the facts of the case is one of the most difficult tasks of the advocate.[45] However difficult, this task is unavoidable and indispensable. It is beyond the power of any jurist, lawyer, or teacher to overemphasize the importance of the facts. It is not inaccurate to speak of the *supremacy of the facts* in giving rise to law. The phrase *ex facto oritur jus*—the law arises from the fact—expresses a truism that cannot be forgotten by the brief writer.

The skilled and experienced trial lawyer is only too well aware of the devastating force of a single fact. Although the layman may believe that lawyers concentrate on *the law*, lawyers know that usually they must concentrate on *the facts*. A lawyer may be able to demonstrate quite convincingly that a given principle of law does not apply to certain facts, or that a given principle of law should be modified or limited, but the facts are not as flexible. Facts are stubborn and unchangeable.

Not even the most able lawyer can give a valid opinion on *the law* unless the facts are fully grasped and understood. For this reason, the competent lawyer is justified in refusing to give a "curbstone opinion." Since the opinion is given gratis, it is sometimes said that it is worth exactly what is paid for it. The remark, although facetious, is nevertheless true. Since no time would have been devoted to the understanding of *the facts* that gave rise to the question, and since the facts would not have been properly sifted and analyzed, the *legal conclusion* would have been worthless.

b. Duty to State Facts; Benefit to Court and Client

Regardless of scholarship, erudition, and legal acumen, judges do not know the facts until they are informed by the lawyer. Though the judge may be presumed to know the law, it may never be presumed that the judge knows the facts. It is the lawyer's duty to inform the court of the facts of the case.

Although the duty to state the facts fairly and understandably is common to all advocates, no two lawyers will discharge this duty in precisely the same fashion. It is expected that brief writers will present the facts in a light most favorable to their clients. As with the entire brief, the advocate will endeavor to have the statement of facts read sympathetically.

---

45 "Every experienced advocate will tell you that *mastering the facts* of a case is the most difficult part of his work . . . . Knowing all of the facts, he must confine his presentation to those which are most cogent and persuasive. His power of selection, of arrangement and of emphasis will be the measure of his genius." Arthur T. Vanderbilt, *Forensic Persuasion*, 7 WASH. & LEE L. REV. 123, 126–27 (1950).

c. Methods for Presentation of Facts

Bearing in mind what has been previously stated about accuracy, brevity, and clarity,[46] one may, nevertheless, ask, "What is the best way to present a condensed version of the facts of the case?"

Professor Llewellyn, in discussing appellate argument, has stated:

> It is a question of making the facts talk. For of course it is the facts, not the advocate's expressed opinions, which must do the talking. The court is interested not in listening to any lawyer rant, but in seeing, or better, in discovering, from and in the facts, where sense and justice lie.[47]

As corollaries, Professor Llewellyn added the following:

> It is trite that it is in the statement of facts that the advocate has his first, best, and most precious access to the court's attention. The court does not know the facts and it wants to. It is trite, among good advocates, that the statement of the facts can, and should, in the very process of statement, frame the legal issue, and can, and should, simultaneously produce the conviction that there is only one sound outcome.
>
> It is yet less generally perceived as a conscious matter that the *pattern of the facts* as stated must be a *simple* pattern, with its lines of simplicity never lost under detail; else attention wanders or (which is as bad) the effect is drowned in the court's effort to follow the presentation or to organize the material for itself.[48]

The following methods of presentation will assure an orderly, understandable, and effective statement of the facts.

i. Chronological

It has been suggested that in "making your statement of facts, always keep in mind the three 'c's'; chronology, candor, and clarity. Begin at the beginning and face the facts as they developed. Be objective lest your adversary point out an obvious omission."[49] Although no talismanic formula can be offered, experience in writing statements of facts will indicate that, in most cases, a chronological presentation of the facts is the most suitable method of presentation. This is not only an easy method to follow, but it also helps to develop the factual situation being presented.

The chronological presentation of the facts necessitates placing the facts in the order of the time of their occurrence regardless of the order in which the facts were presented at the trial through the testimony of witnesses and other evidence. The brief writer must gather the facts from the record and organize them into the desired order of presentation.

---

46   *See supra* pp. 4–8.

47   Karl N. Llewellyn, *The Modern Approach to Counselling and Advocacy*, 46 COLUM. L. REV. 167 (1946), *quoted in* KARL N. LLEWELLYN, THE COMMON LAW TRADITION 238 (1960).

48   *Id.*; *see also* KARL N. LLEWELLYN, COMMERCIAL TRANSACTIONS 20 (1946).

49   Samuel E. Gates, *Hot Bench or Cold Bench*, in COUNSEL ON APPEAL 129 (Arthur A. Charpentier ed., 1968).

ii. Informative and Understandable

In order to make the presentation more informative and more easily understood, it is often desirable to start the presentation with the *key fact*. After stating this "key fact," which serves as an orientation, the brief writer proceeds to show how that fact came about. For example:

> Plaintiff, a minor sixteen years of age, at approximately 5:30 in the afternoon on March 10, 1987, was seriously injured while endeavoring to board the "X" train at the defendant's terminal on 42nd Street.

The preceding statement tells the court the "key" facts—*what* occurred, *when*, *where*, and *to whom*. The facts thereafter relate how the plaintiff was injured.

If the subject matter were to deal with the commission of the crime of larceny, the following statement might precede the chronological statement of the facts:

> The defendant has been convicted upon five counts of Grand Larceny for sums obtained from John Goodhart between May 10 and July 20, 1990.

iii. Distinguish Between Disputed and Undisputed "Facts"

In condensing the evidence, as it appears in the record, counsel must *properly* present the evidence in the case. Propriety, in this sense, implies a presentation that is accurate and candid. The facts should not be "overstated." It is inexcusable to state that such and such is a fact if the assertion is based solely upon the testimony of the appellant when the testimony was seriously contradicted by the respondent and other witnesses.

The facts, as gathered from the evidence produced at the trial and found in the record, must be stated in such a way that the appellate court entertains no doubt as to the conceded or clearly established facts, and matters of conflicting testimony. When there is a conflict, what the facts are is *itself* a question of fact to be determined by the triers of the facts. This question of fact arises whenever there is conflicting testimony (which may involve a question of credibility or accuracy of observation), and when from the undisputed facts reasonable persons may draw conflicting inferences. To fail to apprise the court of the dispute is to misstate the facts of the case. It is, in any event, an inexcusable inaccuracy.

For example, in the case of the minor who was seriously injured while endeavoring to board a train owned and operated by the defendant, the plaintiff-appellant's "Statement of Facts" in the brief can unqualifiedly state that the plaintiff paid the fare, entered the station, and walked to the station platform, which was crowded with people. Those facts are not disputed. But it cannot be said that "calmly and without pushing," plaintiff endeavored to board the train, if there was testimony to the effect that the plaintiff "pushed and shoved."

The following statement of facts are taken from decided cases. Are they clear and understandable? Were you to rewrite them, what changes, if any, would you make?

Statement of Facts

Plaintiff, a Vietnamese, alleges that in November 1962, he was recruited by the CIA to participate in a program of covert military operations against North Vietnam. According to plaintiff, the CIA agreed to compensate him for his services as a saboteur, and, if he were captured or imprisoned while behind enemy lines, the United States would promptly rescue him. If rescue attempts should fail, his wife would continue to receive his pay during his imprisonment.

Plaintiff alleges that on March 15, 1964, while on a sabotage mission at the mouth of the Giang River in North Vietnam, he was captured by North Vietnamese forces. The United States Department of Defense, which had assumed control of the CIA operations against North Vietnam in 1964, failed to rescue him and stopped paying his wife his monthly salary after March 1965.

On January 17, 1980, plaintiff escaped from prison, returned to his village, and rejoined his family. In the spring of 1980, he left Vietnam by boat, and eventually made his way to the United States.[50]

Statement of Facts

On October 5, 1981, institutional disciplinary charges were presented against plaintiff-appellee, Gary Wayne Freeman, a prisoner at the Woodstock Correctional Facility. Freeman was accused of assaulting another prison inmate, Jeffrey Price. The charges were filed by defendant-appellant, Richard Rideout, a prison correctional officer at the facility. As a result of the charges filed by Rideout, a prison disciplinary hearing was conducted on the institutional charges the following day. Freeman was not informed of the identity of his accuser, nor was the alleged assault victim allowed to testify at the hearing. In part, because of the perceived need to protect Price from retaliation, Price was not permitted to testify at the disciplinary hearing.

After the prison disciplinary hearing, Freeman was found guilty and was sentenced to 30 days of "segregation" from the general prison population. The evidence upon which the finding of guilty was based consisted of three documents: an incident report written by defendant-appellant, Richard Rideout; a report written by Correctional Officer John Honnymar; and the unsworn statement of Douglas Pratt, another prison inmate.[51]

Within the bounds of fairness and accuracy, advocates may present the facts in a manner most favorable to their cause.

iv. Topical Subdivision of Facts; Other Aids

Occasionally, a factual situation is encountered that presents transactions and events that seem to defy brevity of presentation. The problem is one of organization. The facts should be subdivided into topics with appropriate section head-

---

50   Guong v. United States, 860 F.2d 1063, 1064 (Fed. Cir. 1988); *see* Appendix D.
51   Freeman v. Rideout, 808 F.2d 949, 950 (2d Cir. 1986).

ings. However, since this may necessitate the presentation of the facts in a nonchronological manner, and in segments, care should be taken that the various parts of the factual presentation are woven into one pattern. This may be accomplished by appropriate introductory or concluding statements.

The insertion of a topical heading is a helpful device. It permits the reader to know at a glance how much attention has been devoted to a particular topic and to reread and review a particular matter without reading through several pages. In the words of Professor Lile, "catch lines" serve as "mental resting places."[52]

Another effective device is the breaking up of a long statement into short paragraphs. The paragraph assists the reader to *see* and *grasp* each of the writer's ideas. It also affords a welcomed pause at the end of each paragraph. Generally, the writer can decide whether a new paragraph is warranted by finding what teachers of English composition call the *topic sentence*. This sentence, which expresses the central theme of the paragraph, is usually the first sentence of the paragraph and will introduce new matter or a new thought.[53]

6. The Argument

a. Scope of the Argument

The *points of law* that will be argued in the brief will be set forth under appropriate *point headings*. These points will be consecutively numbered and will be treated in that order. The previous parts of the brief have furnished the background for the legal argument. The court has been advised of the history of the litigation, the facts of the case, and the issue that it is called upon to decide. Counsel must now convince the court that, by the application of "the law" to the facts of the case, the decision of the lower court should be reversed or affirmed—depending upon whether the brief is written for the appellant or respondent.

The initial problem in the presentation of the argument is one of organization. It is suggested that an outline be made indicating all matters that may be argued. How will the argument commence? How will it proceed? The argument should start at the most effective point, should indicate the merit of the contentions by reference to principle and authorities, and should proceed logically and directly to the desired conclusion.

---

52 WILLIAM M. LILE, SOME PRACTICAL HINTS FOR THE BEGINNER IN THE MAKING OF A BRIEF 16 (1915).

53 "We may think of the topic sentence as a kind of backbone, or spine, which supports the body of the paragraph and around which the rest of the structure is formed." CLEANTH BROOKS & ROBERT PENN WARREN, FUNDAMENTALS OF GOOD WRITING 292 (1950).

b. Preliminary Considerations

Before deciding what matters *may* or *should* be treated, the following self-imposed questions should be answered:

(1) What is the applicable principle of law?

(2) What was the origin of the principle?

(3) What were the reasons that led to the existence of the principle?

(4) What were the original limitations upon the applicability of the principle?

(5) Have any exceptions to the principle come into being?

(6) Does the specific factual situation bring the case within the principle or within one of its acknowledged exceptions?

(7) Does the factual pattern *warrant* the creation of a *new* exception?

(8) Has the passing of time rendered the principle archaic or obsolete?

(9) Has the applicability of the principle been affected by the conduct of the parties (*e.g.*, laches, unclean hands, waiver, estoppel)?

(10) What decision or result would be required by the demands of justice?[54]

(11) Does the "applicable" principle lead to the "just" result?

(12) If not, is there another principle of law that will lead to the "just" result?

(13) If another principle of law will give a "just" result, is not this latter principle (or should it not be) the *applicable* principle of law?

(14) Considering *all factors*, what is the "desirable" result?[55]

(15) Specifically, on what ground or grounds is it contended that the decision of the lower court is right or wrong?

The foregoing questions are intended to cause counsel to *think* about the points to be treated in the brief.

For the brief writer, a key function is one of *identifying* error and determining whether that error, in appellate practice, constitutes *reversible* error.

c. Draft and Outline of Points and Point Headings

Once the brief writer has decided what matters will be set forth and urged in the argument, the various points must be arranged under appropriate point headings.

A "point" is a specific ground or contention urged in support of counsel's position on appeal. Each point will be presented under an appropriate point heading.

---

54   *See* discussion of *stare decisis* and the moral element of the judicial process, *supra* pp. 80–81.

55   *See* discussion of "Search for the Desirable Result," *supra* pp. 81–82.

In view of the importance of the argument, the brief writer should write an outline of the points and should write several drafts of the point headings. If the outline contains too many point headings, they should be reexamined to ascertain whether they are not merely subdivisions of other headings instead of separate headings in themselves. For example, an outline of an argument on appeal may initially contain five or more point headings.

A reexamination of the content of the argument may cause the writer to reorganize the materials into only three point headings.

A case is not necessarily strengthened by urging numerous grounds for reversal.[56]

The story is told of the neophyte who, arguing for the appellant, commenced oral argument by saying:

"May it please the court. There are seven grounds upon which this case should be reversed." One of the judges (who, perhaps, was not happy with the prospect of listening to the *seven* grounds) immediately interrupted: "Counselor, please state to the court your main and best ground. If we will not reverse on that ground, we will not reverse on the others." The incident may be apocryphal, but the point is clear. The court wishes to know the *best* reason in support of the position urged. One point, fortified by reason and authority, well written and effectively documented, may be sufficient to cause the appellate court to reverse the judgment or order of the lower court; whereas, four or five points, inadequately developed and without supporting reasons and authority, may fall short of the mark.

d. "Summary of Argument"

The "Summary of Argument" is an overview or synopsis of the legal argument. Traditionally, in appellate brief writing, this section of the brief has consisted simply of the various point headings in sentence form, set forth in the order in which they appear in the brief.

The "Summary of Argument" is included in the brief as a matter of custom or practice, or because it may be required by rule of court. It brings to the attention of the reader a brief summary of the legal argument or legal position of the author of the brief. The main, if not sole, purpose of the "Summary of Argument" is to give the court a succinct overview of counsel's legal argument on appeal.

The "Summary of Argument" ought to bring each segment of the argument into a complete whole and should help the court see the interrelationship of one point to another, and to the entire argument. It should assist the court to follow the logic of counsel's entire legal argument made in the body of the brief.

This broad panorama of the argument also serves to demonstrate the logical progression of counsel's position from the initial premise to the ultimate conclusion.

---

56 "Frivolous issues cast a shadow of doubt on meritorious ones." Rahdert & Roth, *supra* note 15, at 857.

The court is thereby placed in a position to see at a glance the entire legal syllogism. Like the strategic map, no detail is contained but the reader is permitted to view the entire area.

When counsel, in the "Summary of Argument," set forth their point headings in chronological order, the full benefit of the "Summary of Argument" will not be realized unless the point headings are effective and presented in logical order. If the point headings are sufficiently clear and effectively summarize counsels' legal argument on the appeal, the enumeration of the point headings under the "Summary of Argument" section of the brief is helpful to the reader.

If the point headings do not accomplish the purpose of clearly and effectively summarizing the legal argument, a brief narrative or *a concise synopsis* of the legal argument is preferable. This view finds support in subdivision (h) of Rule 24.1 of the United States Supreme Court Rules, which requires that briefs on the merits shall contain "[a] summary of the argument, suitably paragraphed . . . [which] should be a clear and concise condensation of the argument made in the body of the brief . . . ." Indeed, this rule concludes by stating that the "Summary of Argument" should not be "[a] mere repetition of the headings under which the argument is arranged . . . ."

Although previous editions of the Federal Rules of Appellate Procedure made inclusion of a "Summary of Argument" optional, Rules 28(a)(8) and 28(b) now *require* the appellant's and appellee's briefs each to contain a summary of the argument. Furthermore, the local rules of many of the federal courts specifically require a "Summary of Argument" in all submitted briefs. Note for example, that the rules of the Court of Appeals for the Federal Circuit specifically require the "Summary of Argument" to precede the argument.[57] Hence, a brief submitted to the Federal Circuit not only would contain a "Summary of Argument," but the "Summary of Argument" would follow the "Statement of Facts" and would precede the point headings and points.

The rules of other courts may require the "Summary of Argument" to precede the "Statement of Facts." Counsel should examine the applicable local rule to ensure proper placement of the "Summary of Argument" in the brief.

Note the following "Summary of Argument" in the case of *Spalding v. Agri-Risk Services*.[58] In *Spalding*, the Court of Appeals stated that the question presented was whether, "under Missouri law, there is a material question of fact sufficient to defeat a motion for summary judgment as to whether the insurance company, by its silence or inaction, has either waived its rights, or is estopped from asserting a condition of the insurance contract which provides for the cancellation of the coverage if the insured animal is castrated."[59]

---

57   FED. CIR. R. 28(a).

58   855 F.2d 586 (8th Cir. 1988).

59   *Id.* at 587.

Summary of Argument

The District Court erred in failing to consider Plaintiff's argument that Defendants were estopped from relying upon the terms of the insurance policy which prohibited castration. The principle of estoppel applies whether or not Plaintiff had notice of the terms of the policy. Furthermore, the facts of the case and the conduct of Defendants fulfill all of the elements of either estoppel or waiver. Hence, estoppel or waiver were questions of fact that should have prevented the District Court from granting summary judgment for the Defendants.[60]

e. Point Headings

The "point heading" is a succinct argumentative statement that applies a specific legal principle to the facts of the particular case. Its appearance in bold type in the brief should give a clear idea of the importance of the point heading.

The point heading should be a clear and complete statement, forcefully written. It should not be a statement of an abstract principle of law but rather should contain the conclusion that must follow the application of a principle of law to the facts of the case. Since the brief writer wishes to induce the reader to read the statements in support of the point heading, the point heading must be interesting and informative. It cannot be simply a statement of fact, of law, or a conclusion. The effective point heading must contain all three—preferably in one sentence.

Note the following headings:

I

The complaint does not state a cause of action.

II

The complaint should be dismissed.

III

The complaint is legally insufficient.

IV

The complaint fails to allege that the plaintiff performed its part of the contract.

V

The plaintiff cannot recover since the complaint does not allege performance by the plaintiff.

The above headings may be correct as applied to the actual case, but are they effective? Consider the advantages of the following three headings over the previous ones:

VI

Because the plaintiff does not allege performance, or any excuse for nonperformance, it cannot recover in this action for breach of contract.

---

60 *See* "Summary of Argument" in Appendix C.

VII

The plaintiff cannot recover in this action for breach of contract because it has not alleged performance or any excuse for nonperformance.

VIII

Because plaintiff sues for breach of contract, the complaint is insufficient in law as it does not allege performance by the plaintiff or any excuse for his nonperformance.

Point headings VI, VII, and VIII are more effective. The law is pinpointed to the specific case, and the conclusion flows from its application to the facts.

Consider the following point headings in an action by a plaintiff for breach of contract where the defendant-appellant maintains that no contract came into existence since the defendant did not make an offer but merely notified potential purchasers that it had certain goods for sale:

I

The motion to dismiss the plaintiff's complaint should have been granted.

II

It was error to deny defendant's motion to dismiss.

III

No contract came into being.

IV

The defendant made no offer to the plaintiff.

V

There was no offer that the plaintiff could have accepted.

VI

Since the defendant's circular addressed to plaintiff did not constitute an offer, because it stated neither quantity nor price of the goods, it was impossible for the plaintiff to accept and form a contract.

VII

Because defendant's circular addressed to plaintiff contained no statement as to quantity or price of the goods advertised, it did not constitute an offer that could have been accepted by plaintiff.

VIII

Because defendant's circular did not state any terms as to the quantity or price of the goods advertised, it was not an offer that could have been accepted by plaintiff.

The first five headings are too general to be effective. They are not keyed to the specific case. An experienced brief writer has referred to such point headings as "blind headnotes," since they are "so unenlightening and undistinguished that they might fit any one of a hundred records."[61]

Headings VI through VIII, although more lengthy, highlight the specific issue and state unequivocally the specific contention of counsel.

Note the following point headings in a specific performance action brought by a purchaser of realty three years after the defendant refused to convey. The defendant decided to retain the premises. However, the buyer did not sue for the specific performance until the value of the premises increased appreciably. Under the law of the particular jurisdiction, the defense of laches is recognized, and an action for damages for breach of contract must be commenced within six years.

I

The plaintiff cannot bring this action.

II

The plaintiff is barred by the doctrine of laches.

III

The plaintiff's action for specific performance is barred by laches.

IV

Because plaintiff delayed over three years before commencing suit for specific performance, the suit is barred by laches.

It would seem obvious that point heading IV is more effective than the others.

i. Noninformative Point Headings

As has been demonstrated by some of the previous point headings, if the heading is too general it is not effective. The following are common examples of point headings that are too general to be informative and effective:

The complaint should be dismissed.

The complaint states a valid cause of action.

These headings are mere conclusions and do not help the court. The court's attention is not focused upon a specific legal problem arising from the facts of the case. After reading these general or broad point headings, the court will not know what matters will be discussed under the point.

ii. Burdensome Point Headings

Unduly lengthy point headings must also be avoided. The point heading must be specific; it cannot be clumsy and hard to grasp. It must be an interesting *headline* that will catch the reader's eye and induce the reader to read further. For example, in the specific performance action referred to previously, point heading IV is more

---

61   J. Paxton Blair, *Appellate Briefs and Advocacy*, 18 FORDHAM L. REV. 30, 38 (1949).

effective because it applies the rule of law to the facts of the case. Although terse, it expresses a complete *point*. It reads:

> Because plaintiff delayed three years before commencing suit for specific performance, the suit is barred by laches.

Suppose the brief-writer had written:

> Because the plaintiff delayed three years before commencing suit for specific performance, the suit is barred by laches, and the doctrine of laches is independent of the statute of limitations.

The objection to this heading would not be that what is said in the heading is incorrect but rather that perhaps too much is said. The force or emphasis of the heading is dissipated. Would it not be better if the heading mentioned only the main point, viz., that the suit is barred by laches? Then, under that heading, the discussion would indicate that the two doctrines are distinct and that, although the statute of limitations has not expired, a cause of action for specific performance may, nevertheless, be barred by the doctrine of laches.

In all likelihood, the heading is burdensome if it is not readily understandable.

iii. Recapitulation: The Effective Heading

In recapitulation, it may be stated that since the point heading, like the headline of a newspaper, serves to attract attention, it must be interesting and easy to grasp. It will fail if it is not informative. It will fail if it is not argumentative. It will also fail if it is overburdened and crowded with information.

f. Contents of Points

i. Outline of Argument; Subordinate Propositions; Order of Points

Before commencing to write the body of the points, it is suggested that the outline of the argument be reexamined. This outline, consisting of the point headings with their supporting reasons, will permit the advocate to visualize and evaluate the argument. The outline may show that supporting reasons have been set forth as separate point headings. Occasionally, two separate matters are set forth under the same point. Unless the matters discussed under a particular heading support that heading, the writer must decide whether to list the reasons separately, change the heading, or eliminate a portion of the discussion.

Generally the propositions contained in a point heading will be supported by several subordinate propositions. These subordinate propositions must be established to supply the appropriate foundation for the main proposition contained in the point heading. Since these subordinate propositions are included to demonstrate the merit of the point heading, they are important pillars in support of the argument.

The outline of the argument will help the writer determine whether the *order* in which the points appear is necessarily the most effective. If three points are to be discussed, are all three points of equal importance? Is the position of the advocate secure on all points? Is counsel appealing on alternate theories of equal legal soundness?

The brief writer must decide the order in which the points will be discussed. Which point will be discussed first, and which will be discussed last? The goal, of course, is to present the argument in such a way as to lead to the conclusion that is urged upon the court. Yet, the question persists: What is the most *effective* way to present the points? Effectiveness implies a presentation that is logical, clear, and understandable, and one that will cause the reader to agree with the position urged by the brief writer.

Most lawyers would advise the novice to place one's "best foot forward." It is stated that after reading counsel's best point, the court will read the brief sympathetically. This is probably sound advice. Of course, no point should be urged that does not have some merit. It is foolish to follow a point that is sustainable and sound with one that is untenable. Whatever psychological benefit may have been earned by the reading of the previous point may be lost by the subsequent point. One cannot assume that the court will be so impressed with the one point that it will not read further. A point without merit has no place in a brief.

ii. Factual Statement Contained in Points

Many rules of court require that the statement of the case be followed by the propositions of law and the authorities relied on to support them. The "propositions of law and the authorities relied on to support them" refer to the *points* in the brief. The advocate, however, should not be misled by the phraseology of the requirement. The points cannot be a mere abstract discussion of propositions of law. They should treat a legal proposition *only insofar as it relates to the specific factual situation of the case*. Even if the court were to agree with the propositions of law advanced by counsel, nothing would be accomplished unless it is applicable to the facts of the case. Therefore, under each point the brief writer should set forth the facts that are relevant to the discussion of the particular legal proposition in that point.

Since unnecessary repetition is objectionable in a brief, care should be taken that under each point no more facts be stated than are absolutely necessary to show the relationship between the facts and the legal proposition. The goal is to restate only those facts that pertain directly to the legal discussion in the point.

It is not intended to convey the impression that the factual statement in the points is to be set forth independently of the legal principle. The facts, insofar as they are relevant to a full understanding of the point, ought to be integrated with the legal proposition. This technique was also recommended for the point heading. Although the point heading need not be repeated in the point, it should be borne in mind that the heading was most effective when it was sufficiently specific in its reference to the facts of the particular case that the reader was able to judge or appreciate the exact relationship between the facts and the legal proposition urged. The effectiveness of the argument in the points is tested by the same standard. An abstract legal discussion in the points is a discussion *in vacuo*. The discussion in the points, to serve its purpose, must be concrete. This is accomplished by including the key facts which gave rise to the legal problem discussed in the brief.

iii. Suggestions for Persuasive Argument

It may be said that an argument is as effective as it is helpful to the court. Does the argument, whether written or oral, help the court decide the question presented?

Before committing thought to writing, counsel must answer two questions:

1. What is the best and the most persuasive authority to support counsel's position?

2. What is the best authority that supports the position of counsel's opponent?

These authorities, both in support and in opposition to counsel's position, must be mastered. In the brief, as in oral argument, counsel must strive to persuade the court that the hostile or opposing authority is inapplicable, and that the supporting authority requires the decision urged on appeal. Hence, counsel must stress, and explain, the strongest favorable point and answer the strongest opposing point.

Neither time nor space should be wasted on answering points that are obviously weak or devoid of merit. The effort must be designed to stress why counsel's position is valid and should prevail. The discussion in the points must be specific and relate to the particular question on appeal.

General platitudes, cliches, and useless metaphors must be avoided. Do not state: "To grant the plaintiff specific performance is unfair, unjust, inequitable, and unconscionable." State the reason why the granting of specific performance would be *unjust*. The additional words used almost as interchangeable synonyms do not lend weight to the assertion. If the reason is clearly shown, the court, in its own mind, will add the appropriate synonyms.

On the other hand, care should be taken that the argument is not overstated. The overstatement of the argument is as bad as the substitution of general platitudes for specific supporting reasons. Counsel must know the limitations of the proposition that is being urged. The advocate who states propositions categorically, when there are acknowledged exceptions, injures very seriously the integrity of the brief. Even in the most favorable light, the overstatement is an indication of ignorance of the limitations and exceptions.

iv. Treatment of Authority in Points

If the research undertaken has been thorough, the advocate will usually find that there is a great deal of legal literature on the subject. Obviously, not all of it (decisions, statutes, treatises, articles) will be favorable to one's position. How should it be treated—if at all? How pertinent are the materials to the case on appeal? The cardinal rule is that authorities must be dealt with fairly and frankly. The court should neither be confused nor left in doubt as to counsel's position.

(a) Analysis of Cases to Support Main Propositions

If cases are relied on to sustain a main proposition, it is insufficient merely to cite them. Mere citation of cases is an invitation to the court to examine them for itself and ascertain their relevance to the point urged. It has been stated—with a remarkable degree of accuracy when one considers the overburdened state of some appellate calendars—that this is "a task which few judges will undertake, and one peculiarly incumbent upon counsel."[62]

Every case relied on to support a main proposition should be *analyzed.* An analysis of a case requires an accurate digest of the case. This involves a terse statement of the facts as they relate to the point for which the case is cited, together with the *holding* of the case.[63] The court will also welcome a statement containing the *reasoning* of the decision, the *ratio decidendi,* as distinguished from the *dicta* of the case. This can be accomplished by a *short* quotation from the opinion. Once this is done the court may judge for itself the extent to which the case relied on supports counsel's contention.

If counsel wishes to show that courts have adhered to a given principle for many years and can prove the statement by ten cases, need all of the cases be analyzed? It is sufficient to analyze only a few representative cases. Others may be cited. It will be more effective if the writer first analyzes the most recent case and then indicates that the rule has existed for many years by analyzing an early case and another decided years later. If numerous cases can be cited, the writer should select only those cases in which the factual patterns most closely resemble the case on appeal.

If counsel maintains that the authority of a decided case has been seriously weakened, the presentation should show that subsequent decisions have restricted its application or that changed conditions have rendered the precedent obsolete.

(b) Citation of Authority for Collateral Propositions

If a proposition is merely collateral or subordinate, the citation of a case is sufficient without the analysis referred to previously. This is a rule of necessity, to prevent the brief from becoming unduly voluminous and to prevent the discussion from being bogged down by collateral issues. However, if the status of the main proposition is precarious without supporting reasons, the analysis of a case to sustain the subordinate proposition may also be necessary.

(c) Lengthy Quotations

Lengthy quotations from opinions are to be avoided. The advocate must cultivate the ability to summarize lengthy passages. Instead of quoting an entire paragraph, the writer should state in capsule form the thought or core of the para-

---

62   LILE, *supra* note 52, at 14.

63   The holding of a case should include the legal issues raised by the facts and the court's disposition of the case (relief granted or denied) pertaining to those issues. *See* Rahdert & Roth, *supra* note 15, at 857.

graph. There are always exceptions. A quotation may be so clear and so well written that a paraphrasing would detract from its forcefulness. It may contain a felicitous phrase or the language of a great jurist whose wisdom is revered by the appellate court. An outstanding quotation will lend emphasis to the argument.

If the quotation is long, and does not possess exceptional value, it should not be reproduced in the brief. The advocate should constantly bear in mind that what is being written is a *brief,* and not an explanatory text, article, or treatise. It is possible to shorten a quotation by omitting irrelevant portions. The omission is indicated by the use of ellipses.

If counsel decides to quote a portion of an opinion, quotation marks should be used and, if the quotation is lengthy, it should be indented so as to distinguish clearly between the quoted matter and the language of the brief writer. In a typewritten brief, indented quotations are usually single-spaced.

v. Unfavorable Cases and Authority

In deciding whether to discuss ostensibly adverse or hostile authority, the first consideration should be counsel's professional responsibility. Reference has already been made to Rule 3.3(a)(3) of the Model Rules of Professional Conduct, which expressly provides that "[a] lawyer shall not knowingly: . . . fail to disclose to the tribunal legal authority in the controlling jurisdiction known to the lawyer to be directly adverse to the position of the client and not disclosed by opposing counsel."[64] But once the adverse authority has been disclosed, counsel is free to challenge its soundness.

In the process of distinguishing cases, it is generally more effective (and easier) to distinguish an unfavorable precedent *on its facts* rather than to argue that the case was erroneously decided. In the usual case, counsel will have undertaken a prodigious task of doubtful success in trying to persuade the court to overrule existing authority. Occasionally, however, courts will overrule existing authority and counsel must adopt this approach when no other path is open.

vi. Citation of Judicial Dicta

It is entirely proper to cite a case for favorable judicial dicta. Of course, counsel must let it be known that the case is cited for dicta contained in the opinion. Judicial dicta constitute persuasive authority and, in the absence of imperative authority to the contrary, may very well be deemed controlling. Surely this result may follow if the dicta represented the considered opinion of an able jurist in a case that examined thoroughly the state of the law on the particular subject.

Judicial dicta can be cited with the most promising results in a case where no direct authority can be found or as additional support for other authorities. Most

---

64   See the discussion of candor, *supra* pp. 94–95, and the discussion by Chief Justice Vanderbilt in *In re Greenberg*, 104 A.2d 46 (N.J. 1954).

practitioners will agree that a judicial dictum of an appellate court is likely to be more persuasive than the writings of even the most able authors.

The distinction between judicial dicta and obiter dicta, as made by Professor Llewellyn,[65] although not often recognized, should not be overlooked. The distinction is made on the basis of the *relevance* of the dictum to the issue presented to the court for decision. Since the judicial dictum is more closely related to the issue presented for decision than the dictum that is merely obiter, the former commands greater respect than the latter.

Whatever a judge may write in an opinion must be read with specific reference to the case being decided. Hence, the persuasive authority of dicta may be said to be in the same proportion as the relevance of the dicta to the specific issue of the case. From this standpoint, it is inadequate to know that the words uttered were dicta. The case should be analyzed with such care and skill that the advocate should be able to indicate to the court the degree of authority to which the words are entitled.

vii. Commentaries, Treatises, and Other Legal and "Nonlegal" Writings

As indicated previously,[66] not all authorities are of equal weight from the standpoint of being either imperative or persuasive. The persuasiveness of a comment in a particular periodical may be so negligible as to render its citation useless. This, however, should not deter the brief writer from citing standard works, or even well-written treatises, as supplementary authority. It may be possible to find a sentence or two in a text that is precisely on point. Of course, if the statement is supported by authority, an examination of the authority may cause the brief writer to cite the primary source. On the other hand, if the source cited is not on point and does not support the statement contained in the text, the reference or quotation should be omitted. Its weakness will doubtless be pointed out by opposing counsel, and all authority will thereafter be examined with suspicion.

Common sense dictates that the brief writer grant the most prominent treatment to the best authority. If there is neither a statute nor a domestic case on point, is there a case decided elsewhere? A decision of the highest court of another state is merely persuasive. If the foreign decision is unclear and not directly on point, it may be necessary to resort to commentaries. This should prove helpful if the author of the commentary is widely cited.

In the search for authority, the advocate should not overlook the opportunity of referring to a well-reasoned and persuasive dissenting opinion. A dissent-

---

65   *Id.* See the categories of dicta as found in ROGER W. COOLEY, BRIEF MAKING AND THE USE OF LAW BOOKS 366 *et seq.* (5th ed. 1926) (*obiter dicta, dicta propria, gratis dicta*).

66   *See supra* pp. 82–86.

ing opinion, particularly when written by an eminent jurist, may command great respect.[67]

The advocate's research cannot be thorough until the various law reviews have been examined. With the aid of LexisNexis, Westlaw, and the *Index to Legal Periodicals* (or its CD-ROM or online version), the researcher may be referred to the periodical literature on the topic. Although law review articles are primarily useful for the authority that they have uncovered and the legal analysis of a particular problem, occasionally the article itself may be cited as persuasive or secondary authority.[68] It is no longer uncommon in a judicial opinion to cite, or even to quote from, an outstanding article. A reading of those opinions, however, may show that the articles cited or quoted were usually authored by persons of outstanding professional reputation.[69] Authorship and scholarship are of primary importance.

If the interpretation and application of a statute are required, the advocate must not fail to examine the legislative history of the enactment. Not only must the subsequent history of the statute be examined to ascertain if it has been repealed or amended, but, as indicated in Chapter 5, its prior history may hold the key to the *meaning* of the statute as applied to the particular case.

Informative materials may also be found in the reports of the Law Commissions of the various states. It is not unlikely that an answer to an otherwise unresolved legal problem may be found in a report of a Judicial Council, Law Revision Commission, or, perhaps, a report of the Opinions of the Attorney General.

A discussion of available research materials would be incomplete without a reminder that, in certain cases, materials of a socioeconomic nature may not only be relevant but very persuasive. The classic illustration of the use of "non-legal" materials in a brief is the brief filed by Louis D. Brandeis in the case of *Muller v. Or-*

---

67 *See* ROBERT H. JACKSON, THE SUPREME COURT IN THE AMERICAN SYSTEM OF GOVERNMENT 19 (1955). For a discussion of the function of dissenting opinions, see Stanley H. Fuld, *The Voices of Dissent*, 62 COLUM. L. REV. 923 (1962). *See also* the statement of Chief Justice Hughes, *infra* p. 134.

68 BENJAMIN N. CARDOZO, INTRODUCTION TO SELECTED READINGS ON THE LAW OF CONTRACTS (1931) (compiled and edited by a Committee of the Association of American Law Schools).

69 Many examples can be cited where judges relied on statements of the law as found in articles. See, for example, *Idaho State Bank of Twin Falls, Idaho v. Hooper Sugar Co.*, 276 P. 659 (Utah 1929); *Geffine v. Thompson*, 62 N.E.2d 590 (Ohio Ct. App. 1945), wherein the judge wrote: "There is an excellent article in 22 Michigan Law Review, 521, on *'The assignability of easements in gross in American law,'* by Lewis M. Simes, now a professor of law in the University of Michigan," and proceeded to discuss the article and concluded, "The writer of this opinion is in accord with the views expressed in the above article by Professor Simes." *See, e.g.*, Roberson v. Rochester Folding Box Co., 64 N.E. 442 (N.Y. 1902) (referencing to the famous article on *The Right to Privacy* by Warren and Brandeis in 4 HARV. L. REV. 193 (1890)).

egon.[70] In this famous Supreme Court case, which sustained the validity of a statute of Oregon that limited the hours of labor for women, the brief contained "extracts from over ninety reports of committees, bureaus of statistics, commissioners of hygiene, inspectors of factories, both in this country and in Europe, to the effect that long hours of labor are dangerous for women primarily because of their special physical organization."[71] Justice Brewer, doubtless impressed with the scholarship and industry displayed by the brief, remarked: "In patent cases counsel are apt to open the argument with a discussion of the state of the art. It may not be amiss, in the present case, before examining the constitutional questions to notice the course of legislation, *as well as expressions of opinion from other than judicial sources.* In the brief filed by Mr. Louis D. Brandeis for the defendant in error is a very copious collection of all these matters, an epitome of which is found in the margin."[72]

g. Citations: Form and Quantity

An examination of briefs will indicate that many brief writers commit two errors in relation to citations: first, the form is not acceptable, and second, too many cases are cited.

The purpose of the citation is to lead the reader to the case or work cited without the necessity of seeking aid or information elsewhere. There is such a thing as a *good citation,*[73] and the importance of good form cannot be underestimated. In addition to the compliance with the rules of court concerning the proper method of citation, the brief writer should follow the method of citation suggested in a standard *citator.*[74] The advocate should not believe that the manner of citation will not be noticed by the courts. The court may even make known its displeasure by denying a successful litigant costs that would otherwise have been granted.

The inclusion in a brief of a long series of citations, the so-called "string cite," has been neatly characterized as "one of the greatest vices of brief writing."[75] Thorough research may have required an examination of the cases cited. In the brief, however, only the most pertinent cases need be cited. Little skill is required to quote a proposition of law stated in an encyclopedia, and, after giving the volume and page number of the work, to add the word "citing" and include a string

---

70 Brief for defendant, Muller v. Oregon, 208 U.S. 412 (1908). *See Brown v. Board of Education,* 347 U.S. 483 (1954), wherein the Supreme Court of the United States rejected the "separate but equal" doctrine of *Plessy v. Ferguson,* 163 U.S. 537 (1896), and, citing nonlegal materials, stated: "Whatever may have been the extent of psychological knowledge at the time of *Plessy v. Ferguson,* this finding is amply supported by modern authority."

71 *Muller,* 208 U.S. at 420 n.1.

72 *Id.* at 419 (emphasis added).

73 MILES O. PRICE, A PRACTICAL MANUAL OF STANDARD LEGAL CITATIONS iii (1950).

74 *See* THE BLUEBOOK: A UNIFORM SYSTEM OF CITATION (17th ed. 2000); LEGAL CITATOR, *infra,* pp. 179–206.

75 MARIO PITTONI, SUGGESTIONS ON BRIEF WRITING AND ARGUMENTATION 39 (1951).

of citations found in the encyclopedia. The encyclopedia served its function by leading the advocate to the cases in point.

It is impossible to state a categorical rule on the number of cases that should be cited. Is it necessary to cite more than three cases for the same proposition of law? If success depends upon establishing a given proposition of law, obviously counsel should marshal the available authority. Judicial authority should be presented in order of its persuasiveness, commencing with what has been termed *mandatory* or *imperative authority.* When there is a great deal of authority for a proposition of law, counsel may wish to cite the earliest or most famous case, and a recent case to emphasize its continuing validity.[76] One or two cases directly on point are more effective than a large number of cases that are peripheral to the legal proposition in question.

h. Citations to Exhibits and Transcripts

Sometimes, the more important or crucial citations are not those to legal authorities but rather to exhibits or transcript pages. No disputed statement of fact should be made without an appropriate and accurate citation to the record. For example, in appeals that challenge the grant of a judgment notwithstanding a verdict, the appellant must direct the court's attention to the evidence that could have supported the jury's verdict. Conversely, an appellee who seeks to uphold a jury verdict must cite the substantial evidence in support of that verdict. Accurate citations to that evidence may be crucial. Nothing is more frustrating for an appellate court than the necessity of searching or combing a record for the evidentiary support for the statements made in a brief. The brief with clear and accurate citations to the record will be both more persuasive and helpful to the appellate court.

An important distinction must be made between a citation and an attempt to incorporate material by reference. While a citation may be appropriate, an incorporation by reference is not. Under the Federal Rules of Appellate Procedure, all arguments must be contained within the brief, which must comply with exact page limits.[77] The practice of incorporating by reference arguments made in other briefs or pleadings undermines these rules. For this reason, appellate courts frequently hold that a party who has incorporated arguments by reference to the appendix did not properly raise those arguments on appeal and has thus waived them.[78]

i. Summation of Points

After a point has been properly developed, by a discussion of the legal proposition advanced together with the authorities to sustain it, it is advisable to con-

---

76   Rahdert & Roth, *supra* note 15, at 858.

77   FED. R. APP. P. 32(a)(7)(A).

78   *See, e.g.*, Graphic Controls Corp. v. Utah Med. Prods., Inc., 149 F.3d 1382, 1385 (Fed. Cir. 1998); Executive Leasing v. Banco Popular de Puerto Rico, 48 F.3d 66, 67–68 (1st Cir. 1995).

clude with a short summation or peroration. For example, if the point heading were to read:

> Since plaintiff delayed three years before suing for specific performance, the suit is barred by laches,

an appropriate summation, or final statement for the point, might be:

> Although the lapse of time is but one of the circumstances to be considered in determining whether a suit for specific performance is barred by laches, there is no doubt that the increased value of the premises, in addition to plaintiff's delay, constitutes laches.

It has been stated that:

> [t]he best argument, in any case, is one made for your client, not by yourself, but by a judge of the same or some other dignified court in the rendition of the opinion and judgment in an analogous case. Seldom would a court considering a case neglect to examine and consider such an argument if called to its attention.[79]

Counsel should also remember the "principle" suggested by Professor Llewellyn regarding "the proffered, phrased opinion-kernel." He states:

> What is wanted is a passage which can be quoted *verbatim* by the court, a passage which so clearly and rightly states and crystallizes the background and the result that it is *recognized* on sight as doing the needed work and as practically demanding to be lifted into the opinion.[80]

This summation of the point seems uniquely suited for the insertion of an "opinion-kernel."

7. Conclusion and Signature

The "Conclusion" of the brief offers counsel the last opportunity of written expression to the court. This "Conclusion" is generally a sentence or two and repeats the relief requested. Without violating the requirement of brevity, it should contain a summary of the essential points of the entire argument.

Note the following conclusions:

CONCLUSION

The order appealed from should be affirmed.

CONCLUSION

The judgment should be affirmed and the complaint should be dismissed.

CONCLUSION

For the foregoing reasons the judgment of the Appellate Division should be affirmed.

---

79   THOMAS C. SPELLING, THE BRIEFER AND LAWFINDER 373 (1931).
80   KARL N. LLEWELLYN, THE COMMON LAW TRADITION 241 (1960).

CONCLUSION

For the foregoing reasons the judgment of the Court of Appeals should be reversed and that of the District Court should be affirmed.

CONCLUSION

For the foregoing reasons the judgment and order on appeal should be affirmed with costs.

These "Conclusions" are all *correct* insofar as they correctly recite the relief requested, but they lack emphasis and appeal. A summarization of the key facts and principle of law *together with the formal conclusion* would be more effective. The court would then close the brief remembering the final summary of the case as well as the relief requested.

The following conclusions are therefore preferable to those that do no more than state the relief requested:

CONCLUSION

Through a circular containing no terms of sale, the defendant advertised certain goods for sale. The authorities clearly establish that a circular offering goods for sale is a mere announcement and not an offer. Plaintiff's letter to defendant was, therefore,not an acceptance of an offer for none had been made. Because there was no contract of sale, judgment for the plaintiff should be reversed.

CONCLUSION

By the use of circulars, the defendant announced that he had certain goods for sale. Except for a description of the goods, the circulars contained none of the terms of sale. Such an announcement does not constitute an offer. Plaintiff's letter to the defendant, therefore, was not an acceptance but an offer. Because the plaintiff does not allege that the defendant accepted the offer, no contract came into being. Judgment for the plaintiff was therefore error and should be reversed.

The "Conclusion" is followed by the signature of the brief writer. Because the brief is respectfully submitted to the court, such a complimentary closing is not only customary but entirely proper. The signature may be typed or printed and need not be handwritten.[81]

The following example shows the manner in which the signature of counsel is customarily set forth:

Respectfully submitted,

William Whitestone
Alberts, Brown and Carlson
Attorneys for Defendant-Appellant

---

81   *See, e.g.*, Thiem v. Hertz, 732 F.2d 1559 (11th Cir. 1984).

C. Rereading and Correcting the Brief: Proofreading

1. Checking Typewritten Brief

The conscientious brief writer has finally completed writing the brief.

The brief writer is satisfied with the final draft and feels confident that it is a good brief that will make a most favorable impression. Everything worth arguing has been presented in a manner calculated to assist the court in deciding the case. However, the task is not over. The typewritten brief must now be *checked for errors*. It cannot be assumed that the typewritten copy will be free from error. This copy should be read very carefully, and the conscientious worker must check all *quotations, citations, record references*, and correct errors of *spelling, grammar,* and *punctuation*.

In checking citations, the careful brief writer will always verify a citation with its original source rather than with previously made notes that also contain the citation. Furthermore, citations should not be verified against a case printed or downloaded from an electronic legal database. There simply is no substitute for consulting the actual volume number, page reference, and date.

2. Proofreading Typeset Brief

If the brief is to be typeset, the chore of further checking cannot safely be delegated to the printer. Someone must proofread the galley sheets carefully. This proofreading phase of brief writing is important and, if delegated, must be delegated to a diligent and conscientious worker. The fact that the chore may be delegated should not mislead either the brief writer or the proofreader to believe that the function is not important. Judge Wilbur F. Pell, of the United States Court of Appeals for the Seventh Circuit, wrote as follows about what could have been corrected by simple proofreading:

> These errors may seem of no great significance. What the brief writer actually meant will ordinarily shine through the obscurantism of possible ineptness, and the distraction is only mild. Yet, there is a gnawing feeling on occasion that the obviousness of the uncorrected errors indicates that the brief, having not been read for these errors, may be equally unreliable in its substantive reasoning or its analysis of authorities.[82]

As soon as the galleys have been proofread, they should be returned promptly to the printer so that there may be ample time to proofread the revised proof. Some old errors will be found and some new ones will have been contributed gratuitously by the printer.[83] All of these errors must be detected and corrected.

---

82   William F. Pell, Jr., *Read Before Signing,* 60 A.B.A. J. 977 (1980).

83   "The most baffling device of the imp [of the perverse] is to cause a new error in the process of correcting an old one. This residuary misprint is one against which there is no complete pro-

The final printed brief should be read very carefully before it is filed with the court. It must be a perfect document reflecting many hours of research, study, and careful draftsmanship. Errors in a brief—however trivial—tend to destroy the confidence of the court in the substance of the brief itself.[84] Brief writers cannot risk the loss of any of the benefits gained by drafting an effective brief simply because they failed to devote the necessary time to the careful rereading of the printed brief. This final reading serves a dual purpose: first, it is the last opportunity to correct errors; and, second, it is the beginning of the indispensable preparation for oral argument.

---

tection. When General Pillow returned from Mexico he was hailed by a Southern editor as a 'battle-scarred veteran.' The next day the veteran called upon him to demand an apology for the epithet actually printed, 'battle-scared.' What was the horror of the editor, on the following day, to see the expression reappear in his apology as 'bottle-scarred.'" FREDERIC BERNAYS WIENER, BRIEFING AND ARGUING FEDERAL APPEALS 204 (1961) (quoting Harry L. Koopman, *The Perversities of Type*, in THE BOOKLOVER AND HIS BOOKS 152, 157 (1917)).

84　A recent example of the importance of eliminating errors is case where the court, noting that an attorney's papers were "replete with typographical errors," the "careless, to the point of disrespectful," reduced the hourly fee for written work from $300 to $150. Devore v. City of Philadelphia, No. Civ.A. 00-3598, 2004 WL 414085 (E.D. Pa. Feb. 20, 2004), at *2-3.

VIII

RESPONDENT AND REPLY BRIEFS

A. The Respondent's Brief

1. General Observations

The materials previously discussed are applicable to appellate brief writing generally. The fundamental principles that make for an effective brief are the same whether counsel is drafting Appellant's Brief (the opening brief), Respondent's Brief, or a Reply Brief. Certain special considerations, however, should be mentioned for the benefit of counsel whose brief is written in support of the judgment of the lower court. The purpose of this brief is not to urge that the judgment of the lower court was erroneous, and, therefore, should be reversed, but rather to demonstrate that appellant's allegations of error are ill-founded. Respondent's brief will show that since no reversible error was committed, the judgment or order on appeal should be affirmed.

Because the brief of the respondent is to a great extent a refutatory document (from the standpoint of the psychology of persuasion), the brief writer should know the essential differences between the respondent's brief and the opening brief of the appellant.

2. Respondent's Strategic Advantage

Because the respondent has already won in the lower court, the present goal is to retain what has been gained. In this regard, the respondent enjoys certain distinct advantages over the appellant. First, because the judgment enjoys what may be termed a *presumption of correctness*, the burden of establishing error in the lower court rests with the appellant. Second, in a case of grave doubt, and perhaps as an offshoot of the previous advantage, the appellate court is reluctant to upset the judgment of the lower court. The grounds for reversal must be demonstrated by the appellant to the satisfaction of the appellate court. Third, even if appellant succeeds in establishing an error in a ruling of the lower court, the error may not warrant a reversal if the error has been rectified by a subsequent ruling or if it was not prejudicial.[1] Fourth, the respondent is able to study and digest the appellant's brief and is in a perfect position to take advantage of all of the shortcomings and limitations of appellant's brief as indicated either by its content or omission. Fifth, although the respondent knows exactly what are the contentions of the appellant on the appeal and will refute them by demonstrating their weaknesses, respondent can, and will, nevertheless, *argue affirmatively* in support of the judgment or order rendered by the lower court.

---

1   *See* discussions of "Necessity of Indicating Error" and "Is the Error Harmless or Reversible?" *supra* pp. 50–53.

3. Content and Purpose of Respondent's Brief

The respondent's brief must do two things: first, it must weaken or overcome the argument of the appellant; and, second, it must sustain the judgment or decree under attack. This must be done by meeting the appellant's allegations of error and by demonstrating that no error was committed, or that the error had been obviated or was not prejudicial to the appellant. The respondent's brief should indicate any inaccuracy, misstatement, or omission in appellant's brief if relevant to the appeal and, in compliance with the rules of court, must state the propositions of law and authorities relied upon in support of the judgment.

4. Outline of Appellant's Brief

Counsel for the respondent, after reading the appellant's brief carefully and noting the main propositions urged for a reversal of the judgment of the lower court, would do well to write an outline of the appellant's brief. This outline should indicate appellant's main contentions with their supporting reasons. This outline will assist the respondent to visualize appellant's position and will be helpful in drafting the respondent's brief. The outline, which summarizes appellant's contentions, will also serve as a checklist for the respondent. Have all of appellant's points that warrant refutation been answered or otherwise treated in the respondent's brief?

5. The Facts; The Equities

In most cases, the respondent will have no serious problem regarding the statement of the facts. It is not difficult to ascertain the accuracy of the facts as stated in the appellant's brief. If any error exists, it must be indicated. Generally, the sin is one of omission. In the Statement of Facts, has the appellant omitted an essential fact favorable to the respondent? For example, in an action against a railroad, the appellant in the Statement of Facts emphasized the fact that the station was crowded and that "the crowd was unruly and pushed in order to board the train." The appellant did not mention, however, that all witnesses testified, either in direct examination or in cross-examination, that the "plaintiff pushed and shoved."

In stating the facts, it is elementary that counsel for the respondent must state the *equities* that favor the respondent. Therefore, unless there is an agreed statement of facts, or the case is appealed solely on a question of law, it is a mistake simply to copy the appellant's Statement of Facts.

It is important for both respondent and appellant to state the equities in favor of their clients. These equities arise from the facts. They must be stated specifically. It is ineffective simply to declare that "justice and equity demand that the case be affirmed." In a case where after three years plaintiff sues for specific performance of a contract to sell a house and lot, defendant should emphasize that during the three years substantial improvements were made, thus stressing the equities.

The respondent is entitled to the most favorable statement of the facts that the record will justify. The court, however, cannot do justice and equity unless all the various interests and equities of the parties have been brought to its attention for consideration.

6. Respondent's Brief To Be Independent of Appellant's Brief

It must be remembered that appellant chose a particular order for the discussion of the points because that order presented appellant's argument in the most favorable light. Respondent must refute every tenable point made by the appellant but need not discuss them in the identical order adopted by the appellant. For example, since appellant's first point is likely to be the strongest, respondent's refutation will probably be the weakest. Respondent should, therefore, not follow the order of points in appellant's brief and should discuss the weakest point first. Respondent should arrange the points in the manner that is most helpful to the respondent.

Let us suppose that respondent determines that appellant's first point is the only tenable point and that the others are very weak and hence easily answered. In that case, it may be wise to admit readily that the most serious contention is found in appellant's first point and proceed immediately to refute it. This method of frontal attack may prove to be very effective.

If a contention of the appellant is manifestly without merit or clearly erroneous, no benefit accrues from belaboring the obvious. The decision to answer appellant's first point first, however, must be that of the respondent. The choice should be made after having concluded that the particular approach selected is the most effective and most likely to win the appeal.

7. Respondent's Brief Not a Defensive Document

A rather common error committed by counsel for the respondent in the drafting of respondent's brief is the preparation of a purely defensive document. An examination of many briefs will reveal a large number of respondents' briefs that are solely defensive. This ineffective brief for respondent often does no more than change the point headings found in the appellant's brief by the insertion of a negative term. Often this type of brief will use as ineffective a point heading as "The judgment should be affirmed" or "No error was committed." These headings state no reason for the proposition and do not enlighten the court.[2]

Respondent's brief should be an affirmative document, forcefully written. If it were to be characterized, it should be deemed *assertive* rather than defensive. The argument should proceed upon the strength of respondent's position and not merely upon the weakness of appellant's. Lawyers agree that it is better strategy to depend upon the strength of one's own case than upon the weakness of that of

---

2   *See* discussion of "Point Headings," *supra* pp. 118–21.

the adversary. It is for this reason that it has even been suggested that the "respondent's brief should be completed in first draft . . . *before you even read the appellant's brief.*"[3]

It is sometimes very helpful to note the various facts and points over which there is agreement. Frequently, appellants make critical concessions that may provide a basis to resolve a certain issue on appeal. Moreover, if the parties do agree on many of the facts presented, the respondent or appellee need not repeat all of those facts in its brief. For that reason, court rules commonly require that the responding brief state only those facts where respondent disagrees with those set forth in the brief of the appellant. For example, Federal Circuit Rule 28(b) specifically provides that the appellee's jurisdictional statement and statements of the issues, the case, and the standard of review "shall be limited to specific areas of disagreement with those of the appellant." The rule further provides that absent such disagreement, the appellee shall not include any of these statements.

Once the respondent has ascertained the legal propositions in support of the judgment of the lower court, these propositions must be enthusiastically presented to the court. Like the brief for the appellant, the argument in respondent's brief should be urged convincingly and forcefully.

The attitude of counsel for respondent, as manifested in the brief, should be one of firm conviction in the correctness of the decision of the lower court. An attitude of indifference, or overconfidence because of the success below, may prove to be fatal on the appeal.

8. Refutation of Appellant's Argument

A primary objective of respondent's brief is to answer the argument contained in appellant's brief. Generally, the goal of the refutation is to distinguish successfully the cases and other authorities upon which the appellant must rely. However, because the respondent's brief should be a positive and constructive document, the question arises as to the best method to be used to refute appellant's argument.

The refutation of appellant's argument should not be separated from counsel's affirmative presentation of respondent's position on appeal. Rather, the refutation and the affirmative presentation are to be woven into a single argument. The weakness or fallacy in any of the contentions of the appellant should be brought to the attention of the court. In refuting a point made by the appellant, the respondent must indicate specifically the particular point that is being refuted. Unless the weakness is so obvious as to be glaring, the brief writer, who has read appellant's brief carefully and thoroughly, should not presume that the weaknesses are equally apparent to all other readers. Respondent, therefore, should direct the court's attention to the exact point in controversy and should proceed to demon-

---

3   J. Paxton Blair, *Appellate Briefs and Advocacy*, 18 FORDHAM L. REV. 30, 41 (1949) (emphasis in original).

strate the weakness or lack of merit of appellant's position. The respondent will also set forth the reasons that require that the holding of the lower court be affirmed.

A respondent should not feel obliged to refute every fact and point set forth in the appellant's brief. Some attorneys do so to the point of absurdity. Such an inflexible approach weakens their case and their credibility. Counsel should always be willing to acknowledge obvious weak points in their arguments and counter them with their strengths. Sometimes that means agreeing with some of the facts or points made by the appellant. By selectively deciding which critical points to refute, and acknowledging the points over which were is agreement, counsel greatly enhance their credibility before the court.

Respondent, of course, wishes the brief to be read sympathetically. It would, therefore, be a grievous psychological error to indulge in sarcasm or otherwise to disparage unfairly appellant's brief. Respondent is not only entitled, but is under a duty, to point out to the court all serious errors and inaccuracies in appellant's brief. This, however, is not a license to include insult, however subtle, or to indulge in comments about personalities. Although it is permissible to characterize an argument as untenable, unfounded, erroneous, or fallacious, sarcastic remarks have no place in a legal document.

a. Authorities upon Which Appellant Relies

All authorities upon which the appellant relies are presumably authorities hostile to the position of the respondent. In dealing with hostile authorities, the respondent usually enjoys the advantage of having to refute only those authorities that appellant has included in the brief. In all likelihood, the appellant will rely on several cases for authority. The respondent must examine these cases very carefully. The cases must be "Shepardized," and the opinion of the court should be read carefully—always with particular reference to the specific facts of the case. Some of the techniques used to detract from the apparent authority of hostile cases are familiar to the reader.[4] The hostile case must be distinguished from the case on appeal if its holding is opposed to respondent's position.

As indicated previously,[5] a frontal assault upon a hostile case is to be avoided. Unless the authority of a case has been so weakened by subsequent cases that its demise is imminent,[6] it is usually poor strategy to urge that the case upon which appellant relies "was erroneously decided and should be overruled." The chances of success are better if counsel shows the factual differences between the cases and the legal distinctions in the issues presented for decision. The approach that

---

4   *See supra* pp. 79–82.

5   *See supra* p. 123.

6   An example would be the case of *David Lupton's Sons v. Automobile Club of America*, 225 U.S. 489 (1912), whose authority was seriously affected by the *Angel v. Bullington* decision, 330 U.S. 183 (1947), although it was not expressly overruled until June 20, 1949, by the case of *Woods v. Interstate Realty Co.*, 337 U.S. 535 (1949).

shows factual and legal distinctions, rendering the case inapplicable as authority, is more likely to be successful than a suggestion to overrule the prior decision.

Counsel should not overlook the latent possibilities of a trenchant dissenting opinion.[7] A dissenting opinion may indicate the fallacy or weakness of the majority opinion in a more forceful manner than counsel's. To borrow the language of Chief Justice Hughes: "A dissent in a court of last resort is an appeal to the brooding spirit of the law, to the intelligence of a future day, when a later decision may possibly correct the error into which the dissenting judge believes the court to have been betrayed. Nor is this appeal always in vain. In a number of cases dissenting opinions have in time become the law."[8]

b. Inapplicability of Argument of Appellant

Occasionally the respondent will find the argument made by the appellant in the brief to be perfectly correct but inapplicable to the case on appeal. It may either miss the point in issue or omit vital exceptions or limitations to the propositions discussed. Under these circumstances, the respondent should not fall into the error of refuting the correctness of what the appellant has stated. To the contrary, the respondent can safely admit the correctness of the principle stated by the appellant[9] and proceed to demonstrate its inapplicability to the case because of the existence of an exception or limitation. This may be termed the rounding out of appellant's legal argument by the addition of the forensic "but" or "however."

Counsel should be alert to detect these omissions and exceptions when reading the opposing brief. Of course, in order to discover them, counsel must have done extensive research and be thoroughly prepared.

B. The Reply Brief

1. Not To Be Filed Unless Necessary

As with all legal writing, the first question is whether it is *necessary* to write. Counsel must first determine if it is necessary to submit to the appellate court an additional brief on behalf of the appellant. What specific purpose will it serve?

Rules of court usually provide for the filing of a reply brief by the appellant, but may impose limitations upon its content. For example, the Rules of The Illinois Supreme Court provide that "the reply brief, if any, shall be confined strictly to replying to arguments presented in the brief of the appellee and need contain only Argument."[10]

---

7   *See supra* pp. 126–27.
8   CHARLES EVANS HUGHES, THE SUPREME COURT OF THE UNITED STATES 68 (1928).
9   *See generally* discussion of "Opposing a Motion," *supra* pp. 44–45.
10   ILL. SUP. CT. R. 341(g).

Regardless of any limitation by rule upon the right of appellant to file a reply brief, a reply brief should not be filed unless absolutely necessary. The test ought to be whether the respondent's brief has raised new matter that requires a reply.

Although some lawyers believe that there is an advantage in "having the last word," it is extremely doubtful if, in the usual case, any advantage accrues to the appellant by the simple expedient of writing an additional brief—a Reply Brief. Does appellant wish to *reply* to an argument presented by the respondent, or simply to *repeat* something already presented in appellant's opening brief?

If the appellant is of the firm belief that respondent's brief befuddled an otherwise clear-cut issue, or injected an issue that has no relevance to the case, a reply brief may serve to clarify the matter. If the respondent's brief raises an entirely new point, the appellant should not be deprived of the opportunity to answer that point. In sum, the question is not whether a reply brief *may* be filed, but whether there is a good reason that it should be filed.

2. Content and Purpose

If it is decided that a reply brief is necessary, the appellant must examine and digest respondent's brief and the authorities cited with a view toward their refutation. The reply brief must be concise and to the point. It cannot reargue matter previously discussed in the opening brief; nor should it introduce into the case a new line of argument. Courts frequently emphasize that a reply brief should only reply to the brief of the appellee and that it does not present an opportunity to raise, for the first time, an issue for appellate review. As a result, courts do find that a party who first raises an issue in a reply brief has waived that issue on appeal.[11]

In addition to the refutation of respondent's authorities, the reply brief may refer to the crucial points made in the opening brief that were not answered in the respondent's brief. This type of reply brief is effective because, in addition to its brevity, it brings to the court's attention the main points of the appellant's brief that were impliedly admitted by respondent's failure to refute them.

In cases involving cross-appeals, each party will be given the opportunity to file a reply brief. However, the party filing the cross-appeal must be careful to limit its reply brief to the subject matter pertaining to the cross-appeal only. This reply brief does not provide the cross-appellant an opportunity to have the last word concerning the appellant's primary appeal.

---

11   Enercon GmbH v. Int'l Trade Comm'n, 151 F.3d 1376, 1385 (Fed. Cir. 1998) (quoting Amhil Enters., Ltd. v. Wawa, Inc., 81 F.3d 1554, 1563 (Fed. Cir. 1996) and FED. R. APP. P. 28(c)).

Part Four

ORAL ARGUMENT

IX

PREPARATION FOR ORAL ARGUMENT

A. Importance of Oral Argument

"The Koran says, 'A mountain may change its place, but a man will not change his disposition'; yet the end of eloquence is—is it not?—to alter in a pair of hours, perhaps in a half hour's discourse, the convictions and habits of years."[1] With these words Emerson expressed the power of eloquent speech. For the lawyer, speech is not only powerful, it is an invaluable professional tool. Experience has shown that speech may succeed when the printed word has failed. Justice Brennan of the Supreme Court of the United States has said that "[o]ften my whole notion of what a case is about crystallizes at oral argument."[2]

The ability to speak well has traditionally been attributed to members of the legal profession.[3] Nevertheless, it has been said that "although appellate argument is a common occurrence and represents the culminating competitive effort in the legal contest, it is probably a fact that this is the least qualitative accomplishment of the bar as a whole."[4] There are several explanations for this observation. The era of forensic oratory is almost a matter of the past. Counsel does not enjoy the privilege of arguing appeals unhampered by strict limitations of time. For example, in the Supreme Court of the United States, in the early period when cases were few, extended oral argument was permitted. Today, one is rarely privileged to speak for more than half an hour, except by special leave of the court.[5]

Limitation upon the time allowed for oral argument, however, should not be misinterpreted to mean that appellate judges do not consider it important. Justice Jackson, referring to arguments before the Supreme Court of the United States, stated that: "I think the Justices would answer unanimously that now, as tradition-

---

1   Ralph Waldo Emerson, *Essay on Eloquence*, *in* 1 COMPLETE WRITINGS OF RALPH WALDO EMERSON 640 (1929).

2   William Brennan, HARVARD LAW SCHOOL OCCASIONAL PAMPHLET *No. 9*, at 22–23 (1967).

3   Referring to the great lawyers of classical Rome, Judge Wilkin wrote: "These founders of the profession were masters of the word, both spoken and written." ROBERT N. WILKIN, THE SPIRIT OF THE LEGAL PROFESSION 22 (1938).

4   Raymond S.Wilkins, *The Argument of an Appeal*, 33 CORNELL L.Q. 40, 44 (1947).

5   *See* SUP. CT. R. 28.3.

ally, they rely heavily on oral presentation. Most of them form at least a tentative conclusion from it in a large percentage of the cases."[6]

This point of view was reaffirmed by Justice Byron White, in an address given on July 31, 1981, when he said:

> Although we now hear most cases for only one-half hour on a side, oral argument remains an important step in the decision-making process. It is then that all of the Justices are working on the case, having read the briefs and anticipating that they will have to vote very soon, and attempting to clarify their own thinking and perhaps that of some of their colleagues.[7]

The attitude of the Supreme Court is reflected in Rule 28.1, which provides:

> Oral argument should emphasize and clarify the written arguments in the briefs on the merits. Counsel should assume that all Justices have read the briefs before oral argument. Oral argument read from a prepared text is not favored.

Arguments before the Supreme Court of the United States are tape recorded and transcribed. These tapes are available to the Justices and their law clerks for use in the preparation of draft opinions.[8] This practice, which is also followed in other courts, further underscores the importance of oral argument in the decision-making process of appellate courts. Recently, courts have begun to provide litigants, upon request and the payment of a nominal fee, with a copy of the tape recording of the oral argument. It is good practice to have these tapes transcribed in a certified transcription, particularly if the opposing party has made a startling revelation or a critical concession. Moreover, arguments before the Supreme Court of the United States are transcribed and made immediately available through LexisNexis, Westlaw, Findlaw, and the Court's website.[9]

Oral argument is the advocate's "last clear chance" to prevail. It is counsel's sole opportunity "to involve the interest of the judge, to make him a participant, if you

---

6   Robert H. Jackson, *Advocacy Before the Supreme Court: Suggestions for Effective Case Presentation,* 37 A.B.A. J. 801 (1951); *see also* RICHARD A. POSNER, THE FEDERAL COURTS 119 (1985). Judge Posner states unequivocally: "The value of oral argument to judges is high." *Id.*

7   Address by Justice Byron R. White, Jackson Memorial Lecture, National Judicial College (July 31, 1981).

8   *See* ROBERT L. STERN ET AL., SUPREME COURT PRACTICE 585–86 (7th ed. 1993); DELMAR KARLEN, APPELLATE COURTS IN THE UNITED STATES AND ENGLAND 72 (1963).

9   In contrast, the Fifth Circuit is more restrictive about disseminating oral argument transcripts than the Supreme Court. Its rule states in part:

> [W]ith the advance approval of the presiding judge, cousel may arrange, at their own expense, for a qualified court reporter to record and transcribe oral argument. If it is the court reporter's usual practice, the reporter may make and use a sound recording for the sole purpose of preparing an accurate transcript. The reporter then must immediately destroy or erase the recording without making it available to counsel, a party, or any other person for any purpose. The court records oral argument for its exclusive use and does not make the tapes, or copies or transcripts of the recording available to counsel, the parties, or any other person.

5th Cir. Rule 34.7.

will, in the hunt for the just and fair result and not merely an arbiter, aloof and detached."[10]

Chief Justice Rehnquist has made available to advocates a helpful article on oral advocacy before the Supreme Court.[11] In this article, he stresses that oral argument "is the only opportunity that you will have to confront face to face the nine members of the Court who will ponder and decide your case. The opportunity to convince them of the merits of your position is at its highpoint . . . ."[12]

He emphasizes that "it is one of only two occasions on which the judges get together to consider the case. As an oral advocate you should take advantage of this opportunity to be present with the Court when it collegially concentrates on your case."[13]

1. Submission of Case Without Oral Argument

Appellate counsel is generally permitted to submit a case for consideration by an appellate court without benefit of oral argument. This practice, however, is rarely advisable. There is remarkable unanimity among appellate advocates that anyone who has the opportunity to present oral argument but simply submits the case on the briefs has not taken full advantage of the appellate process.[14]

This view was echoed by the Federal Commission on Revision of the Federal Court Appellate System. In considering a proposal to restrict the availability of oral argument, the Commission observed:

> Oral argument is an essential part of the appellate process. It contributes to judicial accountability, it guards against undue reliance upon staff work, and it promotes understanding in ways that cannot be matched by written communication. It assures the litigant that his case has been given consideration by those charged with deciding it. The hearing of argument takes a small proportion of any appellate court's time; the saving of time to be achieved by discouraging oral argument is too small to justify routinely dispensing with oral argument.[15]

---

10 Milton Pollack, *The Civil Appeal*, *in* COUNSEL ON APPEAL 45 (Arthur A. Charpentier ed., 1968). It has been said that "[o]ral argument is valuable for 'establish[ing] a human connection between bench and bar.'" Stephen L. Wasby, *The Functions and Importance of Appellate Oral Argument: Some Views of Lawyers and Judges*, 65 JUDICATURE 341, 345 (1982).

11 William H. Rehnquist, *Oral Advocacy*, 27 S. TEX. L. REV. 289 (1986). For other useful articles that focus specifically on oral advocacy before the Supreme Court, see Warren E. Burger, *Conference on Supreme Court Advocacy*, 35 CATH. U. L. REV. 525 (1984); Rex E. Lee, *Oral Argument in the Supreme Court*, A.B.A. J. (Special Issue) June 15, 1986, at 60; and Stephen M. Shapiro, *Oral Argument in the Supreme Court of the United States*, 35 CATH. U. L. REV. 529 (1984).

12 Rehnquist, *supra* note 11, at 303.

13 *Id.* at 300.

14 *See* Pollack, *supra* note 10, at 44.

15 COMMISSION ON REVISION OF THE FED. COURT APPELLATE SYS., STRUCTURE AND INTERNAL PROCEDURES: RECOMMENDATIONS FOR CHANGE 48 (1975).

Although the time allotted for oral argument may be short, oral argument is still significant. It is the only instance during the appellate process when the lawyers for the parties can command the undivided attention of the appellate court. That opportunity should not be dismissed lightly.

2. Securing the Right to Argue

Despite the acknowledged importance of oral argument, the overwhelming volume of cases being appealed has compelled most appellate courts to adopt rules restricting oral argument. These rules affect the length as well as the availability of argument, and vary considerably from jurisdiction to jurisdiction. Thus, the appellate practitioner must study closely the rules regarding oral argument of the court to which the appeal is taken. A failure to study the rules may leave counsel without adequate time to argue, or may result in an inadvertent waiver of the right to argue.[16]

In the Supreme Court of the United States, oral argument is generally restricted to thirty minutes for each side.[17] Extensions of time may be allowed upon motion filed not later than fifteen days after service of appellant's or petitioner's brief.[18] The Rules of the Supreme Court also provide that "[o]ral argument will not be allowed on behalf of any party for whom a brief has not been filed."[19]

In the United States courts of appeals, the amount of time allowed for oral argument is a matter within the discretion of the court. For example, Rule 34 of the Rules of the United States Court of Appeals for the District of Columbia Circuit provides, in part:

> (b) **Time Allowed For Argument.** Counsel shall be afforded such time for oral argument as the court may provide and will be so advised by order. Requests for enlargement of time may be made by motion filed reasonably in advance of the date fixed for the argument.

The federal courts of appeals may, by local rule, dispense with oral argument entirely in certain circumstances.[20] Since the opportunity to argue before the federal courts of appeals is no longer a matter of right,[21] counsel must be prepared to state the reasons why oral argument would be helpful to the court.

---

16   *See, e.g.*, Section 600.11(f)(1) of the Rules of Practice of the Appellate Division for the First Judicial Department of the Supreme Court of the State of New York, which provides: (f) Time Permitted for Argument. (1) Counsel for the parties shall consult and determine whether they wish to argue or submit. If they wish to argue, the clerk shall be notified by the parties in one writing of the time desired for argument by each party.

17   *See* SUP. CT. R. 28.3.

18   *Id.*

19   SUP. CT. R. 28.6.

20   *See, e.g.*, D.C. CIR. R. 34(j).

21   All of the United States courts of appeals have adopted local rules implementing the practice of screening cases to determine whether oral argument is necessary.

Some of the factors that may influence the court's decision to hear argument are set forth in Chapter 2 of Appendix I of the Rules of the United States Court of Appeals for the Third Circuit, which states:

2.4.1. Experience discloses that judges usually find oral argument unnecessary when:

(a) The issue is tightly constrained, not novel, and the briefs adequately cover the arguments;

(b) The outcome of the appeal is clearly controlled by a decision of the Supreme Court or this court; or

(c) The state of the record will determine the outcome and when the sole issue is either sufficiency of the evidence, the adequacy of jury instructions, or rulings as to admissibility of evidence, and the briefs adequately refer to the record.

2.4.2 Experience discloses that judges usually vote for oral argument when:

(a) The appeal presents a substantial and novel legal issue.

(b) The resolution of an issue presented by the appeal will be of institutional or precedential value;

(c) A judge has questions to ask counsel to clarify an important legal, factual, or procedural point;

(d) A decision, legislation, or an event subsequent to the filing of the last brief may significantly bear on the case; or

(e) An important public interest may be affected.

3. The foregoing criteria shall not be construed to limit any judge's discretion in voting for oral argument.

In most courts of appeals, the parties are given an opportunity to file a separate statement discussing these and any other factors that indicate the need for oral argument.[22] Other courts may direct the parties to include a statement in their briefs setting forth the reasons why oral argument should be heard. Oral argument is particularly helpful in cases involving physical exhibits, which may require a demonstration or explanation. That fact should be emphasized whenever a request is made for oral argument in such cases, primarily because certain exhibits are more suitable for a live presentation than ordinary written documents. Whenever a case presents facts or circumstances that cannot be easily explained in a brief, those reasons should be argued in an effort to obtain oral argument.

In the state courts, counsel's opportunity to argue may also be restricted by local rules that reflect the volume of cases that the appellate court is called upon to de-

---

22   1st Cir. R. 34.1(a); 3d Cir. R. 34.1(b).

cide. A court that must manage an over-crowded calendar is likely to restrict argument more severely than a court that hears fewer cases.[23]

Rules of court also determine the number of lawyers permitted to argue for each side, the order in which the parties will argue, and the rare circumstances in which counsel for an amicus curiae will be heard. These rules vary among jurisdictions, and counsel must examine the rules of the individual court to which an appeal is taken.

B. Do Appellate Courts Read Briefs in Advance of Argument?

Counsel about to prepare for the argument of a case before an appellate court should endeavor to ascertain whether the court will have read the briefs in advance of oral argument or whether it will hear about the case for the first time at the oral argument.[24] Counsel's approach will differ depending upon the practice of the particular court. In view of the strictly limited time allowed for the presentation of oral argument, it would be particularly helpful to know whether counsel is about to *introduce* the court to the case or whether oral argument will *supplement* the court's knowledge of the case.[25]

If the court has read the briefs prior to oral argument, it is referred to by appellate specialists as a "hot bench." A "cold bench" is an appellate court that has not read the briefs before the oral argument. The classification is, of course, inaccurate because not all of the judges on the same court necessarily possess the same work habits.

If it is difficult to ascertain the judicial practice regarding the reading of the briefs, in the absence of reliable information, counsel should approach oral argument fully prepared to impart to the court *the core of the case* upon the assumption that the court will be hearing about it for the first time. Experts will agree that, when in doubt, counsel "must assume that the judge has never heard of the case or of his situation."[26]

Presiding judges on courts that have read the briefs beforehand are likely to inform counsel at the oral argument that they know the facts of the case and would

---

23 For a graphic illustration of this point, compare the rules regarding oral argument of the Appellate Divisions in the four Judicial Departments of the State of New York, 1st Dep't R. 600.11; 2d Dep't R. 670.20; 3d Dep't R. 800.10; and 4th Dep't R. 1000.11.

24 In some instances, court rules will direct the advocate to assume that the court is familiar with the briefs. *See, e.g.*, SUP. CT. R. 28.1; 1ST CIR. R. 34(c)(1); 7TH CIR. R. 34(d).

25 Referring to the practice of the Appellate Division of the New York Supreme Court, First Department, Professor Karlen states: "In view of the fact that the justices have already read the briefs, the attorney for the appellant does not have to spend as much time as he would otherwise in describing the case and the questions raised on appeal. All he needs to do is refresh the court's recollection as to those matters, and he can devote his major effort to an attempt to persuade the court that the judgment below should be reversed or modified." KARLEN, *supra* note 8, at 20.

26 Pollack, *supra* note 10, at 45.

like to hear argument. They may also inform counsel that they have read the briefs and may begin by asking questions that indicate clearly that the court is familiar with the case.[27]

When arguing before a hot bench, flexibility is of the greatest importance.[28] Counsel must be willing and able to discuss those aspects of the case that the court finds crucial or must persuade the court that other factors are actually dispositive of the questions presented. Before a hot bench, an attorney who attempts to adhere to a prepared text will not be able to take full advantage of the time allotted for oral argument or the questions posed by the court.

Occasionally, a presiding judge may be very specific and emphatic, and will leave no doubt that the court is "familiar with the case" and wishes to know counsel's legal position on the question presented. Indeed, counsel ought to be prepared to hear, perhaps at the very beginning of the oral argument: "Counsel, we know the facts of your case. What is the reversible error on this appeal?"

Awareness of the standard of review is also important, because the court does not wish to hear a *retrial* of the case during oral argument. For example, if the granting or denial of the motion by the trial court was committed to the court's discretion, what is there in the record that reveals that the court *abused* its discretion? Hence, it is important to know whether the standard of review is limited and strict, or "plenary" or broad.

C. Preparation for Oral Argument

1. Argument by Appellate Specialist

The question may also arise whether an appellate specialist ought to be engaged to argue the appeal. No categorical statement can be made as to the wisdom or desirability of engaging outside appellate counsel. The answer depends entirely upon the particular circumstances. Does counsel *wish* to argue the case before the appellate court, or would counsel prefer to have the appeal argued by someone else?[29]

An experienced judge has expressed the view that counsel "who knows the record and has the feel of the case [and] . . . the conscience to do the job for the client" is better able to argue the appeal than outside counsel.[30]

---

27 A lawyer who tries to describe the nature of the case or its prior history to a "hot bench" will draw "a few indignant snorts and an admonishment to get on with argument." Gould, *Oral Argument Losing Its Appeal*, NAT'L L.J., Mar. 23, 1981, at 32.

28 Samuel E. Gates, *Hot Bench or Cold Bench*, in COUNSEL ON APPEAL 109, 132 (Arthur A. Charpentier ed., 1968).

29 *See* discussions of "The Appellate Specialist" and "Who Will Author the Brief?" *supra* pp. 75–76, 78.

30 Pollack, *supra* note 10, at 31, 58.

On that assumption, all will agree that there is no need to engage an appellate specialist. The conscientious advocate who has a thorough knowledge of the record, and "a feel" both for the client and the cause, is well qualified to argue the appeal.

Chief Justice Burger referred to the "tendency to appoint a new lawyer on appeal" as a "large factor in the excessive cost and excessive delay in criminal appeals." Noting that time and money would be saved by requiring trial counsel to conduct the appeal, he added:

> No lawyer should be appointed by the court in any criminal case in any federal court unless he is competent and willing to conduct the case to its final disposition if there is an appeal.[31]

2. Knowledge of the Record

The most eloquent public speaker would be unable to deliver even the simplest talk without a knowledge of the subject matter. In appellate advocacy, this implies that counsel must have a complete mastery and understanding of the facts of the case and the relevant principles of law. This understanding is acquired by reading and rereading the record and briefs.

It would hardly seem necessary to emphasize that counsel on appeal, whether for the appellant or the respondent, must be thoroughly familiar with every word and every aspect of the opinion of the lower court.[32]

The appellant must be able to state clearly and succinctly the precise reversible error or errors in that opinion that warrant a reversal. What is the prejudicial error that is revealed in the lower court's decision? It is not sufficient for the appellant to point out some weakness in the opinion of the lower court. Counsel must specifically call the attention of the appellate court to the kind of error that is material and prejudicial. The error must be of sufficient gravity to warrant a *reversal*.[33]

Notwithstanding the advantages that are enjoyed by the respondent on appeal, counsel for respondent must be fully prepared to indicate with vigor and clarity the reasons that require an affirmance of the judgment. Justice Thurgood Marshall, speaking of the appellee, expressed his disappointment "by the failure of lawyers to use a beautiful opinion by the lower court, scholarly done, bursting with research."[34] He added that it "is sad to see an appellee or respondent prepare his brief, finish his oral argument, and never once rely on the opinion of the judge below."[35]

---

31   Warren E. Burger, *The State of the Federal Judiciary—1971*, 57 A.B.A. J. 855, 858 (1971).

32   *See* discussion of "Necessity of Indicating Error," *supra* pp. 50–53.

33   *See supra* pp. 51–53.

34   Thurgood Marshall, *The Federal Appeal, in* COUNSEL ON APPEAL 141, 152 (Arthur A. Charpentier ed., 1968).

35   *Id.*

Because of time limitations, counsel will probably be unable to discuss every aspect of the case during argument. Justice Jackson stated that "one of the first tests of a discriminating advocate is to select the question, or questions"[36] that will be presented orally. Even the advocate who chooses wisely, however, must be thoroughly familiar with the entire record. It is impossible to anticipate every question that the appellate court may ask or to predict the course that the argument will follow. Hence, counsel must be ready to discuss with the court every part of the record and every aspect of the case.

The knowledge of the record acquired while writing the brief prepares the brief writer for oral argument. As an oral advocate, however, counsel must know not only *what* is in the record but also *where* it is to be found in the record. Counsel must be able to locate, without undue delay, and direct the court's attention to the pleadings, essential exhibits, materials in the briefs, the opinions below, and pertinent testimony. Counsel can facilitate the process of retrieving information and documents by indexing and tabbing the record. Quick and accurate reference to the record inspires confidence in counsel's knowledge of the case.

3. Use of Written Notes

Although the use of written notes is strongly recommended, oral arguments written in their entirety are discouraged for two reasons. First, the advocate in possession of a written text may be tempted to read it. An oral argument that is read is seldom effective or appreciated by the court. The negative reaction to the reading of an oral argument is abundantly clear in the Rules of the Supreme Court, which state: *"Oral argument read from a prepared text is not favored."*[37] Second, even if the entire argument were memorized perfectly, making reading unnecessary, the resulting lack of flexibility could be counsel's undoing. One difficult question from the court, or any unexpected event, may unnerve the speaker and disrupt the prepared address.

On the reading of briefs at oral argument, Chief Justice William H. Rehnquist offers very clear and valuable advice. He states: "The oral argument you make must necessarily be structured by what is covered by your brief, but under no circumstances should you simply recite, summarize, or selectively read from your brief and consider it a satisfactory oral argument."[38]

Simple notes, on the other hand, help the speaker visualize the course of the argument and give the advocate additional assurance and poise. Notes help the advocate overcome the nervous tension that inevitably arises when counsel ad-

---

36   Jackson, *supra* note 6, at 803.

37   SUP. CT. R. 28.1. "I have even heard attorneys upon review read their printed briefs. No greater waste of time can be conceived." JOHN A. APPLEMAN, SUCCESSFUL APPELLATE TECHNIQUES 1009 (1953).

38   Rehnquist, *supra* note 11, at 298.

dresses the court. They assure that the speaker will "think of the right thing to say" and cover everything that is essential.

Although the specific nature of the notes to be used by counsel is a matter of individual preference, two sentences should be written out completely. The first is the opening sentence, to assure the speaker a good start and to help overcome initial nervousness and anxiety. Even experienced appellate advocates "believe in the technique of a very carefully phrased opening sentence on an argument."[39] The second is the closing sentence, to leave the court with the central theme of the argument. Other portions of the argument may be written in the notes in topic sentence form. Some speakers, however, prefer one or two key words or a catch phrase as a guide.

The admonition against reading the argument is equally applicable to the reading of long quotations. Unless a quotation is a short key phrase, or otherwise lends emphasis to the point being made, reading quotations or lengthy passages from the record or cited cases is to be avoided.

4. Content of Notes; Parts of the Argument

It has already been suggested that counsel use notes as a guide during oral argument and that the notes contain opening and closing remarks. What other matters should go into the notes? What are the necessary parts of the argument and how should they be presented?

As a preliminary matter, counsel must decide which question or questions will be discussed during oral argument. In most cases, time limitations simply will not allow the advocate to discuss every issue. Counsel must "confine oral argument to one or two salient, important points."[40] It is better to "select the one point on which you think the decision should turn and hammer away,"[41] than to treat numerous issues superficially.

Once the points to be argued have been selected, counsel can prepare for the argument. Counsel should assemble the notes that will cover the essentials of the case. It is suggested that the notes contain words or phrases to remind the speaker to state:

(1) the nature of the case;

(2) the essential or key facts;

(3) the specific issue to be decided;

(4) the governing legal principles; and

(5) the legal basis for the relief requested.

---

39   Gates, *supra* note 28, at 135.
40   Gould, *supra* note 27, at 32, col. 1
41   *Id.*

Although the order of the presentation should be flexible, counsel should not postpone telling the court what the case is about. As indicated earlier, the amount of time spent describing the nature of the case and stating the facts depends upon whether or not the court has read the briefs prior to argument.[42] Even if the court has read the briefs, however, counsel should not hesitate to stress those facts necessary to inform the court of the *equities* in favor of the client. A proper statement of the equities probably does more to assure a sympathetic audience than perfection of delivery.

Counsel, at the commencement of oral argument, should state the points that will be discussed. In addition to serving as a guide, both for counsel and the court, a statement of the issues gives the court an early opportunity to raise additional issues or ask questions that it feels may be important. The additional points or questions raised by the court may require a modification of counsel's prepared argument. This, however, is preferable to having the case decided on an issue that was neither addressed by counsel nor raised by the court during oral argument.

In what order should the points be presented?

The order in which the points of law will be discussed must be determined in the light of the medium of expression. Perhaps a legally "weak" point may have a special appeal when delivered orally. If there are three points, does counsel wish to argue the strongest first? The weakest? For oral argument, it may be suggested that counsel urge the best argument last and the second best first. Of course, the categorization of the strength of the arguments must be accurate. Unless a point has *some appeal*, it should not be argued. The oral advocate must be *selective*. Counsel may very well decide to discuss only a single point during oral argument, even though the brief contains several points.

The closing statement may usually be an adaptation of the "Conclusion" stated in the brief. Several short sentences summing up the main facts and contentions, followed by the relief requested are preferable to a long sentence containing the necessary information.

5. Time Allowed for Oral Argument and Reserved Rebuttal Time

Keeping in mind exactly how much time the applicable rules of court allow for oral argument, the appellant must give thought to the possibility of reserving some time for *rebuttal*. Court rules may or may not permit reservation of time for rebuttal. Even if rebuttal is permitted, counsel should never withhold substantive issues from the opening argument, intending to raise them on rebuttal.[43] Rebuttal time should be used only to respond to unanticipated argument or to correct an error in the presentation of the respondent.

---

42 *See supra* pp. 148–49.

43 *See* Sup. Ct. R. 28.5.

If the respondent has fairly presented the case, and no new element has been raised during argument, it is good policy to waive the reserved rebuttal time. Waiving rebuttal time is preferable to repeating an argument that has already been presented. Unless there is something important to say, no particular benefit flows from having the last word.

6. Sharing Time with Co-Counsel

An additional matter that requires careful consideration is whether counsel may wish to share the time allowed for oral argument with co-counsel or an associate. The court rules must be examined to determine if it is permissible to share the allotted time and whether special permission is required. Assuming, however, that the practice is permitted, it is nevertheless generally recommended that counsel not divide or share the argument with co-counsel. Note, for example, Rule 28.4 of the Rules of the Supreme Court of the United States, which states that "[d]ivided argument is not favored." In those rare instances when a divided argument is deemed necessary, there ought to be a clear understanding of the specific area that each counsel will discuss in order to prevent repetition or confusion.

When oral argument shared with co-counsel is permitted, counsel should announce to the court the areas that each will cover. During oral argument, if the court were to ask a question in an area to be covered by co-counsel, counsel ought to give a brief reply and state that a fuller response will be given by co-counsel. Notwithstanding thorough preparation, if counsel is not able to respond, counsel may state: "Your honor, that aspect of the case will be covered by my co-counsel, Mr. Brown."

7. Rehearsal of Argument

After counsel is fully prepared to argue the case and is satisfied with the notes outlining the argument, counsel should rehearse the argument. This is an opportunity that no appellate counsel can afford to miss. Even the most able advocates find it necessary to plan, rehearse, and time the argument.[44]

The rehearsal may be before a real or imaginary audience. An experienced lawyer of critical inclination would make a good listener for the rehearsal. An astute listener is in a position to offer constructive criticism, both of the legal content of the argument and its oral presentation. Helpful suggestions may also be obtained from any intelligent person who is willing to listen. If an audience cannot be found, a rehearsal in a closed room is nevertheless beneficial. The rehearsal famil-

---

44 "Do not think it beneath you to rehearse for an argument . . . . I used to say that, as Solicitor General, I made three arguments of every case. First came the one that I planned—as I thought, logical, coherent, complete. Second was the one actually presented—interrupted, incoherent, disjointed, disappointing. The third was the utterly devastating argument that I thought of after going to bed that night!" Robert H. Jackson, *Advocacy Before the United States Supreme Court*, 37 CORNELL L.Q. 1, 6, 9 (1951).

iarizes counsel with the notes, is an invaluable aid to memory, and permits counsel to time the argument.

After the first rehearsal, counsel may wish to rearrange the points, or perhaps eliminate a discussion of one or more points in order to bring the argument within the allotted time.

8. Visit to Courtroom; Presence of Client

Several additional suggestions may prove to be helpful. Counsel would do well to visit the appellate courtroom prior to the date of oral argument. If the court is located in another city, counsel ought to arrive the day before argument. This prior visit will give the advocate an opportunity to become familiar with the physical environment. It is also advisable to arrive sufficiently in advance of the scheduled time for argument to hear other arguments presented to the court.

Counsel ought also to ascertain the exact position on the bench where each judge sits. It would be helpful, particularly in answering questions by the court, to know the names of all of the judges and the position that each one of them occupies on the bench.

During this preliminary visit to the court, counsel ought to ascertain if there is a clock in the courtroom, or a device on the lectern that will indicate the time that remains for oral argument.

During this visit, understand exactly where counsel should sit and stand. While tables are often marked "plaintiff" or "appellant," if they are not, counsel for the plaintiff should stand on the side closest to the witness box in the courtroom. On appeal, counsel for the appellant sits at the table to the right of the lectern, and counsel for the appellee to the left.

Counsel should always arrive early for oral argument. Many courts require that counsel check in advance to ensure attendance by all counsel of record. In some courts, such as the United States Court of Appeals for the Federal Circuit, the names of the judges who will be sitting on the panel are not made public until the day of oral argument. Thus, counsel may have only an hour or so to learn any specific information about any of the judges who will hear the oral argument.

Because many courts decide motions first through tentative rulings, it is critical that counsel arrive early for oral argument to obtain and study a copy of that tentative ruling, which can sometimes be quite lengthy. Any oral argument must then be limited solely to the tentative ruling. If the ruling is favorable, counsel need only answer any questions asked by the court. If the ruling is adverse, counsel must then address specific statements made in the tentative ruling in an attempt to show that the court erred in its ruling.

It may be added that most appellate advocates recommend strongly against being accompanied to the oral argument by one's client or the party in interest.

Judge Medina spoke of an "iron rule" that he "would never under any circumstances" argue an appeal with his client in the courtroom.[45]

Justice Jackson gave some of the reasons why it is not wise to have one's client present in the courtroom during argument. He stated:

> I doubt whether it is wise to have clients or parties in interest attend the argument if it can be avoided. Clients unfortunately desire, and their presence is apt to encourage, qualities in an argument that are least admired by judges. When I hear counsel launch into personal attacks on the opposition or praise of a client, I instinctively look about to see if I can identify the client in the room and often succeed . . . . The case that is argued to please a client . . . will not often make a favorable impression on the Bench.[46]

9. Use of Visual Aids

In preparing for oral argument, counsel should carefully decide whether any visual aid could assist the court at oral argument. Visual aids include illustrative models, specimens, samples, charts, diagrams, or any other exhibit which is blown up or modified for simplicity or clarity. In certain cases, visual aids could become the focal point of an oral argument, and counsel must thoroughly rehearse exactly how that aid will be introduced and used at oral argument. Because visual aids are very helpful in technically complex cases, the United States Court of Appeals for the Federal Circuit, the appellate court with exclusive subject matter jurisdiction over appeals in patent cases, provides for the use of visual aids.[47]

To ensure that counsel will be able to use a visual aid, counsel should closely follow local rules with regard to the use of visual aids. Court rules may provide that counsel notify the court in advance as to the use of visual aids. Rules may also require that one's opposing counsel be given copies well in advance of the argument to allow time for the filing of any possible motion or objection concerning the use of those visual aids. The courts may, like the Federal Circuit, set forth specific time periods for providing notice or objections depending upon whether the visual aid was used in the trial court or was created specifically for the appellate argument. Regardless of whether there is a specific rule governing the use of visual aids, it is always a safe course for counsel to provide copies of the visual aids to opposing counsel in advance of the oral argument. Judges routinely disallow the use of visual aids if counsel has not provided notice to all parties concerning the use of those visual aids.

---

45   Harold R. Medina, *The Oral Argument on Appeal*, 20 A.B.A. J. 139, 142 (1934).
46   Jackson, *supra* note 6, at 861.
47   *See* FED. CIR. R. 34(c).

X

PRESENTATION OF ORAL ARGUMENT

A. Generally

1. Effective Public Speaking and Oral Argument

Unquestionably, the principles of effective public speaking are applicable to the argument of an appeal. These principles include principles of psychology, and, although perhaps basic and elementary, the frequency of their violation justifies their restatement or repetition at this juncture.

Although the object of speech generally is to influence the listener in some manner, in argumentation, the specific object is to *persuade*. The psychology of persuasion requires that the speaker obtain a favorable response from the audience. In order to obtain this favorable response, and to succeed in causing the beliefs of the audience to be harmonized and ultimately to be identical with those of the speaker, a few basic matters should constantly be borne in mind.

a. ABC's of Oral Argument

Commencing with the first edition, this book has stressed the ABC's of Legal Writing. The letters refer to Accuracy, Brevity, and Clarity, qualities that describe all good legal writing. In preparing for oral argument we may now refer to a principle that may be called the ABC's of all advocacy. Here the letters refer to Always Be Candid, a reminder that candor instills confidence and respect, and that lack of candor breeds distrust and disbelief. Although elaboration would not seem to be necessary for such a fundamental principle of professional conduct, its importance warrants discussion in a text on advocacy.

In general terms, it is correct to say that oral argument supplements the briefs. It is usually the very last opportunity to explain, expand, or clarify what has been submitted in the brief. For the respondent, it affords the special opportunity to respond to points or arguments that the appellant has advanced in appellant's Reply Brief. This may be accomplished by incorporating the response in respondent's oral argument or by a specific statement that counsel wishes to respond to a point or a statement made in appellant's Reply Brief.

b. Think of the Court

In addition to a knowledge of the subject, a public speaker cannot speak effectively without knowing something about the audience. To whom will the speech be delivered? The interests of the speaker cannot be united with those of the audience unless the speaker knows the audience.[1]

---

1   It has been suggested that the speaker should ask: "What have I to say that is of interest to this audience?" HARRY A. OVERSTREET, INFLUENCING HUMAN BEHAVIOR 71 *et seq.* (1925).

It is a sound practice to learn as much as possible about the members of the court who will hear the appeal. It has been stated that the "more you know about them [the judges who will hear the appeal] and their backgrounds, the more likely it is that you can touch a responsive chord."[2] Justice Marshall stated:

> Indeed, knowledge of a judge's recent opinions aside, knowing the panel members, their background and interests, provides valuable clues that will enable you to an-swer questions in a way that will as the late Karl Llewellyn once said "capture the court."[3]

When addressing a court of distinguished jurists, the advocate's attitude must be respectful. Counsel is addressing a court with a keen sense of *relevance*. It would, therefore, be inappropriate to endeavor to play solely upon the emotions rather than to make a logical, orderly appeal to reason. Courts may indeed be moved to sympathy, but this response must emanate from the statement of the facts and not from sentimental platitudes and generalities.

Although they were uttered with particular reference to criminal appeals, the following thoughts are worthy of quotation:

> [T]he appellant does not come to the court seeking abstract justice, but he com-plains that he is the victim of injustice, in the form of a specific violation of his substantial rights. One can only right an injustice by doing something about it. This sense of injustice starts a swelling motion when it is properly conveyed.[4]

c. Addressing the Court

Oral argument should be presented to the court, not to a sheet of paper, a card, a wall, or an open window. No feeling of ease or cordiality can arise between court and counsel unless counsel *addresses the court*. This means looking directly at the members of the court. The importance of eye contact in oral communication is widely acknowledged, and it is no less important when addressing a distinguished panel of judges.

Counsel has already been advised against reading the argument.[5] "Never read the argument" is one of the cardinal rules of appellate advocacy. Reading creates a barrier between counsel and the court. By reading, just as by looking elsewhere, counsel loses the advantage to be gained by making a *personal* appearance before the court.

---

2   Samuel E. Gates, *Hot Bench or Cold Bench*, *in* COUNSEL ON APPEAL (Arthur A. Charpentier ed., 1968).

3   Thurgood Marshall, *The Federal Appeal*, *in* COUNSEL ON APPEAL, *supra* note 2, at 141, 144.

4   Harris B. Steinberg, *The Criminal Appeal*, *in* COUNSEL ON APPEAL, *supra* note 2, at 3, 14.

5   *See supra* pp. 151–52.

d. Respectful Attitude Toward Court

The only proper attitude on the part of any speaker toward an audience is one of mutual cooperation in the common pursuit of the subject. An improper attitude may be offensive and may breed resentment.

For an appellate advocate, the only proper attitude toward the court is one of "respectful intellectual equality."[6] No other course of conduct should be pursued. Oral argument should be inspired "with a single and sincere desire to be helpful to the court."[7] Oral argument is intended to help the court decide the case, and a helpful and respectful attitude will benefit both counsel and the cause on appeal.

e. The Voice of the Advocate

In order to persuade the court, counsel must be heard. The voice, therefore, is as important as the words used. If counsel's voice is not easily heard, the lucidity, concreteness, and thought-conveying power of the argument may be completely lost. It is elementary that the speaker's voice must be sufficiently loud.[8] Whether or not the courtroom is equipped with microphones, it should not be necessary for the court to ask counsel to "speak up."

Counsel must also be careful not to mumble words or let the voice fade away toward the end of a sentence. An advocate must speak loudly enough to be heard and distinctly enough to be understood. It is not for the court to strain to hear or understand what counsel is saying. Not all judges will make the effort.

Counsel should appreciate that a pleasing, well-modulated voice is a powerful factor. A squeaky, nasal, or raspy voice is a handicap to the public speaker and the advocate. To a lawyer, who contemplates the trial and argument of cases, a pleasant voice is almost as valuable as the ability to read and write.

A discussion of language ought to include a reference to the sounds of words. Sound images are important in all forms of public speaking.

Since not all ideas or words are of equal importance, the advocate must develop the ability to emphasize certain ideas over others. An address cannot be monotonous if it is to keep the interest of the audience.

The advocate should accentuate key words and phrases and pause before and after a climactic sentence. Just as appropriate punctuation is important to good writing, the tone of voice, inflection, and the pause are important to good speaking.

---

6 FREDERICK BERNAYS WIENER, BRIEFING AND ARGUING FEDERAL APPEALS 299 (1967).

7 John W. Davis, *The Argument of an Appeal*, 26 A.B.A. J. 895, 896 (1940).

8 "[C]ounsel should speak in a voice which is loud enough to be heard and confident in tone but which does not amount to shouting to the court." Michael Closen & Marc Ginsberg, *Preparation and Presentation of the Oral Argument in a Court of Review*, 13 NEW ENG. L. REV. 265, 277 (1977).

f. The Demeanor, "Habits," and Appearance of the Advocate

Successful public speakers know that their dress must be appropriate to the occasion. The attire must indicate an awareness of the importance of the event. It should be neither bizarre nor offensive. It must be remembered that the process of evaluation may commence even before a single word is uttered, and, therefore, counsel should be well groomed and appropriately dressed.

A word of advice may be given to the advocate who has acquired certain habits or mannerisms. Otherwise insignificant habits may assume importance in the courtroom because they distract the court. They may spoil the favorable impression created by an agreeable appearance. Some of the mannerisms particularly to be avoided are toying with eyeglasses, stroking one's hair, fumbling with papers, twirling a watch chain, and the excessive use of a pointer. To this list may be added needless pacing and the use of admonishing or distracting gestures.

A distressing habit possessed by some speakers is the filling in of a pause by "ah" or "er." Such a sound destroys the benefits of the pause. During a pause, the speaker should think—silently. The "er" evidences a lack of self-control and creates the impression that the advocate is unprepared and groping for ideas. Since this habit is antithetical to eloquent speech, it should be eliminated.

Clearly, during oral argument, counsel must not do or say anything that may be considered in bad taste. Counsel for respondent, for example, should not minimize the merit of appellant's argument by assuming a facetious attitude. The argument of an appeal is a serious matter. While an impromptu witticism may make for warmth and congeniality, intentional humor or levity has no place in an appellate court.

g. Advocacy and Emotion

Sophisticated and experienced appellate lawyers know that a successful argument is one that draws out the desired emotion from the listener. The goal of the appellate advocate is to make the judges care about the disposition of the appeal. One way to accomplish this goal is by delivering the argument with feeling, sincerity, and conviction, so that the judges feel most comfortable in believing your argument. On the other hand, lawyers should not present an unrestrained visceral argument because many appellate judges resent such a display of feeling in a courtroom.[9]

2. Questions by the Court

The ability to answer questions asked by the court is perhaps the supreme test of the advocate's skill. In this phase of the argument counsel reaps a full harvest from thorough preparation and general understanding of the peripheral facets of the problems being discussed. A lawyer's competence, experience, and scholarship become manifest in the extemporaneous answers given to a judge in reply to a question.

---

9   John C. Shepherd & Jordan B. Cherrick, *Advocacy and Emotion*, 138 F.R.D. 619, 626 (1991).

During the preparation for oral argument, counsel should try to anticipate both probable and possible questions by the court. The answer to a question that has been explored and deliberated will be smooth and forceful. If the question is one that the court will probably ask, counsel should not wait for the question but should embody the answer in the argument. As to possible questions, counsel should formulate answers with supporting arguments that can be used if needed.

Questions by the court should be welcomed. They are the most reliable test of the court's reaction to the argument. They prove that counsel has succeeded in arousing the interest of the court. Moreover, they also help alleviate whatever artificiality or formality may be present in the courtroom. In the answer, counsel has an opportunity to *speak with* the court in an informal, conversational manner. Questions induce spontaneity and candor. As in all serious conversation, one should think carefully before speaking.

There is, at least, one other important benefit to be derived from questioning by the court. In questioning the advocate, the court reveals its own thought processes. From the viewpoint of the advocate, if in the course of argument there should occur to some judge a theory that would do counsel "no good," it is better to know of it through a question from the bench than to have it "remain a masked battery" for counsel's later undoing.[10] It has been pointed out that "a question affords you your only chance to penetrate the mind of the court . . . and . . . dispel a doubt as soon as it arises."[11]

a. Responsive Answers

Counsel should always *respond to the question directly*, either by answering it, or by conceding a "present unreadiness to answer."[12] One thing is sure—*never* postpone an answer. If the question is going to be discussed fully under a different heading and counsel does not wish to disrupt the presentation, a short answer, accompanied by a statement that the question will be discussed more fully later, may be appropriate. It is preferable, however, to discuss the point at the time the question is raised by the court. The structure of the oral argument should be flexible enough to permit a transposition during the argument so that counsel may take advantage of the court's questions instead of being befuddled by them.

b. Postponing an Answer

A request to postpone an answer may lead the court to believe that counsel is resorting to evasive tactics. The following remarks, written about Chief Justice

---

10   John T. Loughran, *The Argument of an Appeal in the Court of Appeals*, 12 FORDHAM L. REV. 1, 6 (1943).

11   Davis, *supra* note 7, at 897.

12   Loughran, *supra* note 10, at 6.

Hughes, may serve to emphasize the importance of prompt answers to court questions:

> [T]he Chief favored questions from the bench, believing that they tend to bring out the weak points of oral argument, which are usually the important points in a case. Nothing irked him so much as the common answer that counsel would reach the point raised by the question at the appropriate point in his argument. When some other justice received such an answer, one often would find the Chief boring in on counsel with the same question in slightly different form, and it was not often that *he* failed to get an answer.[13]

c. Failure to Answer a Question

Even more serious than postponing an answer is the unfulfilled promise to answer a question. If counsel fails to answer a question, the court may assume that counsel did not answer because the reply would have been detrimental to the client's position. It is to no avail that the reason was sheer forgetfulness or lack of time.

If a question is obviously important to a judge, and counsel is unable to answer the question intelligently, a difficult tactical problem is presented. Should counsel give an off-hand answer, or should counsel state the inability to answer? It is suggested that if a question raises an "undigested difficulty," it is preferable to admit that counsel has not thought of that matter, rather than weaken or detract from the high caliber of a well-reasoned argument by a poor answer. This is especially true if the question is only tangential to the issue. Counsel may also offer to submit a *supplemental memorandum* on that particular point. However, if the court insists on an answer, counsel must answer in the best way possible under the circumstances.

In admitting that counsel does not know the answer to a question, it is important not to offer an excuse for that inability to answer. One excuse that is occasionally made is that counsel did not present or handle the case in the trial court. That sort of excuse is simply unacceptable, particularly if the answer could be determined from the written record. If counsel must admit that the answer is unknown, counsel should simply do so and continue with the argument.

d. When the Question Seems Unclear

When a question seems unclear to counsel, it is proper to say, "Your Honor, I am sorry that I have not understood the question." Counsel, however, should not invoke this response too often since it may be interpreted as a dilatory tactic.

e. Listen Carefully to the Question

Although it may seem trite, it is essential to remind counsel that, prior to responding, counsel must *listen* to the question carefully and must *think* before

---

13 Edwin McElwain, *The Supreme Court's Business Under Hughes*, 63 HARV. L. REV. 5, 17 (1949).

speaking. The solid advice of "think before you speak" has special application to oral argument.

Chief Justice William H. Rehnquist has made certain observations that bear repetition. "If you are going to be able to intelligently answer a question, you must first *listen* to the question."[14] He states that "it is surprising how often appellate advocates, just like many people in private conversation, seem to hear only part of the question, and respond to the part of it they heard even though the answer they give may not be an adequate response to the entire question."[15] In addition to urging counsel to listen to the question and answer the question asked, Chief Justice Rehnquist offers the following valuable advice: "Whether the question is hostile or friendly, first understand the question, and then give the best answer you can for the purpose of advancing your cause."[16]

f. Answering "Hostile" Questions

In addition to urging that counsel "must understand the question before you start to answer," former Solicitor General of the United States Rex E. Lee counsels against an "adversarial relationship with any member of the Court." Specifically, Solicitor General Lee makes two valuable points:

> Do not assume that the question is hostile. Many are. But some are neutral and some are helpful. . . . No matter how unmistakably hostile the question, your response should never be hostile or adversarial, even to someone you know will not vote in your favor. Firmness and confidence, yes; summary treatment, sometimes; hostility, no. [17]

Counsel ought to be prepared to answer difficult questions, and, indeed, difficult questions are to be expected. Questions by the court, however, should neither discourage nor discomfit counsel. It is perhaps natural that the court will focus upon the weakest components of the advocate's case. Counsel should, therefore, welcome the opportunity to overcome any difficulties that the court may have with any aspect of the case.

On occasion, the training of judges as advocates may lead them into what may seem to be argumentation with counsel. When this happens, counsel should respectfully, but firmly, maintain counsel's position on the issues discussed. At times, some judges may indicate that they are not persuaded by the advocate's presentation. This is no excuse, however, for failing to articulate the case in a competent and professional manner. Attempting to discern the ultimate disposition of the case from the court's questions and comments at oral argument, while

---

14 William H. Rehnquist, *Oral Advocacy*, 27 S. TEX. L. REV. 289, 302 (1986) (emphasis in original).

15 *Id.*

16 *Id.*

17 Rex E. Lee, *Oral Argument in the Supreme Court*, 72 A.B.A. J. 60, 60 (Special Issue June 15, 1986).

tempting, is generally not a fruitful endeavor. Thus, notwithstanding any damaging answer or point that may have been raised, counsel should continue to present the case with professional confidence and conviction.

Occasionally, judges will specifically point out some failure of the lawyer or the client in showing the weakness of an argument. It is important for counsel always to accept the court's criticism if it accurately reflects the facts. Counsel should not attempt to transfer the criticism or blame onto another, such as an associate, a paralegal, or co-counsel at another firm. As the lawyers arguing the case, they must accept full responsibility for any action or inaction taken on behalf of their clients. If one does not know the cause for a particular problem, simply explain to the court and ask if it is a matter that can be rectified. If it cannot be rectified, counsel should accept the blame if warranted, but never attempt to shift the blame to others.

g. Cooperative and Helpful Attitude

Throughout this book, the view has been emphasized that the process of deciding cases is a cooperative effort of bench and bar. Hence, during the questioning by the court, and throughout oral argument, counsel ought to remember that the "process of deciding cases on appeal involves the joint efforts of counsel and the court."[18] It is clearly the responsibility of counsel to assist the court in arriving at a just result.[19]

It is also important for counsel to realize that, by asking questions, the court is actively seeking assistance. In the words of an experienced jurist: "The first thing that a court wants is help."[20]

3. Professional Courtesies and Modes of Address

Counsel's inexperience is most readily revealed by the inability to address the members of the court and opposing counsel properly. Counsel should always rise when addressing the court. Each attorney will commence the oral argument by saying: "May it please the court . . ." or "If the court please . . ."

It is important to remember that judges act on behalf of their respective courts. Counsel should resist referring to a particular judge whenever that judge was acting on behalf of the court as a whole. For example, it is preferable to say "in light of this court's ruling, . . ." and not "in light of your ruling, or Judge Jones' ruling, ..."

---

18 *In re* Greenberg, 132 A.2d 46, 49 (N.J. 1954), *quoted in* Edward D. Re, *The Partnership of Bench and Bar*, 16 CATH. LAW. 194, 204 (1970); *see also* Edward D. Re, *The Lawyer as a Lawmaker*, 52 A.B.A. J. 159 (1966).

19 Edward D. Re, *The Partnership of Bench and Bar*, 16 CATH. LAW. 194, 204–05 (1970). "It is often forgotten that by the competent, professional handling of a case, the lawyer is performing, and has the duty to perform, a role that must assist the judge in deciding the case, justly and according to law." *Id.*

20 Judge Charles D. Breitel of the New York Court of Appeals in *A Summing Up*, *in* COUNSEL ON APPEAL, *supra* note 2, at 195.

Lawyers frequently overuse the expression "Your Honor." That phrase should be used as a form of address only, and not as a personal pronoun. For example, in a proper use, counsel should say: "Your Honor, my answer is . . ." rather than "My answer to Your Honor's question is . . . ."

Counsel should refer to a member of the court other than the one with whom counsel is speaking as follows: "Justice Jones previously asked . . . ," or "I agree with the view expressed by the Chief Justice," or "In answer to the question asked by Judge Smith, I stated . . . ."

In answer to a question by a member of the court, instead of a categorical or curt "Yes" or "No" answer, a "Yes, Your Honor" or "No, Your Honor" is preferable.

When referring to associate counsel, the advocate should state: "Ms. Jones, my associate, has discussed the double jeopardy phase of this case," or "My associate, Ms. Jones will discuss . . . " or simply, "My associate."

Reference to opposing counsel should always be devoid of the slightest trace of sarcasm or insult. It is proper to refer to a lawyer as "the opposing counsel." It is unpardonable, however, to speak of "My *learned* opponent" or "The *learned* opposing counsel" when the word "learned" is prolonged so as to create the impression of sarcasm or ridicule. The safest practice is to eliminate the adjective and to state simply "Counsel for plaintiff . . . ," "Counsel for the respondent . . . ," or "Mr. Brown, counsel for the appellant, has urged that the judgment should be reversed."

a. Interrupting Opposing Counsel or the Court

A breach of courtesy that may occur during oral argument is interrupting opposing counsel or even a member of the court. To interrupt someone who is speaking is discourteous and undignified. If opposing counsel makes a material misstatement or remark, counsel will have an opportunity to bring the matter to the court's attention. If the remark is improper, counsel should remain calm and restrained and should not, in turn, commit the same error by manifesting a resentful attitude. If there is justification to resent the remarks of opposing counsel, one is usually vindicated by the fact that the court will also resent them.

Although it may seem unnecessary, it is nevertheless important to remind counsel that "The Court is not your competition. When one of the justices wants center stage, give it up. No matter how brilliant or how telling the point you are making, when one of the justices says something, you should stop talking and start listening."[21]

A calm and dignified attitude is essential throughout the argument. Whether the argument of opposing counsel is excellent or obviously ineffective and poor, the advocate should always listen with courtesy and dignity.

---

21   Lee, *supra* note 17, at 62.

b. Seeming Inattention by the Court

Sometimes, the members of the court may converse with one another during the oral argument. Although the judges are probably discussing some phase of the case, counsel faces a serious problem. Should counsel pause and wait for the court's attention? Judge Harold R. Medina does not recommend that counsel pause, for it may be interpreted as a criticism of the judges. It is apt to irritate them because they may very well be discussing the case, and "they naturally feel that counsel should make no objection to their doing this."[22] Judge Medina offers sound advice when he states the "the better course to pursue would seem to be to go right ahead with the argument, looking at the judge or judges who happen to be disengaged and who are apparently listening."[23]

c. Necessity of Civility

It is interesting to note that matters of courtesy have, on occasion, been discussed by the Supreme Court. In a case interpreting Rule 46 of the Federal Rules of Appellate Procedure, *In re Snyder*,[24] the Supreme Court noted that Rule 46 "reflects the burdens inherent in the attorney's dual obligations to clients and to the system of justice," and emphasized that the "necessity for civility in the inherently contentious setting of the adversary process suggests that members of the bar cast criticisms of the system in a professional and civil tone."[25]

Civility and decorum are not only good manners, but also necessary for successful advocacy. Unfortunately, lawyers need to be reminded of the importance of civility during oral argument. Counsel should never impugn the motives or actions of opposing counsel. Rather, if necessary, counsel should attribute all acts and failings to the adverse party. Moreover, counsel should refrain from using emotional terms in disparaging the adverse party's argument. Words such as "unbelievable," "incredible," "ridiculous," "stupid," or "silly" are simply unprofessional and expose one's inexperience. Rather, if justified, an argument should be called meritless, or without foundation in the record.

Unfortunately, tension at oral argument sometimes causes even the most experienced counsel to lose their tempers. In a recent case, a court of appeal warned counsel for inappropriately pointing a finger at opposing counsel, and arguing that the lawyers were dishonest and unethical. The court noted the difference between hearing an appropriate forceful argument and an unacceptable outburst caused by losing one's composure.[26]

---

22   Harold R. Medina, *The Oral Argument on Appeal*, 20 A.B.A. J. 139, 184 (1934).
23   *Id.*
24   472 U.S. 634 (1985).
25   *Id.* at 647.
26   Nordberg, Inc. v. Telsmith, Inc., 82 F.3d 394, 398 (Fed. Cir. 1996).

4. Citation of Authority During Argument

An appreciation of the limitations of the spoken word as a medium for the conveyance of detailed information will cause the advocate to desist from the citation of cases in oral argument. If too many cases are cited by name, volume, page, and date, the oral argument assumes the nature of a brief orally delivered. It cannot be repeated too often that minute details tend to confuse rather than clarify an oral presentation. Matters that are necessary in the brief may have no place in oral argument.

If a principle of law is well established, the citation of authority is unnecessary. The fact that cases have been cited in the brief for a proposition of law does not imply that those cases must be cited during oral argument. Oral argument should be *conversational*. The smoothness and continuity of thought of the conversation will be harmed by a prologue or afterword such as "Runningfoot versus Charleston, one hundred twenty-six New York page three hundred sixty-two, decided by the Court of Appeals in eighteen ninety-one." The citation may not look as bulky in the brief, primarily because of the use of numbers, but the reading of those numbers is cumbersome.

If a case must be discussed in oral argument, it is proper to state: "The application of the principle is made clear by the case of Jones versus Adamson, discussed on page six of the appellant's brief"; or "John versus Smith held that . . . ;" or "Robertson versus Brown, decided recently by the Supreme Court, and discussed in both briefs, involved a factual situation diametrically opposed to that of the case at bar"; or "This principle dates back to the case of Duke of Brunswick versus The King of Hanover, decided by the House of Lords in eighteen forty-four"; or "Counsel for the appellant has stated that . . . . However, the case of Williams versus Hardy reported in two hundred New York is authority to the contrary." The latter case may thereafter be referred to simply as the *Williams* case.

The first time that an important case is mentioned, counsel ought to indicate where the case is analyzed in the brief. This should be done for the purpose of identifying the case and in lieu of giving its full citation. The statement should not sound like a suggestion to the court to read the discussion of that case in the brief during argument. If the statement is so construed, it will be distressing to counsel to have the court read a portion of the brief during argument.

a. Simplify Citations

The advice regarding the *simplification of the citation* of cases during oral argument is equally applicable to references to other authorities and statutes. It is unnecessary to say: "Joseph Story, in his *Commentaries on Equity Jurisprudence as Administered in England and America*, on page three hundred fifty-three of the Fourteenth Edition, states that . . . ." It is more effective to state: "Discussing the mutality of mistake necessary for reformation, Story, in his work on Equity stated that . . . "; or "Although Pomeroy in his treatise on Equity declares that . . . ., Dean Ames, in an article in the *Harvard Law Review*, stated the rule somewhat differently." Although counsel does not give the specific volume and page number, the reference should be reproduced in full on the cards containing the advocate's notes so that it will be available if requested by the court.

When referring to a statute for purposes of oral argument, it is advisable to give a simplified citation. Generally, the "short title" is adequate to describe the statute. This simplified reference permits the court to concentrate on the substance or content of the statute.

b. Recent or "Late" Cases

On occasion, a case germane to counsel's argument will be handed down between the time that the brief was filed and the date of oral argument. The court may be notified by letter, or, if counsel wishes to cite or discuss the case during oral argument, it is proper to offer copies of the opinion to members of the court and to counsel's adversary at the argument. This possibility is discussed in Chapter 11, which treats "Briefs After Oral Argument." Rather than to risk that the court will read the case submitted at the oral argument during counsel's argument, it may be better to request permission to submit the case together with a "letter brief" *after* the oral argument. This will permit counsel to refer to the case and state its pertinence to the case on appeal without unduly disrupting the prepared oral argument.

After oral argument and submission, but before the issuance of a decision, a recent case may still have to be brought to the attention of the court. A letter brief may be appropriate, and, once again, rules or local rules may authorize or require these post argument submissions. An example is Fed. R. App. P. 28(j).

Rather than assume that the court will discover or learn of the recent case on its own, counsel should provide the court with a copy of the opinion and explain its relevance to the appeal under consideration. Often, counsel for the parties may have completely different views of the relevance of recent authority. Hence, counsel should not miss the opportunity to set forth counsel's view or contention of the relevance of the case and its effect on the question presented for decision.

B. Respondent's Oral Argument

All that has been stated about the principles of good public speaking and effective advocacy is equally applicable to the respondent. The reader is also referred to the suggestions pertaining to the respondent's brief.[27] However, a few observations will be made that are particularly applicable to respondent's oral argument.

As soon as counsel for the appellant has stated the conclusion and has finished speaking, counsel for the respondent should proceed to the lectern and should be prepared to commence. The respondent does not wish to avoid or evade appel-

---

27   *See supra* pp. 135–40.

lant's argument. To the contrary, it is the attitude of the respondent that, by meeting the argument of the appellant directly, head-on, the court will perceive the soundness of the position maintained by the respondent.

It should be apparent that, at the end of appellant's oral argument, the court is reasonably familiar with the case. If the facts have been stated correctly by the appellant, no time should be spent in repeating the facts. It is preferable to repeat only a few key facts, having edited the statement in such a manner as to bring out *the equities* of the respondent's case.

During appellant's opening argument, counsel for respondent should take notes indicating exactly what matters of fact or principles of law have been erroneously stated by the appellant. Counsel should also detect appellant's omissions of material facts. These discrepancies, if important, must be brought to the attention of the court. Once this foundation has been laid, counsel should immediately respond to the heart of appellant's case.

If the facts have been properly stated and the court has been given an accurate idea of the issue before it, counsel for the respondent should immediately answer appellant's strongest point. If respondent can refute appellant's strongest point, appellant's position is precarious. Again it is urged, as in brief writing, that the refutation of the appellant's argument is only one phase of respondent's argument.

For success, counsel for the respondent should rely on the *strength of respondent's case* rather than merely on the weaknesses of the appellant's. The court should be asked to vote for an affirmance of the judgment *because the judgment is correct,* not necessarily because the contentions of appellant are wrong. If the judgment is *right*, it is not difficult to show that the appellant is *wrong*.

1. Advantages of the Respondent

As in brief writing, the respondent on oral argument enjoys certain advantages over the appellant. From the questions asked by the court, respondent should have gathered what matters or points the court wishes discussed. Often the court may indicate precisely what *it* considers to be the question presented. Here again, the advantage of a *flexible presentation* is evident. Respondent should be prepared to modify the order of the prepared presentation according to the needs of the situation. If the court indicated agreement with point I, then there is no need to discuss it. The time may be spent more profitably in endeavoring to convince the court that the respondent's position on point II is justified on reason, principle, and authority.

If the court asked a question of the appellant that either was not answered or was answered in an unsatisfactory manner, the respondent should try to answer the question by including the answer in the presentation. The answer given will be favorable to the respondent, and it is reasonable for the court to assume that the appellant did not respond for that reason.

If the appellant has submitted a reply brief, it is proper for respondent to point out to the court that appellant has failed to answer certain material arguments or propositions made in the respondent's brief. It is also proper to indicate that the reply brief is not responsive. This demonstrates to the court the strength of respondent's case and that counsel for appellant did not reply to a given point because the point made by the respondent is correct.

At a minimum, respondent should use the oral argument as an opportunity to respond to the reply brief. While judges frequently warn counsel not to repeat anything already stated in the briefs, respondent's counsel should always point out the need to respond to points made in the reply brief, particularly if those points were not addressed in respondent's brief. Even the most impatient judge or panel on appeal would understand the need for respondent's counsel to address points made in a reply brief.

2. Professional Manner of Respondent's Counsel

If counsel for the appellant, during the opening argument, made statements that were scandalous, unfounded, or improper, counsel for the respondent should resist the temptation to express anger. Respondent's counsel, in a calm and objective manner, should point out misstatements of material facts and assertions that are not supported by the record. Appellate courts are keenly aware of professional proprieties, and a breach by either side will undoubtedly be noted. Hence, respondent's counsel should ignore provocation and should respond in a dignified and professional manner. No part of the limited time allowed for oral argument should be used to express displeasure or annoyance with the demeanor of opposing counsel.

3. Court's Termination of Argument

In some instances, the court may interrupt counsel for respondent with a statement to the effect that the court does not wish to hear further argument. In that event, it would be futile to insist upon completing one's argument. Generally, such a remark to a respondent indicates that the court entertains no doubt as to the correctness of the judgment below. The court is not likely to refuse to hear a party who is about to be denied relief. Except in the most unusual case, it is a welcomed statement heralding victory.

C. Appellant's Rebuttal

The rules of most courts, such as Rule 34(c) of the Federal Rules of Appellate Procedure, provide that "[t]he appellant opens and concludes the argument." Although it is wise for counsel to reserve time for rebuttal, this does not mean that appellant will necessarily deliver a rebuttal.[28] The question is *whether the rebuttal*

---

28   *See supra* p. 153–54.

is necessary and will serve a purpose. The answer to the question depends upon the nature and effectiveness of the respondent's argument.

Has the respondent misstated or blurred the facts of the case? Is there a confusion that must be clarified? If so, rebuttal is necessary. On the other hand, a rebuttal is not required to answer an obviously ineffective argument by the respondent. A superfluous rebuttal is not only a waste of time but may be counterproductive.

Former Solicitor General Rex E. Lee offers sound advice on the importance of rebuttal arguments. He recommends reserving rebuttal time in all cases. He states, however, that "[v]ery rarely will you need more than two or three minutes for rebuttal, but you should save it if only because of the effect its existence may have on your opponent's willingness to stray from objectivity."[29]

Of the various options in the proper utilization of reserved time, beyond clarifying statements made by opposing counsel, Solicitor General Lee mentions the possibility of simply saying, "Unless the Court has questions, I have nothing further."[30] He concludes by saying, "[D]on't overlook the possibility that the best way to use your rebuttal time is to waive it."[31]

D. Summary of Essentials of Oral Argument

This book discusses the basic principles of oral argument and makes suggestions for the delivery of an effective oral argument before an appellate court. After an appreciation of the essentials, the refinements and subtleties of the art of persuasion must be learned by practice. The following essentials will be restated in the nature of a checklist. No advocate can afford to ignore them.[32]

1. *Thorough preparation*: Counsel must know the record. An advocate, who has not prepared in a manner befitting a diligent practitioner by mastering the facts and the law, is not prepared to discharge the professional responsibility owed to the client and to the court.

2. *Favorable first impression*: The attire and respectful attitude of the advocate should create a favorable impression from the moment counsel rises to address the court. Counsel should speak clearly and distinctly in a voice sufficiently loud.

3. *Effective opening*: Since the first few moments of the argument are perhaps the most difficult, counsel should have a prepared introduction or preliminary statement that generally states the nature of the case and the question presented on appeal. The effective opening must stimulate the court's interest in the case.

---

29   Lee, *supra* note 17, at 62.

30   *Id.*

31   *Id.*

32   For a helpful summary of an effective oral presentation, see Michael Paul Thomas, *Say What's Necessary, and Say Nothing More*, L.A. DAILY J., May 21, 1991, at 7.

4. *Statement of the issue*: Counsel should tell the court the specific issue that it is called upon to decide. The preliminary statement should make the issue intelligible and concrete. Unless the facts of the case are simple and few, counsel should avoid stating the facts of the case prior to informing the court of the issue. The court will thereafter listen to the facts in relation to the issue that must be decided.

5. *Statement of cardinal or key facts*: The statement of the facts should be limited to the prominent and essential facts. Counsel should remember Professor Llewellyn's admonition that "the pattern of the facts as stated must be a simple pattern." Counsel, however, must state the equities in favor of the client together with those facts that are salient and persuasive.

6. *Argument must be concrete*: The argument of the case must be specific and concrete. Principles of law should not be discussed abstractly, but in relation to the particular facts of the case. Although counsel should endeavor to persuade by reason and principle, reference must be made to the specific legal authority upon which counsel relies for affirmance or reversal.

7. *Argument must stimulate interest*: Counsel must interest the court in the justice of the cause. The presentation should be animated and enthusiastic. It must indicate sincerity of purpose and a desire to assist the court to arrive at the just and proper result. The interest created must continue throughout the argument.

8. *Counsel must not divert attention of the court*: Throughout the argument, counsel should not divert the attention of the court by distracting mannerisms, distressing and unexpressive gestures, long quotations, unnecessary citation of cases, or the discussion of details and other peripheral matters. Details of cited cases also cause confusion. Characterizations and insinuations are irrelevant and improper, and have no place in the courtroom.

9. *Questions by court to be welcomed*: Since questions by the court permit the court to participate actively in the argument of the case, they bring about a closer relationship between counsel and the court. Counsel is thereby assured of the interest of the court. Questions lend vitality to the argument and afford counsel the finest opportunity to demonstrate mastery of the case and justification for the position argued.

10. *Closing to be sharp and emphatic*: The length of time permitted by the rules of the court for the oral argument is a statement of the maximum time allowed. It does not imply that counsel must speak for the full length of time nor does it "constitute a contract with the court to listen for that length of time."[33]

During the argument, time is truly of the essence. Counsel should make no more use of it than is absolutely necessary. Once counsel has stated all that is germane to the appeal, the argument must be concluded.

---

33   Davis, *supra* note 7, at 898.

The conclusion is a dramatic moment. It should contain a vivid peroration of the main points discussed. This concluding summary forms the basis of the final sentence, which states the specific relief requested on the appeal. The request may be simply to affirm or reverse the judgment of the lower court. The last sentence should climax a memorable argument reminiscent of the highest traditions of the bar.

XI

CONSIDERATIONS AFTER ORAL ARGUMENT

A. Briefs After Oral Argument

It has been indicated that, regardless of the provisions of the particular rules of court, a reply brief is not to be submitted unless absolutely necessary. The submission of a document must *help* the cause, and it is never helpful to burden the court unnecessarily. After the submission of respondent's brief and appellant's reply brief, counsel must resist all temptations to file additional materials with the court.

Occasionally, during or after oral argument, the court will request additional information. Counsel may comply with the court's request by filing a supplemental brief or memorandum containing the desired information. The court may request that counsel submit a "letter brief," *i.e.,* a discussion in letter form of a particular point. Regardless of the form chosen, counsel should always indicate that the document is being filed "pursuant to the court's request."

Often the questioning during oral argument may clearly indicate that a supplemental memorandum is desired, although there has been no specific request by the court. For example, if during oral argument the court were to ask whether counsel intended to submit a supplemental memorandum on a particular point, such an inquiry "is the equivalent of a command."[1] If any member of the court were to ask a question that counsel is unable to answer, counsel should ask if the court wishes the submission of a supplemental memorandum.[2] If permission is granted, the supplemental memorandum will indicate that it is being submitted "pursuant to permission granted by the court during oral argument." The memorandum should set forth the specific question that will be discussed and the discussion must be limited to that matter.[3]

B. After Appeal Is Decided

1. Petition for Rehearing

In due course, the appellate court will decide the appeal. For counsel, however, the work is not yet over. Counsel who has won may still be faced with a petition for rehearing or another appeal by the losing party. Losing counsel must consider whether additional steps ought to be taken.

---

1   FREDERICK BERNAYS WIENER, BRIEFING AND ARGUING FEDERAL APPEALS 263 (1961).
2   *See* discussion of "Questions by the Court," *supra* pp. 160–64.
3   *See* discussion of "Memorandum of Law for Court," *supra* pp. 41–43.

The first thing that must be done is to study the appellate decision with great care and thoroughness. Every case cited must be read carefully. Do the authorities relied upon support the conclusion and holding of the court? If, after a thorough study of the appellate decision, counsel concludes that the court "overlooked" or "misapprehended" certain material points raised on the appeal, counsel may decide to petition the court for a rehearing.

In the words of Rule 40(a) of the Federal Rules of Appellate Procedure, the petition for rehearing "must state with particularity each point of law or fact that the petitioner believes the court has overlooked or misapprehended and must argue in support of the petition, oral argument is not permitted."

Clearly, counsel should not petition for rehearing simply because of dissatisfaction with the result or disagreement with the reasoning of the appellate opinion. What are the material points of law or fact that the court has "overlooked" or "misapprehended"? A petition is in order if the court, in its decision, sets forth a material and controlling misstatement of fact. Another example may be found if the decision of the court is based upon points that have neither been briefed nor argued by any of the parties.[4]

An additional basis for a rehearing is found in Rule 44.2 of the Rules of the Supreme Court of the United States. With particular reference to petitions for rehearings of orders denying a petition for a writ of certiorari, the rule requires that the grounds "be limited to intervening circumstances of a substantial or controlling effect or to other substantial grounds not previously presented."

The rules of the various state courts do not differ materially with respect to the bases for rehearing or reargument. For example, the applicable rule of the Court of Appeals of the State of New York provides that a motion for reargument "shall state briefly the ground upon which reargument is asked and the points claimed to have been overlooked or misapprehended by the court, with proper reference to the particular portions of the record and to the authorities relied upon."[5] It adds that the motion "may not be based on the assertion for the first time of new points."[6]

In describing a case as "that rarity in which the losing litigant has raised sufficient questions to warrant granting the petition and providing for rebriefing and reargument," Chief Judge Markey, of the Court of Appeals for the Federal Circuit, wrote:

> All the federal courts of appeals and the Supreme Court provide for petitions for rehearing, the rationale being that "a court which is final must also be careful: it

---

4   *See* Petition for Rehearing in Beauharnais v. Illinois, 343 U.S. 988 (1952). For further treatment, see ROBERT L. STERN ET AL., SUPREME COURT PRACTICE 610–35 (7th ed. 1993).

5   Rules of Practice of the New York Court of Appeals § 500.11(g)(1).

6   *Id.* § 500.11(g)(3); *see* discussion of "New Questions Barred on Appeal," *supra* pp. 72–73.

must admit of the possibility that error may occur and that original decisions may not always be the best possible decisions."[7]

Petitions for rehearing or reargument are seldom successful.[8] Nevertheless, counsel may be firmly convinced that there are grounds that warrant petitioning for rehearing. Under such circumstances the lawyer should prepare the petition in accordance with the pertinent rules of court.

A petition for rehearing may never introduce a theory that was not raised on appeal, either in the briefing or during oral argument.[9] As a result, an appellate court will decline to address a new theory raised for the first time in a petition for rehearing.[10]

2. Hearing or Rehearing En Banc

Counsel may also wish to consider the feasibility of seeking a hearing or rehearing en banc, *i.e.*, before all the judges of the court.[11] This possibility exists in courts such as the United States courts of appeals, where cases may be heard by a panel of judges rather than the full bench. Although the possibility is indeed remote in the ordinary case, counsel ought to nevertheless examine the applicable rule of court.[12]

3. Further Appeal

Counsel's responsibility to a client who has lost an appeal is not fully discharged until thorough consideration has been given to the possibility of further appeal. Justice Jackson acknowledged that even the most learned appellate courts sometimes err when he said of the Supreme Court of the United States: "We are not final because we are infallible, but we are infallible only because we are final."[13] Therefore, counsel should not hesitate to appeal, when possible, to a higher court if there are reasonable grounds to believe that an appeal will be successful.

---

7   Farrell Lines, Inc. v. United States, 667 F.2d 1017 (C.C.P.A. 1982) (Markey, C. J., dissenting) (on petition for rehearing). David W. Louisell & Ronan E. Degnan, *Rehearing in American Appellate Courts*, 44 CALIF. L. REV. 627, 632 (1956).

8   "As you know, very rarely is a motion for reargument successful, and I think that is the universal experience." Judge Rifkind, during question and answer period, *in* COUNSEL ON APPEAL 189 (Arthur A. Charpentier ed., 1968).

9   *See, e.g.*, FED. R. APP. P. 40(a).

10 *See* Pentax Corp. v. Robison, 135 F.3d 760, 762 (Fed. Cir. 1998) (citing United States v. Bongiorno, 110 F.3d 132, 133 (1st Cir. 1997) and Wells v. Rushsing, 760 F.2d 660, 661 (5th Cir. 1985)).

11 *See also* FED. R. APP. P. 35 En Banc Determination
    (a) When Hearing or Rehearing En Banc May Be Ordered
    (b) Petition for Hearing or Rehearing En Banc

12 *See, e.g., id.* 35(b).

13 Brown v. Allen, 344 U.S. 443, 540 (1953) (Jackson, J.).

Deciding whether a further appeal to a higher court should be undertaken will take the reader back to the beginning. Is there such a possibility? Is the appeal as of right, or need one seek leave to appeal? These questions have already been treated in this book.[14]

---

14   *See supra* p. 53–55.

Part Five

LEGAL CITATOR

XII

CITATION OF AUTHORITIES

A. Nature and Purpose

1. Definition

In legal writing or argument, a "citation" is a reference to a case or other legal authority for the purpose of establishing or supporting a proposition of law. The word "citation" is derived from the Latin *citare* which means "to call" or "to summon." True to its meaning, the advocate, when offering a citation, is summoning the aid of courts, legislatures, and legal scholars in an attempt to fortify or confirm a proposition of law. In a brief, opposing counsel will *cite* contrary or "hostile" legal authorities to show that the proposition asserted is not a correct statement of the law.

The legal authorities that an advocate may cite in support of a proposition of law include legislation, judicial decisions, administrative rules and regulations, treatises, and legal periodicals. Because not all of these authorities are of equal weight, the citation serves the important function of disclosing to the reader or listener the nature and *source* of the authority upon which the advocate relies. Only by knowing this information can the reader properly assess the merits or legal accuracy of the argument. The imperative or persuasive force of the authority cited depends, in large part, on its source.

In addition to disclosing the nature or type of authority relied on, the citation must also accurately state *where* that authority can be found. The citation should "lead its reader to the work cited . . . without enforced recourse to any other source of information."[1] Using a standardized citation form serves the dual purpose of creating a favorable impression on the reader and allowing the author to use shorter citations than would otherwise be possible.[2] The comments and sample citations set forth in this chapter illustrate proper and acceptable legal citation form.

2. Citations in Body or Footnotes

The citation of authorities may be placed either in the body of the work or in footnotes. Law reviews and most treatises and textbooks have adopted the practice of placing all citations in the footnotes. It is believed that this practice facili-

---

1   Price, A Practical Manual of Standard Legal Citations iii (1950).

2   *Id.* The most widely used citation system is that described in The Bluebook: A Uniform System of Citation (18th ed. 2005).

tates the reading of the text because it is not broken up by citations. The footnote method, however, is hardly ever employed in the writing of briefs. In brief writing, the citation is placed in the body of the brief.[3]

3. Typeface Conventions

In court documents and legal memoranda, as opposed to law review articles or books, only two typefaces are used: (1) ordinary roman type, and (2) *italics* or underscoring. Whether to italicize or underscore the appropriate parts of citations is the author's choice. LARGE AND SMALL CAPS, however, are not used in court documents and legal memoranda.[4]

B. Statutory Authority

1. Constitutions

a. United States

U.S. Const. art. VI.

U.S. Const. art. I, § 8.

U.S. Const. art. I, § 8, cl. 3.

U.S. Const. amend. XIV, § 1.

b. State

Ala. Const. art. III, § 2.

Ohio Const. art. V.

2. Treaties, Executive Agreements, Presidential Proclamations, and Executive Orders

a. Treaties and Executive Agreements

A reference to a Treaty or Executive Agreement to which the United States is a party should be accompanied by a citation to the official source and a parallel citation to the Department of State publication in which the document appears. The official source for Treaties and Executive Agreements prior to January 1, 1950, is the United States Statutes at Large. On or after that date, the official source is United States Treaties and Other International Agreements (U.S.T.). The Depart-

---

3   For forms of briefs including citations, see *infra* Appendices B, C, and D.

4   For a more complete discussion of typeface conventions for court documents and legal memoranda, see Rule P.1 in the Practitioner's Notes of THE BLUEBOOK: A UNIFORM SYSTEM OF CITATION (18th ed. 2005).

ment of State publications in which Treaties and Executive Agreements are reproduced include:

1. Treaty Series—T.S.

2. Executive Agreement Series—E.A.S.

3. Treaties and Other International Acts Series T.I.A.S.

The name, date, and parties to the agreement should precede the cite to the series. Thus, the complete citation will appear as follows:

Agreement on Economic Cooperation, Jan. 8, 1952, United States-Yugoslavia, 3 U.S.T. 1, T.I.A.S. No. 2384.

Treaties to which the United States is not a party may be cited to one of the following publications:

League of Nations Treaty Series—L.N.T.S.

United Nations Treaty Series—U.N.T.S.

European Treaty Series—Europ. T.S.

Great Britain Treaty Series—Gr. Brit. T.S.

Other treaty series are similarly abbreviated.

b. Presidential Proclamations and Executive Orders

Presidential Proclamations and Executive Orders are cited to volume 3 of the Code of Federal Regulations:

Proclamation No. 4707, 3 C.F.R. 87 (1979).

If the cited material has not yet appeared in the Code of Federal Regulations, the cite should be made to the Federal Register:

Exec. Order No. 12,303, 46 Fed. Reg. 21,341 (1981).

The citation should indicate if the Order or Proclamation has been reprinted in the United States Code.

3. Legislation

a. Federal

Federal statutes should be cited to the current United States Code, if possible. The year of the official code, published every six years, is included:

National Labor Relations Act § 1, 29 U.S.C. § 151 (1982).

Statutes that are no longer in force or that have not yet been codified are cited to the official session laws:

Antidumping Act of 1921, ch. 14, § 201, 42 Stat. 11 (repealed 1979).

Although the Internal Revenue Code is part of the United States Code, it is usually cited separately. The date of the code need not be included unless the section cited is no longer in force:

I.R.C. § 285.

Federal Rules of Evidence or Procedure:

Fed. R. Evid. 44.

Fed. R. Crim. P. 3.

Fed. R. Civ. P. 8(d).

Fed. R. App. P. 31.

Sup. Ct. R. 9.

2d Cir. R. 34.

b. State

State statutes should be cited to the current state code when possible. The date of the code should appear in parentheses, along with the publisher's name if the code is not published by the state:

N.Y. Bus. Corp. L. § 910 (McKinney 1980).

When not codified, a statutory citation is made to the session laws:

1980 Colo. Sess. Laws, ch.1, § 1.

4. Legislative Documents

a. Congressional Reports

H.R. Rep. No. 104-563, at 324 (1996).

S. Rep. No. 102-401, at 63 (1992).

b. Bills Pending in Congress

H.R. 184, 79th Cong., § 301 (1945).

S. 112, 89th Cong., § 101 (1965).

c. Congressional Record

Reference to a page in a bound volume:

144 Cong. Rec. 1200 (1998).

Reference to a page in a daily edition:

147 Cong. Rec. H2647 (daily ed. May 23, 2001).

d. New York State

Leg. Doc. No. 65(D), Report, N.Y. Law Revision Comm'n 10 (1964).

5. Publications of Administrative Agencies

a. Annual and Semiannual Reports

11 NLRB Ann. Rep. 52 (1946).

18 FCSC Semiann. Rep. 4 (Jan.–June 1963).

b. Federal Register

Exec. Order 11,246, 62 Fed. Reg. 44,174, 44,179 (1997).

c. Opinions of Attorney General

43 Op. Att'y Gen. 88 (1977).

16 Op. Off. Legal Counsel 41, 43–44 (1993).

d. Code of Federal Regulations

5 C.F.R. § 3801.103 (2003).

32 C.F.R. § 1201.1 (Supp. 1943).

e. Department of State Bulletin

22 Dep't St. Bull. 399 (1950).

C. Judicial and Administrative Decisions

1. United States Courts

a. U.S. Supreme Court

Ware v. Hylton, 21 U.S. (3 Dall.) 568 (1796).

Vacco v. Quill, 521 U.S. 793 (1997).

It may be desirable to include a parallel citation to an unofficial but available report. Refer to a particular court's Local Rules to determine if inclusion of a parallel citation is required or otherwise appropriate:

United States v. Pink, 315 U.S. 203, 62 S. Ct. 552 (1942).

The Lawyers' Edition may be cited in addition to or in lieu of the Supreme Court citation:

United States v. Pink, 315 U.S. 203, 62 S. Ct. 552, 86 L. Ed. 796 (1942).

b. U.S. Courts of Appeals

Franklin Sugar Ref. Co. v. Egerton, 288 F. 698, 701 (4th Cir. 1923).

United States v. Wellman, 830 F.2d 1453, 1463 (7th Cir. 1987).

Bruneau v. South Kortright Cent. Sch. Dist., 163 F.3d 749, 751–52 (2d Cir. 1998).

c. U.S. Court of Appeals for the Federal Circuit (formerly the U.S. Court of Claims and the U.S. Court of Customs and Patent Appeals)

Hunter Douglas, Inc. v. Harmonic Design, Inc., 153 F.3d 1318, 1324 (Fed. Cir. 1998).

Citations to the U.S. Court of Customs and Patent Appeals should be to the Federal Reports:

Jacques Isler Corp. v. United States, 433 F.2d 1399 (C.C.P.A. 1970).

If the opinion cited does not appear in the Federal Reports, cite the *official* reporter of the particular court involved:

United States v. Twin Wintons, 63 C.C.P.A. 84 (1976).

d. U.S. District Courts

Duffy v. Ranger Sec. Corp., 346 F. Supp. 1401 (E.D.N.Y. 1972).

M&F Supermarket, Inc. v. Owens, 997 F. Supp. 908, 912 (S.D. Ohio 1997).

e. U.S. Court of Federal Claims (formerly the Trial Division of the U.S. Court of Claims and the U.S. Claims Court)

Flexible Metal Hose Mfg. Co. v. United States, 4 Cl. Ct. 522 (1984).

Citations to the U.S. Court of Claims should be to the Federal Reports:

Inland Empire Builders, Inc. v. United States, 424 F.2d 64 (Ct. Cl. 1970).

If the opinion cited does not appear in the Federal Reports, cite the *official* reporter of the court:

United States v. Southern Ute Tribe, 191 Ct. Cl. 1 (1970).

f. U.S. Court of International Trade (formerly the U.S. Customs Court)

Royal Bus. Machs., Inc. v. United States, 507 F. Supp. 1007 (Ct. Int'l Trade 1980).

If the opinion cited does not appear in the Federal Supplement, cite the *official* reports:

Farr Mann & Co. v. United States, 1 Ct. Int'l Trade 104 (1980).

Citations to opinions of the Customs Court should be to the Federal Supplement or the Customs Court Reports:

C.B.S. Imports Corp. v. United States, 450 F. Supp. 724 (Cust. Ct. 1978).

Amerimex Corp. v. United States, 80 Cust. Ct. 74 (1978).

g. U.S. Court of Military Appeals

United States v. Adams, 18 C.M.A. 439 (1969).

h. U.S. Tax Court

Lucky Stores, Inc. v. Comm'r of Internal Revenue, 105 T.C. 420 (1995).

i. Federal Rules Decisions

Crumpacker v. Civiletti, 90 F.R.D. 326 (N.D. Ind. 1981).

2. Courts of New York State

a. Court of Appeals

Sabine v. Paine, 223 N.Y. 401, 119 N.E. 849 (1918).

People v. Santana, 80 N.Y.2d 92, 600 N.E.2d 201, 587 N.Y.S.2d 570 (1992).

b. Appellate Division

Hurley v. Union Trust Co., 244 A.D. 590, 280 N.Y.S. 474 (3d Dep't 1935).

In re Jacob, 210 A.D.2d 876, 620 N.Y.S.2d 640 (4th Dep't 1994).

c. Miscellaneous Courts

(i) Supreme Court

Larschen v. Lantzes, 115 Misc. 616, 189 N.Y.S. 137 (App. Term N.Y. County 1921).

People v. Cantos, 174 Misc. 2d 598, 665 N.Y.S.2d 815 (Sup. Ct. Queens County 1997).

(ii) Surrogate's Court

In re Talmadge, 109 Misc. 696, 181 N.Y.S. 336 (Surr. Ct. N.Y. County 1919).

In re Adoption of Michael, 166 Misc. 2d 973, 636 N.Y.S.2d 608 (Surr. Ct. Bronx County 1996).

(iii) Court of Claims

Mosher v. State, 43 Misc. 2d 69, 250 N.Y.S.2d 239 (Ct. Cl. 1963).

d. Courts of County and Municipal Jurisdiction

(i) County Courts

De Paso v. Cooper, 43 Misc. 2d 160, 250 N.Y.S.2d 556 (Westchester County Ct. 1964).

People v. Brown, 170 Misc. 2d 266, 648 N.Y.S.2d 283 (Allegany County Ct. 1996).

(ii) Civil Court of the City of New York

City & Suburban Delivery Sys., Inc. v. Green's Cards & Gifts, Inc., 167 Misc. 2d 283, 639 N.Y.S.2d 681 (N.Y. Civ. Ct. 1996).

(iii) Criminal Court of the City of New York

People v. Price, 178 Misc. 2d 778, 683 N.Y.S.2d 417 (N.Y. Crim. Ct. 1998).

Note: A case in the *New York Law Journal* is cited thus:

Johnson v. Equitable Life Assurance Soc'y, 153 N.Y. L.J., Feb. 2, 1965, at 1, col. 1 (App. Div. 1st Dep't Dec. 3, 1964).

3. Courts of Other States

Dickey v. Vann, 81 Ala. 425, 8 So. 195 (1896).

Robertson v. Robertson, 144 Ark. 556, 223 S.W. 32 (1920).

Bubb v. Evans Constr. Co., 255 Ill. App. 3d 673, 627 N.E.2d 1160 (1993).

Urman v. South Boston Sav. Bank, 424 Mass. 165, 674 N.E.2d 1078 (1997).

Guenther v. City of Onalaska, 223 Wis. 2d 206, 588 N.W.2d 375 (1998).

If the case is not reported officially but is available only in a National Reporter, indicate the State thus:

Ex parte Lewis, 38 S.W. 1150 (Tex. 1896).

The same rule applies to state reports which carry only the name of the report editor:

Lowry v. Stowe, 7 Port. 483 (Ala. 1838).

4. English Decisions

Luther v. Sagor, [1921] 1 K.B. 456.

Mighell v. Sultan of Johore, [1894] 1 Q.B. 149.

Young v. Grote, 4 Bing. 254, 130 Eng. Rep. 764 (Ex. 1827).

5. Administrative Decisions

In re Otis & Co., 31 S.E.C. 380 (1950).

Tennessee Intrastate Rates & Charges, 266 I.C.C. 41 (1952).

Beverly-Fairfax Area Case, 8 C.A.B. 360 (1947).

El Paso Natural Gas Co., 23 F.P.C. 364 (1960).

American Cyanamid Co., 60 F.T.C. 1881 (1962).

Addison Shoe Corp., 27 Ad. L. 2d 650, 184 N.L.R.B. No. 35 (1970).

Whitney Tel. Answering Serv., 20 Ad. L. 2d 72, 1 F.C.C. 2d 1346 (1966).

Am. Hydrotherm Corp. v. Hydrotherm, Inc. (P.O. T.M. App. Bd.) 164 U.S.P.Q. 143, 60 T.M.R. 255 (1969).

6. Citations to Electronic Databases

Cite to cases that are available only on an electronic database, such as LEXIS or WESTLAW, as follows:

Levi Strauss & Co. v. United States, No. 97-1536, 1998 U.S. App. LEXIS 23350, at *5 (Fed. Cir. Sept. 22, 1998).

Mahon v. Credit Bureau of Placer County, Inc., No. 97-17298, 1999 WL 123725, at *4 (9th Cir. Mar. 10, 1999).

D. Treatises and Related Publications

1. Treatises

11 Samuel Williston & Walter H. E. Jaeger, *Williston on Contracts* § 30:19 (4th ed. 2003).

9A Charles Alan Wright & Arthur R. Miller, *Federal Practice and Procedure* § 2459 (3d ed. 1995).

8 James W. Moore et al., *Moore's Federal Practice* § 38.10[2][b] (3d ed. 1998).

3 Melville B. Nimmer & David Nimmer, *Nimmer on Copyright* § 8D.06[D] (2003).

2. Pamphlets

Romuald Szumski, *Labor and the Soviet System* 16 (1950).

3. American Law Institute Publications

Restatement of Conflict of Laws § 249 (1996).

Restatement (Second) of Torts §§ 401–402 (1994).

Restatement (Second) of Conflict of Laws § 10 comment a (1958).

Restatement of Contracts, N.Y. Annot. § 19 (1933).

Model Code of Evidence Rule 304 (1942).

4. Encyclopedias

20 Am. Jur. 2d *Evidence* § 495 (1994).

31 C.J. *Husband and Wife* § 1375 (1923).

20 C.J.S. *Counterfeiting* § 8 (Supp. 2003).

4 Encyc. Soc. Sci. 183–87 (1931).

5. Annotations

Annot., 4 A.L.R.2d 466 (1949).

Annot., 20 L.R.A. (n.s.) 513 (1909).

6. Newspapers

Elizabeth Olson, *New Flare-Up in U.S.-European Banana Fight*, N.Y. Times, Mar. 3, 1999, at A3.

7. Magazines

Brad Stone, *From Here to There: The Physics of Time Travel*, Newsweek , Mar. 16, 1998, at 8.

Articles in books are cited as follows:

Harold McNiece, *Freedom and The Law, in Concept of Freedom* 172 (Carl W. Grindel ed. 1955).

Milton Pollack, *The Civil Appeal, in Counsel on Appeal* 44 (Arthur Charpentier ed. 1968).

Edward D. Re, *The Presettlement Adjudication of International Claims, in International Arbitration: Liber Amicorum for Martin Domke* 214 (Pieter Sanders ed. 1967).

8. Dictionaries

Cite like Treatises.

E. Law Reviews and Legal Periodicals

1. Articles

Erwin N. Griswold, *Renvoi Revisited*, 51 Harv. L. Rev. 1165 (1938).

Jean R. Sternlight, *Forum Shopping for Arbitration Decisions: Federal Courts' Use of Antisuit Injunctions Against State Courts* , 147 U. Pa. L. Rev. 91, 108 (1998).

Jerome J. Shestack, *Taking Professionalism Seriously* , 84 A.B.A. J. 70 (1998).

A reference or quotation from a particular page in the article is indicated as follows:

Erwin N. Griswold, *Renvoi Revisited*, 51 Harv. L. Rev. 1165, 1168 (1938).

2. Student Notes and Comments

Erica G. Franklin, Note, *Waiving Prosecutorial Disclosure in the Guilty Plea Process: A Debate on the Merits of "Discovery" Waivers* , 51 Stan. L. Rev. 567, 572 (1999).

Ian Ayres & Eric Talley, Comment, *Distinguishing Between Consensual and Nonconsensual Advantages of Liability Rules* , 105 Yale L.J. 235, 238 (1995).

3. Legislation Notes

Legislation, 26 Cornell L.Q. 692 (1941).

4. Recent Decisions

27 St. John's L. Rev. 139.

If the case is cited together with the Recent Decision, cite thus:

Kaufman v. Societe Internationale, 343 U.S. 156 (1952), 27 St. John's L. Rev. 139.

If the date of the Recent Decision differs from that of the case it should be added to the citation.

5. Book Reviews

Although seldom cited in briefs, if it is desired to cite a signed Book Review, the name used is that of the reviewer and not that of the author of the book:

Paul W. Bruton, Book Review, 53 Colum. L. Rev. 755 (1953).

Note: If the pages of a bound volume of legal periodicals are not numbered consecutively, give the month or number of the particular issue cited.

Leo R. Friedman, *Trial Brief in a Criminal Case*, Prac. Law, Mar. 1963, at 61.

F. Foreign Legal Materials

In citing foreign legal materials generally, one of the methods recommended for its simplicity is the following:

1. Constitutions

For constitutions in English, cite by country with the word "Const." Add parenthicals as necessary.

Example:

Can. Const. (Constitution Act 1982) pt. I (Canadian Charter of Rights and Freedoms), § 1.

For constitutions, not in English, add "[Constitution]" if needed for clarity.

Example:

Grundgesetz [GG] [Constitution], art. 14 (F.R.G.).

2. Codes

Cite to country; article or section; code name; date.

Example:

Belgium: Sec. 1, art. 412, C. Civ. [Code civil] (1804). France: Bk 1, Title VI, Sec. 1, art. 1, C. Com. [Code de commerce] (1863).

3. Statutes

Cite to country; the word "law"; date; wherein published.

Example:

Netherlands: Law, May 25, 1937, Stb. [Staatsblad van het Koninkrijk der Nederlanden] 801. Russian Federation: Federal Law on Real Estate (Pledge of Real Estate), Sobr. Zakonod, RF, 1998, no. 102-FZ (July 16, 1998).

4. Decisions

Cite to country; the names of the parties if given at the head of the decision, otherwise the word "decision"; court; date; official or unofficial report wherein published.

Example:

France: Decision, Cass. crim. [Cour de Cassation, Chambre criminelle], July 1, 1970, Gazette du Palais 1, 5 (Jurisprudence, Jan.–Feb. 1971).

Italy: Moffo v. Tebales, Corte cost: [Corte Costituzionale], 1959, 4 Rac. uff. corte cost. 441 (1959).

5. Law Reviews, Legal Periodicals, and Treatises

Citations should follow the American method of citing secondary materials.

Example:

Julien-Laferriere, Francois, *Problèmes Juridiques Relatifs au Controle de L'Administration au Chili*, 22 Revue Internationale de Droit Comparé, 341–357 (Apr.–June 1970).

Francesco Calasso, *Medio Evo Del Diritto* 618 (1954).

G. International Legal Materials

1. Materials Contained in Domestic Sources

a. Treaties and executive agreements may be found in a number of publications. Since 1950, the official series has been the United States Treaties and Other International Agreements (U.S.T.). A convenient unofficial series (since 1945) is the Treaties and Other International Acts Series (T.I.A.S.).

Cite to short title and type of agreement; date of signature (or, as the case may be, of other action taken); official and, facultatively, unofficial reporter.

Example:

Offenses and Certain Other Acts Committed on Board Aircraft, multilateral convention, done Sept. 14, 1963, 20 U.S.T. 2941 (1969), T.I.A.S. No. 6768.

b. A valuable source of material of international interest is The Department of State Bulletin, published weekly.

Cite to volume, page, date.

Example:

20 Dep't St. Bull. 577 (1949).

2. Materials Contained in Publications of International Bodies

a. International Court of Justice ("World Court")

Cite to name of case, year, official reporter: The Corfu Channel Case, 1949 I.C.J. 4.

b. United Nations and other worldwide international organizations

(i) Charter

Cite to organization, article, paragraph:

U.N. Charter art. 35, para. 2.

(ii) United Nations Publications

The United Nations has several "principal organs" (e.g., General Assembly; Security Council, etc.), numerous "specialized agencies" and "subsidiary organs," which publish a vast number of documents. For citation form, the reader is referred to *The Bluebook: A Uniform System of Citation* (18th ed. 2005).

c. League of Nations (defunct as of 1946), predecessor of the United Nations, is also the source of numerous publications.

Citation of its official journal should follow the standard method of citing law review sources:

12 League of Nations O. J. 56 (1931).

3. Regional Materials

Much attention has been paid to the various publications of the European Economic Community (abbr. as EEC, known as "Common Market"). One of the convenient unofficial reporters of cases decided by the Court of European Communities is the Common Market Law Reports (Comm. Mkt. L.R.).

Cite to case; court; case number; full date unless year same as volume; volume; year.

Example:

EEC Comm'n v. German Fed. Rep., Ct. of Justice of the Eur. Comm. (case 20/62, Oct. 10, 1962), 2 Comm. Mkt. L.R. (1963).

For a good guide of citations of international legal materials, see *International and Foreign Law Citator*, 6 Va. J. Int'l L. i–xiv app. (1966).

H. Abbreviations

1. General

For a list of abbreviations commonly used in legal works, see *Black's Law Dictionary* 1623–38 (6th ed. 1990); Jacobstein & Mersky, *Fundamentals of Legal Research* app. A (5th ed. 1998); *The Bluebook: A Uniform System of Citation* (18th ed. 2005).

Although it is recommended that abbreviations not be used in the text, they are extensively used in footnotes.

2. National Reporter Series

	1st Series	2d Series	3d Series
Atlantic	A.	A.2d	—
Federal	F.	F.2d	F.3d
New York Supplement	N.Y.S.	N.Y.S.2d	—
Northeastern	N.E.	N.E.2d	—
Northwestern	N.W.	N.W.2d	—
Pacific	P.	P.2d	P.3d
Southern	So.	So. 2d	—
Southeastern	S.E.	S.E.2d	—
Southwestern	S.W.	S.W.2d	S.W.3d

3. Periodicals

The abbreviations of the various legal periodicals and law reviews can be found in *The Bluebook: A Uniform System of Citation* (18th ed. 2005).

4. Names of Certain Courts

Appellate Division	—A.D.
Appellate Term	—App. Term
Bankruptcy Court	—Bankr. Ct.
Chancery	—Ch.
Children's Court	—Child. Ct.
Circuit Court of Appeals (federal)	—Cir.
City Court	—[Name of City] City Ct.
Civil Court	—Civ. Ct.
Claims Court	—Cl. Ct.
County Court	—[Name of County] County Ct.
Court of Appeal (English)	—C.A.
Court of Appeal[s] (state)	—Ct. App.
Court of Claims	—Ct. Cl.
Court of Customs and Patent Appeals	—C.C.P.A.
Court of Errors and Appeals	—Ct. Err. & App.
Court of Federal Claims	—Fed. Cl.
Court of General Sessions	—Ct. Gen. Sess.
Court of International Trade	—Ct. Int'l Trade
Court of Military Appeals	—C.M.A.
Court of Special Sessions	—Ct. Spec. Sess.

Criminal Court	—Crim. Ct.
Customs Court	—Cust. Ct.
District Court (federal)	—D.
District Court (state)	—Dist.
Domestic Relations Court	—Dom. Rel. Ct.
Family Court	—Fam. Ct.
House of Lords	—H.L.
Municipal Court	—[Name of City] Mun. Ct.
Probate Court	—P. Ct.
Superior Court	—Super. Ct.
Supreme Court of the United States	—U.S.
Supreme Court (local)	—Sup. Ct.
Surrogate's Court	—Surr. Ct.
Tax Court	—T.C.

I. Repeating Citations

1. Documentation in Text

a. If the citation of a case has been given in the text of a brief or other legal writing, and it is thereafter referred to by name, *"supra"* (meaning "above") may be used instead of repeating the citation.

Jones v. Brown, supra.

Note, however, that the excessive use of *"supra"* may have a disruptive effect. See discussion on p. 10 of this book.

b. Often it may be desired to refer to a particular page of a previously given citation. For example, the text gave the following citation: *Underhill v. Hernandez*, 168 U.S. 250 (1897). A subsequent reference to or quotation from page 252 is given as follows:

Underhill v. Hernandez, 168 U.S. at 252.

2. Documentation in Footnotes

If citations are given in footnotes, the following rules represent standard practice:

a. A whole footnote is repeated thus:

See supra note 10.

b. The citation to a case cited in a previous footnote is generally repeated. However, if the footnote is on the same page, the following form may be used:

Jones v. Brown, *supra* note 10.

c. Where the immediately preceding citation is to be repeated, simply cite:

Id .

d. If the only change in the immediately preceding citation is the page, cite:

Id . at 274.

If the immediately preceding citation is a case with parallel citations, cite:

Id. at 274, 109 N.E. at 732.

e. If a book has been previously referred to in the footnotes, the repetition of the title of the work is avoided by the following citation:

2 Beale, *supra* note 24, at 826.

1 Williston, *supra* note 24, § 84.

f. If an article has been previously referred to, use:

Griswold, *supra* note 24, at 1168.

J. Explanations and Signals

For a more complete explanation of this topic, see *The Bluebook: A Uniform System of Citation* (18th ed. 2005).

The following signals, which precede the citation, indicate the purpose of the citation:

1. No Signal Used

No signal is used if the name of a case is given in the text and the report is cited in the footnote, or when a direct quotation is made in the text and the citation is given in the footnote.

2. "Accord"

The signal "*accord*" precedes a case citation that *clearly supports* the proposition quoted in the text, taken from another case. Additionally, the law of one jurisdiction may be cited as being in accord with that of another jurisdiction.

Holzman, Cohen & Co. v. Teague, 172 A.D. 75, 158 N.Y.S. 211 (1st Dep't 1916); *accord* Trust Co. of Am. v. Conklin, 65 Misc. 1, 119 N.Y.S. 367 (Sup. Ct. 1909).

3. "Cf."

For the citation of a case that contains a legal proposition different from but sufficiently analogous to the proposition for which cited, use:

Jones v. Brown, 168 U.S. 250 (1897); *cf.* Abel v. Doe, 164 U.S. 225 (1882).

4. "See"

The signal "*see*" should be used when the cited authority directly states or clearly supports the proposition.

See Practice Mgmt. Info. Corp. v. Am. Med. Ass'n, 121 F.3d 516 (9th Cir. 1997).

See Oliphant, *The Theory of Money in the Law of Commercial Instruments*, 29 Yale L.J. 609 (1920).

The word "see" is not italicized when used in its ordinary sense as the verb of a sentence, such as:

See discussion of N.Y. Civ. Prac. Act § 344-a in Sommerich & Busch, *The Expert Witness and the Proof of Foreign Law*, 38 Cornell L.Q. 125 (1953).

5. "See also"

The signal "*See also*" should precede cited authority that constitutes additional source material that supports the proposition. This signal is commonly used to cite an authority supporting a proposition when authorities that state or directly support the proposition already have been cited or discussed.

See Kesserling v. F/T Arctic Hero, 95 F.3d 23, 24 (9th Cir. 1996); *see also* Hartman v. Duffey, 88 F.3d 1232, 1235 (D.C. Cir. 1996).

6. "But see"

"*But see*" precedes cited authority that directly states or clearly supports a proposition contrary to the main proposition.

Jones v. Brown, 168 U.S. 250 (1897). *But see* Doe v. White, 166 U.S. 224, 226 (1895).

7. Explanation or Comment in Citations (Parentheticals)

If it is desired to make a comment pertaining to a case cited, the comment or remark is enclosed in parentheses.

Imperial Corp. of Am. v. Shields, 167 F.R.D. 447, 454 (S.D. Cal. 1995) (finding that counsel had waived work product protection).

8. Subsequent or Prior History

It may be necessary or desirable to include the subsequent or prior history of a cited case. This is done as follows:

Lockwood v. Am. Airlines, Inc., 107 F.3d 1565 (Fed. Cir. 1997), *aff'g* 834 F. Supp. 1246 (S.D. Cal. 1993), *and aff'g* 877 F. Supp. 500 (S.D. Cal. 1994), *on mandamus sub. nom.* In re Lockwood, 50 F.3d 966 (Fed. Cir.), *cert. granted* sub. nom., Am. Airlines, Inc. v. Lockwood, 515 U.S. 1121, *vacated*, 515 U.S. 1182 (1995).

Other statements indicating the history of a case include:

aff'd,
aff'd mem.,
aff'd on other grounds,
amended by
appeal denied,
appeal dismissed,
cert. denied,
modifying
overruled by
reh'g denied, ·
rev'd,
rev'd on other grounds,
rev'd per curiam,
rev'g
sub nom. (indicates change of name on appeal)
withdrawn,

Since the sixteenth edition of *The Bluebook: A Uniform System of Citation*, denials of certiorari or denials of similar discretionary appeals need no longer be indicated unless the decision is less than two years old or the denial is particularly relevant. See Rule 10.7 of the eighteenth edition of *The Bluebook* for further discussion.

K. Sequence of Citations

1. Generally

The following rules are generally observed in determining the citation order:

a. Cite official reports before unofficial reports.

b. Cite primary authorities (cases and statutes) before secondary authorities.

2. Decisions

a. Cases in the same group are cited in the following order:

1. Decisions of the U.S. Supreme Court.

2. Decisions of the lower United States Courts—Courts of Appeal cases and then District Court cases.

3. State court cases (alphabetically according to state).

4. Decisions of English courts.

b. Within each group, unless it is desirable to cite cases according to order of importance, cases are cited beginning with the most recent case.

c. If cases are to be cited in a "string," set each full citation apart by a semicolon.

Zimmerman v. Sutherland, 274 U.S. 253 (1927); Deutsche Bank v. Humphrey, 272 U.S. 517 (1926).

If a contrary citation is used, such as *"But see"* and the like, it should start a new sentence.

City Nat'l Bank v. Roberts, 266 Mass. 239, 165 N.E. 470 (1929). *But see* Holiday State Bank v. Hoffman, 85 Kan. 71, 116 P. 239 (1911).

Authorities preceded by *no signal* and authorities preceded by *accord* , *see* , *see also* , and *cf.* should be separated from each other by semicolons.

Jones v. Brown, 168 U.S. 250 (1897); *cf.* Abel v. Doe, 164 U.S. 225 (1882).

These rules should be followed when cases or other authority are cited consecutively in a "string."

L. Miscellany

1. Title of Reported Case

a. First Names and Initials

The title of a case must be set forth as it appears in the official report, except that initials or first names preceding the surname of an individual are omitted. Hence, James R. Seward v. Joseph Tringali, is simply Seward v. Tringali.

b. Corporate Name

Where a corporate name ends in "Co., Inc." the "Inc." may be omitted. Hence, Robertson Publishing Co., Inc. v. Jones, is cited as Robertson Publishing Co. v. Jones.

2. Proper Word Usage

It may be helpful to point out certain words that are occasionally confused or misused in legal writing. Particular care should be taken not to confuse the following:

accept	except
affect	effect
enormity	enormousness
adverse	averse
allusion	illusion

bloc	block
capital	capitol
complement	compliment
discreet	discrete
founder	flounder
kind	type
principal	principle
then	than
parameter	perimeter

Other words often misused in briefs include: invariably, inapposite, assumedly, and peruse.

3. Spelling and Hyphenation

For the correct and accepted spelling and hyphenation of words, refer to any current standard dictionary and the *U.S. Government Printing Office Style Manual* (29th ed. 2000).

Note the spelling of the following, often misspelled, words:

accommodate
acknowledgment
ascent (rise)
   assent (consent)
believe
breach (break)
   breech (lower part)
deceive
defendant
device (contrivance)
   devise (convey)
exceed
extraordinary
grievous
indict
irreparable
judgment
loath (reluctant)
   loathe (detest)
perceive
preceding
proceed

recommend
relieve
rescission
separate
spacious (large)
   specious (plausible)
stationary (fixed)
   stationery (paper)
succeed
supersede
warrant

The following examples are also noted because of their particular relevance and applicability to brief writing:

cross-examination
cross-interrogatory
direct examination
re-cross-examination
redirect examination
re-redirect examination

4. Capitalization

a. Capitalize names of persons.

b. Capitalize titles of rank or of honor immediately preceding the name of a person:

Judge Underhill
Colonel Robertson
Professor Wallington

c. Capitalize titles of an office when used in place of the name of a specific incumbent:

the Secretary of Commerce
the Governor of New York

d. Capitalize the names of days of the week, months, and holidays:

Tuesday; March; Christmas

e. Capitalize names of governmental bodies, commissions, boards, agencies, clubs, associations, companies, schools, and churches when they are used with a proper name:

Congress of the United States

Civil Service Commission
Ohio State University
Acme Food Company
Gotham Bus Company

f. Capitalize names of streets, buildings, monuments, parks, etc.:

Park Avenue
Sheraton Arms
Lincoln Memorial
Central Park

g. Capitalize all principal words in titles of books, treatises, magazines, news-papers, and reports:

Cases and Materials on Remedies

The word *the* is capitalized only if it is the first word of the title:

The Growth of the Law

5. Punctuation

Punctuation is of great importance in the preparation and interpretation of legal documents and it should not be used carelessly. For rules governing the use of punctuation, the reader is referred to the *U.S. Government Printing Office Style Manual* (rev. ed. 1984).

6. Quotation Marks

a. Use quotation marks for quoted matter whether written or spoken.

b. Indicate omission of words from quoted passage by an ellipsis: "The defen-dant . . . was convicted."

c. Place periods or commas within quotation marks. (Note example in b.)

d. A quotation within a quotation is enclosed in single quotation marks:

"A learned judge," said the professor, "used to say: 'never submit a case on briefs.'"

7. Numbers

a. As a general rule, words are used for numbers less than 10. (The general *Blue-book* rule is to use words for amounts of less than 100.)

b. A number beginning a sentence is expressed in words: Nineteen persons attended.

c. Figures are used for dates, page, section, and footnote numbers:

August 1986
January 10, 1972
On page 8 in footnote 6 it is stated

d. Street numbers except *one* are written in figures:

One Maiden Lane
328 Chauncey Street
19 Broadway

e. Quantities and measurements are expressed in figures. When numerals are used as unit modifiers or numerical compounds, insert a hyphen. Some examples follow:

10 months; *but* 10-month delay
3 years
1 year, 10 months, 16 days
9 months; *but* the first three quarters of 1986
82-year-old man; *but* at the age of 65 ("years" is implied)
3 gallons, 6 1/2 gallons
7 miles; *but* zero miles
6 inches; *but* 3/4-inch pipe; two 6-inch pipes
8- by 10-inch photograph; *but* 8 by 10 inches
25 percent
4 to 1 ratio
5-to-4 vote; *but* the vote was 5 to 4

f. Meridian or clock time is written as follows:

10 o'clock
10:30 a.m.
12 a.m. or midnight
12 p.m. or noon; *not* 12 noon
half past 6

8. Italicization

a. Italicize sparingly.

b. Italicize (in a typewritten brief or other legal writing underline to indicate italics) the names of cases.

c. Italicize titles of all publications appearing in the text, in textual matter within footnotes or when cited in footnotes. Example: Paxton Blair, *Appellate Briefs and Advocacy*, 18 Fordham L. Rev. 30 (1949).

d. Words used to emphasize the author's meaning may be italicized.

e. Latin or foreign words and phrases are in italics when they are not in common English usage.

f. In briefs, the following are not italicized:

amicus curiae	pendente lite
bona fide	per capita
causa mortis	per curiam
certiorari	per stirpes
coram nobis	prima facie
de facto	pro forma
de novo	quasi in rem
dictum	quo warranto
en banc	res judicata
forum non conveniens	stare decisis
habeas corpus	status quo
in banc	subpoena
in personam	sub silentio
in rem	sui generis
inter vivos	ultra vires
lex loci	verbatim
mandamus	vis-à-vis

g. In briefs, the following are italicized:

ad hoc	*infra*
e.g.	*inter alia*
et seq.	*inter se*
ex parte	*nolo contendere*
ex rel.	*quaere*
i.e.	*semble*
ibid.	*sic*
id.	*sub nom.*
in re	*supra*

9. Instructions To Printer

a. Both in a typewritten manuscript, and in one that will be typeset, underline once all words that should be in *italics*.

b. Underline twice all words that are to appear in SMALL CAPITALS.

c. Words that are to appear in HI-LO CAPS should be underlined twice, with the letters that are to appear in large caps underlined a third time.

d. Underline three times all words that are to appear in CAPITALS.

Example 1: Typewritten Manuscript:

Hyde, <u>Compensation for Expropriations,</u> 33 <u>Am. J. Int'l L.</u> 108 (1939).

Print:

Hyde, *Compensation for Expropriations* , 33 AM. J. INT'L L. 108 (1939).

Example 2: Typewritten Manuscript:

<u>Walsh, Equity</u> § 19 (1930).

Print:

WALSH, EQUITY § 19 (1930).

Example 3: Typewritten Manuscript:

<u>Chapter Ten-Conclusion</u>

Print:

CHAPTER TEN—CONCLUSION.

10. Proofreader's Marks and Notations

The following marks are in common usage and may be used in correcting either a typewritten manuscript or printed galley. For additional marks, and for a valuable presentation of typographical practice in general, see *The Chicago Manual of Style* (15th ed., U. Chi. Press 2003) and in the *New York Times Manual of Style and Usage* (rev. and expanded 1st ed., Times Books 1999).

Mark	Meaning	Mark	Meaning
℈	Delete	ᵉᵐ/	Insert em dash
℈̂	Delete and close up	ᵉⁿ /	Insert en dash
℈	Reverse	∧	Insert semicolon
◡	Close up	⊙	Insert colon and en quad
#	Insert space	⊙	Insert period and en quad
◡/#	Close up and insert space	?/	Insert interrogation point
⁋	Paragraph	⑦	Query to author—in margin
❑	Indent 1 em	⌒	Use ligature
⊏	Move to left	⑤	Spell out
⊐	Move to right	tr	Transpose
⊔	Lower	wf	Wrong font
⊓	Raise	bf	Set in **boldface** type
∧	Insert marginal addition	rom	Set in roman type
V∧	Space evenly	ital	Set in *italic* type
✗	Broken letter—used in	caps	Set in CAPITALS
	Margin	sc	Set in SMALL CAPITALS
↓	Push down space	lc	Set in lower case
▬	Straighten line	ℓ	Lower-case letter
‖	Align type	stet	Let it stand: restore words
∧	Insert comma		crossed out

11. Division of Words

Although the division of words at the ends of lines is undesirable, both in a type-written manuscript and in print, it is often unavoidable. The division should be according to the American pronunciation of the word and never in a way that is misleading as to meaning.

It is the general rule of word division that a word is to be divided among syllables:

ne/go/ti/ate

For the rules concerning division of words and an alphabetical list of words showing their accepted divisions, the reader is referred to Word Division, a supplement to the *U.S. Government Printing Office Style Manual* (2000).

APPENDIX A:
Federal Rules of Appellate Procedure

FEDERAL RULES OF APPELLATE PROCEDURE

Amendments received to December 1, 2003*

TITLE I. APPLICABILITY OF RULES

---

* STAFF OF HOUSE COMM. ON THE JUDICIARY, 108TH CONG., FEDERAL RULES OF APPELLATE PROCEDURE (Comm. Print 2004).

TITLE I. APPLICABILITY OF RULES

Rule 1. Scope of Rules; Title

(a) Scope of Rules.

(1) These rules govern procedure in the United States courts of appeals.

(2) When these rules provide for filing a motion or other document in the district court, the procedure must comply with the practice of the district court.

(b) [Abrogated.]

(c) Title. These rules are to be known as the Federal Rules of Appellate Procedure.

Rule 2. Suspension of Rules

On its own or a party's motion, a court of appeals may—to expedite its decision or for other good cause—suspend any provision of these rules in a particular case and order proceedings as it directs, except as otherwise provided in Rule 26(b).

TITLE II. APPEAL FROM A JUDGMENT OR ORDER OF A DISTRICT COURT

Rule 3. Appeal as of Right—How Taken

(a) Filing the Notice of Appeal.

(1) An appeal permitted by law as of right from a district court to a court of appeals may be taken only by filing a notice of appeal with the district clerk within the time allowed by Rule 4. At the time of filing, the appellant must furnish the clerk with enough copies of the notice to enable the clerk to comply with Rule 3(d).

(2) An appellant's failure to take any step other than the timely filing of a notice of appeal does not affect the validity of the appeal, but is ground only for the court of appeals to act as it considers appropriate, including dismissing the appeal.

(3) An appeal from a judgment by a magistrate judge in a civil case is taken in the same way as an appeal from any other district court judgment.

(4) An appeal by permission under 28 U.S.C. § 1292(b) or an appeal in a bankruptcy case may be taken only in the manner prescribed by Rules 5 and 6, respectively.

(b) Joint or Consolidated Appeals.

(1) When two or more parties are entitled to appeal from a district-court judgment or order, and their interests make joinder practicable, they may file a joint notice of appeal. They may then proceed on appeal as a single appellant.

(2) When the parties have filed separate timely notices of appeal, the appeals may be joined or consolidated by the court of appeals.

(c) Contents of the Notice of Appeal.

(1) The notice of appeal must:

(A) specify the party or parties taking the appeal by naming each one in the caption or body of the notice, but an attorney representing more than one party may describe those parties with such terms as "all plaintiffs," "the defendants," "the plaintiffs A, B, et al.," or "all defendants except X";

(B) designate the judgment, order, or part thereof being appealed; and

(C) name the court to which the appeal is taken.

(2) A pro se notice of appeal is considered filed on behalf of the signer and the signer's spouse and minor children (if they are parties), unless the notice clearly indicates otherwise.

(3) In a class action, whether or not the class has been certified, the notice of appeal is sufficient if it names one person qualified to bring the appeal as representative of the class.

(4) An appeal must not be dismissed for informality of form or title of the notice of appeal, or for failure to name a party whose intent to appeal is otherwise clear from the notice.

(5) Form 1 in the Appendix of Forms is a suggested form of a notice of appeal.

(d) Serving the Notice of Appeal.

(1) The district clerk must serve notice of the filing of a notice of appeal by mailing a copy to each party's counsel of record—excluding the appellant's—or, if a party is proceeding pro se, to the party's last known address. When a defendant in a criminal case appeals, the clerk must also serve a copy of the notice of appeal on the defendant, either by personal service or by mail addressed to the defendant. The clerk must promptly send a copy of the notice of appeal and of the docket entries—and any later docket entries—to the clerk of the court of appeals named in the notice. The district clerk must note, on each copy, the date when the notice of appeal was filed.

(2) If an inmate confined in an institution files a notice of appeal in the manner provided by Rule 4(c), the district clerk must also note the date when the clerk docketed the notice.

(3) The district clerk's failure to serve notice does not affect the validity of the appeal. The clerk must note on the docket the names of the parties to whom the clerk mails copies, with the date of mailing. Service is sufficient despite the death of a party or the party's counsel.

(e) Payment of Fees. Upon filing a notice of appeal, the appellant must pay the district clerk all required fees. The district clerk receives the appellate docket fee on behalf of the court of appeals.

Rule 4. Appeal as of Right—When Taken

(a) Appeal in a Civil Case.

(1) Time for Filing a Notice of Appeal.

(A) In a civil case, except as provided in Rules 4(a)(1)(B), 4(a)(4), and 4(c), the notice of appeal required by Rule 3 must be filed with the district clerk within 30 days after the judgment or order appealed from is entered.

(B) When the United States or its officer or agency is a party, the notice of appeal may be filed by any party within 60 days after the judgment or order appealed from is entered.

(C) An appeal from an order granting or denying an application for a writ of error coram nobis is an appeal in a civil case for purposes of Rule 4(a).

(2) Filing Before Entry of Judgment. A notice of appeal filed after the court announces a decision or order—but before the entry of the judgment or order—is treated as filed on the date of and after the entry.

(3) Multiple Appeals. If one party timely files a notice of appeal, any other party may file a notice of appeal within 14 days after the date when the first notice was filed, or within the time otherwise prescribed by this Rule 4(a), whichever period ends later.

(4) Effect of a Motion on a Notice of Appeal.

(A) If a party timely files in the district court any of the following motions under the Federal Rules of Civil Procedure, the time to file an appeal runs for all parties from the entry of the order disposing of the last such remaining motion:

(i) for judgment under Rule 50(b);

(ii) to amend or make additional factual findings under Rule 52(b), whether or not granting the motion would alter the judgment;

(iii) for attorney's fees under Rule 54 if the district court extends the time to appeal under Rule 58;

(iv) to alter or amend the judgment under Rule 59;

(v) for a new trial under Rule 59; or

(vi) for relief under Rule 60 if the motion is filed no later than 10 days after the judgment is entered.

(B)(i) If a party files a notice of appeal after the court announces or enters a judgment—but before it disposes of any motion listed in Rule 4(a)(4)(A)—the notice becomes effective to appeal a judgment or order, in whole or in part, when the order disposing of the last such remaining motion is entered.

(ii) A party intending to challenge an order disposing of any motion listed in Rule 4(a)(4)(A), or a judgment altered or amended upon such a motion, must file a notice of appeal, or an amended notice of appeal—in compliance with Rule 3(c)—within the time prescribed by this Rule measured from the entry of the order disposing of the last such remaining motion.

(iii) No additional fee is required to file an amended notice.

(5) Motion for Extension of Time.

(A) The district court may extend the time to file a notice of appeal if:

(i) a party so moves no later than 30 days after the time prescribed by this Rule 4(a) expires; and

(ii) regardless of whether its motion is filed before or during the 30 days after the time prescribed by this Rule 4(a) expires, that party shows excusable neglect or good cause.

(B) A motion filed before the expiration of the time prescribed in Rule 4(a)(1) or (3) may be ex parte unless the court requires otherwise. If the motion is filed after the expiration of the prescribed time, notice must be given to the other parties in accordance with local rules.

(C) No extension under this Rule 4(a)(5) may exceed 30 days after the prescribed time or 10 days after the date when the order granting the motion is entered, whichever is later.

(6) Reopening the Time to File an Appeal.

The district court may reopen the time to file an appeal for a period of 14 days after the date when its order to reopen is entered, but only if all the following conditions are satisfied:

(A) the motion is filed within 180 days after the judgment or order is entered or within 7 days after the moving party receives notice of the entry, whichever us earlier;

(B) the court finds that the moving party was entitled to notice of the entry of the judgment or order sought to be appealed but did not receive the notice from the district court or any party within 21 days after entry; and

(C) the court finds that no party would be prejudiced.

(7) Entry Defined.

(A) A judgment or order is entered for purposes of this Rule 4(a):

(i) if Federal Rule of Civil Procedure 58(a)(1) does not require a separate document, when the judgment or order is entered in the civil docket under Federal Rule of Civil Procedure 79(a); or

(ii) if Federal Rule of Civil Procedure 58(a)(1) requires a separate document, when the judgment or order is entered in the civil docket under Federal Rule of Civil Procedure 79(a) and when the earlier of these events occurs:

- the judgment or order is set forth on a separate document, or

- 150 days have run from entry of the judgment or order in the civil docket under Federal Rule of Civil Procedure 79(a).

(B) A failure to set forth a judgment or order on a separate document when required by Federal Rule of Civil Procedure 58(a)(1) does not affect the validity of an appeal from that judgment or order.

(b) Appeal in a Criminal Case.

(1) Time for Filing a Notice of Appeal.

(A) In a criminal case, a defendant's notice of appeal must be filed in the district court within 10 days after the later of:

(i) the entry of either the judgment or the order being appealed; or

(ii) the filing of the government's notice of appeal.

(B) When the government is entitled to appeal, its notice of appeal must be filed in the district court within 30 days after the later of:

(i) the entry of the judgment or order being appealed; or

(ii) the filing of a notice of appeal by any defendant.

* * *

Rule 10. The Record on Appeal

(a) Composition of the Record on Appeal. The following items constitute the record on appeal:

(1) the original papers and exhibits filed in the district court;

(2) the transcript of proceedings, if any; and

(3) a certified copy of the docket entries prepared by the district clerk.

(b) The Transcript of Proceedings.

(1) Appellant's Duty to Order. Within 10 days after filing the notice of appeal or entry of an order disposing of the last timely remaining motion of a type specified in Rule 4(a)(4)(A), whichever is later, the appellant must do either of the following:

(A) order from the reporter a transcript of such parts of the proceedings not already on file as the appellant considers necessary, subject to a local rule of the court of appeals and with the following qualifications:

(i) the order must be in writing;

(ii) if the cost of the transcript is to be paid by the United States under the Criminal Justice Act, the order must so state; and

(iii) the appellant must, within the same period, file a copy of the order with the district clerk; or

(B) file a certificate stating that no transcript will be ordered.

(2) Unsupported Finding or Conclusion. If the appellant intends to urge on appeal that a finding or conclusion is unsupported by the evidence or is contrary to the evidence, the appellant must include in the record a transcript of all evidence relevant to that finding or conclusion.

(3) Partial Transcript. Unless the entire transcript is ordered:

(A) the appellant must—within the 10 days provided in Rule 10(b)(1)—file a statement of the issues that the appellant intends to present on the appeal and must serve on the appellee a copy of both the order or certificate and the statement.

(B) if the appellee considers it necessary to have a transcript of other parts of the proceedings, the appellee must, within 10 days after the service of the order or certificate and the statement of the issues, file and serve on the appellant a designation of additional parts to be ordered; and

(C) unless within 10 days after service of that designation the appellant has ordered all such parts, and has so notified the appellee, the appellee may within the following 10 days either order the parts or move in the district court for an order requiring the appellant to do so.

(4) Payment. At the time of ordering, a party must make satisfactory arrangements with the reporter for paying the cost of the transcript.

(c) Statement of the Evidence When the Proceedings Were Not Recorded or When a Transcript Is Unavailable. If the transcript of a hearing or trial is unavailable, the appellant may prepare a statement of the evidence or proceedings from the best available means, including the appellant's recollection. The statement must be served on the appellee, who may serve objections or proposed amendments within 10 days after being served. The statement and any objections or proposed amendments must then be submitted to the district court for settlement and approval. As settled and approved, the statement must be included by the district clerk in the record on appeal.

(d) Agreed Statement as the Record on Appeal. In place of the record on appeal as defined in Rule 10(a), the parties may prepare, sign, and submit to the district court a statement of the case showing how the issues presented by the appeal arose and were decided in the district court. The statement must set forth only those facts averred and proved or sought to be proved that are essential to the court's resolution of the issues. If the statement is truthful, it—together with any additions that the district court may consider necessary to a full presentation of the issues on appeal—must be approved by the district court and must then be certified to the court of appeals as the record on appeal. The district clerk must then send it to the circuit clerk within the time provided by Rule 11. A copy of the agreed statement may be filed in place of the appendix required by Rule 30.

(e) Correction or Modification of the Record.

(1) If any difference arises about whether the record truly discloses what occurred in the district court, the difference must be submitted to and settled by that court and the record conformed accordingly.

(2) If anything material to either party is omitted from or misstated in the record by error or accident, the omission or misstatement may be corrected and a supplemental record may be certified and forwarded:

(A) on stipulation of the parties;

(B) by the district court before or after the record has been forwarded; or

(C) by the court of appeals.

(3) All other questions as to the form and content of the record must be presented to the court of appeals.

Rule 11. Forwarding the Record

(a) Appellant's Duty. An appellant filing a notice of appeal must comply with Rule 10(b) and must do whatever else is necessary to enable the clerk to assemble and forward the record. If there are multiple appeals from a judgment or order, the clerk must forward a single record.

* * *

TITLE III. REVIEW OF A DECISION OF THE UNITED STATES TAX COURT

Rule 13. Review of a Decision of the Tax Court

* * *

TITLE IV. REVIEW OR ENFORCEMENT OF AN ORDER OF AN ADMINISTRATIVE AGENCY, BOARD, COMMISSION, OR OFFICER

* * *

TITLE V. EXTRAORDINARY WRITS

* * *

TITLE VI. HABEAS CORPUS; PROCEEDINGS IN FORMA PAUPERIS

* * *

TITLE VII. GENERAL PROVISIONS

Rule 25. Filing and Service

(a) Filing.

(1) Filing with the Clerk. A paper required or permitted to be filed in a court of appeals must be filed with the clerk.

(2) Filing: Method and Timeliness.

(A) In general. Filing may be accomplished by mail addressed to the clerk, but filing is not timely unless the clerk receives the papers within the time fixed for filing.

(B) A brief or appendix. A brief or appendix is timely filed, however, if on or before the last day for filing, it is:

(i) mailed to the clerk by First-Class Mail, or other class of mail that is at least as expeditious, postage prepaid; or

(ii) dispatched to a third-party commercial carrier for delivery to the clerk within 3 calendar days.

* * *

Rule 28. Briefs

(a) Appellant's Brief. The appellant's brief must contain, under appropriate headings and in the order indicated:

(1) a corporate disclosure statement if required by Rule 26.1;

(2) a table of contents, with page references;

(3) a table of authorities—cases (alphabetically arranged), statutes, and other authorities—with references to the pages of the brief where they are cited;

(4) a jurisdictional statement, including:

(A) the basis for the district court's or agency's subject-matter jurisdiction, with citations to applicable statutory provisions and stating relevant facts establishing jurisdiction;

(B) the basis for the court of appeals' jurisdiction, with citations to applicable statutory provisions and stating relevant facts establishing jurisdiction;

(C) the filing dates establishing the timeliness of the appeal or petition for review; and

(D) an assertion that the appeal is from a final order or judgment that disposes of all parties claims, or information establishing the court of appeals' jurisdiction on some other basis;

(5) a statement of the issues presented for review;

(6) a statement of the case briefly indicating the nature of the case, the course of proceedings, and the disposition below;

(7) a statement of facts relevant to the issue submitted for review with appropriate references to the record (see Rule 28(e));

(8) a summary of the argument, which must contain a succinct, clear, and accurate statement of the arguments made in the body of the brief, and which must not merely repeat the argument headings;

(9) the argument, which must contain:

(A) appellant's contentions and the reasons for them, with citations to the authorities and parts of the record on which the appellant relies; and

(B) for each issue, a concise statement of the applicable standard of review (which may appear in the discussion of the issue or under a separate heading placed before the discussion of the issues);

(10) a short conclusion stating the precise relief sought; and

(11) the certificate of compliance, if required by Rule 32(a)(7).

(b) Appellee's Brief. The appellee's brief must conform to the requirements of Rule 28(a)(1)–(9) and (11), except that none of the following need appear unless the appellee is dissatisfied with the appellant's statement:

(1) the jurisdictional statement;

(2) the statement of the issues;

(3) the statement of the case;

(4) the statement of the facts; and

(5) the statement of the standard of review.

(c) Reply Brief. The appellant may file a brief in reply to the appellee's brief. An appellee who has cross-appealed may file a brief in reply to the appellant's response to the issues presented by the cross-appeal. Unless the court permits, no further briefs may be filed. A reply brief must contain a table of contents, with page references, and a table of authorities—cases (alphabetically arranged), statutes, and other authorities—with references to the pages of the reply brief where they are cited.

(d) References to Parties. In briefs and at oral argument, counsel should minimize use of the terms "appellant" and "appellee." To make briefs clear, counsel should use the parties' actual names or the designations used in the lower court or agency proceeding, or such descriptive terms as "the employee," "the injured person," "the taxpayer," "the ship," "the stevedore."

(e) References to the Record. References to the parts of the record contained in the appendix filed with the appellant's brief must be to the pages of the appendix. If the appendix is prepared after the briefs are filed, a party referring to the record must follow one of the methods detailed in Rule 30(c). If the original record is used under Rule 30(f) and is not consecutively paginated, or if the brief refers to an unreproduced part of the record, any reference must be to the page of the original document. For example:

- Answer p. 7;
- Motion for Judgment p. 2;
- Transcript p. 231.

Only clear abbreviations may be used. A party referring to evidence whose admissibility is in controversy must cite the pages of the appendix or of the transcript at which the evidence was identified, offered, and received or rejected.

(f) Reproduction of Statutes, Rules, Regulations, etc. If the court's determination of the issues presented requires the study of statutes, rules, regulations, etc., the relevant parts must be set out in the brief or in an addendum at the end, or may be supplied to the court in pamphlet form.

(g) [Reserved]

(h) Briefs in a Case Involving a Cross-Appeal. If a cross-appeal is filed, the party who files a notice of appeal first is the appellant for the purposes of this rule and Rules 30, 31, and 34. If notices are filed on the same day, the plaintiff in the proceeding below is the appellant. These designations may be modified by agreement of the parties or by court order. With respect to appellee's cross-appeal and response to appellant's brief, appellee's brief must conform to the requirements of Rule 28(a)(1)-(11). But an appellee who is satisfied with appellant's statement need not include a statement of the case or of the facts.

(i) Briefs in a Case Involving Multiple Appellants or Appellees. In a case involving more than one appellant or appellee, including consolidated cases, any number of appellants or appellees may join in a brief, and any party may adopt by reference a part of another's brief. Parties may also join in reply briefs.

(j) Citation of Supplemental Authorities. If pertinent and significant authorities come to a party's attention after the party's brief has been filed—or after oral argument but before decision—a party may promptly advise the circuit clerk by letter, with a copy to all other parties, setting forth the citations. The letter must state the reasons for the supplemental citations, referring either to the page of the brief or to a point argued orally. Any response must be made promptly and must be similarly limited.

Rule 29. Brief of an Amicus Curiae

(a) When Permitted. The United States or its officer or agency, or a State, Territory, Commonwealth, or the District of Columbia may file an amicus-curiae brief without the consent of the parties or leave of court. Any other amicus curiae may file a brief only by leave of court or if the brief states that all parties have consented to its filing.

(b) Motion for Leave to File. The motion must be accompanied by the proposed brief and state:

(1) the movant's interest; and

(2) the reason why an amicus brief is desirable and why the matters asserted are relevant to the disposition of the case.

(c) Contents and Form. An amicus brief must comply with Rule 32. In addition to the requirements of Rule 32, the cover must identify the party or parties supported and indicate whether the brief supports affirmance or reversal. If an amicus curiae is a corporation, the brief must include a disclosure statement like that required of parties by Rule 26.1. An amicus brief need not comply with Rule 28, but must include the following:

(1) a table of contents, with page references;

(2) a table of authorities—cases (alphabetically arranged), statutes and other authorities—with references to the pages of the brief where they are cited;

(3) a concise statement of the identity of the amicus curiae, its interest in the case, and the source of its authority to file;

(4) an argument, which may be preceded by a summary and which need not include a statement of the applicable standard of review; and

(5) a certificate of compliance, if required by Rule 32(a)(7).

(d) Length. Except by the court's permission, an amicus brief may be no more than one-half the maximum lenght authorized by these rules for a party's principal brief. If the court grants a party permission to file a longer brief, that extension does not affect the length of an amicus brief.

(e) Time for Filing. An amicus curiae must file its brief, accompanied by a motion for filing when necessary, no later than 7 days after the principal brief of the party being supported is filed. An amicus curiae that does not support either party must file its brief no later than 7 days after the appellant's or petitioner's principal brief is filed. A court may grant leave for later filing, specifying the time within which an opposing party may answer.

(f) Reply Brief. Except by the court's permission, an amicus curiae may not file a reply brief.

(g) Oral Argument. An amicus curiae may participate in oral argument only with the court's permission.

Rule 30. Appendix to the Briefs

(a) Appellant's Responsibility.

(1) Contents of the Appendix. The appellant must prepare and file an appendix to the briefs containing:

(A) the relevant docket entries in the proceeding below;

(B) the relevant portions of the pleadings, charge, findings, or opinion;

(C) the judgment, order, or decision in question; and

(D) other parts of the record to which the parties wish to direct the court's attention.

(2) Excluded Material. Memoranda of law in the district court should not be included in the appendix unless they have independent relevance. Parts of the record may be relied on by the court or the parties even though not included in the appendix.·

(3) Time to File; Number of Copies. Unless filing is deferred under Rule 30(c), the appellant must file 10 copies of the appendix with the brief and must serve one copy on counsel for each party separately represented. An unrepresented party proceeding in forma pauperis must file 4 legible copies with the clerk, and one copy must be served on counsel for each separately represented party. The court may by local rule or by order in a particular case require the filing or service of a different number.

(b) All Parties' Responsibilities.

(1) Determining the Contents of the Appendix.

The parties are encouraged to agree on the contents of the appendix. In the absence of an agreement, the appellant must, within 10 days after the record is filed, serve on the appellee a designation of the parts of the record the appellant intends to include in the appendix and a statement of the issues the appellant intends to present for review. The appellee may, within 10 days after receiving the designation, serve on the appellant a designation of additional parts to which it wishes to direct the court's attention. The appellant must include the designated parts in the appendix. The parties must not engage in unnecessary designation of parts of the record, because the entire record is available to the court. This paragraph applies also to a cross-appellant and a cross-appellee.

(2) Costs of Appendix. Unless the parties agree otherwise, the appellant must pay the cost of the appendix. If the appellant considers parts of the record designated by the appellee to be unnecessary, the appellant may advise the appellee, who must the advance the cost of including those parts. The cost of the appendix is a taxable cost. But if any party causes unnecessary parts of the record to be included in the appendix, the court may impose the cost of those parts on that party. Each circuit must, by local rule, provide for sanctions against attorneys who unreasonably and vexatiously increase litigation costs by including unnecessary material in the appendix.

(c) Deferred Appendix.

(1) Deferral Until After Briefs Are Filed. The court may provide by rule for classes of cases or by order in a particular case that preparation of the appendix may be deferred until after the briefs have been filed and that the appendix may be filed 21 days after the appellee's brief is served. Even though the filing of the appendix may be deferred, Rule 30(b) applies; except that a party must designate the parts of the record it wants included in the appendix when it serves its brief, and need not include a statement of the issues presented.

(2) References to the Record.

(A) If the deferred appendix is used, the parties may cite in their briefs the pertinent pages of the record. When the appendix is prepared, the record pages cited in the briefs must be indicated by inserting record page numbers, in brackets, at places in the appendix where those pages of the record appear.

(B) A party who wants to refer directly to pages of the appendix may serve and file copies of the brief within the time required by Rule 31(a), containing appropriate references to pertinent pages of the record. In that event, within 14 days after the appendix is filed, the party must serve and file copies of the brief, containing references to the pages of the appendix in place of or in addition to the references to the pertinent pages of the record. Except for the correction of typographical errors, no other changes may be made to the brief.

(d) Format of the Appendix. The appendix must begin with a table of contents identifying the page at which each part begins. The relevant docket entries must follow the table of contents. Other parts of the record must follow chronologically. When pages from the transcript of proceedings are placed in the appendix, the transcript page numbers must be shown in brackets immediately before the included pages. Omissions in the text of papers or of the transcript must be indicated by asterisks. Immaterial formal matters (captions, subscriptions, acknowledgments, etc.) should be omitted.

(e) Reproduction of Exhibits. Exhibits designated for inclusion in the appendix may be reproduced in a separate volume, or volumes, suitably indexed. Four copies must be filed with the appendix, and one copy must be served on counsel for each separately represented party. If a transcript of a proceeding before an administrative agency, board, commission, or officer was used in a district-court action and has been designated for inclusion in the appendix, the transcript must be placed in the appendix as an exhibit.

(f) Appeal on the Original Record Without an Appendix. The court may, either by rule for all cases or classes of cases or by order in a particular case, dispense with the appendix and permit an appeal to proceed on the original record with any copies of the record, or relevant parts, that the court may order the parties to file.

Rule 31. Serving and Filing Briefs

(a) Time to Serve and File a Brief.

(1) The appellant must serve and file a brief within 40 days after the record is filed. The appellee must serve and file a brief within 30 days after the appellant's brief is served. The appellant may serve and file a reply brief within 14 days after service of the appellee's brief but a reply brief must be filed at least 3 days before argument, unless the court, for good cause, allows a later filing.

(2) A court of appeals that routinely considers cases on the merits promptly after the briefs are filed may shorten the time to serve and file briefs, either by local rule or by order in a particular case.

(b) Number of Copies. Twenty-five copies of each brief must be filed with the clerk and 2 copies must be served on each unrepresented party and on counsel for each separately represented party. An unrepresented party proceeding in forma pauperis must file 4 legible copies with the clerk, and one copy must be served on each unrepresented party and on counsel for each separately represented party. The court may by local rule or by order in a particular case require the filing or service of a different number.

(c) Consequence of Failure to File. If an appellant fails to file a brief within the time provided by this rule, or within an extended time, an appellee may move to dismiss the appeal. An appellee who fails to file a brief will not be heard at oral argument unless the court grants permission.

Rule 32. Form of Briefs, Appendices, and Other Papers

(a) Form of a Brief.

(1) Reproduction.

(A) A brief may be reproduced by any process that yields a clear black image on light paper. The paper must be opaque and unglazed. Only one side of the paper may be used.

(B) Text must be reproduced with a clarity that equals or exceeds the output of a laser printer.

(C) Photographs, illustrations, and tables may be reproduced by any method that results in a good copy of the original; a glossy finish is acceptable if the original is glossy.

(2) Cover. Except for filings by unrepresented parties, the cover of the appellant's brief must be blue; the appellee's, red; an intervenor's or amicus curiae's, green; and any reply brief, gray; and any supplemental brief, tan. The front cover of a brief must contain:

(A) the number of the case centered at the top;

(B) the name of the court;

(C) the title of the case (see Rule 12(a));

(D) the nature of the proceeding (e.g., Appeal, Petition for Review) and the name of the court, agency, or board below;

(E) the title of the brief, identifying the party or parties for whom the brief is filed; and

(F) the name, office address, and telephone number of counsel representing the party for whom the brief is filed.

(3) Binding. The brief must be bound in any manner that is secure, does not obscure the text, and permits the brief to lie reasonably flat when open.

(4) Paper Size, Line Spacing, and Margins. The brief must be on 8½ by 11 inch paper. The text must be double-spaced, but quotations more than two lines long may be indented and single-spaced. Headings and footnotes may be single-spaced. Margins must be at least one inch on all four sides. Page numbers may be placed in the margins, but no text may appear there.

(5) Typeface. Either a proportionally spaced or a monospaced face may be used.

(A) A proportionally spaced face must include serifs, but sans-serif type may be used in headings and captions. A proportionally spaced face must be 14-point or larger.

(B) A monospaced face may not contain more than 10½ characters per inch.

(6) Type Styles. A brief must be set in a plain, roman style, although italics or boldface may be used for emphasis. Case names must be italicized or underlined.

(7) Length.

(A) Page limitation. A principal brief may not exceed 30 pages, or a reply brief 15 pages, unless it complies with Rule 32(a)(7)(B) and (C).

(B) Type-volume limitation.

(i) A principal brief is acceptable if:

- it contains no more than 14,000 words; or
- it uses a monospaced face and contains no more than 1,300 lines of text.

(ii) A reply brief is acceptable if it contains no more than half of the type volume specified in Rule 32(a)(7)(B)(i).

(iii) Headings, footnotes, and quotations count toward the word and line limitations. The corporate disclosure statement, table of contents, table of citations, statement with respect to oral argument, any addendum containing statutes, rules or regulations, and any certificates of counsel do not count toward the limitation.

(C) Certificate of compliance.

(i) A brief submitted under Rule 32(a)(7)(B) must include a certificate by the attorney, or an unrepresented party, that the brief complies with the type-volume limitation. The person preparing the certificate may rely on the word or line count of the word-processing system used to prepare the brief. The certificate must state either:

- the number of words in the brief; or
- the number of lines of monospaced type in the brief.

(ii) Form 6 in the Appendix of Forms is a suggested form of a certificate of compliance. Use of Form 6 must be regarded as sufficient to meet the requirements of Rule 32(a)(7)(C)(i).

(b) Form of an Appendix. An appendix must comply with Rule 32(a)(1), (2), (3), and (4), with the following exceptions:

(1) The cover of a separately bound appendix must be white.

(2) An appendix may include a legible photocopy of any document found in the record or of a printed judicial or agency decision.

(3) When necessary to facilitate inclusion of odd-sized documents such as technical drawings, an appendix may be a size other than 8½ by 11 inches, and need not lie reasonably flat when opened.

(c) Form of Other Papers.

(1) Motion. The form of a motion is governed by Rule 27(d).

(2) Other Papers. Any other paper, including a petition for rehearing and a petition for rehearing en banc, and any response to such a petition, must be reproduced in the manner prescribed by Rule 32(a), with the following exceptions:

(A) a cover is not necessary if the caption and signature page of the paper together contain the information required by Rule 32(a)(2). If a cover is used it must be white.

(B) Rule 32(a)(7) does not apply.

(d) Local Variation. Every court of appeals must accept documents that comply with the form requirements of this rule. By local rule or order in a particular case a court of appeals may accept documents that to not meet all of the form requirements of this rule.

Rule 33. Appeal Conferences

The court may direct the attorneys—and, when appropriate, the parties—to participate in one or more conferences to address any matter that may aid in disposing of the proceedings, including simplifying the issues and discussing settlement. A judge or other person designated by the court may preside over the conference, which may be conducted in person or by telephone. Before a settlement conference, the attorneys must consult with their clients and obtain as much authority as feasible to settle the case. The court may, as a result of the conference, enter an order controlling the course of the proceedings or implementing any settlement agreement.

Rule 34. Oral Argument

(a) In General.

(1) Party's Statement. Any party may file, or a court may require by local rule, a statement explaining why oral argument should, or need not, be permitted.

(2) Standards. Oral argument must be allowed in every case unless a panel of three judges who have examined the briefs and record unanimously agrees that oral argument is unnecessary for any of the following reasons:

(A) the appeal is frivolous;

(B) the dispositive issue or issues have been authoritatively decided; or

(C) the facts and legal arguments are adequately presented in the briefs and record, and the decisional process would not be significantly aided by oral argument.

(b) Notice of Argument; Postponement. The clerk must advise all parties whether oral argument will be scheduled, and, if so, the date, time, and place for it, and the time allowed for each side. A motion to postpone the argument or to allow longer argument must be filed reasonably in advance of the hearing date.

(c) Order and Contents of Argument. The appellant opens and concludes the argument. Counsel must not read at length from briefs, records, or authorities.

(d) Cross-Appeals and Separate Appeals. If there is a cross-appeal, Rule 28(h) determines which party is the appellant and which is the appellee for purposes of oral argument. Unless the court directs otherwise, a cross-appeal or separate appeal must be argued when the initial appeal is argued. Separate parties should avoid duplicative argument.

(e) Nonappearance of a Party. If the appellee fails to appear for argument, the court must hear appellant's argument. If the appellant fails to appear for argument, the court may hear the appellee's argument. If neither party appears, the case will be decided on the briefs, unless the court orders otherwise.

(f) Submission on Briefs. The parties may agree to submit a case for decision on the briefs, but the court may direct that the case be argued.

(g) Use of Physical Exhibits at Argument; Removal. Counsel intending to use physical exhibits other than documents at the argument must arrange to place them in the courtroom on the day of the argument before the court convenes. After the argument, counsel must remove the exhibits from the courtroom, unless the court directs otherwise. The clerk may destroy or dispose of the exhibits if counsel does not reclaim them within a reasonable time after the clerk gives notice to remove them.

Rule 35. En Banc Determination

(a) When Hearing or Rehearing En Banc May Be Ordered. A majority of the circuit judges who are in regular active service may order that an appeal or other proceeding be heard or reheard by the court of appeals en banc. An en banc hearing or rehearing is not favored and ordinarily will not be ordered unless:

(1) en banc consideration is necessary to secure or maintain uniformity of the court's decisions; or

(2) the proceeding involves a question of exceptional importance.

(b) Petition for Hearing or Rehearing En Banc.

A party may petition for a hearing or rehearing en banc.

(1) The petition must begin with a statement that either:

(A) the panel decision conflicts with a decision of the United States Supreme Court or of the court to which the petition is addressed (with citation to the conflicting case or cases) and consideration by the full court is therefore necessary to secure and maintain uniformity of the court's decisions; or

(B) the proceeding involves one or more questions of exceptional importance, each of which must be concisely stated; for example, a petition may assert that a proceeding presents a question of exceptional importance if it involves an issue on which the panel decision conflicts with the authoritative decisions of other United States Courts of Appeals that have addressed the issue.

(2) Except by the court's permission, a petition for an en banc hearing or rehearing must not exceed 15 pages, excluding material not counted under Rule 32.

(3) For purposes of the page limit in Rule 35(b)(2), if a party files both a petition for panel rehearing and a petition for rehearing en banc, they are considered a single document even if they are filed separately, unless separate filing is required by local rule.

(c) Time for Petition for Hearing or Rehearing En Banc. A petition that an appeal be heard initially en banc must be filed by the date when the appellee's brief is due. A petition for a rehearing en banc must be filed within the time prescribed by Rule 40 for filing a petition for rehearing.

(d) Number of Copies. The number of copies to be filed must be prescribed by local rule and may be altered by order in a particular case.

(e) Response. No response may be filed to a petition for an en banc consideration unless the court orders a response.

(f) Call for a Vote. A vote need not be taken to determine whether the case will be heard or reheard en banc unless a judge calls for a vote.

Rule 36. Entry of Judgment; Notice

(a) Entry. A judgment is entered when it is noted on the docket. The clerk must prepare, sign, and enter the judgment:

(1) after receiving the court's opinion—but if settlement of the judgment's form is required, after final settlement; or

(2) if a judgment is rendered without an opinion, as the court instructs.

(b) Notice. On the date when judgment is entered, the clerk must serve on all parties a copy of the opinion—or the judgment, if no opinion was written—and a notice of the date when the judgment was entered.

Rule 37. Interest on Judgment

(a) When the Court Affirms. Unless the law provides otherwise, if a money judgment in a civil case is affirmed, whatever interest is allowed by law is payable from the date when the district court's judgment was entered.

(b) When the Court Reverses. If the court modifies or reverses a judgment with a direction that a money judgment be entered in the district court, the mandate must contain instructions about the allowance of interest.

Rule 38. Frivolous Appeal—Damages and Costs

If a court of appeals determines that an appeal is frivolous, it may, after a separately filed motion or notice from the court and reasonable opportunity to respond, award just damages and single or double costs to the appellee.

Rule 39. Costs

(a) Against Whom Assessed. The following rules apply unless the law provides or the court orders otherwise:

(1) if an appeal is dismissed, costs are taxed against the appellant, unless the parties agree otherwise;

(2) if a judgment is affirmed, costs are taxed against the appellant;

(3) if a judgment is reversed, costs are taxed against the appellee;

(4) if a judgment is affirmed in part, reversed in part, modified, or vacated, costs are taxed only as the court orders.

(b) Costs For and Against the United States. Costs for or against the United States, its agency, or officer will be assessed under Rule 39(a) only if authorized by law.

(c) Costs of Copies. Each court of appeals must, by local rule, fix the maximum rate for taxing the cost of producing necessary copies of a brief or appendix, or copies of records authorized by Rule 30(f). The rate must not exceed that generally charged for such work in the area where the clerk's office is located and should encourage economical methods of copying.

(d) Bill of Costs: Objections; Insertion in Mandate.

(1) A party who wants costs taxed must—within 14 days after entry of judgment—file with the circuit clerk, with proof of service, an itemized and verified bill of costs.

(2) Objections must be filed within 10 days after service of the bill of costs, unless the court extends the time.

(3) The clerk must prepare and certify an itemized statement of costs for insertion in the mandate, but issuance of the mandate must not be delayed for taxing costs. If the mandate issues before costs are finally determined, the district clerk must—upon the circuit clerk's request—add the statement of costs, or any amendment of it, to the mandate.

(e) Costs on Appeal Taxable in the District Court. The following costs on appeal are taxable in the district court for the benefit of the party entitled to costs under this rule:

(1) the preparation and transmission of the record;

(2) the reporter's transcript, if needed to determine the appeal;

(3) premiums paid for a supersedeas bond or other bond to preserve rights pending appeal; and

(4) the fee for filing the notice of appeal.

Rule 40. Petition for Panel Rehearing

(a) Time to File; Contents; Answer; Action by the Court if Granted.

(1) Time. Unless the time is shortened or extended by order or local rule, a petition for panel rehearing may be filed within 14 days after entry of judgment. But in a civil case, if the United States or its officer or agency is a party, the time within which any party may seek rehearing is 45 days after entry of judgment, unless an order shortens or extends the time.

(2) Contents. The petition must state with particularity each point of law or fact that the petitioner believes the court has overlooked or misapprehended and must argue in support of the petition. Oral argument is not permitted.

(3) Answer. Unless the court requests, no answer to a petition for panel rehearing is permitted. But ordinarily rehearing will not be granted in the absence of such a request.

(4) Action by the Court. If a petition for panel rehearing is granted, the court may do any of the following:

(A) make a final disposition of the case without reargument;

(B) restore the case to the calendar for reargument or resubmission; or

(C) issue any other appropriate order.

(b) Form of Petition; Length. The petition must comply in form with Rule 32. Copies must be served and filed as Rule 31 prescribes. Unless the court permits or a local rule provides otherwise, a petition for panel rehearing must not exceed 15 pages.

Rule 41. Mandate: Contents; Issuance and Effective Date; Stay

(a) Contents. Unless the court directs that a formal mandate issue, the mandate consists of a certified copy of the judgment, a copy of the court's opinion, if any, and any direction about costs.

(b) When Issued. The court's mandate must issue 7 calendar days after the time to file a petition for rehearing expires, or 7 calendar days after entry of an order denying a timely petition for panel re-hearing, petition for rehearing en banc, or motion for stay of mandate, whichever is later. The court may shorten or extend the time.

(c) Effective Date. The mandate is effective when issued.

(d) Staying the Mandate.

(1) On Petition for Rehearing or Motion. The timely filing of a petition for panel rehearing, petition for rehearing en banc, or motion for stay of mandate, stays the mandate until disposition of the petition or motion, unless the court orders otherwise.

(2) Pending Petition for Certiorari.

(A) A party may move to stay the mandate pending the filing of a petition for a writ of certiorari in the Supreme Court. The motion must be served on all parties and must show that the certiorari petition would present a substantial question and that there is good cause for a stay.

(B) The stay must not exceed 90 days, unless the period is extended for good cause or unless the party who obtained the stay files a petition for the writ and so notifies the circuit clerk in writing within the period of the stay. In that case, the stay continues until the Supreme Court's final disposition.

(C) The court may require a bond or other security as a condition to granting or continuing a stay of the mandate.

(D) The court of appeals must issue the mandate immediately when a copy of a Supreme Court order denying the petition for writ of certiorari is filed.

Rule 42. Voluntary Dismissal

(a) Dismissal in the District Court. Before an appeal has been docketed by the circuit clerk, the district court may dismiss the appeal on the filing of a stipulation signed by all parties or on the appellant's motion with notice to all parties.

(b) Dismissal in the Court of Appeals. The circuit clerk may dismiss a docketed appeal if the parties file a signed dismissal agreement specifying how costs are to be paid and pay any fees that are due. But no mandate or other process may issue without a court order. An appeal may be dismissed on the appellant's motion on terms agreed to by the parties or fixed by the court.

Rule 43. Substitution of Parties

(a) Death of a Party.

(1) After Notice of Appeal Is Filed. If a party dies after a notice of appeal has been filed or while a proceeding is pending in the court of appeals, the decedent's personal representative may be substituted as a party on motion filed with the circuit clerk by the representative or by any party. A party's motion must be served on the representative in accordance with Rule 25. If the decedent has no representative, any party may suggest the death on the record, and the court of appeals may then direct appropriate proceedings.

(2) Before Notice of Appeal Is Filed—Potential Appellant. If a party entitled to appeal dies before filing a notice of appeal, the decedent's personal representative—or, if there is no personal representative, the decedent's attorney of record—may file a notice of appeal within the time prescribed by these rules. After the notice of appeal is filed, substitution must be in accordance with Rule 43(a)(1).

(3) Before Notice of Appeal Is Filed—Potential Appellee. If a party against whom an appeal may be taken dies after entry of a judgment or order in the district court, but before a notice of appeal is filed, an appellant may proceed as if the death had not occurred. After the notice of appeal is filed, substitution must be in accordance with Rule 43(a)(1).

(b) Substitution for a Reason Other Than Death. If a party needs to be substituted for any reason other than death, the procedure prescribed in Rule 43(a) applies.

(c) Public Officer: Identification; Substitution.

(1) Identification of Party. A public officer who is a party to an appeal or other proceeding in an official capacity may be described as a party by the public officer's official title rather than by name. But the court may require the public officer's name to be added.

(2) Automatic Substitution of Officeholder. When a public officer who is a party to an appeal or other proceeding in an official capacity dies, resigns, or otherwise ceases to hold office, the action does not abate. The public officer's successor is automatically substituted as a party. Proceedings following the substitution are to be in the name of the substituted party, but any misnomer that does not affect the substantial rights of the parties may be disregarded. An order of substitution may be entered at any time, but failure to enter an order does not affect the substitution.

Rule 44. Case Involving a Constitutional Question When the United States or the Relevant State is Not a Party

(a) Constitutional Challenge to Federal Statute. If a party questions the constitutionality of an Act of Congress in a proceeding in which the United States or its agency, officer, or employee is not a party in an official capacity, the questioning party must give written notice to the circuit clerk immediately upon the filing of the record or as soon as the question is raised in the court of appeals. The clerk must then certify that fact to the Attorney General.

(b) Constitutional Challenge to State Statute. If a party questions the constitutionality of a statute of a State in a proceeding in which that State or its agency, officer, or employee is not a party in an official capacity, the questioning party must give written notice to the circuit clerk immediately upon the filing of the record or as soon as the question is raised in the court of appeals. The clerk must then certify that fact to the attorney general of the State.

Rule 45. Clerk's Duties

(a) General Provisions.

(1) Qualifications. The circuit clerk must take the oath and post any bond required by law. Neither the clerk nor any deputy clerk may practice as an attorney or counselor in any court while in office.

(2) When Court Is Open. The court of appeals is always open for filing any paper, issuing and returning process, making a motion, and entering an order. The clerk's office with the clerk or a deputy in attendance must be open during business hours on all days except Saturdays, Sundays, and legal holidays. A court may provide by local rule or by order that the clerk's office be open for specified hours on Saturdays or on legal holidays other than New Year's Day, Martin Luther King, Jr.'s Birthday, Presidents' Day, Memorial Day, Independence Day, Labor Day, Columbus Day, Veterans' Day, Thanksgiving Day, and Christmas Day.

(b) Records.

(1) The Docket. The circuit clerk must maintain a docket and an index of all docketed cases in the manner prescribed by the Director of the Administrative Office of the United States Courts. The clerk must record all papers filed with the clerk and all process, orders, and judgments.

(2) Calendar. Under the court's direction, the clerk must prepare a calendar of cases awaiting argument. In placing cases on the calendar for argument, the clerk must give preference to appeals in criminal cases and to other proceedings and appeals entitled to preference by law.

(3) Other Records. The clerk must keep other books and records required by the Director of the Administrative Office of the United States Courts, with the approval of the Judicial Conference of the United States, or by the court.

(c) Notice of an Order or Judgment. Upon the entry of an order or judgment, the circuit clerk must immediately serve a notice of entry on each party, with a copy of any opinion, and must note the date of service on the docket. Service on a party represented by counsel must be made on counsel.

(d) Custody of Records and Papers. The circuit clerk has custody of the court's records and papers. Unless the court orders or instructs otherwise, the clerk must not permit an original record or paper to be taken from the clerk's office. Upon disposition of the case, original papers constituting the record on appeal or review must be returned to the court or agency from which they were received. The clerk must preserve a copy of any brief, appendix, or other paper that has been filed.

Rule 46. Attorneys

(a) Admission to the Bar.

(1) Eligibility. An attorney is eligible for admission to the bar of a court of appeals if that attorney is of good moral and professional character and is admitted to practice before the Supreme Court of the United States, the highest court of a state, another United States court of appeals, or a United States district court (including the district courts for Guam, the Northern Mariana Islands, and the Virgin Islands).

(2) Application. An applicant must file an application for admission, on a form approved by the court that contains the applicant's personal statement showing eligibility for membership. The applicant must subscribe to the following oath or affirmation:

> "I, _____, do solemnly swear [or affirm] that I will conduct myself as an attorney and counselor of this court, uprightly and according to law; and that I will support the Constitution of the United States."

(3) Admission Procedures. On written or oral motion of a member of the court's bar, the court will act on the application. An applicant may be admitted by oral motion in open court. But, unless the court orders otherwise, an applicant need not appear before the court to be admitted. Upon admission, an applicant must pay the clerk the fee prescribed by local rule or court order.

(b) Suspension or Disbarment.

(1) Standard. A member of the court's bar is subject to suspension or disbarment by the court if the member:

(A) has been suspended or disbarred from practice in any other court; or

(B) is guilty of conduct unbecoming a member of the court's bar.

(2) Procedure. The member must be given an opportunity to show good cause, within the time prescribed by the court, why the member should not be suspended or disbarred.

(3) Order. The court must enter an appropriate order after the member responds and a hearing is held, if requested, or after the time prescribed for a response expires, if no response is made.

(c) Discipline. A court of appeals may discipline an attorney who practices before it for conduct unbecoming a member of the bar or for failure to comply with any court rule. First, however, the court must afford the attorney reasonable notice, an opportunity to show cause to the contrary, and, if requested, a hearing.

Rule 47. Local Rules by Courts of Appeals

(a) Local Rules.

(1) Each court of appeals acting by a majority of its judges in regular active service may, after giving appropriate public notice and opportunity for comment, make and amend rules governing its practice. A generally applicable direction to parties or lawyers regarding practice before a court must be in a local rule rather than an internal operating procedure or standing order. A local rule must be consistent with—but not duplicative of—Acts of Congress and rules adopted under 28 U.S.C. § 2072 and must conform to any uniform numbering system prescribed by the Judicial Conference of the United States. Each circuit clerk must send the Administrative Office of the United States Courts a copy of each local rule and internal operating procedure when it is promulgated or amended.

(2) A local rule imposing a requirement of form must not be enforced in a manner that causes a party to lose rights because of a nonwillful failure to comply with the requirement.

(b) Procedure When There Is No Controlling Law. A court of appeals may regulate practice in a particular case in any manner consistent with federal law, these rules, and local rules of the circuit. No sanction or other disadvantage may be imposed for non-compliance with any requirement not in federal law, federal rules, or the local circuit rules unless the alleged violator has been furnished in the particular case with actual notice of the requirement.

Rule 48. Masters

(a) Appointment; Powers. A court of appeals may appoint a special master to hold hearings, if necessary, and to recommend factual findings and disposition in matters ancillary to proceedings in the court. Unless the order referring a matter to a master specifies or limits the master's powers, those powers include, but are not limited to, the following:

(1) regulating all aspects of a hearing;

(2) taking all appropriate action for the efficient performance of the master's duties under the order;

(3) requiring the production of evidence on all matters embraced in the reference; and

(4) administering oaths and examining witnesses and parties.

(b) Compensation. If the master is not a judge or court employee, the court must determine the master's compensation and whether the cost is to be charged to any party.

APPENDIX OF FORMS

Form 1. Notice of Appeal to a Court of Appeals From a Judgment or Order of a District Court

United States District Court for the _____

District of _____

File Number _____

A.B., Plaintiff *v.* C.D., Defendant	} Notice of Appeal

Notice is hereby given that _____(here name all parties taking the appeal)_____, (plaintiffs) (defendants) in the above named case,* hereby appeal to the United States Court of Appeals for the _____ Circuit (from the final judgment) (from an order (describing it)) entered in this action on the ___ day of _____, 20__.

(s)_____
Attorney for _____
Address: _____

* See Rule 3(c) for permissible ways of identifying appellants.

(As amended Apr. 22, 1993, eff. Dec. 1, 1993; Mar. 27, 2003, eff. Dec. 1, 2003.)

Form 2. Notice of Appeal to a Court of Appeals From a Decision of the United States Tax Court

UNITED STATES TAX COURT
Washington, D.C.

A.B., Petitioner *v.* Commissioner of Internal Revenue, Respondent	} Docket No. _____

Notice of Appeal

Notice is hereby given that _____(here name all parties taking the appeal)*_____ hereby appeal to the United States Court of Appeals for the _____ Circuit from (that part of) the decision of this court entered in the above captioned proceeding on the _____ day of _____, 20__ (relating to _____).

(s)_____
Counsel for _____
Address: _____

* See Rule 3(c) for permissible ways of identifying appellants.

(As amended Apr. 22, 1993, eff. Dec. 1, 1993; Mar. 27, 2003, eff. Dec. 1, 2003.)

Form 3. Petition for Review of Order of an Agency, Board, Commission or Officer

United States Court of Appeals for the _____ Circuit

A.B., Petitioner	
v.	Petition for Review
XYZ Commission, Respondent	

_____(here name all parties bringing the petition)*_____ hereby petition the court for review of the Order of the XYZ Commission (describe the order) entered on _____, 20__.

(s)_____,

Attorney for Petitioners

*Address:*_____

* See Rule 15.

(As amended Apr. 22, 1993, eff. Dec. 1, 1993; Mar. 27, 2003, eff. Dec. 1, 2003.)

Form 4. Affidavit Accompanying Motion for Permission to Appeal In Forma Pauperis

Form 4. Affidavit to Accompany Motion for Leave to Appeal in Forma Pauperis

United States District Court for the _____ District of _____

A.B., Plaintiff

v.   Case No. _____

C.D., Defendant

Affidavit in Support of Motion	Instructions
I swear or affirm under penalty of perjury that, because of my poverty, I cannot prepay the docket fees of my appeal or post a bond for them. I believe I am entitled to redress. I swear or affirm under penalty of perjury under United States laws that my answers on this form are true and correct. (28 U.S.C. § 1746; 18 U.S.C § 1621.)	Complete all questions in this application and then sign it. Do not leave any blanks; if the answer to a question is "0," "none," or "not applicable (N/A)," write in that response. If you need more space to answer a question or to explain your answer, attach a separate sheet of paper identified with your name, your case's docket number, and the question number.
Signed: _____	Date: _____

My issues on appeal are:

1. For both you and your spouse estimate the average amount of money received from each of the following sources during the past 12 months. Adjust any amount that was received weekly, biweekly, quarterly, semiannually, or annually to show the monthly rate. Use gross amounts, that is, amounts before any deductions for taxes or otherwise.

Income source	Average monthly amount during the past 12 months		Amount expected next month	
	You	Spouse	You	Spouse
Employment	$_____	$_____	$_____	$_____
Self-employment	$_____	$_____	$_____	$_____
Income from real property (such as rental income)	$_____	$_____	$_____	$_____
Interest and dividends	$_____	$_____	$_____	$_____
Gifts	$_____	$_____	$_____	$_____
Alimony	$_____	$_____	$_____	$_____
Child support	$_____	$_____	$_____	$_____
Retirement (such as social security, pensions, annuities, insurance)	$_____	$_____	$_____	$_____
Disability (such as social security, insurance payments)	$_____	$_____	$_____	$_____
Unemployment payments	$_____	$_____	$_____	$_____
Public-assistance (such as welfare)	$_____	$_____	$_____	$_____
Other (specify):_____	$_____	$_____	$_____	$_____
Total monthly income:	$_____	$_____	$_____	$_____

2. *List your employment history for the past two years, most recent employer first. (Gross monthly pay is before taxes or other deductions.)*

Employer	Address	Dates of employment	Gross monthly pay

3. *List your spouse's employment history for the past two years, most recent employer first. (Gross monthly pay is before taxes or other deductions.)*

Employer	Address	Dates of employment	Gross monthly pay

4. *How much cash do you and your spouse have? $_____*
Below, state any money you or your spouse have in bank accounts or in any other financial institution.

Financial institution	Type of account	Amount you have	Amount your spouse has
		$_____	$_____
		$_____	$_____
		$_____	$_____

If you are a prisoner seeking to appeal a judgment in a civil action or proceeding, you must attach a statement certified by the appropriate institutional officer showing all receipts, expenditures, and balances during the last six months in your institutional accounts. If you have multiple accounts, perhaps because you have been in multiple institutions, attach one certified statement of each account.

5. *List the assets, and their values, which you own or your spouse owns. Do not list clothing and ordinary household furnishings.*

Home	(Value)	Other real estate	(Value)	Motor vehicle #1	(Value)
				Make & year:	
				Model:	
				Registration #:	

Motor vehicle #2	(Value)	Other assets	(Value)	Other assets	(Value)
Make & year:					
Model:					
Registration #:					

6. *State every person, business, or organization owing you or your spouse money, and the amount owed.*

Person owing you or your spouse money	Amount owed to you	Amount owed to your spouse

7. *State the persons who rely on you or your spouse for support.*

Name	Relationship	Age
_____	_____	_____
_____	_____	_____
_____	_____	_____

8. *Estimate the average monthly expenses of you and your family. Show separately the amounts paid by your spouse. Adjust any payments that are made weekly, biweekly, quarterly, semiannually, or annually to show the monthly rate.*

	You	Your Spouse
Rent or home-mortgage payment (include lot rented for mobile home)	$_____	$_____
Are real-estate taxes included? ☐Yes ☐No		
Is property insurance included? ☐Yes ☐No		
Utilities (electricity, heating fuel, water, sewer, and telephone)	$_____	$_____
Home maintenance (repairs and upkeep)	$_____	$_____
Food	$_____	$_____
Clothing	$_____	$_____
Laundry and dry-cleaning	$_____	$_____
Medical and dental expenses	$_____	$_____
Transportation (not including motor vehicle payments)	$_____	$_____
Recreation, entertainment, newspapers, magazines, etc.	$_____	$_____
Insurance (not deducted from wages or included in mortgage payments)	$_____	$_____
Homeowner's or renter's	$_____	$_____
Life	$_____	$_____
Health	$_____	$_____
Motor Vehicle	$_____	$_____
Other: _____	$_____	$_____
Taxes (not deducted from wages or included in mortgage payments) (specify): _____	$_____	$_____
Installment payments	$_____	$_____
Motor Vehicle	$_____	$_____
Credit card (name): _____	$_____	$_____
Department store (name): _____	$_____	$_____
Other: _____	$_____	$_____
Alimony, maintenance, and support paid to others	$_____	$_____
Regular expenses for operation of business, profession, or farm (attach detailed statement)	$_____	$_____
Other (specify): _____	$_____	$_____
Total monthly expenses:	$_____	$_____

9. *Do you expect any major changes to your monthly income or expenses or in your assets or liabilities during the next 12 months?*
   ☐Yes ☐No   If yes, describe on an attached sheet.

10. *Have you paid — or will you be paying — an attorney any money for services in connection with this case, including the completion of this form?* ☐Yes ☐No

   If yes, how much? $_____

   If yes, state the attorney's name, address, and telephone number:

   _____

   _____

   _____

11. *Have you paid — or will you be paying — anyone other than an attorney (such as a paralegal or a typist) any money for services in connection with this case, including the completion of this form?*
    ☐Yes ☐No

   If yes, how much? $_____

   If yes, state the person's name, address, and telephone number:

   _____

   _____

   _____

12. *Provide any other information that will help explain why you cannot pay the docket fees for your appeal.*

13. *State the address of your legal residence.*

   _____

   _____

   Your daytime phone number: (_____) _____

   Your age: _____ Your years of schooling: _____

   Your social-security number: _____

(As amended Apr. 24, 1998, eff. Dec. 1, 1998.)

Form 5. Notice of Appeal to a Court of Appeals from a Judgment or Order of a District Court or a Bankruptcy Appellate Panel

United States District Court for the _____
                    District of _____

In re

_____,

                Debtor

_____,   File No. _____

                Plaintiff

                   v.

_____,

                Defendant

Notice of Appeal to United States Court of Appeals for the
                _____ Circuit

_____, the plaintiff [or defendant or other party] appeals to the United States Court of Appeals for the _____ Circuit from the final judgment [or order or decree] of the district court for the district of _____ [or bankruptcy appellate panel of the _____ circuit], entered in this case on _____, 20___ [here describe the judgment, order, or decree]
_____

The parties to the judgment [or order or decree] appealed from and the names and addresses of their respective attorneys are as follows:

                        Dated _____
                        Signed _____
                               Attorney for Appellant
                        Address: _____
                        _____

(As added Apr. 25, 1989, eff. Dec. 1, 1989; amended Mar. 27, 2003, eff. Dec. 1, 2003.)

Form 6. Certificate of Compliance With Rule 32(a)

Form 6. Certificate of Compliance With Rule 32(a)

Certificate of Compliance With Type-Volume Limitation, Typeface Requirements, and Type Style Requirements

1.   This brief complies with the type-volume limitation of Fed. R. App. P. 32(a)(7)(B) because:

☐ this brief contains [*state the number of*] words, excluding the parts of the brief exempted by Fed. R. App. P. 32(a)(7)(B)(iii), *or*

☐ this brief uses a monospaced typeface and contains [*state the number of*] lines of text, excluding the parts of the brief exempted by Fed. R. App. P. 32(a)(7)(B)(iii).

2.   This brief complies with the typeface requirements of Fed. R. App. P. 32(a)(5) and the type style requirements of Fed. R. App. P. 32(a)(6) because:

☐ this brief has been prepared in a proportionally spaced typeface using [*state name and version of word processing program*] in [*state font size and name of type style*], or

☐ this brief has been prepared in a monospaced typeface using [*state name and version of word processing program*] with [*state number of characters per inch and name of type style*].

(s)_____

Attorney for _____

Dated: _____

(As added Apr. 29, 2002, eff. Dec. 1, 2002.)

APPENDIX B:
Appellant's Brief: New York State Court of Appeals

Time for Argument: 15 Minutes

To be argued by
Mark Dwyer

Court of Appeals *
STATE OF NEW YORK

THE PEOPLE OF THE STATE OF NEW YORK

Appellant,

against

CLARENCE MOORE,

Defendant-Respondent.

APPELLANT'S BRIEF AND APPENDIX

Robert M. Morgenthau
District Attorney
New York County
Attorney for Appellant
155 Leonard Street
New York, New York 10013
(212) 553-9000

Robert M. Pitler
Mark Dwyer
 Assistant District Attorneys
  Of Counsel

*Condensed and edited. For "Content of briefs and appendices," see N.Y. CPLR 5528.

TABLE OF CONTENTS

APPENDIX
[Not Reproduced Here]

Appellant's Brief

Statement

By permission of the Honorable Samuel J. Silverman, granted May 2, 1978, the People of the State of New York appeal from an order of the Appellate Division, First Department, entered April 18, 1978 (opinion by Murphy, P.J.). That order reversed, on the law, a judgment of the Supreme Court, New York County (Leff, J.), rendered November 9, 1976, by which defendant was convicted of Burglary in the Third Degree (Penal Law Section 140.20) and sentenced as a predicate felon to an indeterminate term of imprisonment of from two to four years. The order of the Appellate Division also vacated defendant's guilty plea, granted defendant's motion to suppress evidence, and dismissed the indictment. Defendant had been incarcerated pursuant to the judgment against him but was released following the decision of the Appellate Division.

Question Presented

May a police officer approach and question a man when, during a patrol at night in an area of Manhattan in which numbers of burglaries have recently taken place, the officer observes that man walking at a fast pace, with a noticeable limp, covered with snow and carrying a television set in a pillowcase thrown over his shoulder?

Answer of the court below: No, testimony and circumstances were inadequate to provide the detective with sufficient cause to approach and question the defendant.

Introduction

On the evening of January 22, 1976, defendant Clarence Moore burglarized an apartment on West 149th Street in Manhattan. Defendant stole a television set, a fur coat, and several pieces of jewelry.

Defendant carried those items from the apartment in a pillowcase thrown over his shoulder. Detective John Mattias, on an anti-burglary patrol on Eighth Avenue, observed defendant walking at a rapid pace on that avenue and could see the outline of the television set inside the pillowcase. He also noticed that defendant walked with a limp, and was covered with snow. The detective approached defendant to inquire about his business. After defendant gave vague and evasive answers, stated incorrectly the brand name of the television set, and was discovered also to have a fur coat and jewelry in the pillowcase, Detective Mattias concluded that those items were stolen and took defendant into custody.

Defendant was subsequently indicted for Burglary in the Second Degree and related offenses. On September 17, 1976, the Honorable Richard G. Denzer presided at a suppression hearing on defendant's motion to suppress the television set and the other stolen property recovered on January 22, 1976. Justice Denzer concluded at the close of the hearing that both the decision to question defendant and the decision to arrest him had been reasonable. He therefore denied defendant's suppression motion.

On October 8, 1976, defendant pleaded guilty before the Honorable James J. Leff to Burglary in the Third Degree. On November 9, 1976, defendant was sentenced as a predicate felon to a term of imprisonment of from two to four years.

In an opinion by Presiding Justice Francis T. Murphy, the Appellate Division, First Department, reversed on the law and ordered the suppression of the stolen property recovered from defendant. 62 A.D.2d 155. The court felt that the sight of defendant limping, walking quickly, covered with snow, and carrying a pillowcase in which Detective Mattias believed he could see the outline of a television set, was inadequate to provide the detective with sufficient cause to approach defendant and question him.

Justice Samuel J. Silverman dissented. He first endorsed the determination of Justice Denzer, after the suppression hearing, that the circumstances of the original sighting of defendant provided an objective, credible justification for the minimal intrusion of approaching to request information. Justice Silverman further concluded that defendant's answers to the questions posed, the extraordinary combination of a television set, a fur coat, and jewelry in a pillowcase, and defendant's inability correctly to state the brand name of the television set, had created reasonable cause to take defendant into custody.

On May 2, 1978, after timely application by the People, Justice Silverman issued a certificate granting leave to appeal to this Court. Since the questions before this Court are questions of law, the Court has jurisdiction to hear the instant appeal pursuant to CPL Section 450.90 and 470.35.

THE EVIDENCE AT THE HEARING
ON THE MOTION TO SUPPRESS

The People's Case

On the evening of January 22, 1976, Detective John Mattias and his partner, Officer Douglas Brussell, were assigned to an anti-burglary patrol in an area on Manhattan's upper west side in which a series of burglaries had taken place (A15, A24, A28).[1] At about 7:40 p.m. the officers, who were in a police department taxicab, drove past defendant on Eighth Avenue between 148th Street and 149th Street (A15-16, A18, A20-21). Defendant was the only person on the street (A28). He was walking south toward 148th Street at a fast pace and with a noticeable limp; his hair and his outer garments "from his head to his feet" were covered with snow (A15-16, A18, A19). Defendant was carrying a pillowcase over his shoulder, and Detective Mattias saw the outline of a television set inside that

---

1   Parenthetical references preceded by the letter "A" are to pages of appellant's appendix.

pillowcase (A16, A20, A28). He immediately turned to his partner and stated that defendant appeared to have a television set inside his sack (A16).

Detective Mattias backed up the cab, stepped out into the street, asked defendant to stop, and identified himself as a police officer (A16, A23). The detective asked from where defendant was coming; defendant responded that he had just been to a friend's house on 149th Street (A16, A19, A23-24). The detective asked who the friend was and where he lived; defendant did not reply (A16, A19, A24). At about this time, the detective noticed that defendant had sustained a cut to the left side of his head (A22).

Detective Mattias next asked defendant what he was carrying in his sack. Defendant said he had a television set and a fur coat (A16, A24). When the detective inquired about what type of set defendant was carrying, defendant replied that it was a Sony portable (A16, A24, A27). Detective Mattias asked if he could look into the sack; defendant replied that he could, and opened the pillowcase (A16, A24, A27). When the detective looked inside the pillowcase, he saw that the television set had in fact been made by General Electric, and not by Sony (A16, A24, A27). Also in the pillowcase were a fur coat and some jewelry (A20, A24).

Defendant was taken by Detective Mattias to the 32nd Precinct station house and charged with possession of stolen property (A16-17, A25). Defendant was searched at the station and house, and after a screwdriver was recovered from him, defendant was also charged with possession of burglar's tools (A17, A19). Defendant's head injury was treated that night either at Harlem Hospital or at the station house (A22).

The Defendant's Case

Defendant presented no witnesses.

The Court's Findings and Decision

Justice Denzer stated at the conclusion of the suppression hearing that there was no doubt in his mind that the circumstances of the initial sighting of defendant provided reason for Detective Mattias to stop defendant for questioning. Justice Denzer cited defendant's snow-covered appearance, his limp, the absence of other persons on the street, and the fact that defendant carried a pillowcase in which could be seen the outline of a television set (A33-34). Justice Denzer further found that the subsequent questioning of defendant had been reasonable and had provided ample cause to take defendant into custody. Specifically, the justice referred to defendant's unwillingness to explain from where he had come, his failure to explain where he had obtained the property he carried, and his incorrect identification of the brand name of the television set (A34-35). Justice Denzer concluded:

> The salient flavor of the case, throughout, seems to me the reasonableness of the police officer's action. Everything he did in this case would seem reasonable to any person impartially viewing the conduct of the police officer.

Defendant's motion was, accordingly, denied (A35).

POINT

Detective Mattias acted reasonably in questioning defendant under circumstances indicating that defendant had committed a burglary or was in possession of stolen property.

In *People v. DeBour*, 40 N.Y.2d 210 (1976), this Court confirmed the authority of police officers to make reasonable inquiry of a citizen, even in the absence of circumstances justifying a forcible seizure of that citizen. This case presents an uncomplicated question of whether the facts confronting Detective Mattias on the night of January 22, 1976, were sufficient to justify his decision to approach defendant and make an inquiry. The hearing court found that the facts were sufficient.

The majority in the Appellate Division, however, chose to view this case as a test of whether, after DeBour, a black man can carry a television set about the streets of New York without subjecting himself to interrogation. 62 A.D.2d at 156. Defendant is black; obviously that fact provided no cause for Detective Mattias to question him. But, defendant was not questioned because he was black. Absolutely nothing in the record suggests that the police singled out defendant, a black man in a black neighborhood, for harassment on account of his race. *Cf. People v. Tinsley*, 48 A.D.2d 779 (1st Dept. 1975), *rev'd on dissenting opinion*, 39 N.Y.2d 1028 (1976).

Defendant in fact was questioned because he was carrying a television set in a pillowcase thrown over his shoulder, because he was doing so in a neighborhood in which a series of burglaries had taken place, because he was covered with snow, and because he was walking alone at night at a fast pace and with a limp. Certain of these circumstances of Detective Mattias' sighting of defendant, even considered apart from the others, were highly suspicious and strongly suggested that a burglary had taken place. First, defendant's carrying any sizeable object while walking at a fast pace, and while he was alone after dark in an area in which a number of burglaries had taken place, would have been sufficient at least to call attention to him. Second, Detective Mattias noted as soon as he saw defendant that the object defendant was carrying appeared to be a television set. Portable television sets are frequent targets of burglars. They are not often carried about after dark by their owners, and most certainly the owner of a television set would rarely carry it in a pillow case thrown over his shoulder. Third, defendant was limping, and was covered "from his head down to his feet" with snow. It did not snow in New York City on January 22, 1976, but there was snow on the ground that day.[2]

---

2   This Court can take judicial notice that there was no precipitation in New York City on January 22, 1976. The Court can also notice that 2.7 inches of snow had fallen on the City during the two previous days. *See* "Monthly Summary of New York, New York Local Climatological Data," National Oceanic and Atmospheric Administration, Environmental Data Service (January 1976). Defendant's appearance and his limp thus suggested that if he had not struggled with another, he had at least tumbled to the ground, perhaps after a jump or fall of some distance.

But whether or not Detective Mattias' inquiry would have been justified by any of the individual circumstances he observed, all those circumstances considered together certainly provided cause for questioning. Detective Mattias determined to ask questions after he observed defendant's rapid pace, his limp, and his snow-covered appearance, that defendant in a neighborhood recently beset by burglars was carrying a television set in a sack thrown over his shoulder, and that defendant was alone with his burden after dark. The detective's decision to make an inquiry, rather than arrest defendant or simply allow him to make his escape, is precisely the decision that would be expected of a conscientious police officer attempting, in these circumstances, to do his duty and to obey the rule of *People v. DeBour.*

The majority in the Appellate Division, having suggested that defendant was stopped because of his race, concluded that no other facts could justify Detective Mattias' inquiry by isolating one circumstance of the encounter from all the others. The court dismissed from consideration all facts except that defendant carried a television set in a sack, 62 A.D.2d at 156-57, and held that this single circumstance did not justify an inquiry. If instead all the other circumstances of the encounter are considered along with the fact that defendant was carrying a television set in a sack, it is clear that the ruling of the Appellate Division is incorrect. Justice Denzer, after the suppression hearing, and Justice Silverman, in the Appellate Division, properly took account of all the circumstances of the incident; as a result, both justices concluded that Detective Mattias' actions were reasonable.

This Court has reached the same conclusion in evaluating similar police conduct triggered by circumstances far less suspicious than those of this case. In *People v. DeBour* itself, this Court held that officers had properly questioned the defendant after the defendant, while walking alone at night in a high-crime area, chose to cross the street rather than pass near the officers. In *People v. Rosemond*, 26 N.Y.2d 101 (1970), this Court heard a challenge to a police decision to question two men who entered an apartment building, and shortly afterwards emerged from it with a suitcase and a shopping bag. The Court reasoned:

> [T]he police can and should find out about unusual situations they see, as well as suspicious ones. It is unwise, and perhaps futile, to codify them or to prescribe them precisely in advance as a rule of law. To a very large extent what is unusual enough to call for inquiry must rest in the professional experience of the police.

Id. at 104. The Court then concluded that the inquiry directed to Rosemond and his companion was "undoubtedly lawful." *Id.* at 105; *see also People v. Brown*, 32 N.Y.2d 172 (1973) (upholding the questioning, but not the subsequent arrest, of a man carrying a crowbar and an automobile battery); *People v. Ray*, 62 A.D.2d 772 (1st Dept. 1978); *People v. Wheeler*, 61 A.D.2d 737 (1st Dept. 1978); *People v. Magnifico*, 59 A.D.2d 914 (2d Dept. 1977).

By no means to the contrary is *People v. Davis*, 36 N.Y.2d 280, *cert. denied*, 423 U.S. 876 (1975), cited in the majority opinion below. In *Davis*, a police officer saw the defendant, a male, take matches from a purse and then pass the purse to a female companion. Inside the purse the officer could see papers which, he later testified, could have been either glassine envelopes or candy wrappers. The officer thereupon arrested the defendant. Had Detective Mattias in this case made an immediate arrest of defendant, *Davis* might be relevant to an evaluation of his conduct. But *Davis* has little to say about whether the limited inquiry actually conducted by Detective Mattias was justified.

In short, Detective Mattias' decision to question defendant was reasonable. The inquiry was, moreover, conducted reasonably. The Detective backed up his vehicle, asked defendant to stop, and identified himself as an officer. After stepping out of the vehicle, he asked from where defendant had come. Defendant's only response was "from a friend's house on 149th street." When the detective asked for the friend's name and for his address, defendant did not reply. The detective also asked what defendant had in the pillow case; defendant replied that he had a television set and a fur coat. These questions were "circumscribed in scope to [the detective's] task," *People v. DeBour*, 40 N.Y.2d at 220. Nothing in the record suggests that defendant was in any way subjected to a loss of dignity.

At this point, Detective Mattias had heard from defendant an incomplete and unsatisfactory explanation for his presence and had learned that defendant carried an extraordinary pair of items, a television set and a fur coat, inside his pillowcase. The detective had by now also observed that defendant had received an injury to the left side of his head; that factor, considered with defendant's limp and his snowy appearance, again suggested that defendant had jumped or fallen some distance to the ground. Under these circumstances, Detective Mattias quite understandably determined to conduct a simple test of whether defendant owned the items he carried. He asked defendant the brand name of the television set. Defendant replied that the television was a Sony. The detective asked to see the set; when defendant opened the pillowcase, the detective saw that the television set had in fact been made by General Electric.

This test of ownership was a sensible attempt to establish whether or not defendant had committed a crime, without subjecting him to intimidation or a loss of dignity. The request for a look inside the pillowcase was similar in nature to the police officers' request in the *DeBour* case that Louis DeBour open his jacket so that the officers could determine the cause of the bulge they observed. *See People v. DeBour*, 40 N.Y.2d at 220-21. If Detective Mattias did not, like the officers in *DeBour*, have cause to be concerned for his safety before he put his request to defendant, he nevertheless faced circumstances far more indicative of criminal behavior than those that confronted the officers who questioned DeBour. Moreover, the request that defendant open the pillowcase in which he carried a television set was less intrusive on personal privacy than the request that DeBour open his jacket. In any event, here as in *DeBour* the inspection request was a "minimal intrusion" that was "consonant with the respect and privacy of the individual." *People v. DeBour*, 40 N.Y.2d at 221; *see also People v. Cruz*, 43 N.Y.2d 786 (1977) (holding that the police acted reasonably in inquiring to determine what the defendant held in his hand).

The discovery that defendant had incorrectly identified the brand name of the television set and that the pillowcase contained other valuables that defendant had not mentioned, considered with defendant's failure to explain his possession of the unusual items he carried and with all the preceding circumstances, provided Detective Mattias with probable cause to believe that defendant had committed a crime. Under the circumstances, any reasonable man would have believed that defendant was guilty of burglary, or that defendant at the very least was in possession of stolen property. Defendant was at that point properly taken into custody.

. . . .

People v. DeBour requires that police officers respond in measured fashion to the circumstances they face. While the suspicion engendered by initial observations may not support highly intrusive action, it may nevertheless justify inquiry; as a result of such inquiry,

> the degree of belief possessed at the point of inception may blossom by virtue of responses or other matters which authorize and indeed require additional action as the scenario unfolds.

40 N.Y.2d at 225. The detective in this case acted precisely in accordance with the dictates of *DeBour*; he questioned defendant, and later escalated his inquiry, only in reasonable response to developing circumstances. The conclusion of the court below was that any inquiry was improper. That conclusion denies the police exercise of "a normal power" and fulfillment of "a necessary duty." *People v. Rivera*, 14 N.Y.2d 441, 445 (1964). Or, as the United States Supreme Court expressed it in the context of a stop and frisk, the court below has ruled that the officer was required "to simply shrug his shoulders and allow a crime to occur [and] a criminal to escape." *Adams v. Williams*, 407 U.S. 143, 145 (1972). Neither the State nor the Federal Constitution requires that result, and this Court should not permit it to stand.

Conclusion

The order of the Appellate Division should be reversed and the case remitted to that court for a determination on the facts.

Respectfully submitted,

Robert M. Morgenthau
District Attorney
New York County

Robert M. Pitler
Mark Dwyer
    Assistant District Attorneys
    of Counsel

November 19, 1978

APPENDIX C:
Petition for Writ of Certiorari: Supreme Court of the United States

No. [94-1660]*

IN THE
SUPREME COURT OF THE UNITED STATES
OCTOBER TERM, 1994

AMERICAN AIRLINES, INC.,
Petitioner,
vs.
LAWRENCE B. LOCKWOOD,
Respondent.

Petition for Writ of Certiorari to the
United States Court of Appeals
for the Federal Circuit

PETITION FOR WRIT OF CERTIORARI

Bruce J. Ennis, Jr.

Paul M. Smith

JENNER & BLOCK

601 Thirteenth Street, N.W.

Washington D.C. 20005

(202) 639-6000

Of Counsel:
R. Bruce Wark

Don W. Martens
Counsel of Record

Joseph R. Re

Paul A. Stewart

KNOBBE, MARTENS, OLSON & BEAR

620 Newport Center Drive

Sixteenth Floor

Newport Beach, CA 92660

(714) 760-0404

Attorneys for Petitioner
AMERICAN AIRLINES, INC.

---

* [Editors' Note: This petition is a truncated version of the petition filed and granted in *In re Lockwood*, 50 F.3d 966 (Fed. Cir.), *vacated*, 515 U.S. 1182 (1995). The Court assigns docket number days after the brief is filed. *See* SUP. CT. R. 34(1)(a); *see also* SUP. CT. R. 21 (governing briefs on the merits).]

QUESTION PRESENTED

In an action in which the sole claim to be tried is a claim under the Declaratory Judgment Act to have a patent declared invalid, is there a right to a jury trial under the Seventh Amendment of the United States Constitution?

LIST OF PARTIES TO THE PROCEEDING
PURSUANT TO RULES 14.1(b) AND 29.1

Pursuant to Supreme Court Rule 14.1(b), Petitioner American Airlines, Inc. certifies that the names of all parties to this proceeding appear in the caption of this Petition for Writ of Certiorari.

Pursuant to Supreme Court Rule 29.1, Petitioner American Airlines, Inc. certifies that AMR, Inc. Is the parent company of American Airlines, Inc. There are not subsidiaries or affiliates of American Airlines, Inc. that have issued shares to the public.

TABLE OF CONTENTS

TABLE OF AUTHORITIES

* * *

CONSTITUTIONAL PROVISIONS

STATUTES

BOOKS

PETITION FOR WRIT OF CERTIORARI

Petitioner American Airlines, Inc. ("American") respectfully petitions this Court for a writ of certiorari to review the order of the Court of Appeals for the Federal Circuit mandating a jury trial on American's claim for a declaration that two patents are invalid.

REPORTED DECISIONS

The following decisions and opinions in this case directly relating to the question presented have been reported and are included in the designated appendices:

In re Lockwood, 33 U.S.P.Q.2d (BNA) 1406 (Fed. Cir. 1995) (mandating trial by jury on rehearing and denying rehearing in banc) (App. A, App. B).

In re Lockwood, 33 U.S.P.Q.2d (BNA) 1907 (Fed. Cir. 1995) (Nies, J., dissenting from denial of rehearing in banc) (App. C).

In re Lockwood, 30 U.S.P.Q.2d (BNA) 1292 (Fed. Cir. 1994) (mandating trial by jury) (App. D).

Lockwood v. American Airlines, Inc., 47 Pat. Trademark & Copyright Journal (BNA) No. 1169 (S.D. Cal. 1993) (striking jury demand) (App. E, App. F).

The District Court decisions in this case bifurcating trial, 1992 U.S. Dist. LEXIS 22077, granting partial summary judgment, 834 F. Supp. 1246, *reh'g denied*, 847 F. Supp. 777, and denying entry of judgment, 29 U.S.P.Q.2d (BNA) 1637, have been reported but are not directly relevant to the question presented.

STATEMENT OF JURISDICTION

American seeks review of an order of the Court of Appeals for the Federal Circuit issued January 11, 1995. App. A. That order, issued on rehearing, directed the District Court, by writ of mandamus, to conduct a jury trial in this case.

That same day, the Court of Appeals denied American's suggestion for rehearing in banc. App. B. Circuit Judge Nies, joined by Chief Judge Archer and Circuit Judge Plager, filed an opinion dissenting from the denial of rehearing in banc. App. C.

This Court has jurisdiction under 28 U.S.C. § 1254(1) to review the Court of Appeals' decision by writ of certiorari. The Court of Appeals had jurisdiction to issue the writ of mandamus under the All Writs Act, 28 U.S.C. § 1651. The District Court has jurisdiction over this case under 28 U.S.C. §§ 1331, 1338.

CONSTITUTIONAL PROVISIONS AND STATUTES INVOLVED

The following constitutional provisions and statutes are involved in this case:

United States Constitution, Seventh Amendment

In suits at common law, where the value in controversy shall exceed twenty dollars, the right of trial by jury shall be preserved, and no fact tried by jury, shall be otherwise re-examined in any Court of the United States, than according to the rules of the common law.

Declaratory Judgment Act, 28 U.S.C. § 2201(a)

In a case of actual controversy within its jurisdiction, . . . any court of the United States, upon the filing of an appropriate pleading, may declare the rights and other legal relations of any interested party seeking such declaration, whether or not further relief is or could be sought. Any such declaration shall have the force and effect of a final judgment or decree and shall be reviewable as such.

STATEMENT OF THE CASE

The case underlying this petition is an action to invalidate two patents. This petition, however, involves no issues of patent law. Rather, the issue presented in this petition relates strictly to the interpretation of the Seventh Amendment of the United States Constitution. As Circuit Judge Nies explained below:

> It is rare for patent litigation to present an appellate court with only constitutional issues. This case is that rarity. C1.

In the underlying action, Respondent Lawrence B. Lockwood ("Lockwood") alleged American infringed two patents. Lockwood demanded a jury. American counterclaimed for a declaration that the patents are invalid and not infringed. American did not demand a jury.

The District Court ruled on summary judgment that American does not infringe either of the patents. *See Lockwood v. American Airlines, Inc.*, 834 F. Supp. 1246 (S.D. Cal. 1993), *reh'g denied*, 847 F. Supp. 777 (S.D. Cal. 1994). The District Court's ruling disposed of all of Lockwood's claims for relief and granted American the full relief it requested on its counterclaim for a declaration of noninfringement.

This relief alone, however, was inadequate to resolve the controversy between the parties. American feared further patent litigation by Lockwood. Accordingly, American elected to pursue its counterclaims for a declaration of patent invalidity. The District Court exercised its discretion and retained jurisdiction over these declaratory judgment counterclaims.

American then moved to strike Lockwood's jury demand. The District Court granted American's motion. "[T]he remaining claims," the District Court concluded, "are equitable in nature." E5. Thus, the court held, "the plaintiff is not entitled to a trial by jury as a matter of right." *Id.* The District Court set this case for trial to the court. F2.[1]

Lockwood petitioned the Court of Appeals for the Federal Circuit to review the District Court's ruling by writ of mandamus. Without oral argument, the Federal Circuit granted the writ and directed the District Court to conduct a jury trial.

The Federal Circuit initially issued its decision as a nonprecedential order. App. D. American requested rehearing and rehearing in banc. The Federal Circuit granted the petition for rehearing, vacated its nonprecedential decision, and issued a 30-page precedential opinion. App. C. In that opinion, the Federal Circuit once again ruled that Lockwood has a constitutional right to have a jury decide American's claim for declaratory relief.

The Federal Circuit denied American's suggestion for rehearing in banc. App. B. Circuit Judge Nies authored a 21-page dissent, joined by Chief Judge Archer and Circuit Judge Plager. App. C. In her dissent, Judge Nies wrote that this Court should review the Federal Circuit's decision because of its conflict with the precedents of this Court and the other circuits. C21.

Judge Nies also explained the practical importance of the question presented in this case. Demands for jury trials in patent cases, she wrote, were rarely made twenty-five years ago. C1-C2. Now, however, they are commonplace. C2 & n.1. In light of this change, she stressed:

> No more important nor contentious an issue arises in patent law jurisprudence than the appropriate role of juries in patent litigation. C2.

American now seeks review of the Federal Circuit's order mandating a jury trial on American's claim for declaratory relief. The District Court has scheduled trial for August 15, 1995, and absent the grant of this petition for writ of certiorari by this Court, the trial will be presented to a jury.

SUMMARY OF ARGUMENT

The Federal Circuit held in this case that a patent owner has a Seventh Amendment right to a jury trial in an action where the only claim to be tried is one seeking a declaratory judgment invalidating the patent. This ruling in no way hinged upon the Federal Circuit's special expertise in substantive patent law.

Rather, the Federal Circuit's decision rests entirely upon its outright rejection of this Court's decisions interpreting the Seventh Amendment and the Declaratory Judgment Act. To endorse the claim of a jury right in this case, the Federal Circuit cast aside this Court's basic test for the determination of Seventh Amendment rights, rejected this Court's precedents holding there is no right to a jury

---

1   Lockwood later amended his Complaint to allege infringement of a third patent. The District Court dismissed this claim on summary judgment, ruling the patent invalid and not infringed.

trial in actions to set aside patents and other government grants, and also rejected this Court's precedents holding that declaratory relief is an equitable form of relief. As Judge Nies remarked in dissent, the Federal Circuit's decision "leaves a wide path strewn with the carnage of cases declared overruled or obsolete." C13 n.6.

In addition, the Federal Circuit has created a conflict with its sister circuits in areas outside of its expertise in patent law. Before the Federal Circuit's decision, the circuit courts had uniformly held there is no right to a jury trial in actions to invalidate intellectual property rights, such as trademarks or copyrights. The court also refused to follow the decisions of the Second and Ninth Circuits, as well as the uniform practice of all of the district courts before the merger of law and equity, each of which made clear that there is no right to a jury trial in actions to invalidate patents. Judge Nies correctly observed that "this case creates the type of conflict with other circuits that warrants Supreme Court review." C21.

* * *

REASONS FOR GRANTING THE WRIT

I.

THE QUESTION PRESENTED IS ONE OF EXTRAORDINARY NATIONAL IMPORTANCE THAT THE LOWER COURTS WILL NOT FURTHER ANALYZE

This Court has repeatedly recognized the importance to the public at large of resolving questions of patent invalidity. *Cardinal Chemical Co. v. Morton Int'l, Inc.*, 113 S. Ct. 1967, 1977 (1993) (citing *Blonder-Tongue Labs., Inc. v. University of Illinois Found.*, 402 U.S. 313, 336 (1971)). Unlike the issue of patent infringement, which directly affects only the litigants themselves, a patent's validity affects the public at large. *See Sinclair & Carroll Co. v. Interchemical Corp.*, 325 U.S. 327, 330 (1945); *see also Pope Mfg. Co. v. Gormully & Jeffrey Mfg. Co.*, 144 U.S. 224, 234 (1892). As Judge Nies noted in her dissent in this case, the Federal Circuit itself has recognized that "[t]he grant of a valid patent is primarily of a public concern." C5 (quoting *Patlex Corp. v. Mossinghoff*, 758 F.2d 594, 604 (Fed. Cir. 1985)).

Because the Federal Circuit has exclusive jurisdiction over appeals from all of the district courts in patent cases, 28 U.S.C. § 1295(a)(1), its decision will require juries on demand in all patent validity trials nationwide. As this case demonstrates, the Federal Circuit will mandate jury trials even within circuits having controlling precedent to the contrary. A27 (dismissing Ninth Circuit precedents). This case therefore presents "a matter of special importance to the entire Nation." *Cardinal Chemical*, 113 S. Ct. at 1971.

Now more than ever this Court should take the opportunity to address the right to a jury trial in actions to invalidate patents. Historically, "the overwhelming tendency" was to try patent cases without juries. *Blonder-Tongue*, 402 U.S. at 336.[2] In light of this history, it is not surprising, as Judge Nies noted, that this Court has not addressed the role of juries in patent cases in this century. C1. Today, however, juries are routinely demanded. C2 & n.1.

Unless corrected by this Court, the Federal Circuit's ruling will impose a significant burden on the resources of the federal judiciary by requiring juries where they have never been required before. This burden will extend well beyond patent cases. Departing from all precedent, the Federal Circuit relied upon Lockwood's request for damages in a ***dismissed*** complaint to award him a jury trial on American's claim for declaratory relief. *See* A24-A25. The mere pleading of even a meritless claim for damages, according to the Federal Circuit, gives a patent owner the right to a jury trial.

Because of the Federal Circuit's exclusive nationwide subject matter jurisdiction, and its refusal to rehear this case in banc, this Court will not benefit from further discussion of the question presented by the lower courts. Further debate outside of this Court has been foreclosed by the Federal Circuit. Therefore, there is no reason for this Court to refrain from definitively resolving the question presented now.

II.

THE FEDERAL CIRCUIT'S DECISION CONFLICTS WITH MANY DECISIONS OF THIS COURT AND OTHER CIRCUITS

A. The Federal Circuit Has Rejected Outright This Court's Basic Test For Determining The Scope Of Seventh Amendment Rights

The Seventh Amendment preserves the right to a jury trial only in civil actions "at common law." U.S. Const. amend. VII; *Chauffeurs, Teamsters and Helpers, Local No. 391 v. Terry*, 494 U.S. 558, 564 (1990). An action "at common law" is one which would have been tried to a common law court, not an equity court, in Eighteenth Century England. *Tull v. United States*, 481 U.S. 412, 417 (1987).

This Court has repeatedly instructed the lower courts that they must use a two-part test to determine whether an action is one at common law. The lower courts "must examine ***both*** the nature of the action ***and*** of the remedy sought" to determine whether the Seventh Amendment extends to a particular case. *Id.* (emphasis added). The right to jury trial exists only if "on balance, these two factors indicate that a party is entitled to a jury trial." *Granfinanciera, S.A. v. Nordberg*, 492 U.S. 33, 42 (1989).

---

2   For example, as this Court noted in *Blonder-Tongue*, only 2 of 131 patent cases tried in 1968 were tried to juries. *Blonder-Tongue*, 402 U.S. at 336 n.30.

The Federal Circuit has now repudiated this Court's Seventh Amendment test. According to the Federal Circuit:

> if a particular action entails *either* the adjudication of legal rights, *or, alternatively*, the implementation of legal remedies, the district court *must* honor a jury demand.

A13 (emphasis added, citations omitted). Thus, contrary to this Court's precedents, the Federal Circuit has held that it need not look to both factors, and no balancing is required.

Consistent with its newly formulated test, the Federal Circuit disregarded the nature of the relief sought by American, even though this Court has repeatedly emphasized that the relief requested is the primary factor to be considered in the Seventh Amendment analysis.[3]

As Judge Nies explained in dissent, "[t]he panel's holding is unprecedented." C12. "The panel recognizes the two part test (18th Century analog **AND** remedy) announced repeatedly but changes the 'and' to 'or.'" C11 (as in original). "By completely disregarding any analysis of the remedy sought in this case, the panel is accomplishing in this case what the Court specifically rejected in *Tull*." C12

This Court should grant certiorari to review the Federal Circuit's outright refusal to follow this Court's basic Seventh Amendment test.

B. The Federal Circuit's Decision Is In Direct Conflict With This Court's Precedents Holding That Actions To Set Aside Patents And Other Government Grants Are Equitable Actions

The relief sought by American in this case is a declaration that two patents are invalid. Had the Federal Circuit adhered to this Court's precedents, it would have determined that this is an equitable action for equitable relief. Before the merger of law and equity, this Court twice held that actions to invalidate patents are equitable actions triable in a court of equity.

The first of these decisions was *Mowry v. Whitney*, 81 U.S. (14 Wall.) 434 (1872), in which this Court explained in great detail the history of actions to invalidate patents in both the English and American courts. That history showed to this Court that the traditional actions to set aside patents in both England and the United States were actions in equity.

"The ancient mode of doing this in the English courts," this Court explained, "was by scire facias." *Id.* at 439. "The scire facias to repeal a patent *was brought in chancery* where the patent was of record." *Id.* at 440 (emphasis added). In addition to scire facias, the English equity courts could also invalidate patents by

---

3   *See Wooddell v. I.B.E.W., Local 71*, 502 U.S. 93, 97 (1991); *Chauffeurs*, 494 U.S. at 565; *Granfunanciera*, 492 U.S at 42; *Tull*, 481 U.S. at 421; *Cirtis v. Loether*, 415 U.S. 189, 196 (1974).

bill of chancery. *Id.* (citing *Attorney General v. Vernon,* 1 Vern. 277, and *Jackson v. Lawton,* 10 Johns. 24).

The practice of invalidating patents in courts of equity was carried over into the United States. As this Court explained, "though in this country the writ of scire facias is not in use as a chancery proceeding, *the nature of the chancery jurisdiction and its mode of proceeding have established it as the appropriate tribunal for the annulling of a grant or patent from the government."* *Mowry,* 81 U.S. (14 Wall.) at 440 (emphasis added).

This Court revisited the subject in *United States v. American Bell Telephone Co.,* 128 U.S. 315, 359-73 (1888), and again concluded that the proper forum for an action to invalidate a patent was a court of equity.

Moreover, this Court's decisions in *Mowry* and *American Bell* do not stand alone. They are part of a broader class of this Court's cases holding that actions to set aside government grants must be tried in a court of equity.

The first of these was *Stone v. United States,* 69 U.S. (2 Wall.) 525 (1865), cited by the *Mowry* Court as dispositive. *See Mowry,* 81 U.S. (14 Wall.) at 440. In *Stone,* this Court held that an action to set aside a patent granting title to real property should be brought by "a bill in chancery." *Id.* at 535. This Court reached the same conclusion in *United States v. San Jacinto Tin Co.,* 125 U.S. 273, 281 (1888), citing *Stone* and *Mowry* as dispositive.

Similarly, in *Luria v. United States,* 231 U.S. 9 (1913), this Court held that an action to cancel a certificate of citizenship is "not a suit at common law." *Id.* at 27. Rather, "[t]he right asserted and the remedy sought were essentially equitable, not legal." *Id.* Accordingly, this Court held that there is no right to a jury trial in such actions. *Id.* at 28. This Court cited *Stone, San Jacinto Tin,* and *American Bell* in support of its decision. *Id.* at 28.

In short, this Court's decisions have consistently made clear that actions to set aside government grants, including patents for inventions, must be brought in a court of equity. For Seventh Amendment purposes, all of these actions have been treated alike by this Court, and all of these actions are triable without a jury.[4]

The Federal Circuit, however, rejected precedent and history. It dismissed this Court's decisions in *Mowry* and *American Bell* in a footnote, and did not cite this Court's decisions in *Stone, San Jacinto Tin,* or *Luria* at all. *See* A19 n.9. The Federal Circuit held that *Mowry* and *American Bell* are limited to actions to declare a patent "unenforceable," and do not apply to actions to declare a patent "invalid." A19-A20 n.9. However, as Judge Nies explained in dissent, *Mowry* expressly ap-

---

4   Except for the Federal Circuit, the circuit courts have followed suit, denying requests for jury trials in all actions to set aside government grants. *See, e.g., United States v. Kairys,* 782 F.2d 1374, 1384 (7th Cir.), *cert denied,* 476 U.S. 1153 (1986) (certificate of citizenship); *Anti-Monopoly, Inc. v. General Mills Fun Group,* 611 F.2d 296, 307 (9th Cir. 1979) (trademark); *Shubin v. United States District Court,* 313 F.2d 250, 251-52 (9th Cir.), *cert denied,* 373 U.S. 936 (1963) (patent).

plies to any "unlawful grant" of a patent. C14-C15; *see also Mowry*, 81 U.S. (14 Wall.) at 439. This Court should review the Federal Circuit's refusal to follow this Court's binding precedents.[5]

C. The Federal Circuit's Decision Creates A Conflict Among The Circuits

Typically, the decisions of the Federal Circuit interpreting the substantive patent laws do not create circuit conflicts because the Federal Circuit has exclusive subject matter jurisdiction over patent appeals. *See* 28 U.S.C. § 1295(a)(1). However, the Federal Circuit's decisions can create a circuit conflict on issues not dependent upon an interpretation of the patent laws. That is precisely the case here. The Federal Circuit's decision in this case does not interpret the patent laws. Instead, it purports to rest entirely upon general principles of the Seventh Amendment and the Declaratory Judgment Act.

Because the Federal Circuit's decision creates a circuit conflict in areas well beyond the Federal Circuit's exclusive subject matter jurisdiction, this Court should grant certiorari.

D. The Federal Circuit's Extension Of The Right To Jury Trial To Claims Involving No Request For Monetary Relief Or The Recovery Of Property Is Not Supported By Any Precedent

This case involves no pending claim for money of any kind or for the recovery of property. Nevertheless, the Federal Circuit held that there is a Seventh Amendment right to a jury in this case. In reaching this conclusion, the Federal Circuit again strayed far from precedent.

This Court has explained on many occasions that the traditional form of legal relief is money damages. *See Mertens v. Hewitt Assocs.*, 113 S. Ct. 2063, 2068 (1993); *Chauffeurs*, 494 U.S. at 570. In fact, the only other form of legal relief which this Court has recognized is the recovery of real and personal property. *Pernell v. Southall Realty*, 416 U.S. 363, 370 (1974); *Scott v. Neely*, 140 U.S. 106, 110 (1891); *Whitehead v. Shattuck*, 138 U.S. 146, 151 (1891). For this reason, every case in which this Court has recognized a Seventh Amendment right to trial by jury has involved a claim for monetary relief or for the recovery of property. *See* C20.[6]

---

5   The Federal Circuit also declared that this Court's decisions in *Cochrane v. Deener*, 94 U.S. 780 (1877), and *Root v. Railway Co.*, 105 U.S. 189 (1882), are no longer good law. A29 n.15.

6   Indeed, much of this Court's modern Seventh Amendment jurisprudence has been an effort to classify various actions for monetary relief and the recovery of property as either legal or equitable. *See Tull*, 481 U.S. at 422 (civil penalty); *Pernell*, 416 U.S. at 370 (recovery of real property); *Katchen v. Landy*, 382 U.S. 323, 336-40 (1966) (claims for monetary relief in bankruptcy proceedings); *Dairy Queen, Inc. v. Wood*, 369 U.S. 469, 476-79 (1962) (accounting of profits). This Court has never suggested that the constitutional right to a jury trial extends to cases involving no claim for monetary relief or the recovery of property.

Consistent with this Court's precedents, the circuit courts have held that the presence of a claim for monetary relief is the touchstone of the right to trial by jury.[7] For example, the District of Columbia Circuit has held that a pending claim for damages is "a prerequisite to a claim that [a party] is being deprived of a right to a jury trial."*Filmon Process Corp. v. Sirica*, 379 F.2d 449, 451 (D.C. Cir. 1967). Similarly, the Sixth Circuit has described the distinction between a claim for money and a claim for an injunction as the "key dividing line between law and equity." *Hildebrand v. Board of Trustees of Mich. State Univ.*, 607 F.2d 705, 708 (6th Cir. 1979).[8]

The Federal Circuit's departure from this basic distinction between legal and equitable remedies is unprecedented. The Federal Circuit is apparently the first appellate court ever to find a Seventh Amendment right to a jury trial in a case involving no claim for monetary relief or the recovery of property, and in so holding has put itself squarely in conflict with its sister circuits and this Court. What was once a narrow right applicable to **certain** claims for monetary relief and the recovery of property is now a right of unknown scope, applicable whether or not any traditional legal relief is involved. Again, this Court should review the Federal Circuit's clear departure from precedent and historic practice, and its broad expansion of the Seventh Amendment.

III.

THE FEDERAL CIRCUIT'S DECISION IS IN CONFLICT WITH THIS COURT'S DECLARATORY JUDGMENT JURISPRUDENCE

A. This Court's Precedents Establish That Declaratory Relief Is Essentially Equitable

Since the enactment of the Declaratory Judgment Act, 28 U.S.C. § 2201, this Court has explained on many occasions that declaratory relief is a discretionary, equitable remedy.[9] As this Court explained in *Great Lakes Dredge & Dock Co. v. Huffman*, 319 U.S. 293, 300 (1943), declaratory relief is "essentially an equitable cause of action" and "is analogous to the equity jurisdiction in suits quia timet or for a decree quieting title." Indeed, even before the passage of the Declaratory

---

7   In most cases the circuit courts have overlooked legal actions for the recovery of property, presumably because these actions are so rarely tried in the federal courts today.

8   Commentators have long recognized the same fundamental distinction. For example, Judge Re has written:
   With the exceptions of *ejectment*, for the recovery of the possession of land, *replevin*, for the recovery of the possession of chattels, and the recovery of a *debt*, the ordinary common law remedy consisted of *damages*.
   Edward D. Re, *Remedies* 3 (2d ed. 1987) (emphasis in original); *see also* Jill Martin et al., *Modern Equity* 31 (12th ed. 1985).

9   *See, e.g., Samuels v. Mackell*, 401 U.S. 66, 70-71 (1971); *Abbott Labs. v. Gardner*, 387 U.S. 136, 155 (1967); *Rickover*, 369 U.S. at 112 (declaratory judgment action to invalidate a copyright); *Eccles v. Peoples Bank of Lakewood Village*, 333 U.S. 426, 431 (1948).

Judgment Act, this Court, per Justice Brandeis, explained that declaratory relief "would . . . come under a familiar head of equity jurisdiction." *Willing v. Chicago Auditorium Ass'n*, 277 U.S. 274, 289 (1928).

The Federal Circuit rejected outright these Supreme Court precedents as well. According to the Federal Circuit, these cases do not "stand for the proposition that declaratory judgment actions are always, or even usually, equitable for Seventh Amendment purposes." A32. In the Federal Circuit's view, this Court's declaratory judgment jurisprudence is not relevant because this Court's decisions merely "concern the discretionary nature of the decision to grant declaratory relief in a particular equitable cause of action rather than the Seventh Amendment right to a jury trial." A32 n.17.

The Federal Circuit's reading of this Court's cases is unsupportable. This Court has held, as a matter of historical fact, that declaratory relief is equitable in nature. This Court also has held, as a matter of constitutional law, that there is no right to a jury trial on claims historically tried to courts of equity. These decisions leave no room for genuine debate. Actions for declaratory relief were traditionally tried to courts of equity and therefore do not come within the scope of the Seventh Amendment.

The Federal Circuit was led astray by its misunderstanding of this Court's holding in *Beacon Theatres, Inc. v. Westover*, 359 U.S. 500 (1959). *See* A16. In *Beacon,* this Court held that a legal claim for damages must be tried before any bench trial on a claim for declaratory relief. *Beacon*, 359 U.S. at 503-04; *see also* C12 n.6. A claim for declaratory relief, like any other equitable claim, cannot be used to resolve the merits of a legal claim for damages unless a jury is used. *Beacon,* 359 U.S. at 504; *see also Simler v. Conner*, 372 U.S. 221, 223 (1963).

The procedure mandated by *Beacon* was followed by the District Court in this case. The District Court resolved all of Lockwood's legal claims on summary judgment before ordering a bench trial on American's claim for declaratory relief.

Thus, unlike the plaintiff in *Beacon,* American is not seeking to use its declaratory judgment counterclaim to resolve the merits of Lockwood's legal claim for damages. Lockwood's legal claim has already been resolved by its dismissal. Rather, fearing further litigation, American has sought a remedy which historically fell within equity jurisdiction. American now requests that this Court grant certiorari to make clear that claims for declaratory relief, as in a bill *quia timet*, are equitable.

B. The Federal Circuit Has Shown A Continued Disregard For The Independence Of Actions For Declaratory Relief

* * *

IV.

THE FEDERAL CIRCUIT HAS CREATED ANOTHER CIRCUIT CONFLICT BY PERMITTING A DISMISSED PLEADING TO CONTROL THE RIGHT TO A JURY TRIAL

In *Curtis v. Loether*, 415 U.S. 189, 196 n.11 (1974), this Court reserved judgment on whether the Seventh Amendment right to a jury trial is controlled by the claims which have been pled but dismissed, or the claims which will actually be tried. Since *Curtis,* the First, Fourth, Fifth, Sixth, Ninth, and Eleventh Circuits have each held that dismissed claims can have no impact on the parties' Seventh Amendment rights.[10] Until now, no circuit court had reached a contrary conclusion.

* * *

CONCLUSION

The Federal Circuit has pronounced a rule of pressing national importance. Its ruling, requiring a jury trial where the only claim to be tried is a claim for a declaratory judgment invalidating a patent, directly conflicts with the precedents of this Court and the circuit courts. For each of the reasons set forth above, this Court should grant a writ of certiorari to the Court of Appeals for the Federal Circuit.

Respectfully submitted,

DATED: April 6, 1995

Bruce J. Ennis, Jr.
Paul M. Smith
JENNER & BLOCK
601 Thirteenth Street, N.W.
Washington D.C. 20005
(202) 639-6000

Of Counsel:
R. Bruce Wark

Don W. Martens
Counsel of Record
Joseph R. Re
Paul A. Stewart
KNOBBE, MARTENS, OLSON & BEAR
620 Newport Center Drive
Sixteenth Floor
Newport Beach, CA 92660
(714) 760-0404

Attorneys for Petitioner
AMERICAN AIRLINES, INC.

---

10 [Citations omitted.]

APPENDIX D:
Appellee's Brief: United States Court of Appeals for the Federal Circuit

BRIEF FOR APPELLEE ROUSSEL-UCLAF SA[1]

IN THE
UNITED STATES COURT OF APPEALS
FOR THE FEDERAL CIRCUIT

Appeal No. 96-1246

SCHERING CORPORATION
Plaintiff/Appellant,
and
ROUSS EL-UCLAF SA,
Involuntary Plaintiff/Appellee,
vs.
ZENECA INC. and ZENECA HOLDINGS INC.,
Defendant/Appellee.

ON APPEAL FROM
A JUDGMENT OF THE UNITED STATES DISTRICT
COURT FOR THE DISTRICT OF DELAWARE
IN C.A. NO. 95-566-RRM, ENTERED FEBRUARY 29, 1996
HONORABLE RODERICK R. McKELVIE, DISTRICT JUDGE

DONALD R. DUNNER
JOHN R. THOMAS
**FINNEGAN, HENDERSON,
FARABOW, GARRETT & DUNNER**
1300 Eye Street N.W., Suite 700
Washington, D.C. 20005
(202) 408-4000

JAMES F. LESNIAK
Counsel of Record
JOSEPH R. RE
JOSEPH F. JENNINGS
KNOBBE, MARTENS, OLSON & BEAR
620 Newport Center Drive, 16th Floor
Newport Beach, CA 92660
(714) 760-0404

Attorneys for Involuntary Plaintiff/Appellee
ROUSSEL-UCLAF SA

June 3, 1996

---

1 [Editors' Note: This brief is a truncated version of one appellee brief filed in *Schering Corp. v. Zeneca Inc.*, 104 F.3d 341 (Fed. Cir. 1997). *See* FED. R. APP. P. 28(b) (governing appellee briefs in U.S. circuit courts of appeal).]

CERTIFICATE OF INTEREST

Counsel for Appellee ROUSSEL-UCLAF SA, certify the following information in compliance with Fed. R. App. P. 26.1 and Federal Circuit Rules 26.1 and 47.4:

1. The full name of the party represented by the attorneys listed below is: Roussel-Uclaf SA.

2. Roussel-Uclaf is the real party in interest.

3. Roussel-Uclaf SA is traded on the Paris Stock Exchange. A majority of Roussel-Uclaf SA is owned by Hoechst AG, a public corporation of Germany. Hoechst AG, through its subsidiaries, owns interests in the following companies which have issued shares to the public:

* * *

TABLE OF CONTENTS

Page #

TABLE OF AUTHORITIES

Page #

STATUTES

OTHER AUTHORITIES

STATEMENT OF RELATED CASES

There are no related appeals or cases as set forth in Federal Circuit Rule 47.5.

I. STATEMENT OF THE ISSUES

1. Could paragraph 5 of the Co-Ownership Agreement between Schering and Roussel ever limit the undisputed right of Roussel to grant licenses under the co-owned patent?

2. If paragraph 5 of the Co-Ownership Agreement could limit Roussel's right to grant licenses under the co-owned patent, was it triggered in this case to invalidate Roussel's license to Zeneca?

II. STATEMENT OF THE CASE

Schering's Statement of Facts includes unsupported argument, fails to mention many of the undisputed facts, and mischaracterizes numerous others. Accordingly, Roussel submits its own Statement of the Case.

A. Background Of Roussel's Dispute With Schering And Labrie

The '382 patent at issue and numerous corresponding foreign patents resulted from work performed and funded by Roussel. A479. Schering had no role whatsoever in that work. A475. These patents are sometimes referred to as "combination therapy" patents because they disclose and claim combining an anti-androgen with an LHRH agonist for the treatment of prostate cancer. A5.

Without citation to the record, Schering mischaracterizes paragraph 5 of the 1989 Co-Ownership Agreement as part of an "overall theme of cooperation between the parties" regarding the co-ownership of the '382 patent. Sch. Br. at 8. The undisputed facts are directly to the contrary. As the district court correctly stated, the 1989 Co-Ownership Agreement arose out of a dispute between Roussel, Schering, and one of the inventors of the '382 patent, Fernand Labrie. A10. In 1985, Labrie, unbeknownst to Roussel, assigned his purported U.S. patent rights in the Roussel technology to Schering. A477-78. The dispute concerned Labrie's right to assign those rights to anyone other than Roussel. A479.

The other inventor named in the '382 patent was Jean-Pierre Raynaud, a Roussel employee, who had assigned his rights in the invention to Roussel. A8-9. Based on a written agreement, Roussel maintained that Labrie was also obligated to assign his U.S. patent rights to Roussel, as he had done with the corresponding foreign patents. A479. Labrie and Roussel ultimately resorted to litigation in France to resolve Roussel's ownership of the patent rights. A476.

In August 1988, Schering offered to help Roussel resolve the Labrie litigation, A1014-15, concealing its own interest in the outcome resulting from Labrie's earlier assignment to Schering, A476. In a letter, Roussel declined Schering's offer as unnecessary, stating it was confident it would ultimately prevail in the Labrie litigation. A1016; A477. At that time, Roussel was unaware of the Labrie assignment to Schering. A477.

In the same letter, Roussel also told Schering that they needed to discuss Schering's sale of its anti-androgen (Eulexin) in view of Roussel's combination therapy patents, including the '382 patent. A1016. Shortly thereafter, Steiner Kanstad of Schering suggested to Roussel that Schering "may have" already acquired some rights from Labrie. A477-78. Roussel immediately searched the records of the U.S. Patent and Trademark Office (PTO) and learned that Labrie had executed an assignment of the '382 patent to Schering back in 1985 which Schering had recorded in the PTO. A478; A895-96. Roussel was "shocked, if not furious" upon discovering Schering had, for three years, concealed from Roussel the Labrie assignment. A356 at p. 23; A478-79.

B. Roussel Acknowledges Schering's Co-Ownership To Settle The Dispute

Both Roussel and Schering were interested in resolving the dispute over the Labrie assignment, but for vastly different reasons. Roussel wanted to avoid protracted and expensive litigation. A479-80. Schering needed a license under Roussel's worldwide combination therapy patents to market Eulexin. A482; A600.

Schering and Roussel met in November 1988 and agreed on two basic points: (1) the parties acknowledged each other's co-ownership of the '382 patent, and (2) Roussel agreed to grant a worldwide license to Schering under the combination therapy patents. A601. Moreover, Labrie acknowledged Roussel's complete ownership of all of the foreign patents. *Id.*

C. Schering Never Bargained For Paragraph 5 Of The Co-Ownership Agreement

On February 7, 1989, after several rounds of negotiating the terms of the Labrie/ Roussel Settlement Agreement and Foreign License Agreement, Schering again wrote to Roussel, stating its belief that the "most important points" had been solved. A1021. At the same time, Schering proposed a letter agreement to Roussel to "regulate payments" concerning the "co-owned" patent. A1020. Specifically, Schering introduced the letter agreement to Roussel as follows:

> Also enclosed is a draft of a letter which would *regulate payments* of the *co-owned* patents in the U.S. I think the letter is in line with what we discussed in Paris.

Id. (emphasis added).

This letter agreement, in final form, is now known as the "Co-Ownership Agreement," though the parties never referred to it as such before this litigation.

Because the 1985 Labrie assignment gave an ownership interest to Schering, the so-called Co-Ownership Agreement could not have created the parties' co-ownership interests. For that reason, Schering's proposal to regulate payments referred to the U.S. patents as "co-owned," *id.*, just as Kanstad earlier referred to the parties' co-ownership as a "fait accompli," A1017.

The proposed Co-Ownership Agreement allocated the costs and responsibilities for the co-owned patents. A1022-23. Schering's initial draft contained five paragraphs. The first paragraph merely recognized that the patents were co-owned by Roussel and Schering. The second paragraph assigned to Roussel the responsibility for paying any maintenance fees. The third paragraph provided that Schering shall reimburse Roussel for half of the maintenance fees. Paragraphs 4 and 5 also addressed the payment of maintenance fees.

Roussel later proposed a new draft, adding new paragraph 5, which is now at issue, and combining old paragraphs 4 and 5 into new paragraph 4. A1024-25. The added paragraph 5 reads as follows:

> *Upon the discovery by any party of any infringement* of one or more patents listed above, such party shall notify the other diligently: if the parties agree to do so, appropriate legal action in connection therewith shall be undertaken by the parties jointly. In the event that such action is taken, each party shall contribute equally to the expenses of any such action. If any damages for *infringement* are awarded by a final decree or judgment, then after deducting all expenses arising from the litigation and reimbursing each party for its contributions, the remainder shall be divided equally among the contributing parties. If one party shall not wish to join or continue in any such action, but the other party shall wish to institute or continue such action, said one party shall render all *reasonable assistance* to said other party *in connection therewith at said other party's expense* and said other party shall be entitled to retain all recoveries obtained with respect to such action.

(Emphasis added).

* * *

D. Roussel Always Believed It Had A Right To License The '382 Patent

At the time Roussel entered into the Co-Ownership Agreement, Roussel had been actively searching for a licensee under the '382 patent. In 1983, Roussel's affiliate company had rejected the United States marketing rights for Roussel's anti-androgen nilutamide. A550-51; A1007-09. Thereafter, Roussel continually looked for potential licensees to market nilutamide under the '382 patent. A539-40; *see, e.g.*, A1010-13, 1026. Roussel knew that the only way it could market nilutamide in the United States was to license somebody else. A496. Most importantly, just *three weeks before Roussel signed the Co-Ownership Agreement*, it responded to a license request reaffirming its intention to grant a license under the '382 patent. A1027.

Roussel's licensing efforts continued in the years subsequent to the execution of the Co-Ownership Agreement. A1028-30. Roussel did not find a licensee to market nilutamide until 1995, when Marion Merrill Dow was acquired by Roussel's parent Hoechst and agreed to market the product in the United States. A1005-06.

E. Roussel Considers Zeneca's And Schering's Offers To Buy Rights Under The '382 Patent

* * *

Roussel ultimately chose to grant a nonexclusive license to Zeneca instead of granting exclusive rights to Schering. A499. On March 29, 1995, Roussel called Schering to reject Schering's offer. A86; A279 at p. 83. Early the next month, Roussel informed Zeneca that it would grant Zeneca a license under the '382 patent. A338 at p. 97.

F. Schering Changes Course To Threaten Litigation, While Roussel Negotiates License Terms With Zeneca

Having agreed to license Zeneca, Roussel began negotiating the terms of the license. On May 11, 1995, Roussel received Zeneca's first draft of the license agreement. A99-108. Thereafter, on May 22, 1995, Roussel received Schering's first demand letter, including a notice of Zeneca's "potential infringement." A120-21. Roussel understandably perceived Schering's May 22 letter to represent a dramatic shift in Schering's strategy from an attempt to purchase Roussel's exclusive patent rights to a threat of litigation as if it already had those rights. A502. Roussel therefore proceeded cautiously in an attempt to avoid litigation. A502-03.

* * *

G. Roussel Licensed Zeneca Before Any Possible Infringing Act By Zeneca

By September 15, 1995, Roussel and Zeneca agreed to the basic terms of their license. A14; A335 at p. 60. On October 4, 1995, Zeneca first obtained FDA approval of Casodex. A190. By the next day, Roussel and Zeneca executed the license agreement. A193-201. Zeneca did not begin selling Casodex until October 18, 1995, after it was licensed by Roussel. A15.

H. District Court Proceedings

After executing the license agreement, Zeneca moved for summary judgment on the grounds that the license was a complete defense to Schering's complaint. Roussel joined in the motion. Zeneca's motion was based on two independent grounds: (1) the Co-Ownership Agreement could not limit Roussel's right to license; and (2) even if the agreement could limit Roussel's right to license, the relevant portions of the agreement were not triggered in this case. After a hearing in which the district court considered testimony concerning the license defense, Schering cross-moved for summary judgment that the license was invalid as a matter of law. Although initially expressing a tentative view in support of Schering, the district court entered summary judgment in Zeneca's favor. The district court agreed with Zeneca and Roussel that the Co-Ownership Agreement "does not restrict Roussel from granting a license to Zeneca after notice of infringement" A22. In view of that ruling, the district court correctly saw no need to determine whether Schering's letters to Roussel "constituted proper notice of infringement" to trigger paragraph 5 of the Co-Ownership Agreement. A24.

III. SUMMARY OF ARGUMENT

The district court correctly construed the Co-Ownership Agreement to find it could not impliedly limit Roussel's undisputed right to grant licenses under the co-owned patent. The agreement is not ambiguous and was properly construed on summary judgment. The district court correctly construed the "reasonable assistance" clause of paragraph 5 merely to require Roussel to provide the type of assistance commonly associated with a legal action, but not to forego its undisputed right to grant licenses as a co-owner. Moreover, by merely granting Schering the right to bring suit on its own, Roussel did not waive its own right to grant licenses under the patent. Any such construction of paragraph 5 would be inconsistent with the language and purpose of the agreement, the other contemporaneously executed agreements, and the parties' prior and subsequent course of dealing.

The Sixth Circuit opinion in *Willingham* does not suggest a different result. First, it does not address whether a co-owner has the right to license. It addressed only a standing issue—whether a co-owner could object to involuntary joinder in an infringement suit brought by the co-owner where the co-owners had agreed that each had the right to sue for infringement. The *Willingham* opinion never questioned the co-owners' fundamental right to use, assign or transfer the patented invention, without the consent of the other co-owner. Second, Schering agrees that Roussel had the right to license Zeneca, at least until Schering gave notice of infringement. Schering therefore had to argue that there is some "temporal" limitation to the *Willingham* "doctrine." That reading of the case is completely unsupported by the *Willingham* opinion.

* * *

IV. ARGUMENT

A. The District Court Correctly Held The Co-Ownership Agreement Does Not Limit Roussel's Right To Grant Licenses As A Matter Of Law

Unless there is an agreement to the contrary, a co-owner of a patent is free to make, use, and sell the patented invention without the consent of other owners. 35 U.S.C. § 262. Nor is the consent of other owners required for a patent co-owner to grant licenses under the co-owned patent to third parties. *Talbot v. Quaker-State Oil Refining Co.*, 104 F.2d 967, 968 (3d Cir. 1939).

All parties agree with the district court's holding that no language in the Co-Ownership Agreement explicitly restricts Schering's or Roussel's right to grant licenses under the '382 patent after notice of infringement. A19. The district court also correctly recognized that an acknowledgement of one's co-ownership of the patent implicitly recognizes the party's right to license the patent as well. A 19-20 (citing *Talbot*). Lastly, the district court correctly characterized paragraph 5 as establishing rights and responsibilities with respect to enforcing the '382 patent, but no part of paragraph 5 explicitly mentions licensing or any restriction on licensing. A20.

On appeal, Schering makes two primary arguments attacking the district court's construction of paragraph 5 of the agreement. First, Schering argues that the phrase "reasonable assistance" of paragraph 5 is ambiguous, requiring resolution by a jury. Sch. Br. at 46. Second, it claims that paragraph 5 as a whole is subject to differing interpretations and thus raises a question of fact for the jury. Sch. Br. at 42. Both arguments are contrary to law, the testimony of Schering's own witnesses, and completely unsupported by any other evidence.

1. The "Reasonable Assistance" Clause Did Not Limit The Right To License As A Matter Of Law

Under basic contract law, the parties' intent as expressed in their writing controls. *J.I. Hass Co., Inc. v. Gilbane Bldg. Co.*, 881 F.2d 89, 92 (3d Cir. 1989), cert. denied, 493 U.S. 1080 (1990). A court must construe the contract as a matter of law where its terms are clear and unambiguous. *Cooper Labs, Inc. v. Int'l Surplus Lines Ins. Co.*, 802 F.2d 667, 671 (3d Cir. 1986); *Kaufman v. Provident Life And Casualty Ins. Co.*, 828 F. Supp. 275, 282-83 (D.N.J. 1992), *aff'd*, 993 F.2d 877 (3d Cir. 1993). The initial question of whether a contract term is clear or ambiguous is itself a question of law for the court. *Kaufman*, 828 F. Supp. at 282. No ambiguity exists unless "the terms of the contract are susceptible to at least two *reasonable* alternative interpretations." *Id.*. at 283 (emphasis added); *see also Pennbarr Corp. v. Insurance Co. of North America*, 976 F.2d 145, 150 (3d Cir. 1992). The district court properly found the relevant terms of the Co-Ownership Agreement are not ambiguous and thus properly construed them as a matter of law.[2]

The only language the district court could find in paragraph 5 to even possibly support Schering's alleged restriction on the right to license was the "reasonable assistance" clause:

> If one party shall not wish to join or continue in any such action, but the other party shall wish to institute or continue such action, *said one party shall render all reasonable assistance to said other party in connection therewith at said other party's expense* and said other party shall be entitled to retain all recoveries obtained with respect to such action.

A55-57 ¶ 5. That phrase is the only expression of any obligation placed upon a nonsuing co-owner in the Co-Ownership Agreement. Therefore, the district court correctly focused on this clause.

The district court construed "reasonable assistance" to obligate a nonsuing co-owner to provide litigation support to the other. A21-22. The district court correctly found that the type of assistance referenced by this language is susceptible to only one reasonable interpretation. *Id.* The language, as the district court found, refers to assistance commonly associated with a legal action, such as the production of files, documents, witnesses, etc. *Id.* Kanstad testified that he had the same understanding. A301 at pp. 49, 52-53; A595-97.

This construction is completely consistent with the requirement that the reasonable assistance be "in connection" with a legal action and "at said other party's expense." As the district court correctly found, reimbursement for those expenses comports with the overall purpose of the agreement—to regulate payments—and sensibly compensates a nonsuing co-owner for its time and effort in providing the assistance. A21. The district court noted that these activities result in reasonable and readily quantifiable expenses for which the suing co-owner could reimburse the nonsuing co-owner. *Id.*

The district court correctly determined, as a matter of law, that the phrase "reasonable assistance" could not force either party to bypass an opportunity to license the '382 patent. *Id.* Foregoing the opportunity to license is certainly not readily quantifiable, as are expenses normally associated with litigation support. Moreover, foregoing that opportunity is not "in connection" with any legal action.

2. Paragraph 5 "As A Whole" Did Not Limit The Right To License As A Matter Of Law

Schering's argument that paragraph 5 "as a whole" raises a genuine issue of material fact as to Roussel's right to license ignores the law. Sch. Br. at 40.

---

2   [Footnote omitted.]

Schering cannot overcome the rule of law that the application of contract language is an issue of contract construction for the court to decide as a matter of law. *Cooper Labs., Inc. v. Int'l Surplus Lines Ins. Co.*, 802 F.2d 667, 671 (3d Cir. 1986); *see also United States v. Bills*, 639 F. Supp. 825, 829 (D.N.J. 1986) (summary judgment granted though parties differ on what consequences flow from contract). Schering is actually challenging the legal consequences of the Co-Ownership Agreement. Indeed, Schering is unable to point to any language in paragraph 5 which creates a genuine issue of material fact. Part of Schering's problem is Kanstad's concession that the language of paragraph 5 was "very clear." A575.

Schering now argues on appeal as if Roussel's allowing Schering the procedural right to sue somehow supersedes Roussel's substantive right to license. Sch. Br. at 30. But the language and purpose of the Co-Ownership Agreement, the related agreements forming the overall transaction, the circumstances surroundings those agreements, and the parties' prior and subsequent course of dealing all refute the legal consequence Schering hopes to gain.

Schering stated that the purpose of the Co-Ownership Agreement was to "regulate payments of the co-owned patents in the United States." A1020. Paragraph 5 of the Co-Ownership Agreement did not alter the purpose of the agreement, but was completely consistent with that purpose. Paragraph 5 simply addressed that allocation with respect to an infringement action. If the action is undertaken jointly, the parties share expenses and any recovery. If one party undertakes that action, it pays the expenses and retains the recovery. The plain language of paragraph 5 shows that the equal allocation of damages corresponds to the equal investment the parties would make in any joint litigation, not to any lost opportunities to market the invention, as Schering now argues. Schering Br. at 47-48.

The circumstances surrounding the Co-Ownership Agreement also comport with the district court's construction. The agreement was part of an overall settlement intended to confirm Roussel's ownership rights in the patents and to grant Schering the right to market Eulexin free from those patents. A300 at pp. 44-45. Co-ownership of the '382 patent was simply a convenient method of accomplishing that objective in view of Labrie's earlier assignment. A483. Schering even explained that co-ownership of the '382 patent was, for all practical purposes, the same as if Roussel had full ownership and granted a nonexclusive royalty-free license to Schering. A1018. Schering did not "bargain for" any rights in paragraph 5, let alone the rights it now requests. A574.

Had the parties intended any restriction on licensing, they would have addressed it expressly. A387-88; A302-03. They expressly addressed licensing in the Foreign License Agreement, executed contemporaneously with the Co-Ownership Agreement. A58-66. Roussel granted Schering a nonexclusive non-transferable license "with the right to grant one non-transferable sublicense" in Japan where it had licensed a distributor of Eulexin. A60. Because a nonexclusive license does not normally carry with it the right to sublicense, *PPG Indus., Inc. v. Guardian Indus. Corp.*, 597 F.2d 1090, 1093 (6th Cir.), *cert. denied*, 444 U.S. 930 (1979), it was necessary to draft that agreement accordingly. Correspondingly, because co-ownership does not preclude one co-owner from licensing others, it would have been necessary to draft the Co-Ownership Agreement with terms to restrict the right to license, had that been the parties' intent. The district court found that one treatise even suggests such a provision. A20 (citing 4 *West's Federal Practice Manual* § 3935, at 32 (2d ed. 1989)).

3. Paragraph 5 Should Not Be Construed To Incorporate An Implied Restraint Of Trade

* * *

B. *Willingham* Does Not Limit The Parties' Undisputed Right To License

* * *

C. No Court Has Expressed "Hostility" To A Co-Owner's Right To License

Schering argues that "courts have shown a manifest hostility to any effort by one co-owner to sabotage the litigation by licensing the defendant." Schering Br. at 32. It argues that "a series of cases whose facts are remarkably similar to this one" are exemplary of such judicial hostility. It then cites two cases, one an unpublished opinion, and the other a district court case from 1899. *Molinaro v. Rockwell Int'l*, No. 75-169 (D. Del. Oct. 21, 1977) (unpublished copied in Joint Appendix); *Lalance & Grosjean Mfg. Co. v. Haberman Mfg. Co.*, 93 F. 197, 198 (S.D.N.Y. 1899).

Both of the cases relate to an issue not raised here—whether one co-owner has the right to release an accused infringer from accrued damages for past infringement over the objection of the other co-owner. *See Molinaro* at A831; *Lalance*, 93 F. at 198. Indeed, the *Molinaro* court recognizes the fundamental distinction between a release from accrued damages and a license. The court specifically stated that a co-owner had "complete authority" to grant a license and that the objecting co-owner would have no recourse against either the co-owner or the alleged infringer with respect to the use of the invention pursuant to such a license. *Molinaro* at A830. The only issue in this appeal is Roussel's ability to license for future acts, not a release for any past infringement. Schering's complaint does not even request damages for any past infringements, since there had been no infringement. A185. The complaint merely seeks a declaration of infringement.

* * *

D. Alternatively, Because Paragraph 5 Was Not Triggered, Summary Judgment Would Be Proper

* * *

CONCLUSION

The district court's judgment should be affirmed on either one of two grounds. First, paragraph 5 of the 1989 Co-Ownership Agreement could never limit either party's right to license the co-owned patent. Alternatively, even if paragraph 5 could possibly limit either party's right to license, Schering did not trigger paragraph 5 under the circumstances in this case. Accordingly, the license to Zeneca was valid and this Court should affirm the grant of summary judgment.

Respectfully submitted,

KNOBEE, MARTENS, OLSON & BEAR

Dated: By: _____

James F. Lesniak
Joseph R. Re
Joseph F. Jennings
Attorneys for Appellee, ROUSSEL-UCLAF SA

Of Counsel:

Donald R. Dunner
John R. Thomas
FINNEGAN, HENDERSON,
FARABOW, GARRET & DUNNER

APPENDIX E:
Form of Claim or Demand Letter

FORM OF CLAIM OR DEMAND LETTER

Edwards, Peters & Jones
Attorneys at Law
1600 Washington St.
Stamford, CT 00138

March 11, 2004

Mr. Robert Nearstead
26 Westwood Drive
Stamford, CT 00136

Dear Mr. Nearstead:

My client, your neighbor, Mr. Thomas Bleeker, has informed me that a dispute has arisen as to the fence that you recently erected on the west side of your house near the swimming pool that you have just completed. This fence, which divides your property and that of my client, encroaches two feet onto my client's property.

Mr. Bleeker states, and my examination of a surveyor's report confirms, that the fence extends two feet onto Mr. Bleeker's property. Therefore, on behalf of Mr. Bleeker, I am notifying you that you either remove the fence completely or move it to the correct boundary in accordance with the appropriate survey.

If you have any questions, please feel free to telephone me. I do hope that this problem as to the location of the fence can be resolved quickly and amicably.

Thank you for your prompt attention to this matter.

Sincerely,

Michael Jones

APPENDIX F:
Form of Trial Memorandum

1. Submitted by Plaintiff
2. Submitted by Defendant

FORM OF TRIAL MEMORANDUM
SUBMITTED BY PLAINTIFF DURING TRIAL*

UNITED STATES DISTRICT COURT
FOR THE
EASTERN DISTRICT OF NEW YORK

Martin Marietta Corporation,

Plaintiff,

-against-

Peter Kiewit Sons' Co. and
Slattery Associates, Inc.,   Index No.
individually, and doing business   71 Civ. 246
as Peter Kiewit Sons' Co.-
Slattery Associates, Inc.
(Joint Venture),

Defendants.

PLAINTIFF'S TRIAL MEMORANDUM

Plaintiff has commenced this action to recover $55,252.02 representing damages sustained when the scows FEENEY 20 and HB 130 broke adrift, while in the sole custody and control of the defendants, from a bulkhead operated and maintained by the defendants at Far Rockaway, New York in April 1970. It has been stipulated that the defendants were engaged in a joint venture at the times described hereinbelow, and, consequently, plaintiff seeks judgment holding them jointly and severally liable for the damage sustained by the scows.

---

* See decision in 346 F. Supp. 892 (E.D.N.Y. 1972).

POINT 1

THE DEFENDANTS WERE BAILEES OF
THE SCOWS FEENEY 20 AND HB 130

Edward A. Smith, plaintiff's sales manager, has testified as to a special relationship between plaintiff and defendants. Plaintiff ordinarily sells crushed stone and transports it to a place designated by its customer in scows towed by tugs hired by plaintiff. Mr. Smith has testified and the defendants have conceded that it was impossible for plaintiff's tugs to deliver the scows FEENEY 20 and HB 130 to the defendants' premises in February of 1970 because a tug strike was in progress. Well aware of the strike, defendants offered to pick up the scows with their own tug DOTSIE, which was manned by personnel whose union was based in Philadelphia and was not affected by the strike. Mr. Smith refused to consent to the defendants' request until he had obtained assurances that the scows would be covered by the defendants' insurance. Under these circumstances, defendants owed the scows a special duty of care.

The testimony has revealed that the scows FEENEY 20 and HB 130 were delivered to the defendants' job site by the defendants' tug, unloaded by defendants' employees, and moored to a bulkhead operated and maintained by defendants. There has been no testimony that the plaintiff participated in any of these acts. The scows were unmanned and none of plaintiff's employees were present when the scows went adrift. Under these circumstances defendants were clearly bailees of the scows. Defendants appear to make two arguments in support of their contention that the bailment had been terminated. They argue that they notified plaintiff on February 17 and March 6, 1970, that the cargo had been completely discharged from the scows FEENEY 20 and HB 130, respectively, and that plaintiff was free to pick up the scows. This argument is specious because the tug strike affecting plaintiff's tugs did not end until the day before the casualty here at issue. Moreover, even if tugs had been available, the defendants' obligation to the scows would not have been decreased. As the court noted in *Mid-America Transportation Co. v. St. Louis Barge Fleeting Service*, 229 F. Supp. 409 (E.D. Mo. 1964), *aff'd*, 348 F. 2d 920 (8th Cir. 1965), at page 411:

> Respondent contends that since the libelant was free, at any time, to take possession of its barge and remove it, that respondent never assumed control or custody of libelant's barge (a necessary requirement to establish a bailment). Such a contention is clearly erroneous.

Defendants also argue that periodic visits to the job site by plaintiff's runner, John Lindholm, relieves them of a bailee's obligation. His visits, however, were of the same nature as those of the owner of the deck scow in *Kenny v. City of New York*, 108 F.2d 958 (2d Cir. 1940), where bailee's liability was imposed upon the defendant when the scow went adrift from its dock in a storm.

By virtue of the bailment of the scows FEENEY 20 and HB 130, plaintiff is entitled to a presumption of the defendants' negligence upon proof of delivery in sound condition and the return of the scows in damaged condition. *Mid-America Transp. Co. v. St. Louis Barge Fleeting Serv.*, 229 F. Supp. 409 (E.D. Mo. 1964), *aff'd*, 348 F.2d 920 (8th Cir. 1965).

If the defendants are unable to rebut the presumption, plaintiff must have judgment.

POINT II

THE WEATHER CAN PROVIDE THE DEFENDANTS NO DEFENSE

Mr. Cunningham, defendants' Marine Manager, testified that there were winds of "60-70 miles per hour or knots" when he arrived at the job site at 4:15-4:30 p.m. on the afternoon of the casualty. His amateur opinion is completely at odds with the official weather data recorded by experts at J. F. Kennedy Airport, about three miles northeast of the site of the casualty and at Fort Tilden, about three miles due west thereof. As will be demonstrated at the trial, the weather data recorded at those points on April 2, 1970, was as follows:

TIME	J. F. KENNEDY AIRPORT	FORT TILDEN
14:51 (2:51 p.m.)	23 knots with gusts of 33 knots	
15:00 (3:00 p.m.)		25 knots
15:31	25 knots with gusts of 32 knots	
15:51	30 knots with gusts of 40 knots	
16:05 (4:05 p.m.)	26 knots with gusts of 33 knots	
16:29	25 knots with gusts of 33 knots	
17:00 (5:00 p.m.)		10 knots
17:19	13 knots	

It is readily apparent from the foregoing that the highest recorded wind velocity was 40 knots rather than the 60-70 knots described by Mr. Cunningham. If vessels can be expected to come loose from their moorings on every occasion when winds reach speeds of 40 knots, this court's dockets would be considerably longer.

In fact, most of the vessels secured at defendants' job site did not come loose from their moorings as did scows FEENEY 20 and HB 130. Since each of the vessels was subjected to the same weather conditions, the weather can provide no defense to the plaintiff's claim with respect to those that went adrift.

POINT III

THE PLAINTIFF HAS PROVED ITS DAMAGES

There can be no serious dispute that the plaintiff has established its right to recover for all but two of the items listed in Exhibit A annexed to the pre-trial order. (There was no testimony with respect to the Carl Torner invoice in the amount of $53.00 and the McAllister Bros. invoice for $910.00 because plaintiff was unable to produce a witness with personal knowledge that the invoices have in fact been paid.) Defendants have made a weak attempt to convince the court that some of the damage sustained by the scow FEENEY 20, for which plaintiff seeks to recover, was sustained prior to the casualty here at issue. Their Mr. Cunningham took issue with the expert testimony of Mr. Ganly that the damage surveyed was "new damage." Yet, as Mr. Ganly testified, Mr. Cunningham refused to examine the damaged areas that he claimed were pre-existing. Accordingly, plaintiff should have judgment against the defendants, jointly and severally, in the amount of $54,289.02.

Respectfully submitted,

THACHER, PROFFITT, PRIZER,
CRAWLEY & WOOD
Attorneys for Plaintiff
40 Wall Street
New York, New York 10005

Dwight B. Demeritt, Jr.,
Raymond S. Jackson, Jr.
 Of Counsel

FORM OF TRIAL MEMORANDUM
SUBMITTED BY DEFENDANT DURING TRIAL*

UNITED STATES DISTRICT COURT
FOR THE
EASTERN DISTRICT OF NEW YORK

Martin Marietta Corporation,

Plaintiff,

-against-

Peter Kiewit Sons' Co. and
Slattery Associates, Inc.
individually, and doing business   Index No.
as Peter Kiewit Sons' Co.   71 Civ. 246
Slattery Associates, Inc.
(Joint Venture),

Defendants.

TRIAL MEMORANDUM ON BEHALF OF DEFENDANTS
Statement

This case involves one of the many claimed incidents of damage to harbor scows in the New York area. The plaintiff, Martin Marietta Corporation, alleges that the scows FEENEY 20 and HUGHES BROTHERS 130, which were blown from their place of mooring at Rockaway, New York on April 2, 1970, were damaged as the result of the defendants' negligence.

The defendants, Peter Kiewit Sons' Co. and Slattery Associates, Inc., are construction firms that had formed a joint venture in order to perform certain construction work on the Cross Bay Bridge at Rockaway during the year 1970.

---

*See decision in 346 F. Supp. 892 (E.D.N.Y. 1972).

Prior to the events in suit, the defendants had purchased certain crushed rock and stone from the plaintiff corporation to be used in construction work. Under normal circumstances, the plaintiff would arrange to deliver the stone, in scows that it either owned or controlled, to the construction site and would retrieve the empty scows after the cargo had been removed. In early 1970, however, various New York tugboat unions were on strike, so that the plaintiff was unable to deliver its stone in the normal fashion. Because the defendants owned a tugboat crewed by members of a union not on strike, they agreed to pick up the stone laden scows at the plaintiff's locations and tow the scows to the construction site themselves.

Pursuant to this arrangement, defendants' tug DOTSIE towed the loaded scows FEENEY 20 and HUGHES BROTHERS 130, on February 6 and February 23, 1970, respectively, to its construction site at Broad Channel Drive, Rockaway. Defendants subsequently emptied the stone from the scows and moored them at a wharf leased from the Department of Parks.

On February 17 and March 6, 1970, the defendants notified plaintiff that the scows FEENEY 20 and HUGHES BROTHERS 130, respectively, had been discharged and were ready for pickup.

During the afternoon of April 2, 1970, the defendants again notified plaintiff that the scows FEENEY 20 and HUGHES BROTHERS 130, respectively, had been discharged and were ready for pickup.

During the afternoon of April 2, 1970, at approximately 4:00 p.m., an unpredicted storm of considerable force caused the barges in question to break loose from the moorings and go adrift. Defendants were able to recover and resecure the FEENEY 20, but the HUGHES BROTHERS 130 was blown ashore on an unnamed island in Jamaica Bay. Plaintiff seeks to recover from the defendants damages allegedly resulting from this incident.

POINT I

DEFENDANTS WERE NOT THE INSURERS OF PLAINTIFF'S SCOWS

Plaintiff apparently contends that merely because the scows in question went adrift from the position where the defendants had secured them, that defendants are liable in damages. While there is no question that the defendants moored the barges in question, it is also uncontested that they notified plaintiff that they were through with the scows, and the plaintiff's own employee visited the construction site at regular intervals of at least twice a week during the entire period in which they were so moored, and that he inspected their condition. Plaintiff, therefore, cannot properly argue that the defendants were in complete control of the scows and that it had no control over them.

Even assuming arguendo that the defendants did have complete control over the scows in question, they would still only be required to exercise reasonable or ordinary care to prevent injuries, and in order to recover damages, the plaintiff must prove negligence on the part of the defendants. *M & J Tracy, Inc. v. Marks, Lissenberger & Sons, Inc.*, 283 F. 100, 102 (2d Cir. 1922).

It was stated in the case of *Sisung v. Tiger Pass Shipyard*, 303 F.2d 318, 321-22 (5th Cir. 1962):

> The rule in bailment cases is that the bailee may overcome the influence of negligence arising against it because of delivery in good condition and return in damaged condition by telling all that it knows of the casualty, and that it exercised ordinary care in all that it did with respect to the vessel. This burden, unlike that of persuasion which rested at all times on the appellants, simply required appellee to go forward with evidence sufficient to show that it had no more knowledge of the cause of the casualty than was available to appellants and that it exercised ordinary care. At this juncture the burden of going forward would shift back to the appellants to ultimately persuade the trier of facts of negligence on the part of the appellee approximately causing the casualty.

Furthermore, in the case at bar, it is clear that at least some control over the scows was exercised by the plaintiff, so that the defendants' duties are correspondingly decreased. As the Court held in *Sisung* at page 322:

> [F]urthermore, where the owner maintains some dominion over the vessel, as Sisung did by selecting the place of mooring, there is a corresponding limitation on the duty of the bailee or one in possession. Cf. *Stegemann v. Miami Beach Boat Slips, Inc.*, 5 Cir. 1954, 213 F. 2d 561.

POINT II

DEFENDANTS PROPERLY MOORED THE SCOWS IN QUESTION

It will be demonstrated at trial that the barges in question were properly moored by the defendants and that the cause of their going adrift was an unpredicted storm of such force and magnitude that mooring bitts were pulled completely out of their mountings. The fact that the plaintiff's employee, Mr. Lindholm, visited the scows at regular intervals and made no complaint about the manner in which they were secured, is demonstrative of the fact that they were properly moored.

POINT III

PLAINTIFF HAD ACCEPTED REDELIVERY OF THE SCOWS PRIOR TO THE EVENTS IN SUIT

It is an uncontested fact that defendants notified plaintiff on February 17 and March 6, 1970, that they were finished with the scows FEENEY 20 and HUGHES BROTHERS 130, respectively, and that plaintiff could remove them as of those dates. The facts that plaintiff did not complain of, or reject, this tender, and that its employee attended at the construction site to check on the condition of the scows, demonstrate that plaintiff had in fact accepted the constructive redelivery of these scows.

Plaintiff, having resumed control of the scows, cannot now properly claim that they were under the control of the defendants on April 2, 1970. In spite of the fact that they had redelivered these scows, defendants continued to watch and care for them along with their own scows and those of third parties that happened to moor at the same berthing facility. The mere fact that defendants acted as "good samaritans" in watching and rescuing scows for which they were not legally responsible, should not be interpreted as any admission of responsibility with regard to those scows.

Conclusion

Plaintiff has not proven negligence on the part of defendants, and the complaint should be dismissed.

Respectfully submitted,

HILL, BETTS & NASH
Attorneys for Defendants

David C. Wood,
Edward H. Duggan, Jr.
Of Counsel

APPENDIX G:
Form of Office Memorandum of Law

FORM OF OFFICE MEMORANDUM OF LAW*

TITLE: Tenant's Compensation for Fixtures upon Condemnation of Leased Premises

(Re Inquiry of Client R. W. Smith)

REQUESTED BY: James Kinson

DATE SUBMITTED: June 1, 1992

QUESTION PRESENTED

Whether tenant would be entitled to compensation for trade fixtures in event of condemnation of the leased premises?

BRIEF ANSWER

In the State of New York the tenant's right to compensation for fixtures is recognized notwithstanding paragraphs 19 and 24 of the lease.

STATEMENT OF FACTS

Client operates a machine shop at the premises known as 34 Main Street, Borough of Brooklyn. He is in possession under a 20-year lease executed on May 15, 1991. He has, since 1991, installed valuable machinery in the leased premises. The machinery is bolted to the concrete floor. It now appears that there is a reasonable likelihood that the premises will be condemned in the near future for highway purposes.

Paragraph 19 of the lease provides: "If all, or substantially all, of the leased premises are condemned, then at the option of the Landlord this lease shall become null and void and the estate of the Tenant shall terminate. No part of any award, however, shall belong to the Tenant."

Paragraph 24 of the lease provides: "If after default in payment of rent or violation of any other provision of this lease, or upon the expiration of this lease, the Tenant moves out or is dispossessed and fails to remove any trade fixtures or other property prior to such said default, removal, expiration of lease, or prior to the issuance of the final order or execution of the warrant, then in that event, the said fixtures and property shall be deemed abandoned by the said Tenant and shall become the property of the Landlord."

---

*The memorandum of law may also serve as the basis of counsel's opinion letter to the client.

DISCUSSION

It is well established in New York that the machinery would be characterized as trade fixtures and could be removed at any time before expiration of the term provided the fixtures can be removed without material injury to the realty and provided they are removed prior to expiration of the term. *Matter of the City of New York*, 192 N.Y. 295, 84 N.E. 1105 (1908). The rule is very liberal in favor of the tenant. Apart from common law rights, an examination of the lease indicates that, under paragraph 24, the tenant's continued ownership and right of removal is clearly agreed upon as to any machinery installed by the tenant during the term. The tenant's sole liability is for any damage caused to the leased premises in removing the machinery.

It is also well established that the State must pay compensation for "fixtures," which, although removable by a tenant, would be considered real property if they had been installed by the owner of the fee. *In re Allen Street and First Avenue*, 256 N.Y. 236, 176 N.E. 377 (1931). *See* 51 *N.Y. Juris.*, Eminent Domain §252 (1986). The tenant's right to compensation for fixtures, as against the State, survives the termination of the estate. *Matter of City of New York*, 256 N.Y. 236, 176 N.E. 377 (1931); *Marraro v. State*, 12 N.Y.2d 285, 189 N.E.2d 606 (1963).

Although no New York State Court of Appeals case has been found, it is also clear that paragraph 19 will not defeat the tenant's right to compensation for the machinery in spite of the language employed in the lease. As between the tenant and the State, the machinery is considered realty and just compensation must be paid. However, as between tenant and landlord, the compensation belongs to the tenant in recognition of the continued ownership and in order to avoid unjust enrichment on the part of the landlord. *McClusky v. State*, 16 Misc. 2d 920, 184 N.Y.S.2d 986 (Ct. Cl. 1959); *Antonowsky v. State*, 180 N.Y.S.2d 966 (Ct. Cl. 1958). The cited cases involved leases with virtually identical provisions governing condemnation.

Gristede Bros. v. State, 11 A.D.2d 580, 200 N.Y.S.2d 755 (3d Dep't 1960), is especially relevant in the event of the condemnation. The tenant of premises appropriated by the State for thruway purposes entered a claim for compensation for the value of fixtures. The lease contained the typical form clause denying to the tenant any part of a condemnation award. The court indicated that such a provision "serves only to deprive the tenant of any compensation for value of the *leasehold*. 'Even so, the tenant retains the right to compensation for his interest in any annexations to the real property which, but for the fact that the real property has been taken, he would have had the right to remove at the end of his lease. . . . '" 200 N.Y.S.2d at 756. However, the Court of Claims had dismissed the tenant's claim because the lease provided that any fixtures not removed prior to termination of the lease were to be deemed abandoned by the tenant and were to become the property of the landlord (paragraph 24 in client's lease is identical). The Appellate Division reversed and remanded to determine classification of the property and damages, ruling that the clause providing for abandonment should be restricted to voluntary abandonment of the fixtures and should not govern termination because of condemnation. There was no opportunity for removal, and therefore the tenant was entitled to an award for whatever fixtures constituted true annexations to the realty. The *Gristede* decision is clearly sound in that it protects the tenant in the event of vesting of title in the sovereign without opportunity for removal. Further, it is supported by the common law doctrine recognizing a tenant's right of removal after termination of the estate if the estate was of an indefinite duration or terminated unexpectedly.

It should be noted that the valuation of fixtures in condemnation proceedings is usually measured by the so-called "Unit Rule," under which the leasehold and the improvements are valued as a unit and not separate items. *See generally* 51 *N.Y. Juris.*, Eminent Domain §§ 225, 257 (1986). However, that rule need not be applied in exceptional circumstances. *Cooney Bros.* v. *State*, 24 N.Y.2d 387, 248 N.E.2d 585 (1969); *Marraro* v. *State*, 12 N.Y.2d 285, 189 N.E.2d 606 (1963). These decisions should be reviewed if the fear of condemnation materializes.

CONCLUSION

In the event of condemnation of the leased premises, available authorities recognize tenant's right to compensation for the machinery, provided tenant has no opportunity to remove the machinery prior to condemnation. Tenant's lease with landlord is no bar to compensation in the event of condemnation nor does it prevent tenant from removing the machinery prior to condemnation.

Respectfully submitted,
Robert Reeves

APPENDIX H:
Form of Opinion Letter

FORM OF OPINION LETTER*

CARLTON, DAVIDSON & ROMANO
280 Broadway
New York, NY 10007

May 10, 2004

Abbott & Baker,
Clothing Manufacturing Company
1234 Madison Avenue
New York, NY 10028

Attorney-client confidential communication

Dear Mr. Abbott:

In your letter of May 1st, 2004, you state that you wish to register the mark "Executive Brand" for men's suits manufactured by your company. You indicate that "for the past year or so" you have been sewing labels on certain suits that contain the name "Executive Brand." Specifically, you ask for our legal opinion as to whether the words "Executive Brand," which you refer to in your letter as your trademark, may be registered with the U.S. Patent and Trademark Office (P.T.O.).

As a result of our research, we have concluded that an application for the registration of the mark "Executive Brand" is likely to be refused.

The United States Court of Customs and Patent Appeals has decided an appeal that dealt with a mark consisting of the words "Executive Model." The case appealed a decision of the Trademark Trial and Appeal Board, which had affirmed the action of the Examiner of Trademarks in refusing to register the mark "Executive Model."

The question before the court was whether the mark "Executive Model" so resembled previously registered marks, to wit., "The Executive," "Executive Group," "Young Executive," and "Junior Executive," as to be likely to cause confusion, mistake, or to deceive. The mark "Executive Model" was applied to men's shorts and slacks, whereas the previously registered marks were used for a variety of clothing, including men's suits.

---

* The case relied upon by counsel in the opinion letter that follows is *In re Farah Manufacturing Co.*, 58 CCPA 829, 435 F.2d 594 (1971).

Pursuant to the applicable statutory provisions of law, the P.T.O. shall not refuse registration unless an applicant's mark so resembles a registered mark as to be likely, when applied to the goods of the applicant, "to cause confusion, or to cause mistake, or to deceive as to the source of the goods." The court consequently affirmed the decision, which refused registration of the proposed mark.

The court agreed with the Board's findings that words such as "The" and "Junior" merely emphasize the word "Executive" and that "Executive" was "the dominant feature" of the mark "Executive Model." The court attached little or no importance to the additional word "Model" in the trademark in view of its obvious meaning in the clothing field.

It is clear that the words "Model" and "Brand" convey the same meaning. Therefore, because of the great similarity of the mark and its application to identical goods, men's suits, the holding and reasoning of the court pertaining to "Executive Model" apply equally to your proposed mark "Executive Brand." This assumes that all prior registrations are still in force.

In view of the foregoing, we are of the opinion that you would probably not be able to register the mark "Executive Brand" for the suits manufactured by your company.

This letter deals exclusively with the rights of registration and not with your right to use the mark.

If you are still interested in using this mark, we suggest that the following action be taken:

1) Verify that the prior registrations are still in force; and

2) Investigate the companies that own the registrations to determine whether they are currently using the marks shown in those registrations.

Please call me if you have any questions.

Very truly yours,

John J. Romano

CARLTON, DAVIDSON & ROMANO
By: John J. Romano

INDEX

A

B

C

Charges to Jury

Citation of Authorities,. **81–83, 179–206**

Citations

D

E

G

H

K

L

M

N

O

P

Q

R

T

U

V

W